THE V&A SOURCEBOOK OF

# PATTERN & ORNAMENT

# THE V&A SOURCEBOOK OF

# PATTERN & ORNAMENT

AMELIA CALVER

# CONTENTS



**Frontispiece.** Silk ballgown with appliqué, beadwork and embroidery, Norman Hartnell, London, 1953

# INTRODUCTION

## AMELIA CALVER

The ambition to improve and embellish our environment with pattern and ornament is undoubtedly one of the earliest forms of human endeavour, as we know from the cave markings made by Neanderthals and the elaborately decorated tombs of Ancient Egypt. Patterns not only decorate, they can also convey different meanings across different communities. Checks found on European cloth may convey modernity or affiliation, while in south-western Nigeria, the checkerboard pattern found on indigo resist-dyed cloth made by the Yoruba people and known as *Olokun* denotes the goddess of the sea.

As long as there has been trading between different peoples and cultures, patterns have escaped their original context and traversed the world, as they did along the fluid trade network that connected China and Central Asia to Europe. The influence of the Silk Road, as this route is known, wends its way through every chapter of this book. It is evident from the way that dragons first seen on Imperial Chinese robes began to appear on textiles created on 14th-century Italian looms. It is exemplified by the growth in popularity in Europe of the curved teardrop form of the Indian *buta* or Iranian *boteh* (both referred to in this book as *boteh*), leading to the rise of the 'paisley motif' in the 19th century as the shape was imitated by the British weaving centres of Edinburgh, Norwich and Paisley.

The Victoria and Albert Museum has one of the finest collections of pattern and ornament in the world, and the story of the museum's origin and intended purpose helps to explain the richness and diversity of its objects. The museum first opened its doors to the public in 1852, following the enormous success of the Great Exhibition held in Hyde Park, London, the previous year. Proceeds from the world's first international display of design and manufacturing were used to establish Prince Albert and Sir Henry Cole's grand dream of the Museum of Manufactures. The museum's founding principle was based on three ideals: to make works of art available to all, to educate working people and to inspire British designers and manufacturers.

Prince Albert himself proposed early guidelines for the museum's acquisition of objects, which should 'improve the standards of taste and manufacture by providing constant reference to the best examples of the decorative and fine arts of the past'. Over time, the V&A's ceramics, dress, furniture, glass, ironwork, jewellery, paintings, photographs, prints, sculpture, silver and textiles have come to embody a history of art and design from ancient times to the present day, from the cultures of Europe, Africa, the Americas and Asia.

The V&A, via its Brand Licensing team, offers a tailor-made research and design service, which traces its roots back to Prince Albert and Henry Cole. It operates under the founding mission to provide design resources to manufacturing and retail partners across the world by acting as a knowledgeable interface between the collection and industry. When designers and manufacturers meet the Licensing team – on-site, off-site or online – and start the journey of creating a new product range, they may already have a pattern, technique or art movement in mind. Combining an awareness of current market trends with an in-depth understanding of the museum's galleries, stores and archives, the team brings together a selection of the most appealing and appropriate floral designs, figurative artworks, geometric prints or narrative surface pattern. By the end of the process, a new range of home furnishings or wall art, clothing, jewellery, ceramics or even greeting cards, licensed and endorsed with the prestigious V&A trademark, will have emerged. Designs may appear on new objects very much as they did in the 18th or 19th centuries, or be radically repurposed with a new treatment of colour, scale or substrate. At any one time around 90 companies, across a vast matrix of styles and product types, might be working with the Licensing team. All profits made through these collaborations are returned to the museum.

The contents of this book offer readers an opportunity to gain a similar inspiration. Through its pages, designers, manufacturers and anyone interested in ornament, pattern and design are able to engage with the collection creatively. The cherry-picked selection has been organized into four categories: Plants, Animals, Earth and the Universe, and Abstract Patterns, each offering a fascinating variety of design approaches. The selection spans hundreds of years and includes the output of well-known and lesser-known companies, artisans, artists, designers and makers.

The names of some of the suppliers and manufacturers have changed slightly over time, so for clarity we have chosen to stick to one iteration in some instances. For example, we have streamlined Heal's Fabrics, Heal's Wholesale and Export and Heal & Son as Heal's, and Sanderson, Arthur Sanderson & Sons and Sanderson Fabrics as Sanderson. For ease of reading, we have also dropped the used of Ltd in all company names.

*The V&A Sourcebook of Pattern and Ornament* is a remarkable compendium of the V&A's eclectic and seemingly limitless collections. It is not intended as a comprehensive glossary of design but as a unique catalogue for creativity – who knows what it might inspire?

**Opposite.** *Springboard* screen-printed linen furnishing fabric designed by Lucienne Day for Heal's, England, 1954

# PATTERNING IN PRACTICE

## A CONVERSATION WITH TIMOROUS BEASTIES ABOUT DESIGN AND INSPIRATION

**The award-winning design studio Timorous Beasties was established in Glasgow in 1990 by Alistair McAuley and Paul Simmons, and is noted for its surreal and irreverent textiles and wallpapers. Its edgy, provocative designs are based on the duo's deep understanding of textiles history. In 2010, the company was commissioned to redesign the V&A boardroom. Its design was inspired by the carvings of roses and thistles on the museum building itself. We spoke to Alistair [AM] and Paul [PS] about the contents of this sourcebook and to gather some of their thoughts on the importance of pattern and ornament in their work.**

**What prompted you to set up your studio, and what sort of work were you doing in your first decade together?**

**[AM]** We both graduated from Glasgow School of Art in 1988, under the tutelage of Barbara Santos Shaw and Chuck Mitchell, an inspiring though sometimes dangerous mixture who demanded hard graft, craftsmanship and an understanding of the importance of engaging with the world outside art school. The textile design course was very practical; we were learning a trade and understanding a skill, like an apprenticeship. We were taught to design with the process in mind. This encouraged experimentation, and we experienced the joy of making, starting with an idea and taking it through a process that you alone controlled. Like most final-year students, the work we were doing was indulgent and protected by the art-school environment; we were not concerned with costs. The work was labour-intensive, with lots of screens and a ridiculous number of hours spent drawing and developing a print regime. After graduation, it was evident that our work, while appreciated, was not commercially viable. Desperate to prove a point and more than a little naive, we decided to set up our own studio.

**[PS]** Neither of us could entertain the notion of being dictated to in terms of the designs we wished to create. We both loved nature and were hugely influenced by John James Audubon's *Birds of America* (1827) and Maria Sibylla Merian's *Insects of Surinam* (1705), as well as the engraving-like drawings in the Bromley Hall Pattern Book (*c.*1765–1800; p. 245, fig. 6) – I do urge everyone to see the whole book in the V&A. The V&A collections show how abundantly plants and animals feature in the pattern and ornamentation of interiors, and demonstrate the human need to bring nature into our lives and our homes. From the very outset, we wanted Timorous Beasties to be known for its designs of nature, though not with a saccharine aesthetic. A shrivelled leaf can command as much beauty as a fresh flower in bloom, and that was the 'truth' we wanted to convey. I drew large, brightly coloured designs of eels and fish, insects and gargoyles, entwined and entangled in ornate plant life; what is normally considered unattractive made beautiful through striking juxtapositions. The scale was large, and in the world of textiles, the imagery was shocking. I wanted people to look at my work and think, in the words of W.B. Yeats: 'A terrible beauty is born.'

But at that time, a large iguana munching on insects right in the centre of the textile was not exactly commercially viable, and we had a tough time as we struggled to carve out our niche. It often felt like we were digging at the coal face with a plastic spoon! It was financially tough, and in that first decade, we took on every job we could. Ironically, that meant designing for those very commercial companies we were kicking against.

**[AM]** We set up a 20-metre (65-foot) print table, the biggest we could afford, in a converted church in Maryhill in Glasgow. Now that we were covering the costs, the merits of two- to maybe three-colour prints (rather than the ten- or twelve-screen efforts that we enjoyed at art school) were very apparent. Having the facilities to print our designs, however, highlighted the bespoke element of our offering. We began working with interior designers, producing fabrics and wallpapers for unique hospitality projects, and this gave us good market visibility – it introduced us to the world as designer-makers.

**Timorous Beasties was formed in the 1990s when the general style was unobtrusive, low-key decor. Your designs were undoubtedly ahead of the times. What drove you to buck the trend with such vigour?**

**[AM]** Arguably, we started our business at the worst possible time. We were two graduates with no business experience, selling luxury goods that nobody needed. It was a minimalist heyday, and there was an economic depression. An interior was only considered successful if it went unnoticed – and it's that attitude that has driven us to buck the trend ever since.

**[PS]** In our view, it's a dead end to jump on the bandwagon because it's the fashion. We weren't interested in the prosaic furnishing market of the early 1990s. And we were right because sometimes the gaps in the market are more significant than what is readily available. We wanted the freedom to bring craftsmanship back to the design process and, above all, we aimed to change the market. Yes, past designers' influence was huge for us, but it seemed pointless to simply mimic. For example, we quite often took from William Morris's imagery but, in the process, we transformed it. For instance, our *Fruit Looters* design from 2009 (p. 10) is a nudge and a wink to Morris's *Strawberry Thief* (p. 99, fig. 5).

**Opposite.** *Glasgow Toile* in red, wallpaper digitally printed on 170gsm non-woven paper, 2004

**[AM]** We were utterly convinced and determined that we were doing the right thing, and we were encouraged by the right people at the right time. When I told Humphrey Boyle, head of Wallcoverings International, that we were setting up a 40-metre (131-foot) print table, he said we would probably be bankrupt within a year. But he still encouraged us to do it, and supported us by buying some cloth to make a sarong and offering advice over the years.

**You gained widespread recognition in 2004 for your *Glasgow Toile* (p. 9), which takes its cue from the toile de Jouy pastoral patterns developed in 18th-century France. Tell us how that came about.**

**[PS]** In 2004 we had the chance to exhibit in London as part of Designersblock at 100% Design. At the time, we were both living in council flats in Glasgow and we were broke. Initially, we tried to design a genuine toile depicting bucolic scenes of shepherdesses tending their flocks or lovers on a flower-entwined swing. We noticed, however, that some of the original French toiles were quite macabre, depicting murders, battles and enslavement, whether as moral tales or historical events. When most of the population was illiterate, they might be hung as curtains to tell stories, real or imagined, in homes and public buildings. Our last-minute inspiration was to create a literal take on this style of toile de Jouy by including contemporary images of the city that we lived in. The *Glasgow Toile* has an immediacy that people relate to. One can call our toiles social commentary or social realism, but that was never our initial agenda.

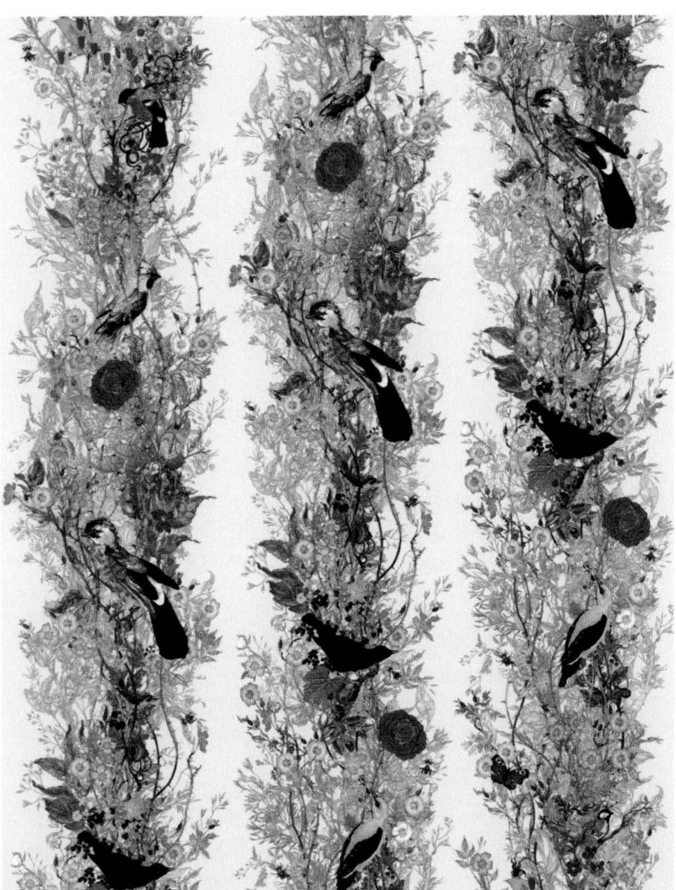

**[AM]** The success of *Glasgow Toile* was a total surprise. We had made a couple of toile-style prints for private clients in the past, but the *Glasgow Toile* had simplicity, relevance and timing. It depicted real scenes from around Glasgow and our old studio, reflecting not only some pretty dark social circumstances but also the positive trajectory that the city was on. We used it on a privacy screen and a small Victorian bedroom chair, creating an intentionally unremarkable and subtle installation. At first glance, the viewer thinks they are looking at a common rehash of a tired style but, true to original toiles, we were telling the story of a particular time in a particular place. As the truth slowly revealed itself, it turned our 14-year struggle into an overnight success.

**[PS]** The concept of a toile can, of course, be applied and expanded in many ways. The *London Toile* was produced in 2005, followed by the *Edinburgh Toile* commissioned for the Edinburgh Festival in 2007. Other toile-orientated commissions have followed: for vodka bottles, book covers, ceramics, T-shirts – the variety, and the contents themed from past to present, is endless. We even produced a golf-themed toile for Nike for the 2019 British Open Golf Championship at Portrush in Ireland. We found our inspiration in the history and landmarks of Portrush and depicted a complex scene in silhouette.

**Why do you think your approach to design has struck such a chord with a contemporary audience?**

**[PS]** People love images that tell stories and, when it comes to pattern, they enjoy the nostalgic resonances from the past. Our work satisfies both these feelings. And because our images are often large-scale detailed drawings, the observer can take subconscious pleasure in recognizing the time and skill spent creating it.

**[AM]** I would like to think that the contemporary audience appreciates our approach because it shares our irreverence and because it acknowledges the value of the labour involved. We are conscientious and deliberate in our undertakings. We don't design what we think will sell. We just try to do our best and do what we like. People are far more informed about design and sustainability than they were 30 years ago and are less likely to be content with common offerings. That said, the designs that don't sell as well are just as important in our library because they cater to a niche with a different outlook, and they draw the attention of the interested audience. Clearly, some people will not like what we do, and that's important too. If we appealed to everyone that would make us mainstream, and the world doesn't need that.

**You have taken on several special commissions, ranging from one-off exhibitions at Normanby Hall in Lincolnshire and Harewood House in West Yorkshire to product packaging (for brands including Fortnum & Mason and Johnnie Walker) and complete interiors, such as the smoking room at Bowhill House in the Scottish Borders and the boardroom at the V&A. What is your starting point with each commission, and to what sort of historical design references are you particularly drawn?**

**Left.** *Fruit Looters* in lichen, furnishing fabric digitally printed on 100% linen, 2009

**[PS]** Our starting point is always talking to the client, then researching the company, the site or the product. Sometimes the right imagery is there straight away. For example, at Bowhill, it was a smoking room, so billows of smoke and pelmets made of cigars were key ideas. Other designs, such as the packaging for Fortnum & Mason, fell into place quite quickly: dark woodland for dark chocolates, stem ginger conjured tropical imagery, and so on.

Normanby Hall, a stunning regency manor, approached us in 2019 to commission a fabric as part of their exhibition *Artists in the Hall*. The historic estate displays several contemporary artworks that draw attention to some of the overlooked cultural influences found in the hall's designs and decoration. Our first step was to pick out elements from the hall and render them in meticulous detail (p. 13). We then developed them into a *trompe-l'oeil* design in which these objects seem to burst out of rips in the fabric (p. 12). The illustrations represent the numerous styles of art and ornamentation that feature in the house. Our final design was hand-printed on to silk with a black base and gold detailing and made into curtains that took pride of place in the exhibition and will remain in place as a permanent fixture of the hall.

**[AM]** Brands, organizations or individuals that approach us already like what we do, but it's important to understand their aspirations and expectations of what they think we can bring to a project – it's a wonderful exchange. To see how others see us is to be valued. First impressions can be inspirational; the first review can sometimes be disappointing, but the process of being a designer is to navigate a way to the most intelligent and beautiful outcome.

**This book shows that pattern and ornamentation have always been relevant. The work of some pattern designers – notably William Morris – is never entirely out of fashion and regularly undergoes a significant revival. Why do you think pattern has always played such an important role in our lives, and what does it say about the human psyche?**

**[PS]** Pattern has been with us from the earliest days of humanity. Some of the first cave paintings show patterns that seem to illustrate time passing – a view before this moment and a projection beyond this moment. Pattern repeats eternally, and maybe there is a primeval instinct to look for patterns in things – but you would probably have to ask an anthropologist or a psychoanalyst to elaborate on that!

There does seem to be a collective link with pattern. Patterns reflect the moods of the times: spiky fifties such as Lucienne Day's *Herb Anthony* (p. 124, fig. 2); psychedelic sixties such as Nigel Quiney's designs on pages 376–7 (figs 4, 6 and 7); geometric seventies such as Barbara Brown's *Complex* (p. 356, fig. 2); doodle-splat eighties; minimal nineties and so on. Like all art, it reflects the time it is created, but there is also a nostalgic timeline that we register through pattern. Think of the rumoured last words of the great aesthete Oscar Wilde: 'This wallpaper and I are fighting a duel to the death. Either it goes or I do!'

**[AM]** I must have been absent the day we did 'pattern and the human psyche', so I can only reflect on what it means to me. I grew up in a 1970s council estate on the outskirts of Glasgow. My mother decorated the house, and no combination of pattern was forbidden – though some have since been outlawed. Pattern humanizes a space and allows for individuality. It brings comfort – it helps us predict and expect what is coming. The continual resurgence of William Morris and other classic designers is perhaps a reflection on the repetition of time and an appreciation of quality in design and craftsmanship. There is recognizable nostalgia in pattern; it takes time to forgive and forget, then it's back – the same but different.

**Most of your designs do not offer the interior decorator a neutral background against which to place objects. Indeed many speak as if demanding to be heard, and some even invoke an active dialogue with the viewer. How much is this intentional on your part? Do you think pattern has played this role during other interludes in history or in different cultures?**

**[PS]** Pattern can add a strong aesthetic, mood, warmth and feel to a room. Of course, our designs are intentional, but the way they are used is out of our hands. I often find our aesthetic works best on one feature wall, but again that depends on where it is placed and how it is put together.

**[AM]** If there was a hierarchy of interior products back in the early '90s, we surely would have been down at the bottom, probably as a result of our determination to go against the grain. Perhaps as a consequence of that rebuff in our early years, we have intentionally tried to make our product the feature of the room, and we don't think we should apologize for that.

Pattern and decoration have played a massive role in history and culture. They inform, they create an expectation and they amplify individuality. Cultures are defined and identified by pattern and the use of it. The fact that you can tell where something is from by a collection of marks and colours speaks volumes of the relevance of pattern in human history.

**Your designs often challenge conventional ideas about scale, to the extent that some of your wallpapers have such minimal repeats that they are almost like paintings, and a sofa fabric might have only one repeat. Can you tell us your views on scale, repeat and detail?**

**[PS]** I don't know exactly why but I love designing on a large scale. Let's say that when dealing with an image that is already dramatic, one may as well go the whole way and be dramatic oneself. Playing with scale can completely change the preconceived notion of a design. Florals don't have to be delicate, perfectly formed and small – they can be big, sculptural and dramatic.

**[AM]** All of these aspects are to be enjoyed and played with. There are no rules in any of this, only surprises, and it is up to the individual to decide if something is good. Scale, repeat and detail are all related and finding a balance between them can be liberating – and often difficult. In fact, if it's not difficult, then you're not doing it right.

**Why do you think some motifs and patterns, for example the *boteh* or the Greek key, have longevity and universal appeal? Are there other motifs that you feel have a resonance that is shared globally and through different periods?**

**[PS]** The Victorians used the motif of the *boteh* on an industrial scale and renamed it the paisley pattern because it was produced in Paisley,

Scotland. It is a motif that has survived and been resurrected time and time again. It may have originated from early humans printing with the side of their fists or as a very early symbol of life growing from a bud – who knows? Like the Greek key, its history goes back so far that its appeal is deeply embedded in our collective unconscious.

The bee is another universal motif that appears time and again. In Europe, it was used by the first French kings, then by the Barberini popes of Rome, then by Napoleon. Today it manifests as the emblem of the city of Manchester, symbolizing hard work and collective endeavour. Within our own Timorous Beasties history, it has a strategic position as the B in our logo, and a significant Beastie in our name, as well as featuring consistently in our work. The classic shapes of the damask and stylized flowers like the chrysanthemum, lily and, of course, the rose can all be interpreted in so many ways and have often contributed to our idiosyncratic appeal.

**Most design and production can now be created digitally. Yet much of your work is still produced using traditional, more labour-intensive (and likely more expensive) methods – why do you take this approach?**

**[PS]** It is important to be informed about how something is made to design well for it. Whether it's digital, hand-print, lace, jacquard, carpet, textiles or wallcoverings – design for process is essential. We started out hand-printing and we still hand-print, but we have always embraced new processes. Digital technologies have brought new ways of printing that would not have been possible decades ago. In recent years the digital process was used to make prototypes, but now the prototype has become the final product. The number of colours available and the scale of repeats is utterly new. Some wallpapers we hand-print on top of a digital print in a high-tech meets low-tech way. The challenge is to push the boundaries and use the best qualities of each process to its greatest advantage.

**[AM]** We were trained to hand-print, and if the electricity goes off, we can still get on with stuff. Technology does not make you creative – ideas can be expressed with a simple drawing and usually are.

**How important are collections of pattern and ornamentation, such as those at the V&A, to today's designers? Are you drawn to such collections as a source of inspiration?**

**[PS]** The V&A has one of the richest archives of pattern and ornamentation in the world and has always been, and always will be, a never-ending source of inspiration and awe. For me, one of the finest examples of a printed fabric in the V&A is a Robert Jones & Co. piece showing a rural scene with birds amid a rugged landscape and ruins (p. 243, fig. 4). It inspired the title for our exhibition, *Peacocks Among the Ruins*, which we curated at Dundee Contemporary Arts in 2007.

**[AM]** As production methods advance and new ways of doing things are brought to light, it's important to remember that they are progressions from something that was done earlier. Collections such as the V&A are invaluable as they give us an understanding of what we do now by understanding what came before. We must not forget techniques and skills by ignoring their relevance. Access to these resources will always bring surprises.

**What advice would you give to today's emerging designers or those studying design? Where should they look for inspiration? Is there much to be learned by looking back through history or from other cultures, as well as focusing on what is happening today?**

**[AM]** It's a cliché, but inspiration is everywhere. Over time we have had to research all sorts of stuff, not all interesting. At some point, you have to find the moment of inspiration. It is elusive, can be in disguise and is rarely instant. Sometimes you have to work harder and not doubt yourself.

**[PS]** I would say that you have to know your past to realize your future, and look for inspiration in the gaps and cracks in the market. Look for things that are not there, rather than what already exists. Stick doggedly with your own truth. Truth is a thing of beauty and, as Keats tells us: 'A thing of beauty is a joy for ever.'

**Left.** Textile created for *Artists in the Hall* at Normanby Hall, hand-printed on gold silk, 2019

**Opposite.** Artwork for textile created for *Artists in the Hall* at Normanby Hall, pen on paper, 2019

Sharpie

# PLANTS

**Opposite.** *Palamos* furnishing fabric, designed by Sylvia Chalmers for Elizabeth Eaton, London, 1953

1

2

3

1 *Wild Centuries* was designed by botanical artist Charles Raymond for Edinburgh Weavers, Carlisle, in 1960. The roses and leaves on this screen-printed cotton are painted in soft textures.

2 This monochromatic rose design is one of 616 lithographic prints of textile designs published under the title *Dessins Nouveautés* in 1880–1 by French publishers Lechartier et Paul.

3 Arts and Crafts designer Allan Francis Vigers created this woodblock-printed wallpaper, *Japanese Rose*, for English manufacturers Jeffrey & Co. at the turn of the 20th century.

4 William Morris's 1864 woodblock-print wallpaper *Trellis* was inspired by his garden at Red House in Kent. The simple formalized flat pattern is typical of his early work. Philip Webb, architect of Red House, drew the birds.

5 Probably made in England in the early 17th century, this gold locket case was designed to hold a portrait miniature. The enamelled decoration centres on a red Tudor rose.

6 Published as a lithograph in *Dessins Nouveautés* by Lechartier et Paul in the late 19th century, the flat, two-tone roses in this pattern are embellished with a delicate, lace-like frill.

7 This illustration for a dress fabric was published in 1925-6 in *Art-Goût-Beauté: Feuillets d'Élégance Feminine*, an haute couture magazine founded by textile manufacturer Albert Godde, Beddin & Cie in 1920.

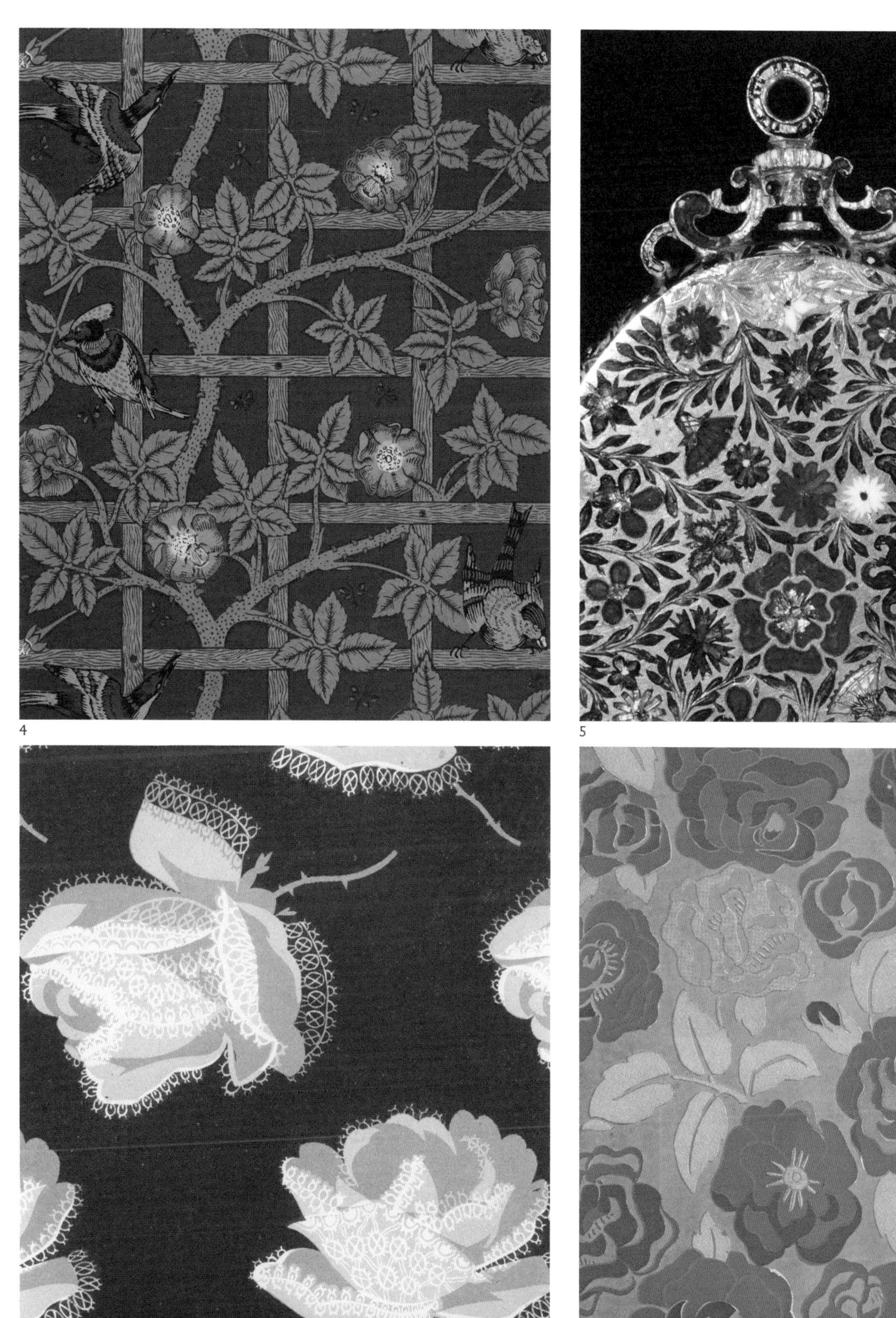

4

5

6

7

1

1 Possibly made by Herrburger & Rhomberg, Austria, in about 1910, this cotton damask tablecloth features a geometric pattern of flower, leaf and thorn motifs.

2 Horrockses Fashions, Lancashire, was a ready-to-wear clothing label specializing in high-quality full-skirted cotton dresses. Its glory years were the 1940s and 1950s and its trademark was bold and bright, often floral patterns.

3 This dress fabric was created by the Calico Printers' Association, Manchester, in about 1911. The pattern uses highly stylized roses on a pale background. Fabrics such as this were popular for summer dresses in Britain in the early 20th century.

4 In contrast to the taste for naturalistic patterns in the 19th century, the roses on this printed cotton from around 1850 are simplified and geometric, like motifs used for heraldic devices. It was printed for the London firm Charles Hindley & Sons.

5 This highly structured and robust 1909 wallpaper pattern, *Chancellor*, by A.F. Vigers, depicts a Gothic-style rose in an ogival lattice framework, reminiscent of the silk-velvet textiles exported between Turkey and Italy in the 17th and 18th centuries.

6 William Morris's symmetrical pattern *Rose* was registered as a printed cotton in 1883. Morris's interest in wildlife and flowers, as well as his garden at Kelmscott Manor in rural Oxfordshire, had a great influence on his work.

2

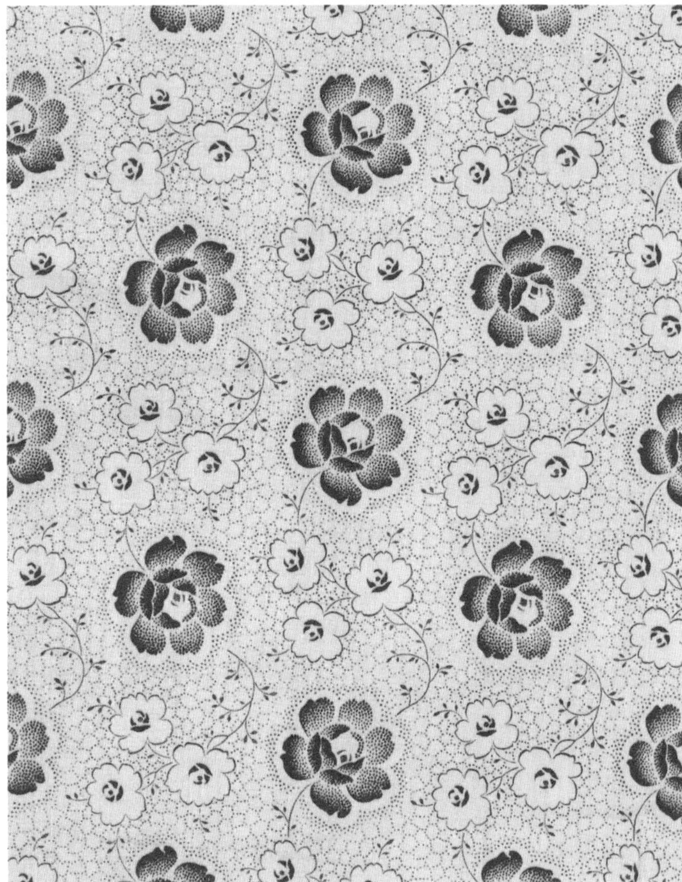

3

4

5

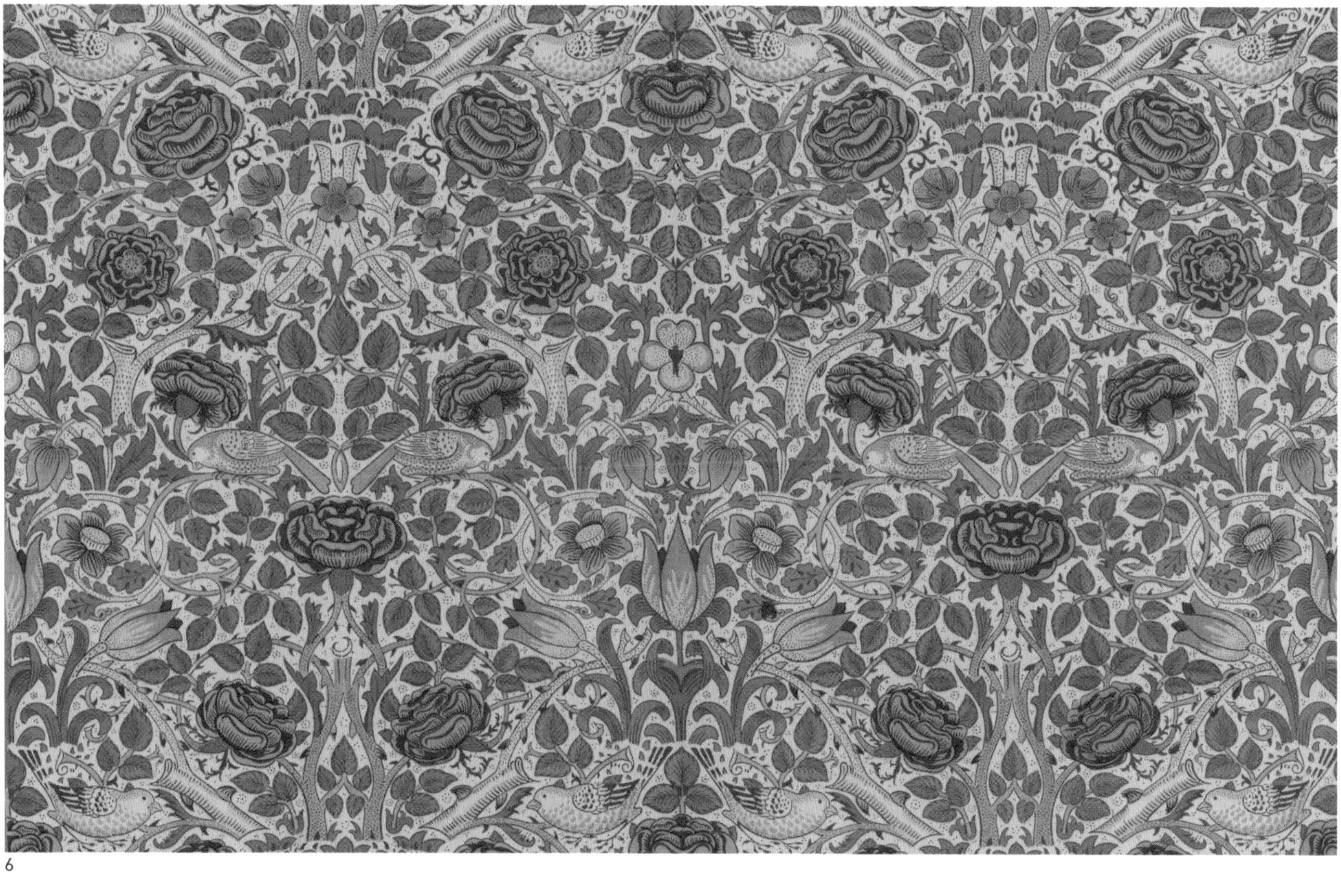

6

1

2

3

1 The simple repeating pattern of *Briar*, drawn at the height of C.F.A. Voysey's career in 1901, was originally produced as a wallpaper. The pattern incorporates one of Voysey's signature motifs – the rose and bramble.

2 This delightful printed cotton, made in Britain, has a traditional floral design of freshly picked roses. Fashionable for summer furnishings in the mid-19th century, the textile brings the garden into a room.

3 Printed in Lancashire or Manchester, this dress fabric from 1913 is patterned with stylized roses similar to motifs used by the Glasgow School artists, who influenced the development of the Art Nouveau style in Belgium and France.

4 Intended for furnishings, this glazed cotton chintz features naturalistic sprays of overblown roses on a stippled ground. Many variations of this popular style were hand-block and roller printed in Lancashire factories in the mid-19th century.

5 Well known as an illustrator of children's books in England, Walter Crane returned to fairy-tale themes throughout his career as a wallpaper designer. *Rose Bush* wallpaper from 1900 might depict the enchanted briar that springs up around Sleeping Beauty's castle.

6 Arborescent designs, with ribbon trails and floral sprays on a background of foliage, were printed on high-quality British mid-19th-century cotton fabrics. Their production demanded the finest technical printing skills.

4

5

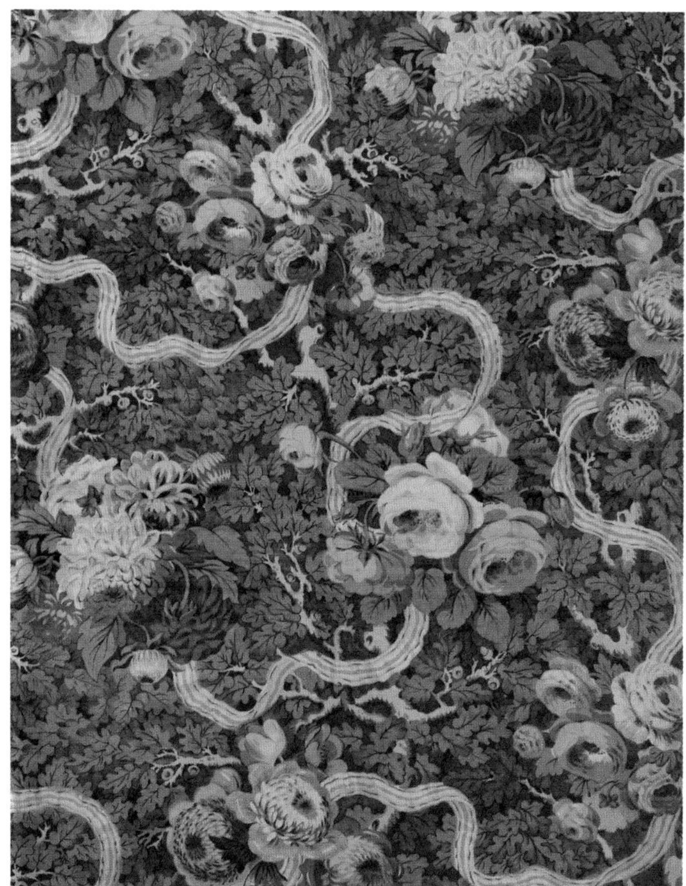

6

1

2

3

1 This superb design was created by Graham Sutherland for the 1934 *Modern Art for the Table* exhibition at Harrods, London. The pattern is called *White Rose,* and the egg cup was made in Staffordshire by E. Brain & Co. (Foley China).

2 English designer Pat Albeck worked for Horrockses Fashions, Lancashire, after leaving the Royal College of Art, London, producing many witty and sharply drawn variations of stripes and flora for the firm's charming printed cotton dresses, including this fabric dating from 1953 titled *Engraved Rose*.

3 The prestigious London furnishings company Hindley & Wilkinson retailed this printed cotton chintz around 1890. Patterns using naturalistic plant motifs were sometimes produced using printing blocks made decades earlier.

4 Woven in Spitalfields, London, a centre of English silk weaving, this late 19th-century skirt is brocaded with life-like roses and larkspur. The flower stems are arranged as individual specimens, as if the blooms had been selected for flower arranging.

1 The *Tulip* chair (1956–7), by Eero Saarinen for American firm Knoll, was named for its resemblance to the flower; yet it is often considered 'space age' for its futuristic curves.

2 With its bold design of tulips with sinuous flowing stems, this printed cotton exemplifies the cutting-edge Art Nouveau style. It was made by the Lancashire firm of F. Steiner & Co. in 1906.

3 Jacob Dimoldenberg moved from Paris to Manchester, a centre of the cotton industry, in the 1920s to create designs, such as this one, for ties, shirts, scarves and women's clothing.

4 *Garden Tulip* wallpaper from 1885 by William Morris is a fine floral trail of elegant, elongated stems and tulips, with a background of tiny flowers.

5 Turkish domestic embroidery designs, such as this linen hanging, were based on Ottoman silk textiles and used the same iconography of floral motifs, including tulips, throughout the 16th and 17th centuries.

6 This 1935 dress fabric of silk crêpe de chine was designed by the Calico Printers' Association, Manchester.

7 Sanderson, England, established a reputation for bold, floral furnishing fabrics and wallpaper from the 1860s. This distinctive design is from 1929.

8 This printed cotton is from the archive of Morton Sundour, a British company known for its bright 'unfadeable' dyes. With its graphic tulip motif in spectacular colours, it probably dates from the 1960s.

1

2

3

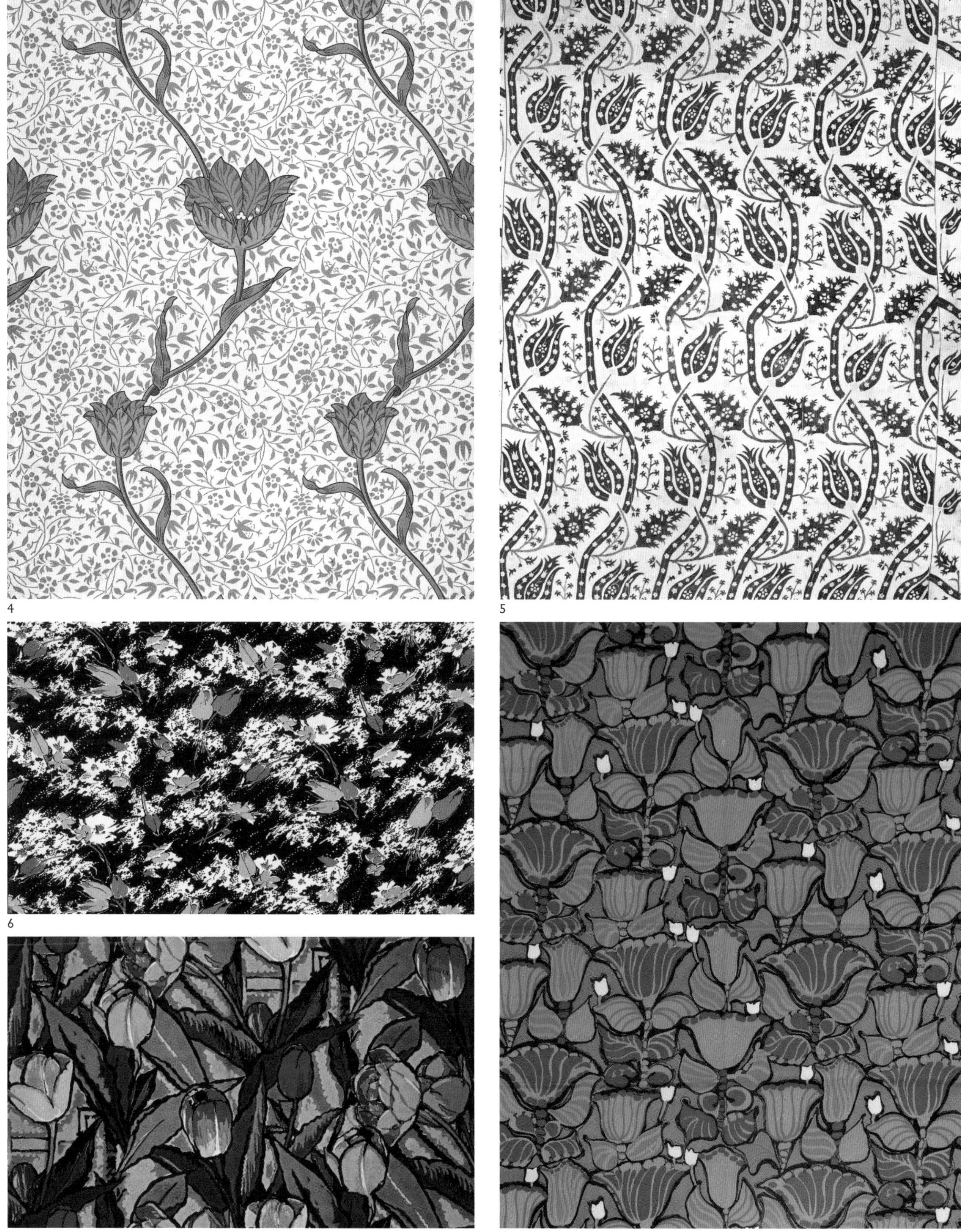

4

5

6

7

8

1

1 The randomly distributed flowers on this fashionable screen-printed crêpe are suggestive of tulips rather than a precise rendition. It was made by the Calico Printers' Association, Manchester.

2 Made by the Sèvres porcelain factory, France, between 1760 and 1768, this is one of a pair of porcelain wall sconces, each with three tulip-shaped candle holders in gilt bronze.

3 *Tulip* woollen furnishing textile designed by John Henry Dearle was made by Morris & Co., England, in 1900. Some of the firm's most successful woven textiles were produced under Dearle's direction.

4 Arthur Silver's design for a furnishing textile for the Silver Studio dates from around 1894. The light colourway gives the stylized tulip flowers and leaves a more naturalistic appearance.

5 This beautiful tulip custard cup with moulded hand-painted decoration is richly gilded, inside and out. It was made by Spode Ceramic Works, England, around 1815–20.

6 The Art Nouveau style is used here for a washable wallpaper, *Flaming Tulips*, designed in 1903 by Arthur L. Gwatkin and made by Scottish firm Wylie & Lochhead, known for its artistic design and craftsmanship.

7 This textile design by Helen Sampson from 1932 to 1933, with a pattern of tulips against a background of abstract shapes, is an example of the trend towards Art Deco in Britain for textiles and wallpaper.

2

3

4

5

6

7

1

2

1 This design for a printed textile, *The Braunton*, by Harry Napper from 1902, is in typical Art Nouveau style, featuring flattened, hard-edged flower forms in vigorous, spiralling curves of leaves.

2 J.H. Dearle's 1898 *Tulip and Net* design for Morris & Co. consists of alternating rows of tulips, a repeating device combining elements of historical patterns from Italy, Iran and Turkey.

3 *The Nure* by C.F.A. Voysey was produced as wallpaper by Essex & Co., England, in 1899, and by G.P. & J. Baker as a textile.

4 Many Sanderson designs, such as this example from 1930, are based on hand-drawn flowers, stylized, enlarged and printed in bright colours for home furnishings.

5 A cotton and viscose satin dress fabric printed by the Calico Printers' Association in 1933 features bright tulips, energized with white streaks.

6 This floriform vase from around 1895 was part of Louis Comfort Tiffany's *Favrile* range of art-glass made at the Corona glassworks, Long Island, New York.

7 An early 18th-century man's *patka* (sash) from India is decorated with a row of finely drawn and dyed tulips, outlined with silver-gilt thread embroidery.

8 The designer of this 1902 furnishing fabric for F. Steiner & Co. used typically Art Nouveau flowers and leaves to create a compressed geometric pattern in the pale colours popular in the Edwardian period.

3

4

5

6

7

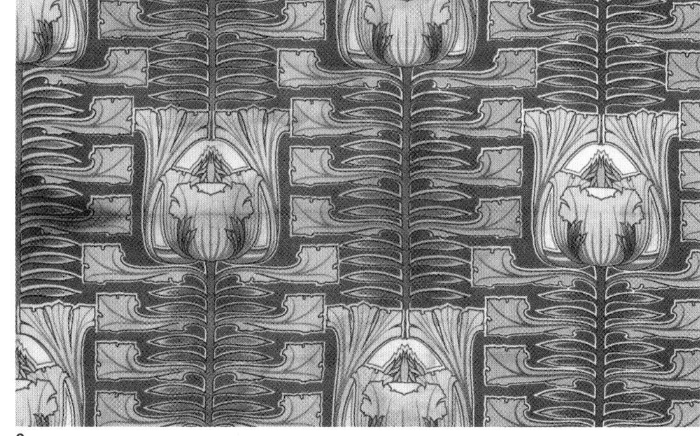
8

1

2

3

4

1 The queen of plants may be depicted as a stylized fleur-de-lis, which can be in a variety of different forms, or as the natural flower. Walter Crane's *Lily* wallpaper, produced by Jeffrey & Co., England, in 1900 sits between the two.

2 Walter Crane's 1894 *Lily and Rose* wallpaper pattern of elegant Easter lily and Tudor rose uses medieval art as the basis for its design. Many stylized versions of the lily are represented as a fleur-de-lis in heraldic practice.

3 The day lily (*Hemerocallis*) produces elegant trumpet-like blooms in summer, each lasting for only one day. Crane has captured the day lily-like burst against a large golden orb, representing the sun's passage across the sky, in his 1897 wallpaper design *Day Lily*.

4 Lindsay Phillip Butterfield was one of the most successful freelance designers working in the Arts and Crafts style. A keen gardener, he used his first-hand knowledge of plants as a source for his designs, as this 1896 watercolour, *Tiger Lily*, shows. The pattern was printed as a textile by G.P. & J. Baker.

5 Composed of sinuous motifs, this enamelled Jugendstil pendant was probably made in Germany around 1900.

6 This wallpaper frieze by Walter Crane was intended for use with his *Lily and Rose* wallpaper. Both were produced by Jeffrey & Co., London, 1894.

5

6

1

2

1 The 1897 wallpaper *Golden Lily*, which depicts lilies intertwined with wildflowers, is one of numerous Iranian-influenced repeating patterns designed by J.H. Dearle for Morris & Co.

2 A bold embroidered spray of lilies, by the Parisian embroidery company Lesage, is incorporated on the front of a 1940 evening gown by the provocative Italian fashion designer Elsa Schiaparelli.

3 *Rose and Lily* was designed by J.H. Dearle in 1893 and woven in wool and silk. A talented embroiderer and artist, Dearle was head designer of Morris & Co. and responsible for handling the company's woven textiles.

4 This high-quality silk, designed with lilies on a ribbed ground, was intended for either dress or furnishings and probably woven in the 1870s on a loom with a jacquard attachment.

5 The curving branches and formalized plant motifs of Walter Crane's *Francesca* wallpaper from 1902 show the influence of the Art Nouveau style that was fashionable at the time this was produced.

6 Naturalistic jewellery was popular in the 19th century, influenced by the Romantic movement, and often included the fashionable lily. This diamond tiara from around 1835 could be perched on the head or worn around the neck.

7 *Turk's Cap* wallpaper design from 1890 by Lewis Foreman Day is based on the Turk's cap lily, whose petals spring open and curl back in a turban shape.

3

4

5

6

7

1

2

3

4

5

1 Enid Marx designed *Pansy* in 1946 while representing the field of textile design on the Utility Furniture Advisory Committee panel. Produced by Morton Sundour, Carlisle, the fabric met the criteria for designs that could be made in Britain under post-war austerity measures.

2 The wild pansy, or heartsease, is the subject of this woven sample by Luther Hooper from 1920 to 1930. Originally a wood engraver and wallpaper designer, Hooper founded the Ipswich (or English) Silk Weaving Company, a handloom silk-weaving firm, in 1896.

3 Part of a range of chintzes introduced by Edinburgh Weavers, Olive Sullivan's *Pansies* from 1958 is in the long-favoured tradition of floral cottons for home furnishings, but its large scale and bright colours update its appeal.

4 This fan was decorated by French fan painter Ronot-Tutin in the 1890s. Floriography, the language of flowers, was popular with the Victorians, so these pansies may have conveyed a message; or they may just have matched a particular dress.

5 The intricate repeating pattern of this cotton furnishing fabric was produced using engraved metal rollers around 1818 by Samuel Matley & Sons at their print and dye works in Cheshire.

6 This porcelain vase dates from around 1830, during the Flight, Barr & Barr period of the Worcester porcelain factory (1813–40). Embellished with gilt handles, it is patterned with a hand-painted pansy or viola.

6

1

2

1 Many manufacturers stocked books of botanical illustrations as resources for their designers. The botanical forms in this French furnishing fabric of printed cotton from 1850 to 1875 show a close study of the beauty and order of the colour and pattern in nature's systems.

2 Informed by his skills as an illuminator, A.F. Vigers specialized in intricate florals simply and accurately depicted and arranged in artful synchronized pattern formations. The title of the 1904 wallpaper, *Shrewsbury*, might refer to a species of violet found in Shropshire, England, where Shrewsbury is the county town.

3 A.F. Vigers began his career as an architect, but became well known as a designer of textiles, furniture and especially wallpaper for the likes of Jeffrey & Co. and Liberty, London. His *Pansy* wallpaper dates from 1899 to 1909.

4 In the 1960s, under the direction of Tom Worthington, Heal's in London invested in contemporary textiles by working with freelance designers and art school graduates. Howard Carter, a student at the Royal College of Art, London, designed *Pansies* in 1962, which was printed on a textured cotton cloth.

3

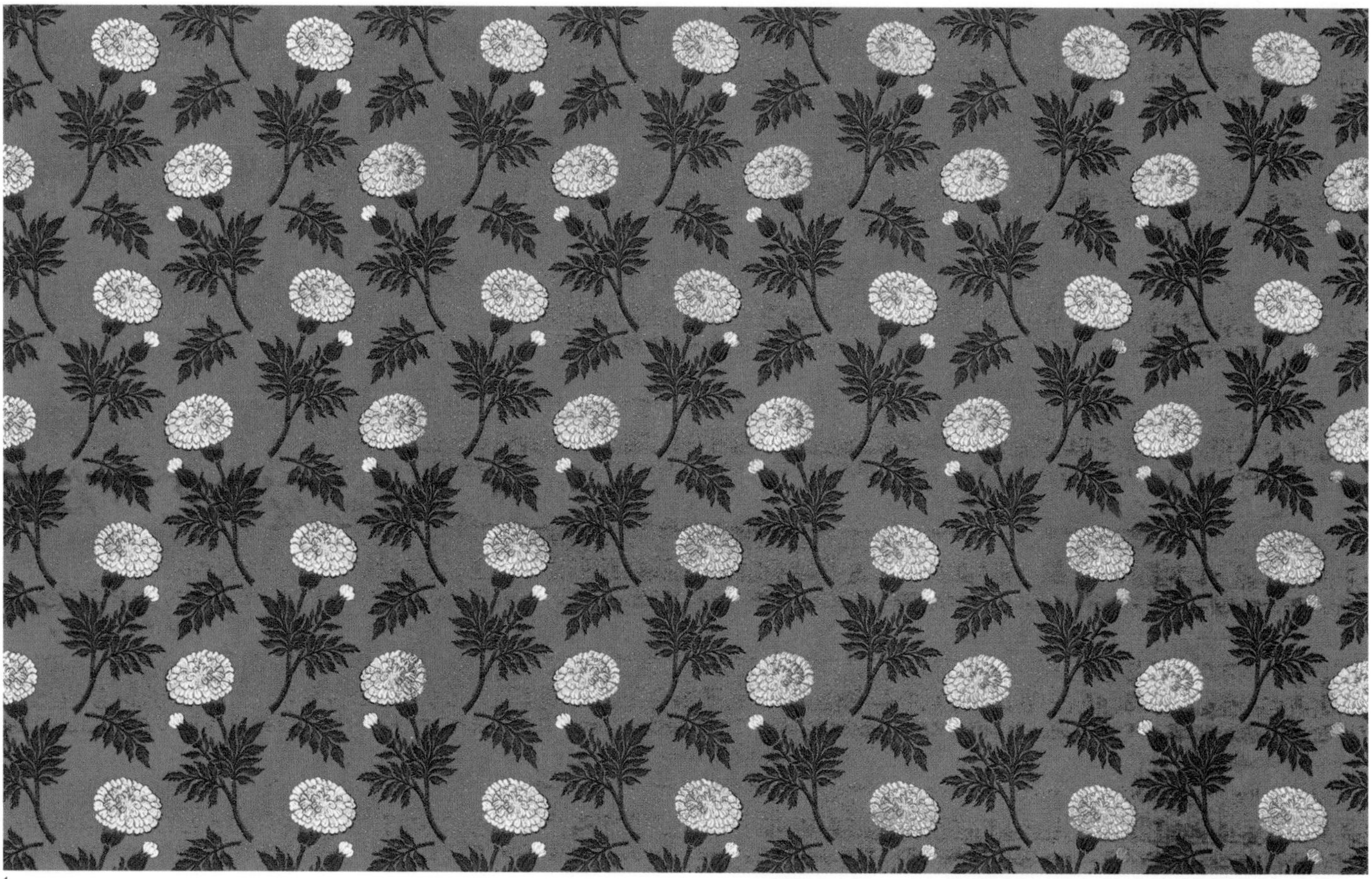

1

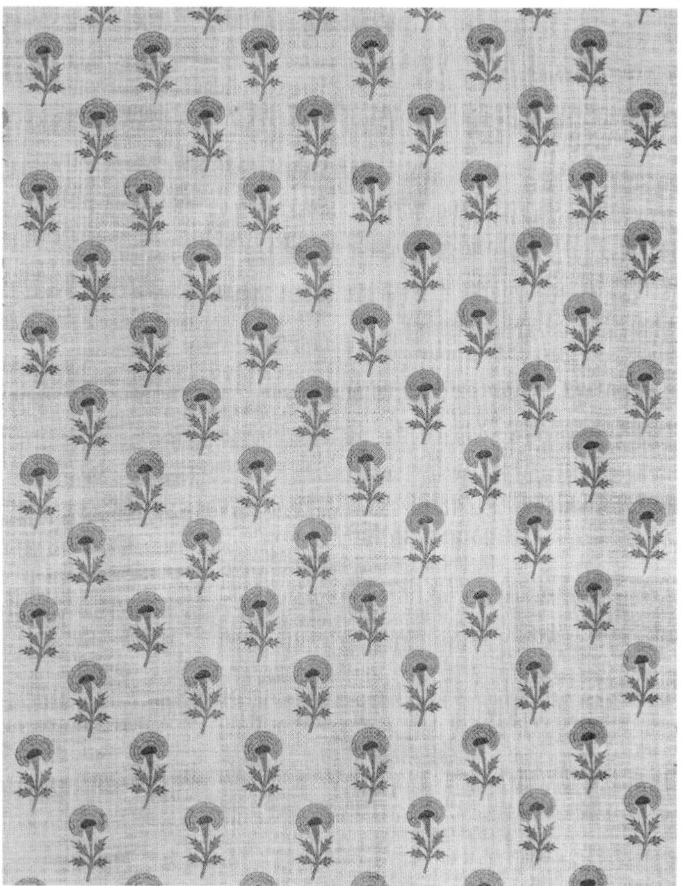

2

1 With its pattern of marigold sprigs, this jacquard-woven silk fabric was made in Switzerland in the 1980s for Hayes Textiles, London, to be exported to Nigeria for use as *gele*, women's head-ties or scarves, worn in West Africa.

2 This is a detail of an almost 10-metre- (33-foot-) long cloth produced in Rajasthan, a region of India renowned for its block printing. The cotton fabric was probably intended to be made into a man's robe and may date to as early as 1772.

3 *African Marigold* furnishing textile is an example of William Morris's ability to create flowing patterns that evoke the vitality of the natural world. The design was printed using woodblocks by Wardle & Co. for Morris & Co., England, in 1876.

1

2

3

4

5

1 This detail from an outer kimono (*uchikake*) depicts peonies created with appliqué and embroidery in silk and gold-wrapped thread, as well as other motifs relating to a kabuki play. The kimono was probably made in Kyoto around 1860–80.

2 A Chelsea Porcelain fruit dish from around 1753 is naturalistically modelled as a crimson- and brown-fringed peony blossom and bud resting between leaves with a stalk-shaped handle.

3 Dating from around 1910, this textile by the British designer Lindsay P. Butterfield is likely to have been inspired by the art of Japan, as the pattern depicts peony flowers with branches of *Prunus* blossom, both having great cultural significance in Asia.

4 Made in Japan in the 19th century, this textile fragment of woven silk is patterned with scrolling stems bearing peonies.

5 This panel of polychrome woven silk with a design of peonies was probably used in a Buddhist temple. The peonies are woven against a sumptuous gold ground, which would have glimmered in the candlelight of the temple.

6 Yasujirō Yamaguchi, a master weaver of Kyoto, made this *karaori*, a type of outer robe worn by actors playing female roles in the classical Nō theatre of Japan, in 1980. Large-scale colourful peonies float across the silk robe's green ground. The composition of auspicious motifs was created for the theatrical role of a beautiful high-ranking younger woman.

6

1

2

1 Made in south-eastern India, this 18th-century palampore (a large bed or wall cover or hanging) was produced specifically for the Western market, using a complex combination of drawing, resist dyeing and mordant. The flowering tree motif is typical of the chintz furnishings exported to Europe at this time.

2 This detail is from a richly embroidered shawl, with floral motifs and peonies on silk crêpe, dating from around 1870 to 1920. Historically, this type of shawl was made in Canton (now Guangzhou), China, and was popular in Europe between 1840 and 1910.

3 During the 18th century, wallpaper was hand-painted in China for the export market. This example was most likely worked in the port city of Canton (Guangzhou) between 1810 and 1830. Peonies have been combined with other flowers and peacocks.

4 The Korean peninsula has a long history of crafting high-quality lacquerware. This lacquered five-tiered wooden box with inlaid decoration of peony scrolls in shimmering mother-of-pearl was made between 1550 and 1599.

5 Among flowering plants, the peony was associated with certain high official ranks in imperial China. The decoration of embroidered peonies covering the surface of this silk panel from 1900 to 1930, used as a hanging or a cover, reflects an appropriate elegance.

3

4

5

1 Symbolizing autumn, chrysanthemums are a very popular motif in Japan. These golden blooms were woven in the 19th century.

2 These autumn-flowering herbaceous perennials are native to East Asia and north-eastern Europe. This chrysanthemum-patterned fragment of silk was woven in China between 1500 and 1799.

3 William Morris's 1883 *Windrush* furnishing fabric shows winding chrysanthemum heads on a leafy background.

4 Chrysanthemums decorate this women's ceremonial robe (*changyi*) from the Tongzhi period (1862–74) of China's Qing dynasty.

5 Designed by William Morris in 1877, *Chrysanthemum* wallpaper shows a mix of flattened leaves and a hint of three-dimensional flowerheads.

6 The complicated *Cray* furnishing fabric pattern, designed by William Morris in 1884, is based on natural forms and inspired by a 17th-century cut velvet Morris had seen at the V&A.

7 In Japan, the chrysanthemum also came to be associated with the imperial family. Depicting two types of chrysanthemum, this cloisonné enamel vase has the mark of the Ando Company, Nagoya, and was made around 1912–26.

1

2

3

4

5

6

7

1

2

3

4

1 This is a detail from a kimono of embroidered and resist-dyed silk crêpe, Japan, 1800–50. The dense pattern of peonies, chrysanthemums and hollyhocks combined with a key-fret pattern is characteristic of kimono worn by women of samurai families.

2 Designed by Émile Gallé, this vase was shown at the 1900 Paris Exposition. Gallé was influenced by Japanese design, and was also a trained botanist; these two interests are combined in the detail shown here.

3 Walter Crane's chrysanthemum design wallpaper was made around 1875, a period that coincides with the Aesthetic Movement in Britain, which was influenced by the displays of Japanese craftsmanship at the V&A in 1862 and in Paris in 1867.

4 Made in the 1960s, this Asian metallic jersey dress is decorated to great effect with large, bold chrysanthemums.

5 The opulence of this figured satin silk kimono made in Japan between 1800 and 1870 suggests it was probably worn by a bride. The shimmering white ground is embroidered with chrysanthemums and other flowers and large butterflies, no two of which are the same.

6 This almost absinthe-coloured printed cotton fabric with a design of intricately connected stems and chrysanthemum heads was manufactured by F. Steiner & Co. in 1903 in Lancashire. It is characteristic of the dynamic Art Nouveau textiles popular in Europe at this time.

5

6

1

1 A 17th-century Ottoman voided silk velvet and metal-thread cushion cover (*yastik*) from Bursa or Istanbul, Turkey, features a central medallion surrounded by carnations.

2 This detail is from a wall hanging depicting carnations and acanthus designed by William Morris around 1880, and worked by May Morris and others between 1900 and 1910.

3 Made of luxurious woven pashm (Tibetan goat hair), prized across South Asia, this fragment of twill-tapestry fabric featuring carnations was recovered from a coat belonging to Tipu Sultan, who ruled the kingdom of Mysore in south India from 1782 to 1799.

4 This small bowl was made in 1893 by the leading enameller of his day, Fernand Thesmar, in Paris. The Ottoman-inspired motifs are expertly created in *plique-à-jour*, a technique that allows light to shine through translucent enamel.

5 British textile and wallpaper designer Sidney Mawson had a long and successful career thanks to his ability to adapt to the fashions of the times and the individual tastes of manufacturers. This naturalistic design was produced by Morton Sundour and sold through Liberty in the 1890s.

6 Lewis Foreman Day created this textile design in 1888 for the leading and innovative textile manufacturer Turnbull & Stockdale of Lancashire. The pattern uses sprays of acanthus leaves and carnations.

2

3

4

5

6

1 This dress fabric sample of silk crêpe de chine with a pattern of *Dianthus* flowers (the genus incorporating pinks and carnations) was produced by the silk-weaving manufacturer Bianchini-Férier in Lyon, France, in 1935.

2 Bianchini-Férier, Lyon, also produced this dress fabric sample with a pattern of *Dianthus* flowers in 1935.

3 Registered by John Trumble and Co. in 1858, *Persian Sprig* wallpaper reflects its designer Owen Jones's interest in Islamic design and his theories that all direct representations of nature in paper hangings should be avoided and natural forms 'conventionalized', or stylized.

4 *Compton* wallpaper was produced in 1896 and is recognized as a collaboration between J.H. Dearle and William Morris, with large-scale flowers resembling gillyflowers similar to the carnation (also known as the clove pink).

5 A tangle of carnations, tulips and saz (*reed*) leaves embellishes a colourful fritware dish from Turkey. Such flowers were used as decorative elements on Iznik pottery of the 16th and 17th centuries.

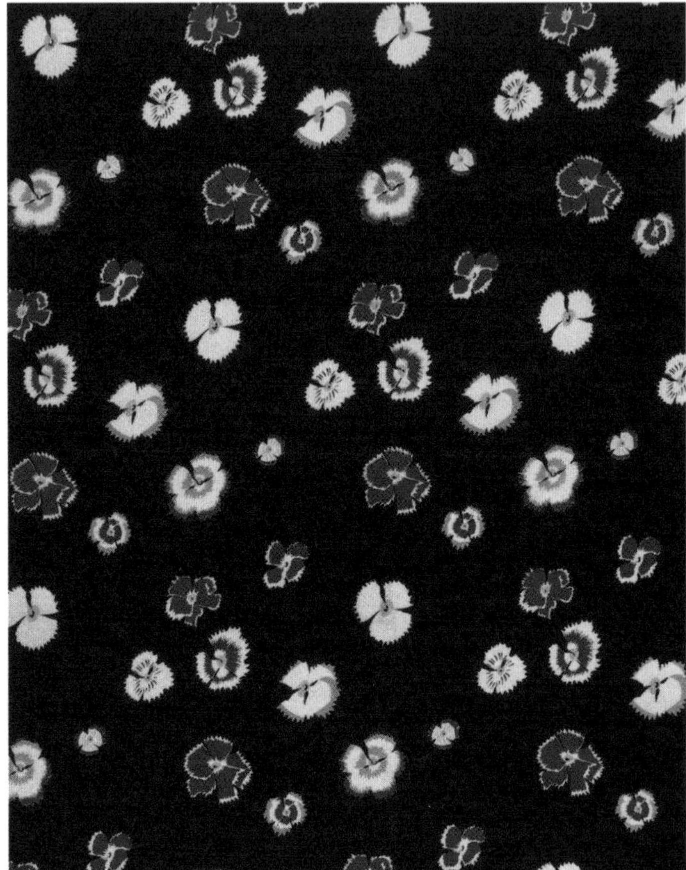

1

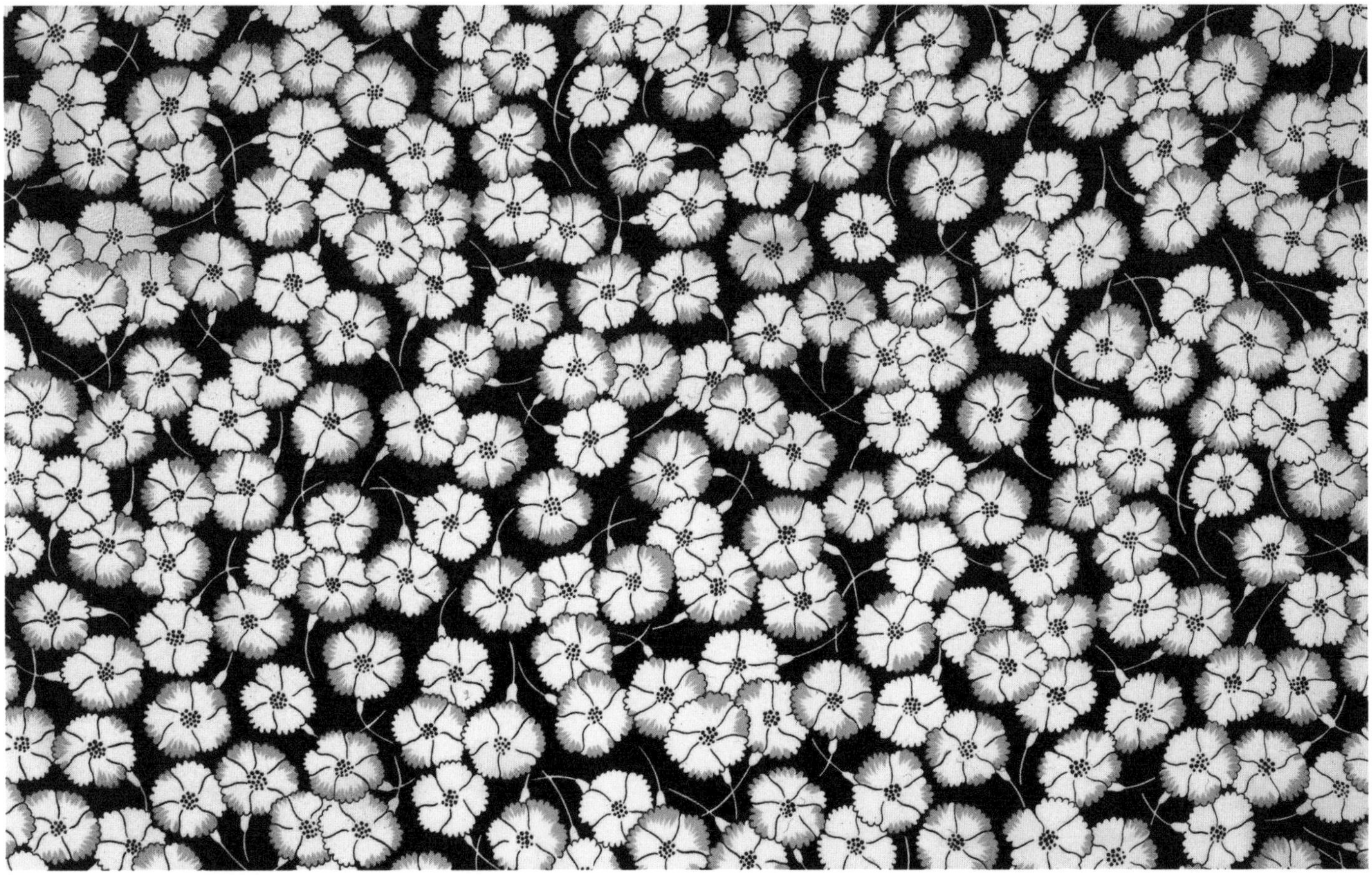

2

3

4

5

1 This Hungarian Art Nouveau-style bowl, probably designed by chemist Vinsce Wartha, was made at the Zsolnay Ceramic Works in 1900, using a glaze that gave an iridescent effect.

2 The crocus design of this fabric by Sanderson from 1932 sits well with the 1930s London Underground posters promoting parks and gardens made accessible by the Tube.

3 Saffron comes from the flower of the saffron crocus, and this 1903 furnishing fabric by George Charles Haité, made by G.P. & J. Baker, portrays its trademark spicy yellow.

4 Crocuses mark the arrival of spring and vary dramatically in colour, as depicted in this 1932 furnishing fabric by Sanderson.

5 Stylized daffodils alternate with more Iranian-style flowers and framework in this wallpaper by J.H. Dearle for Morris & Co., England, from 1903.

6 This incredible headdress was worn by a showgirl at Murray's Cabaret Club, London, in the 1960s. The beads make the headdress extraordinarily heavy.

7 The *Daffodil and Bluebell* carpet design from around 1896, by Walter Crane for James Templeton & Co., demonstrates the interest of Arts and Crafts designers in the forms and colours of British garden flowers.

8 Walter Crane, a founder member and first president of the Arts and Crafts Exhibition Society, designed *Fairy Garden* wallpaper in 1890.

1

2

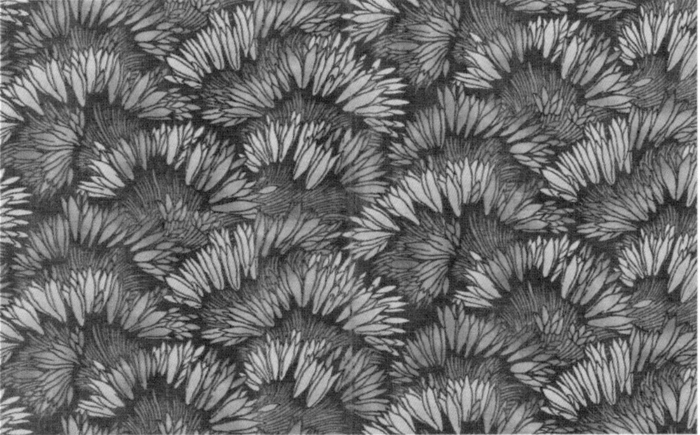

3

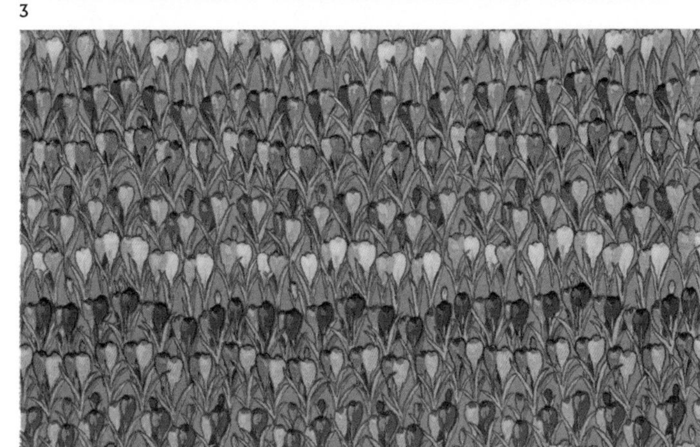

4

5

6

7

8

1 This silk damask, with a regular foliate pattern of stylized iris-like motifs, was jacquard-woven in Bavaria, Germany, in 1870–5.

2 *Iris* printed cotton furnishing fabric was designed by William Morris and manufactured by Thomas Wardle for Morris & Co., England, in 1876.

3 Irises with curved stems and transparent leaves are picked out in white on a grey spotted ground in this furnishing fabric of roller-printed cotton, probably designed by the Silver Studio, London, around 1895.

4 J.H. Dearle designed *Iris* in 1887; it was his first wallpaper design for Morris & Co. Distinctly Dearle, the pattern is more naturalistic than Morris's 1876 printed textile of the same name.

5 The iris was often used as a decorative design in the Aesthetic, Art Nouveau, and Arts and Crafts movements. This wallpaper frieze of flat stylized iris flowers from 1877 is by Walter Crane.

6 This wallpaper frieze in a pale colourway uses highly stylized irises and was designed by Walter Crane in 1877 to accompany his *Iris and Kingfisher* wallpaper.

7 *Iris pallida*, the Dalmatian iris or sweet iris, is depicted flowering in Mary Harper's 1958 *Pallida* furnishing fabric design for Edinburgh Weavers, Carlisle.

8 For this 17th-century Iranian lustreware bowl, an iridescent design of ruby-coloured irises and poppies was created by a second firing of metallic glaze.

1

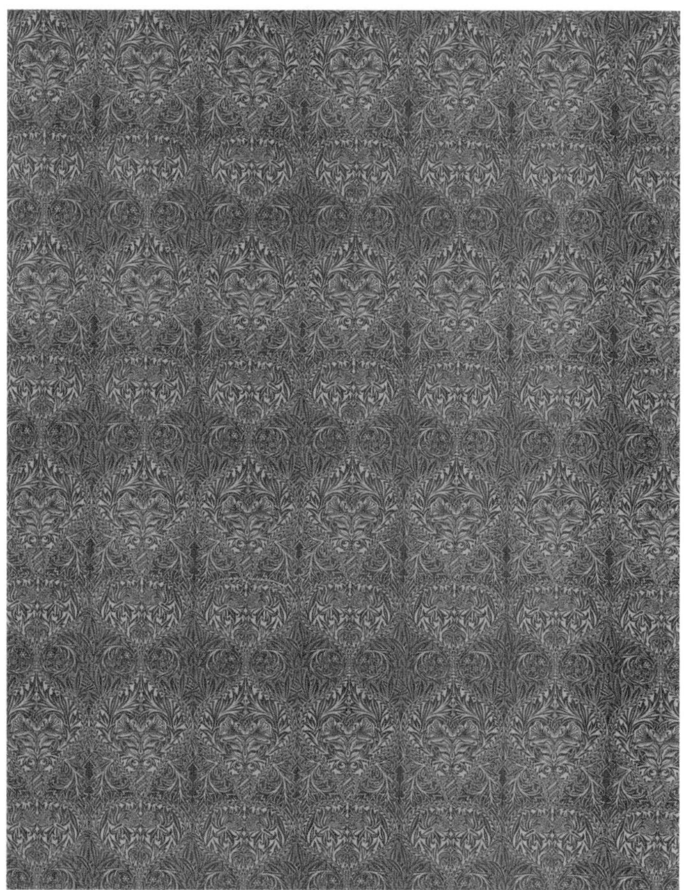

2

3

4

5

6

7

8

1

2

3

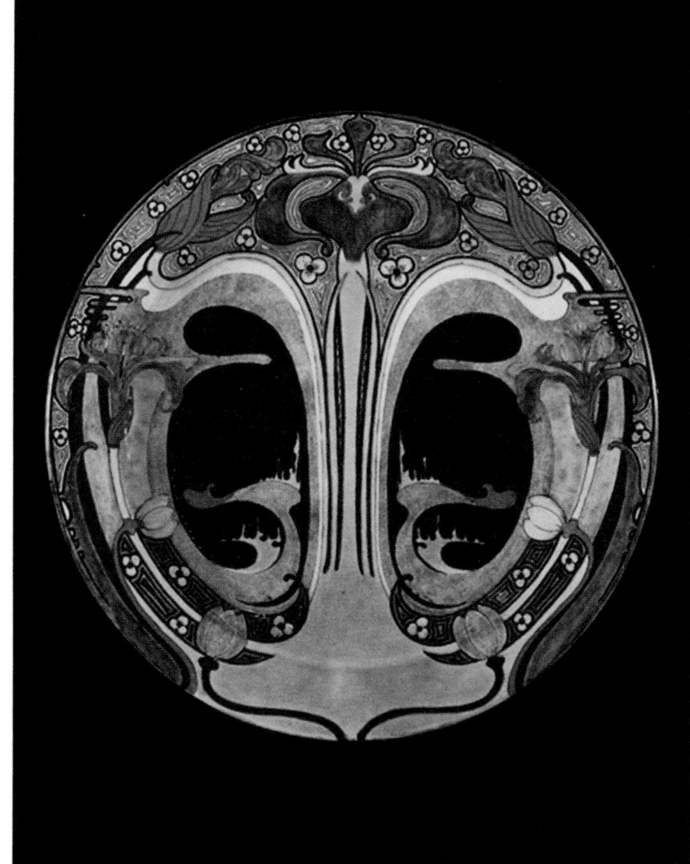
4

1 Irises were one of the most persistent motifs in Japanese art. This buckle by René Lalique, made in Paris in about 1895, is a fine example of the influence of Japan on Art Nouveau design.

2 This is a furnishing fabric by Lindsay P. Butterfield, Britain, from about 1900. The irises are designed in a highly typical Art Nouveau style.

3 This Japanese-inspired wallpaper design dating from 1877, *Iris and Kingfisher*, is by Walter Crane. The fascination with water motifs came from the influence of Japanese design on European decorative arts after the reopening of Japan to trade around 1854.

4 The Brantjes factory in the Netherlands produced this earthenware dish in about 1900, using a stylized iris design probably taken from the pattern books of the Swiss decorative artist Eugène Grasset.

5 In the late 19th century, heavily stylized flowers and leaves such as these were popular Art Nouveau motifs. This design was created by Arthur Silver for the Silver Studio, London.

6 Lacemakers from Burano, near Venice, revived the skill of handmade needle lace, creating copies of historical pieces as well as this highly fashionable and luxurious stole of about 1900, worked in linen thread.

5

6

1

2

3

4

5

1 This detail is from a bed hanging embroidered in a technique known as crewelwork, popular through much of the 17th century. Coiling stems with floral motifs – honeysuckle and other English flowers – formed the most popular designs.

2 William Morris's distinctive, detailed work was largely inspired by the English countryside. Designed in 1876, *Honeysuckle* furnishing fabric combines twining honeysuckle with tulips and acanthus leaves.

3 An Arts and Crafts-style pattern, this furnishing fabric of intertwined leafing and flowering stems with pairs of birds was designed by Sidney Mawson, produced by the Lancashire firm of Turnbull & Stockdale in 1909 and retailed by Liberty in London.

4 Needlework 'slips' were designs depicting plants or floral motifs, often copied from 17th-century herbals, appliquéd on fabric to embellish a larger piece of cloth. This embroidered canvas in coloured silks from around 1600 hovers between botanical literalism and stylized motif.

5 Designed by May Morris in 1883 for wallpaper, *Honeysuckle* features wild and rambling English cottage garden flowers, unlike her father's more woody and stylized version.

6 The flowing style of this gown was popular in the mid-18th century. This example from the 1760s was made with yellow silk brocaded with delicate trails of honeysuckle and rosebuds, woven in Spitalfields, London.

6

1

2

3

4

5

1 Manufacturer Hull Traders of Lancashire was formed in 1957 and won several awards for its fabric designs. John Drummond designed *Hydrangea* furnishing fabric featuring blowsy blue flower heads for the company in 1959.

2 Renowned cloisonné artist Namikawa Yasuyuki of Kyoto, Japan, created this vase around 1875–80.

3 Shown at the Great Exhibition of 1851 by London retailer Jackson & Graham, this Victorian roller-printed and glazed cotton is an example of the most expensive and popular form of summer furnishing fabric available in mid-19th-century Britain.

4 *Jasmine* wallpaper, designed in 1872 by William Morris, features an all-over background pattern of hawthorn leaves overlaid with blossoms and a meandering jasmine trail over the top.

5 This pattern of climbing jasmine was produced for retailers Charles Hindley & Sons, London, in 1845–65.

6 The Art Nouveau enamelled gold brooch seen here, featuring jasmine, was made in Germany around 1903.

7 *Jasmine Trail* furnishing fabric of hand-block-printed chintz was designed by William Morris for Morris & Co., England, in 1868–70. It is thought to be his first design for a printed cotton and was based on an 1830s pattern.

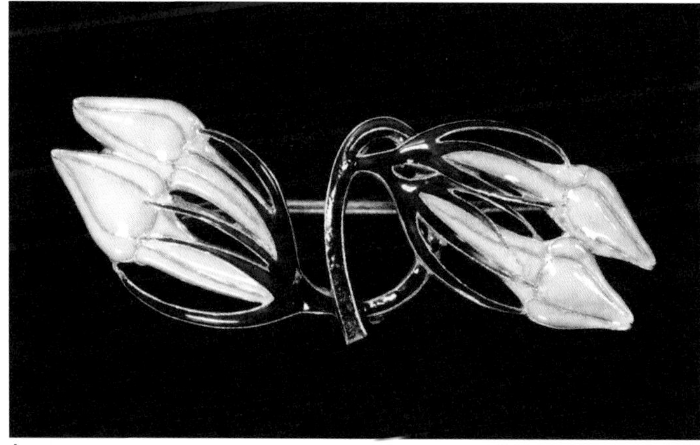
6

7

1

1 Mary Harper was employed at Edinburgh Weavers in 1955 to satisfy the demand for floral chintzes. Her 1958 *Poppies* composition combines larger-than-life screen-printed blooms with a glazed cotton finish.

2 The flowers on this silk georgette dress fabric in a French Modernist style, produced by the British Calico Printers' Association in 1933, shine with fresh life and vigour.

3 William Morris designed this *Poppy* wallpaper in 1881, and it was manufactured by Jeffrey & Co., London.

4 Carl Almquist, known for his stained-glass designs, was commissioned by the Lancaster firm Shrigley & Hunt to design windows for the nursery at Pownall Hall in Wilmslow, Cheshire. He designed this panel, depicting poppies and bats, around 1886.

5 This design for *Poppy Head* wallpaper frieze by English designer Lewis Foreman Day, from about 1891–2, shows the seed pods of the opium poppy.

6 This 1901 *Poppies* furnishing fabric by Lindsay P. Butterfield is representative of the second generation of the Arts and Crafts Movement. It shows the fine draughtsmanship and passion for gardens that was a common feature of the movement's designers.

7 *Poppyland* furnishing textile was designed and retailed by Liberty, London. It features a meadow of poppies and is typical of the retailer's style in the early 1900s.

2

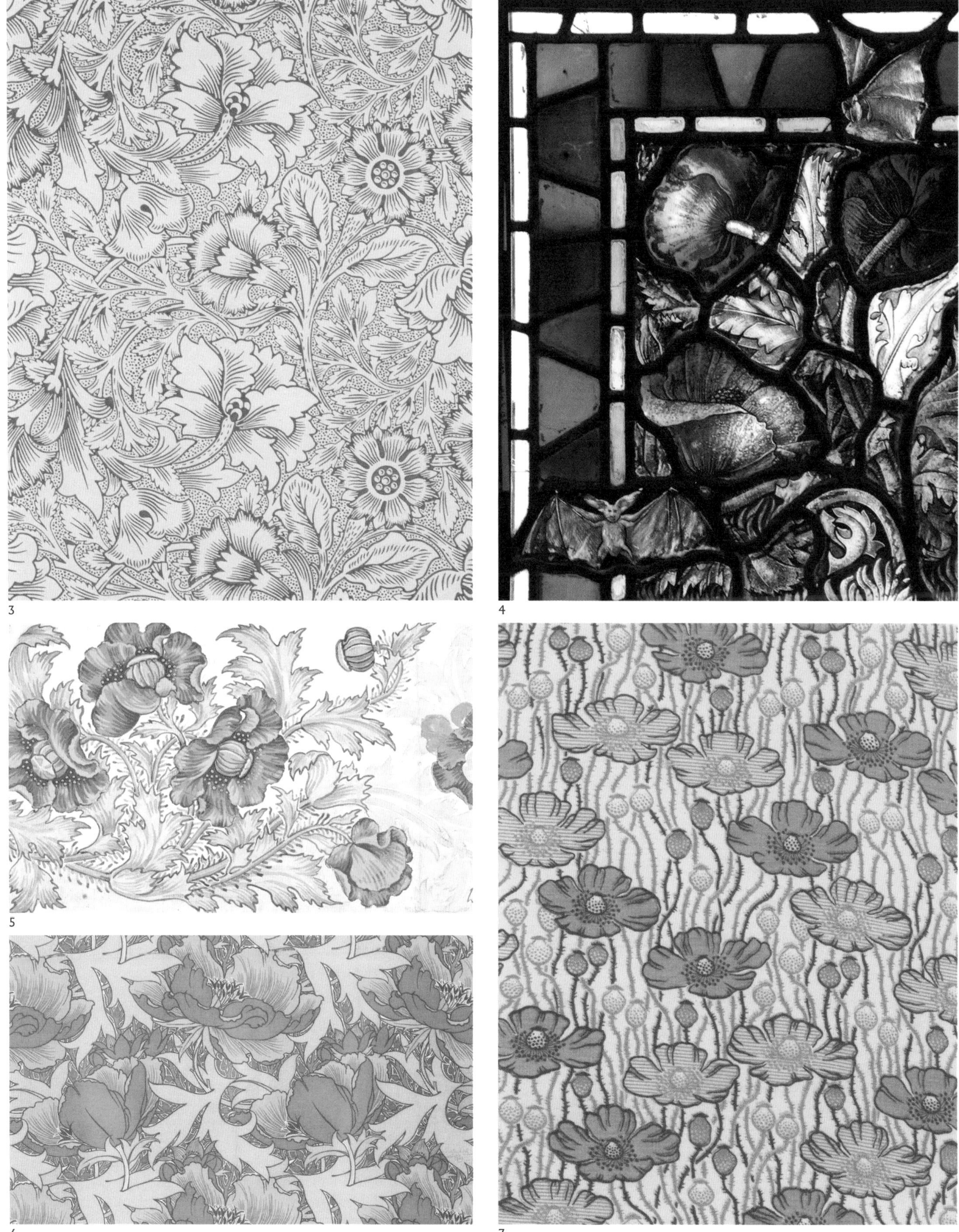

3

4

5

6

7

1

2

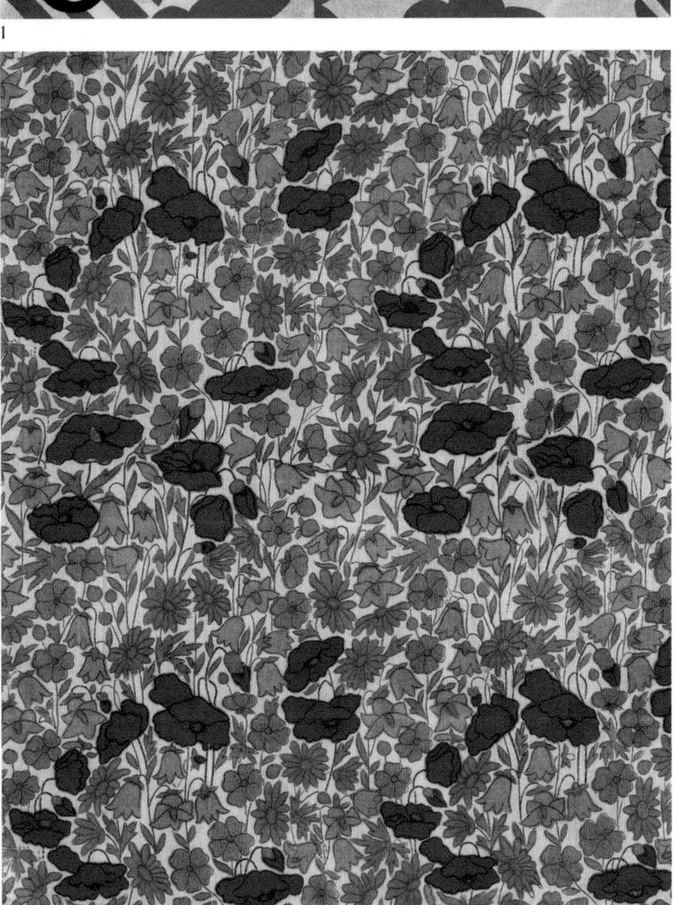
3

1 Ossie Clark was one of Britain's most influential fashion designers of the 1960s and 1970s. Throughout his career he used the textiles designed by his wife, Celia Birtwell. This man's shirt from 1968 to 1970 features one of her vibrant patterns, mingling swirls with poppies.

2 Poppies can be found in the summer months in English fields and hedgerows. This pattern was created by British textile designer Mary Yonge in the 1960s–70s and uses a variety of wild flowers arranged in a rhythmic repeating pattern.

3 The field poppies on this *Poppy and Daisy* block-printed silk handkerchief, produced and sold by the fashionable London-based retailer Liberty in 1929–30, suggest the fragility of nature.

4 British manufacturer F. Steiner & Co. bought Art Nouveau-style patterns from freelance designers in France and Belgium. The poppy's frilled petals and elongated leaves were often adapted for the firm's designs in the early 20th century.

5 The careful arrangement of the finely drawn sprays of poppies in this F. Steiner & Co. 1903 furnishing textile emphasizes their stylistic properties over their humble meadow origins.

6 Here, a sequence of abstracted poppy petals and leaves creates a fluid, swirling design in unusual colours. It was produced in 1903 by F. Steiner & Co.

7 This vase by English potter William Moorcroft from the 1920s has a big poppy design over a mottled background.

4

5

6

7

1

2

3

1 Carl Almquist created this section of a window around 1886 for Shrigley & Hunt, Lancaster, makers of stained glass, for the nursery at Pownall Hall in Cheshire.

2 This woven silk fabric with a sunflower repeat was designed around 1880 by Bruce J. Talbert for Warner & Ramm. The pattern's name, *Nagasaki*, shows the influence of Japanese design.

3 *Sunflowers* is a woven wool and cotton furnishing fabric designed by C.F.A. Voysey around 1895. Many of Voysey's patterns echo William Morris's use of plant motifs.

4 The intense, geometric patterns of Japanese art inspired Bruce J. Talbert's design for this silk curtain (*c.*1870-80), probably woven in Essex or Suffolk.

5 Howard Carter's 1961 fabric for Heal's, London, features a life-size sunflower, just as its petals become dry and the seeds turn black. *Sunflower* was a Council of Industrial Design award winner in 1962.

6 This section of railing is from the Japanese Pavilion at the Centennial Exhibition of 1876 in Philadelphia and the 1878 Exposition Universelle, Paris. The wrought- and cast-iron pavilion designed by Thomas Jeckyll was made by Barnard, Bishop and Barnard of Norwich.

7 Grautex Fabrics of Copenhagen was a leading Danish textile company from the 1950s to the 1970s, often producing designs resulting from collaborations with well-known artists and designers. The striking *Sunflower* dates from 1951.

4

5

6

7

1

2

3

4

5

1 The stylish Art Nouveau sketch shown here depicts hemlock and thistles. It is a design for a printed textile, possibly by Harry Napper for the Silver Studio, manufactured by G.P. & J. Baker in 1900.

2 This woven cotton furnishing fabric with a pattern of spiky plant forms was designed by Harry Napper and produced around 1895 by the Silver Studio, a commercial design practice in Hammersmith, London.

3 Designed by Émile Gallé in 1889, this vase has an asymmetrical, informal arrangement of thistles that derives from Japanese prints. The thistle was also a symbol for the Lorraine area of France, Gallé's home region.

4 This huge, bold print of teasels was created by Jane Daniels for Heal's in 1960. Although the teasel does not belong to the thistle tribe, they both have sharp leaves and purple flowers. Daniels's painterly interpretation captures the dried seed heads.

5 Miles & Edwards opened on London's Oxford Street in 1822. It specialized in fabric for curtains and furniture, fringes and cords. This panel of chintz fits with the craze for the Scottish countryside led by Queen Victoria and Prince Albert in the 1840s and 1850s.

6 *Villa Louis Persian Thistle* is a 2001 reproduction of an 1880s textile by Thomas Wardle produced by Scalamandré for the refurbishment of the Villa Louis historic house museum in Wisconsin. The pattern is screen printed on cotton velveteen.

6

1

1 Mary Oliver based this 1976 printed cotton *Lily Pond* furnishing fabric for Heal's on a photograph. A newsprint effect is created with tones and half-tones in leaf-green dots on a white ground.

2 The writhing stems and bright colours in this 1903 F. Steiner & Co. printed cotton furnishing fabric give it a dynamic Art Nouveau character, more typical of continental European than British textiles of this time.

3 This majolica-style water lily plate moulded in low relief was produced by John Adams & Co. in Hanley, Staffordshire, in 1865–73.

4 William Morris's *Lotus* design of 1875 combines the Asian lotus motif with his characteristic acanthus leaves and stylized flowers for this embroidered hanging. It was worked in the 1880s by Margaret Beale in silks on canvas purchased in kit form from Morris & Co, England.

5 A detail from a large fragment of chintz hanging, finely printed with lotus plants and insects, produced in south-eastern India in the early 18th century for the European market.

6 This opal glass decorated with enamel was probably made in Stourbridge, Worcestershire, around 1850. The design of water lilies makes reference to the goblet's intended use as a table glass for water.

2

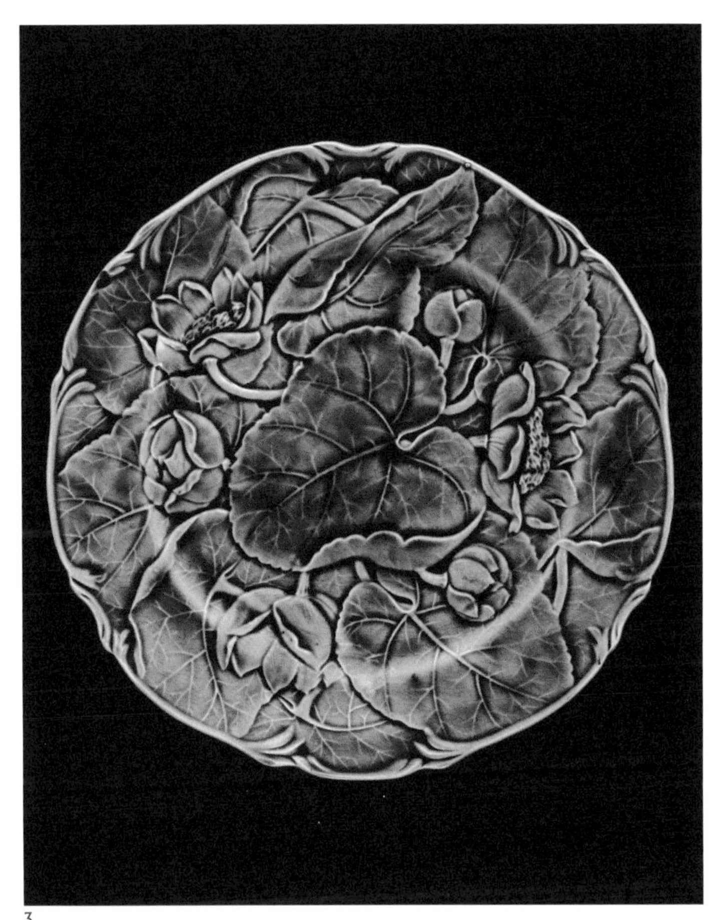
3

4

5

6

1 Grace Sullivan's design for printed cotton was produced by Heal's, London, for curtains and soft furnishings in 1972. It is based on an Asian motif, with a small waterlily and leaves creating a repeating grid pattern.

2 Sinuous stems, a typical element of the Art Nouveau style, were ingeniously arranged to form a symmetrical pattern on this printed furnishing fabric, *Waterlilies*, from around 1900 by Harry Napper for G.P. & J. Baker.

3 Lotus plants with pink flowers offset against a swastika pattern in gold decorate this 19th-century Chinese robe tapestry woven in silk.

4 First issued in 1915, G.P. & J. Baker's *Nympheus* furnishing fabric became an all-time favourite. The original design by William Turner was based on a Ming dynasty (1368–1644) painted silk scroll depicting an egret sheltering beneath lotus leaves.

5 The stylized lotus motif in this 1858 wallpaper pattern by British architect and designer Owen Jones was inspired by the Ancient Egyptian symbol of creation or rebirth.

6 The underside of a lotus flower is moulded in relief and painted and gilded on this Qing dynasty porcelain snuff bottle dating from around 1750.

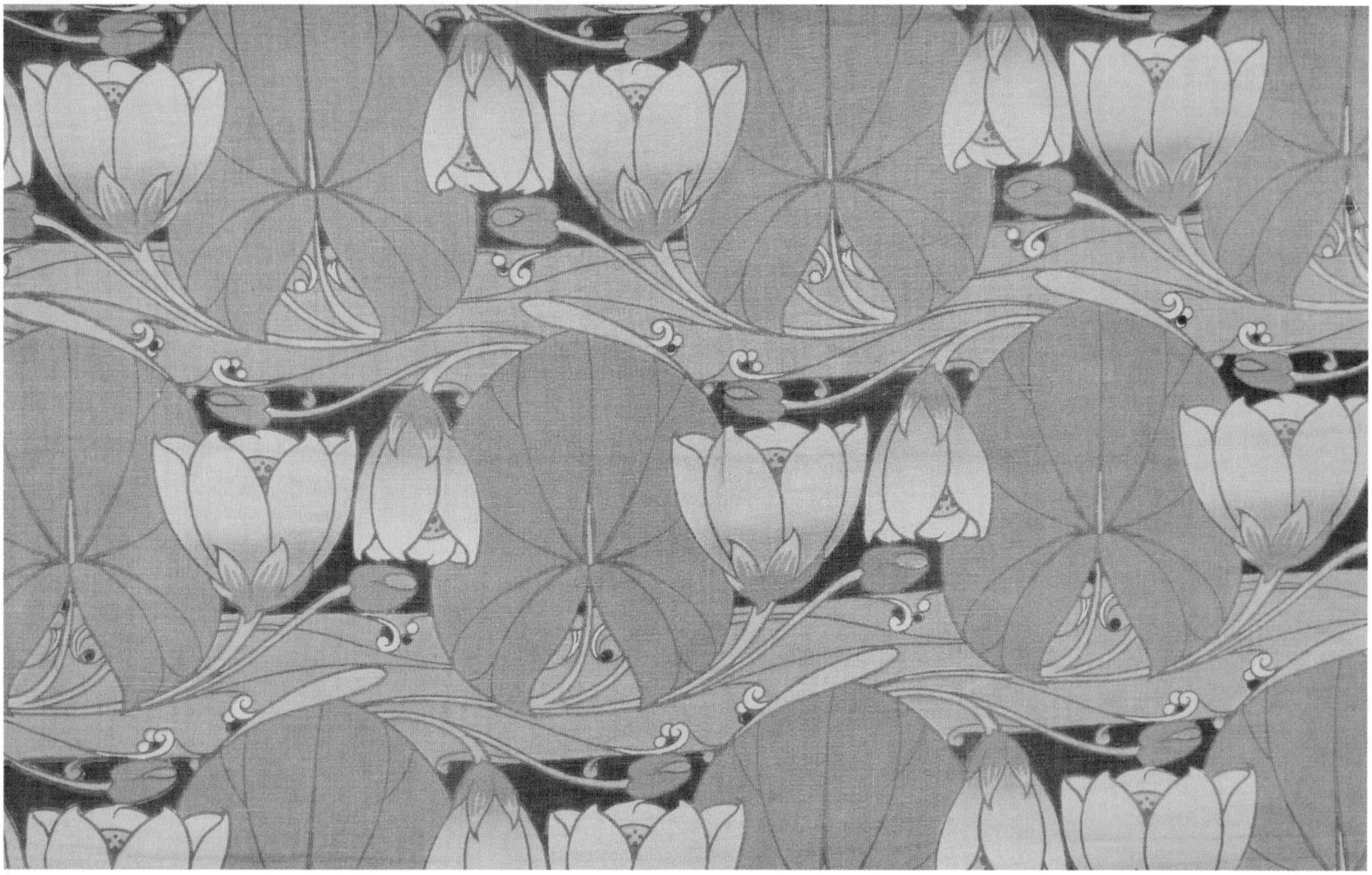

1

2

3

4

5

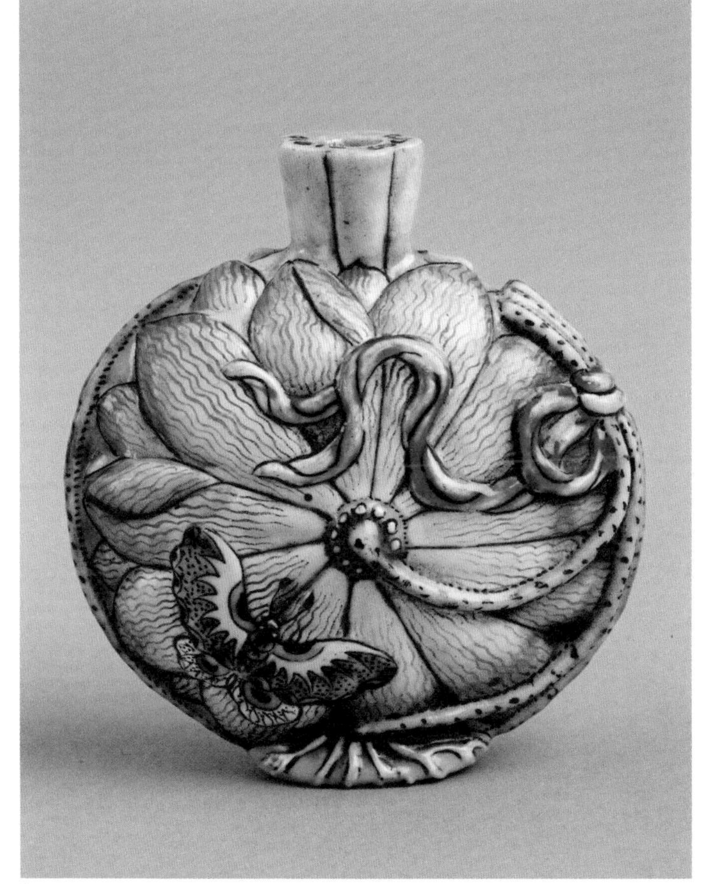
6

1

2

3

4

1 In the 1860s Owen Jones published a book on what he identified as Chinese ornament. Many of the pattern motifs were sourced from the V&A's early holdings. This design is based on a cloisonné enamel vase.

2 J.H. Dearle designed *Clover* wallpaper for Morris & Co. in 1903. The pattern combines clover flowers and tree blossom.

3 This wallpaper from 1875–8 by Bruce J. Talbert for Jeffrey & Co., London, is an example of the Anglo-Japanese style of the Aesthetic Movement, with a crowded pattern of blossom.

4 Daphne Barder's patterns are often based on naturalistic plant forms; however, as this textile design from the 1960s to 1970s shows, she could also invent her own motifs. This Marimekko-like pattern captures the British preoccupation with Scandinavian design.

5 Cloisonné enamels are one of the great glories of Meiji-period craftsmanship (1868–1912). This elegant unsigned vase (*c.*1900) was recognized as one of his own works by Nagoya-based cloisonné artist Ando Jubei on his visit to the V&A in 1910.

6 Some Japanese kimono were made specifically for export to the West around the turn of the 20th century. This example, owned by wealthy American socialite Emilie Grigsby, is decorated with opulent wisteria embroidery.

7 A spray of wisteria is given an Aesthetic refinement by Walter Crane in this wallpaper border of around 1875 to 1910.

5

6

7

1

2

1 British designers have been inspired by the Japanese stylization of nature since the 1870s. The blossom and wave design on this F. Steiner & Co. cotton satin furnishing fabric from 1902 is an example of the Japanese influence on design persisting into the early 20th century.

2 This detail from a lavish kimono for a young unmarried woman (*furisode*), made in Kyoto in 2014, has an overall design of peonies, chrysanthemums and plum blossom among gold clouds and bamboo.

3 These waves of blossom are from an album of synthetic and silk fabric swatches of kimono fabric produced by the Oka Trading Company, Japan, in 1938.

4 The decoration of *Prunus* blossoms and branches against a background of cracked ice may signify that this porcelain jar was intended as a present for the New Year. It was produced in Jingdezhen, China, between 1683 and 1710. Chinese jars such as this were very popular in the late 19th century in Europe, where they were known as 'ginger jars'.

5 Made in Manchester by the Calico Printers' Association in 1911, this fabric, probably for furnishings, has an all-over pattern that evokes a Japanese aesthetic, by then assimilated into British design.

3

4

5

2

3

1 William Turner's textiles and wallpapers adopted a Chinese feel as he studied the East Asia collections of the V&A and the British Museum, London. This wallpaper is based on an 18th-century Chinese panel housed in the V&A, and adapted to suit British taste.

2 This late 18th-century textile design is painted in gouache. The unusual small-scale patterning was a speciality of Peter, a French textile merchant and dyeworks.

3 This 18th-century textile design of stylized blossom is another example from Peter. It might have been produced as a jacket lining.

4 Although this hand-painted gouache textile design was created by Peter in the 1790s, it looks very late 1960s in style. The *ramoneur* (chimney sweep) background used in designs such as this could be dark brown or bronze coloured but was usually black.

4

1

2

3

4

1 Flowers from both field and garden featured in Morris & Co.'s designs. *Garden* wallpaper by J.H. Dearle from 1899 is typical of the Arts and Crafts period, featuring a symmetrical pattern of forget-me-nots, foliage and lilies.

2 By the 19th century, Indian makers were producing painted wood and papier-mâché goods, including chairs, for Western tourists. This Kashmiri armchair from 1870 has never been used, so its 'thousand flowers' decoration is beautifully preserved.

3 This gold lamé evening bag dating from 1934–1940 is embroidered with a garden-path design and cottage flowers made of green velvet appliqué, moulded glass gems and beads.

4 *Flower Bed* was designed by Trenton Doyle Hancock in 2003. This screen print on vinyl-coated paper is part of a body of work that explores extensive fantastical narratives through parables about good and evil.

5 This Derby Porcelain Factory bottle has an explosion of floral forms encrusted on the body. Sometimes described as a scent bottle, it is impractical for use, as the decoration is far too delicate and sharp for regular handling. It dates to around 1840.

6 Bianchini-Férier is the longest continuously running silk mill in Europe. Founded in Lyon, France, in 1888, the firm was renowned for its silk velvets and brocades for haute couture. This silk dress fabric featuring asters and daisies dates to 1935.

5

6

1

1 This design for a textile by Lindsay P. Butterfield from about 1910 features a pattern of floral sprigs that look as if they take their inspiration from early 17th-century herbals and English embroidered slips.

2 *Spiralling Meadow*, an acrylic handbag, features a carved motif of insects and wild flowers, hand-dyed and lightly hand-painted. The technique of internal carving in acrylic creates an effect of fine cut glass with three-dimensional motifs.

3 This is one of a group of designs by the merchant Peter, who produced fast-dyed chintzes at his factory in France in the 18th and early 19th centuries.

4 Named after the flowering herb, this small-scale pattern, *Eyebright*, was designed by William Morris for Morris & Co., England, in 1883.

5 Produced by Turnbull & Stockdale, this printed cotton features a dense design of herbaceous flowers. The Lancashire firm produced fabrics used for Arts and Crafts interiors in the late 19th and early 20th centuries.

6 This dress fabric of printed silk was designed and made by Bianchini-Férier, Lyon, France, in 1935. The company produced thousands of bold floral designs for dressmakers and couturiers during the 20th century.

7 Featuring the garden annual love-in-a-mist, this furnishing fabric of printed cotton was produced by Newman, Smith & Newman, England, in 1909.

2

3

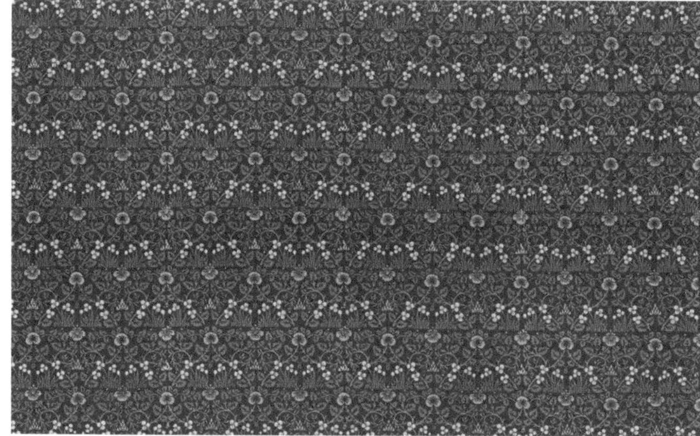
4

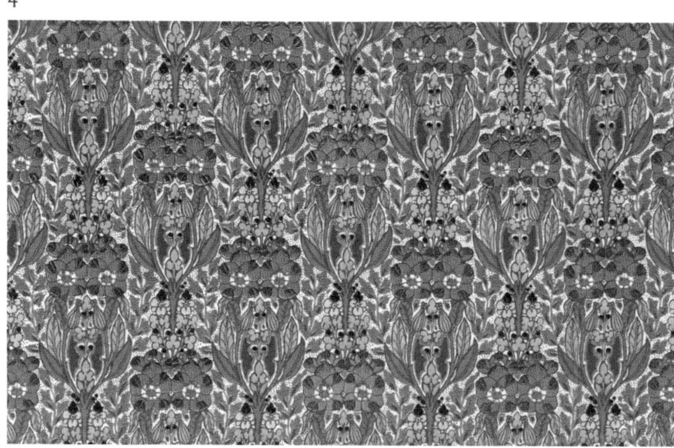
5

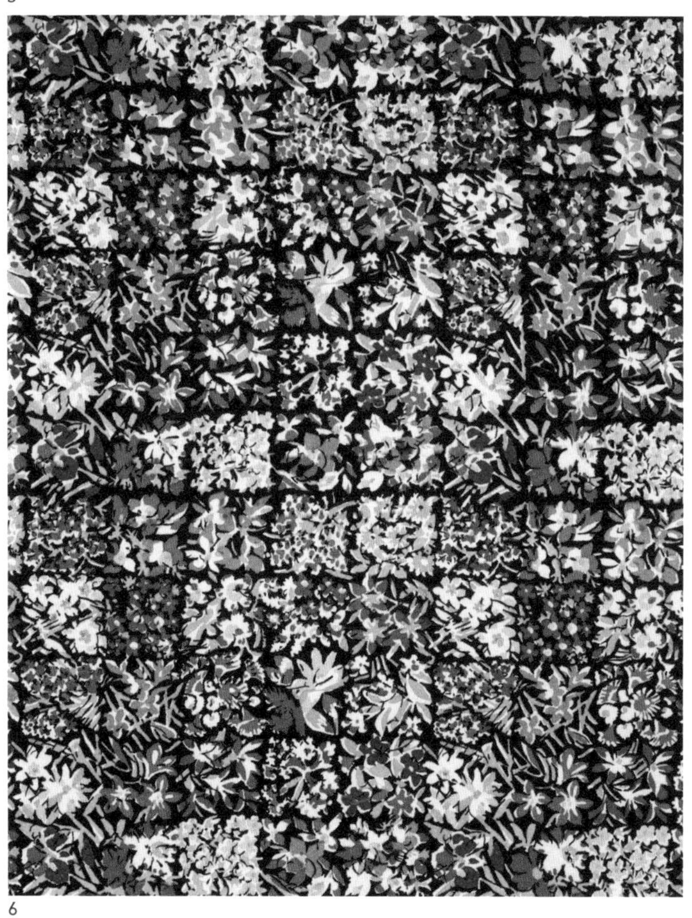
6

7

1

2

3

4

5

1 This is a detail from a day dress from about 1830 made of block-printed cotton. The vivid Turkey-red background is scattered with naturalistically rendered sprigs of heather and stems of marigolds and valerian.

2 This delicate design for a printed textile was created by the textile merchant and dyeworks Peter in France in 1794. The chintz pattern uses *bonnes herbes* (small flowers and leaves) motifs arranged on a *ramoneur* (chimney sweep) background. *Ramoneur* backgrounds used in designs such as this could be black, dark brown or bronze.

3 *Matthiola bicornis*, commonly known as evening stock, night-scented stock or perfume plant, is the perfect choice for a cottage garden. Its tall, sturdy flowering stems are depicted on this printed cotton sample from 1936 by the Calico Printers' Association, Manchester.

4 Produced by the Lyonnais textile manufacturer Bianchini-Férier around 1935, this silk dress fabric has a pattern of daisies, their white petals radiating out from a sunny yellow centre.

5 *Cow Parsley*, from 1954, is Annette McClintock's mid-century interpretation of love-in-a-mist and white umbellifers for a Liberty furnishing fabric. The ethereal flowers float above the cocoa-coloured ground.

6 With its colourful pattern of daisies, this is another sample of printed cotton dress fabric by the Calico Printers' Association, from 1932.

6

1

1 Designed by J.H. Dearle in 1912 for Morris & Co., England, this *Michaelmas Daisy* wallpaper pattern depicts the asters, or Michaelmas daisies, that grow in late summer and autumn arranged in a curving trellis design.

2 A member of the Arts and Crafts Movement, A.F. Vigers created the *Mallow* wallpaper pattern around 1899–1909. The design reflects the movement's interest in simple yet pleasing colour schemes and motifs drawn from native British wildflowers.

3 This is a detail from a summer mini-dress designed by French fashion designer André Courrèges in 1967. Raised pink daisies are applied in a repeating pattern over the whole of the nylon organza dress, each with a glimmering centre of iridescent Perspex.

4 Produced in the 1830s, this finely printed cotton furnishing fabric of meadow flowers has a timeless appeal. The design includes cornflower, poppy, scabious, hawkweed and grasses.

2

3

2

3

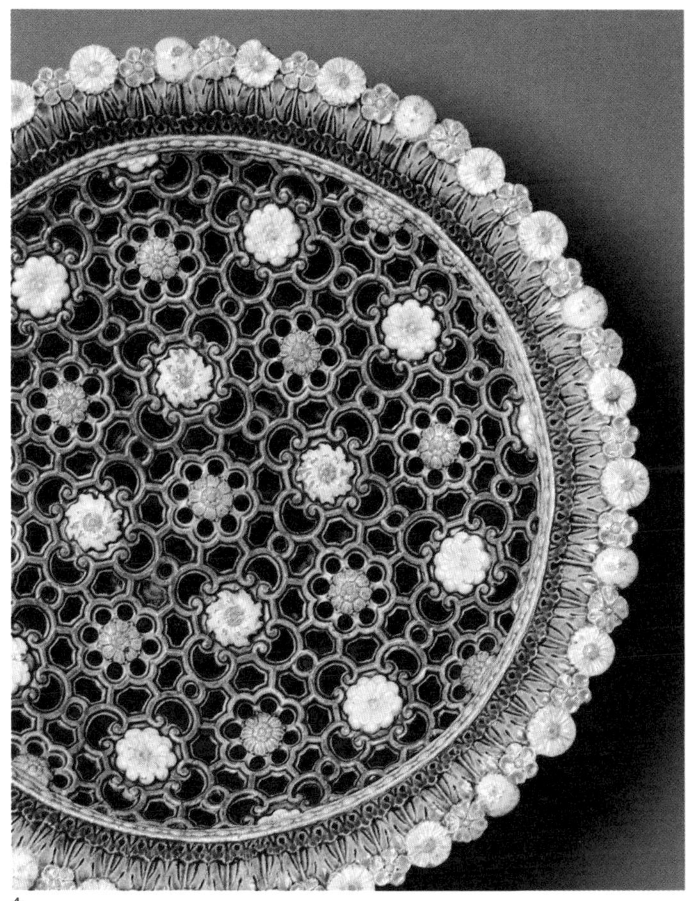
4

1 This beautiful *Columbine* wallpaper was one of several designed by A.F. Vigers in the late 1890s to early 1900s. The delphinium, love-in-a-mist and aquilegia illustrations are stylized just enough to avoid disturbing the Arts and Crafts Movement's distaste for realism.

2 Mary Yonge's characteristic use of bold colour and naturally inspired forms is evident in this textile design of the 1960s–70s. A melange of ivy, bark and tropical daisies makes it seem both exotic and suburban at the same time.

3 Rayon crêpe was especially suitable as a fabric for the fluid bias-cut dresses of the 1930s. This example with an all-over pattern of daisies was screen printed by the Calico Printers' Association, Manchester, in 1935.

4 The pierced clay decoration in this dish incorporates a motif of daisies, or marguerites, which were popular in France at the time it was made in the first half of the 17th century.

5 *Meadow Flowers* by Walter Crane from 1896 is a dense design of flora in jewel-tone colours, which impart a calming and comforting influence. Typical of Crane's designs, there is pattern everywhere, with no blank spaces to be found.

5

1

2

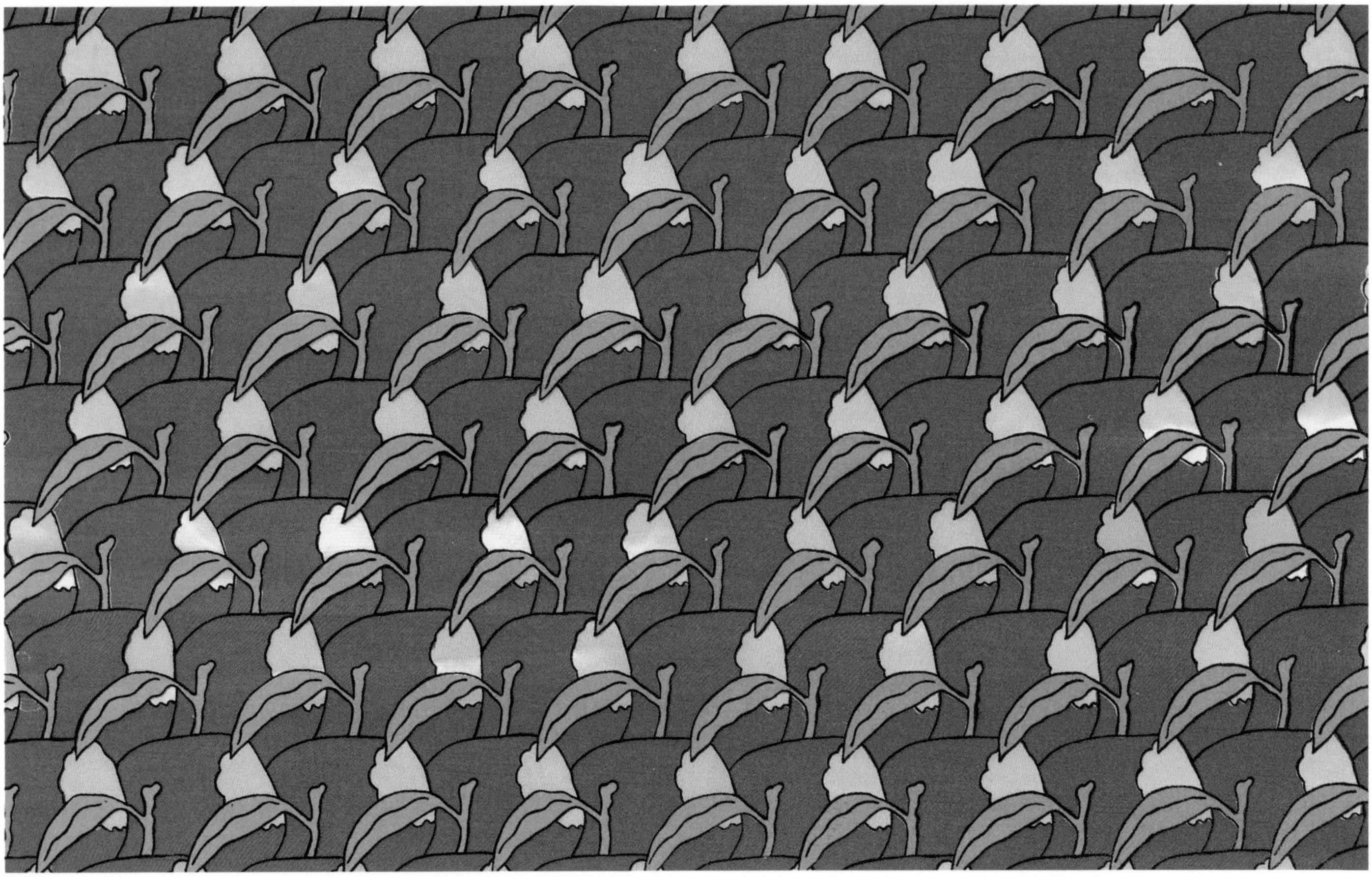

3

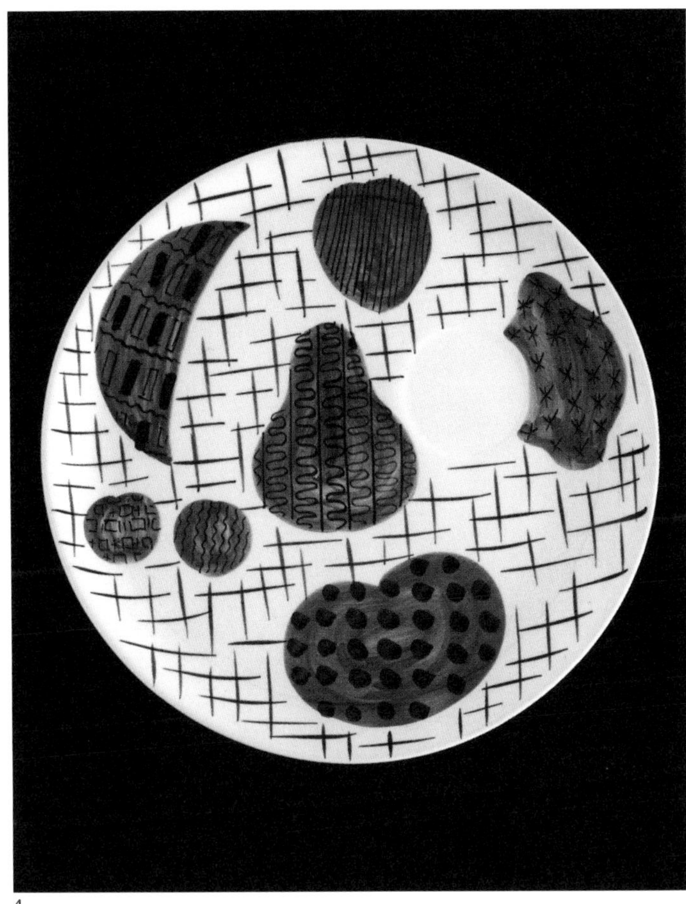

4

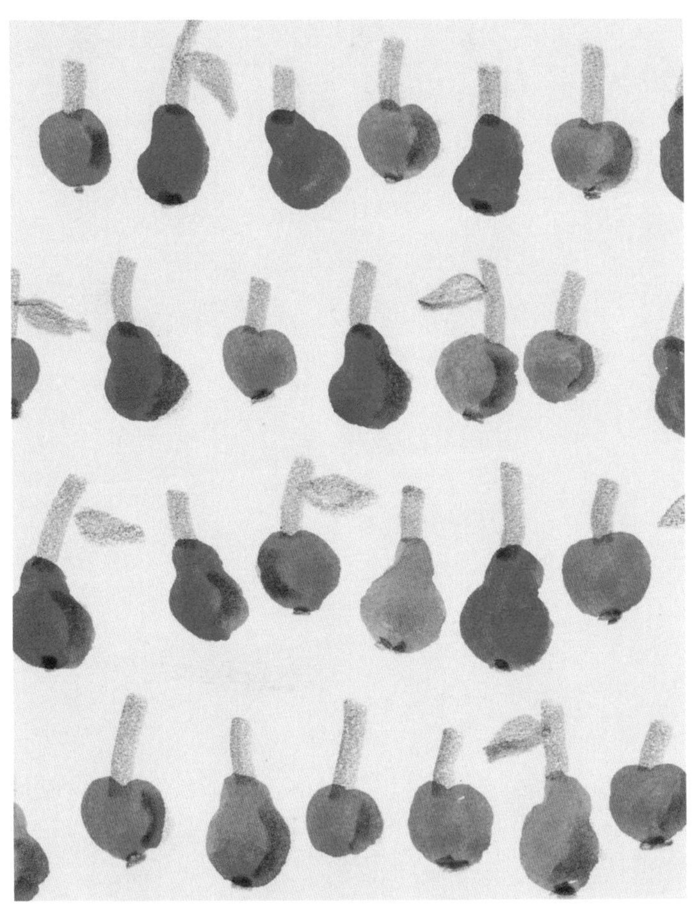

5

1 This joyful 1970s ink and watercolour design for a textile is by Mary Yonge. Previously Head of Studio at Courtaulds, Yonge freelanced from the 1960s for companies such as Liberty, London, and Edinburgh Weavers, Carlisle.

2 This is another 1970s ink and watercolour textile design by Mary Yonge. While working at Courtaulds, Yonge also taught one day a week at the Central School of Art and Design, London, where she had been a student.

3 A cheeky bite has been taken out of each red apple in this pattern from 1973. *Apples*, designed by Jane Wentworth for OK Textiles of London, is printed here on satin furnishing fabric.

4 Made in Italy around 1955, this hand-painted plate and its accompanying cup (not pictured) were created specially for meals eaten in front of the television.

5 Joyce Badrocke was a textile designer for Horrockses Fashions, Lancashire, in the late 1940s and 1950s. This simple, sweet design of apples and pears is from her archive.

6 *Appia*, this printed furnishing fabric with cheerful motifs of cross-sections of fruit in bold colours, was produced by British textile manufacturer Morton Sundour, Carlisle, around 1960.

6

1 This enamelled 14th-century Italian pomander, resembling an apple, would originally have held aromatic spices and hung from a long girdle worn at the waist or hips.

2 William Morris designed *Apple* wallpaper in 1877. The pattern combines apples and scrolling acanthus leaves against a background of foliage.

3 Robert Tierney experimented with a variety of stylistic idioms in his screen-printed fabrics for Edinburgh Weavers, Carlisle. His harmonious *Pears* design dates from 1961.

4 J.H. Dearle's designs often adapt motifs taken from earlier patterns by Morris. Here the large swirling leaves of *Orchard* (1899) are inspired by Morris's *Acanthus*, and the background recalls *Daisy*, the first wallpaper issued by Morris & Co.

5 *Kier*, from 1954, showcases Robert Stewart's strong design identity with its combination of fruit motifs set within a geometric composition and its vibrant colour palette.

6 This lid from an ivory box was made around 1800–50 by an unknown artist in France.

7 Lindsay P. Butterfield's designs were based on plant forms that were recognizable but subtly stylized, such as this wallpaper frieze from 1905.

8 Butterfield used his skilled draughtsmanship working for design firms that produced patterns for wallpapers and textiles, such as this 1898 *Apple* design for G.P. & J. Baker.

1

2

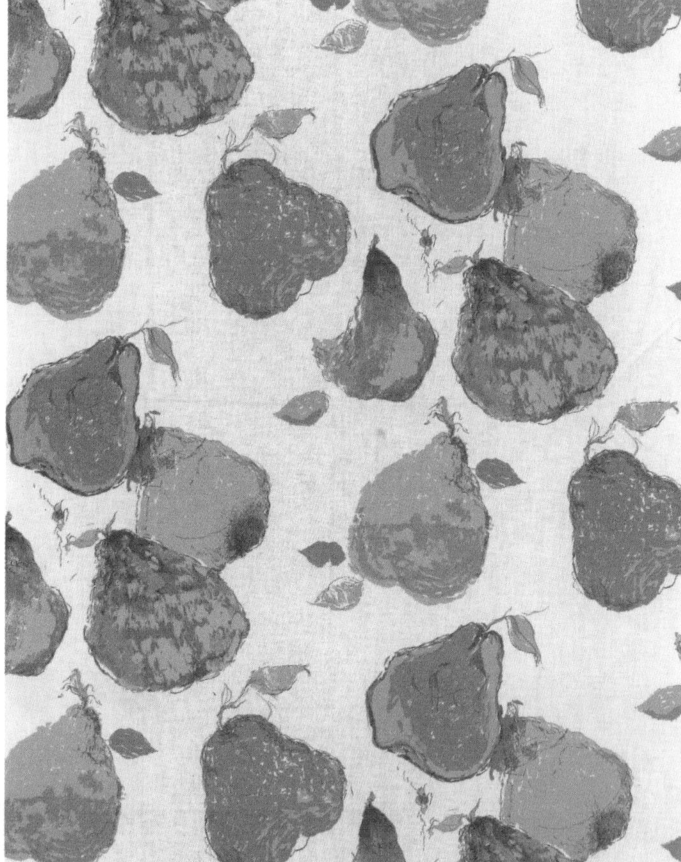

3

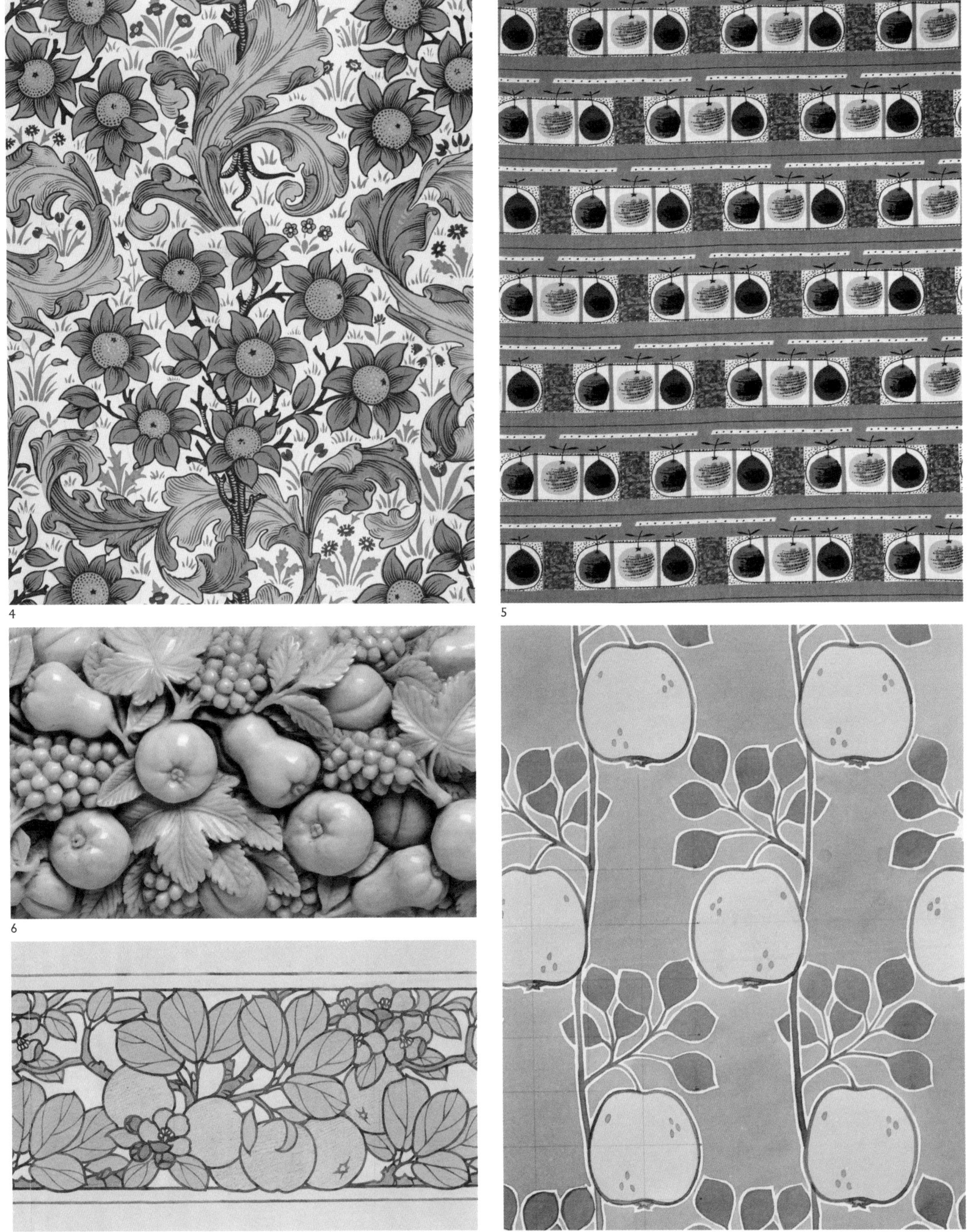

4

5

6

7

8

1

2

1 Depicting fruiting boughs and orange fruits, this Aesthetic Movement wallpaper panel by Lewis Foreman Day was made in London by Jeffrey & Co. in 1874.

2 Elizabethan 'slips' are small motifs cut out and applied to larger pieces of fabric, such as bed curtains. Often naive in design and out of scale, they are carefully worked with shaded colours. This example stitched in silk on linen canvas from around 1600 depicts a lemon branch.

3 This 1890s dinner dress with its distinctive design would have been dramatic when worn. The realistic pattern was woven with a jacquard loom, perhaps in the Spitalfields area of London.

4 The *Appelsiini*, or *Citrus*, pattern bursts off this printed cotton fabric designed by Maija Isola in 1956 and produced in Helsinki, Finland, by Printex. Finnish textiles were at the forefront in modern interiors in post-war Europe.

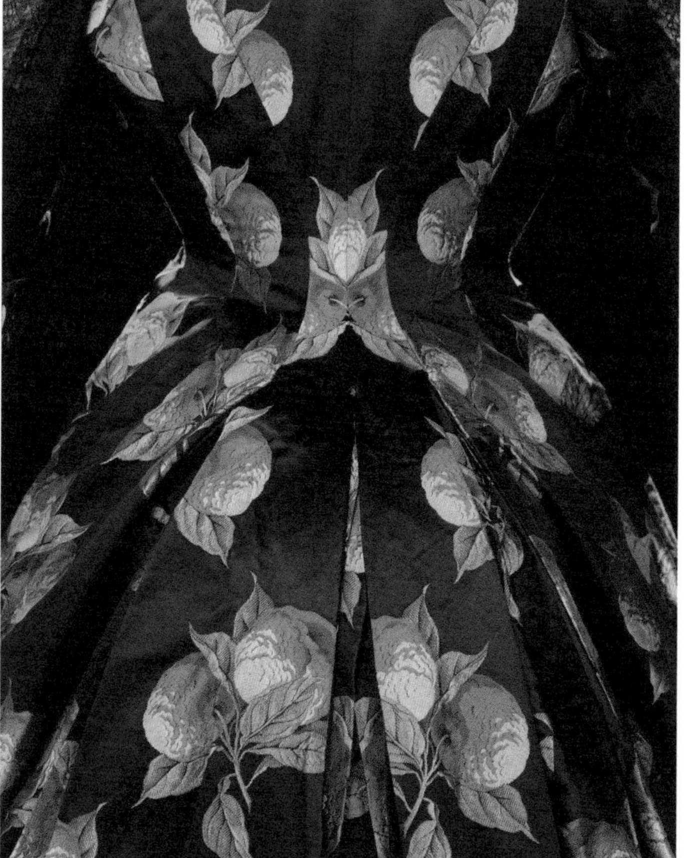

3

1

2

3

4

5

1 C.F.A. Voysey's mastery of pattern design is evident in this exuberant example filled with fruiting foliage and dating from around 1919.

2 This Aesthetic Movement tile with fruiting orange boughs was made at Minton's China Works, Stoke-on-Trent, England, around 1885–90.

3 Dating from around 1924, this fabric sample with a design of fruit and flowering branches was produced by the Ramsden Wood Print Works, Todmorden, Lancashire.

4 Liberty embraced a more modern approach to fabric design after the Festival of Britain in 1951. The stylized motifs of *Fruit Delight*, designed by Arthur Stuart, evoke a recipe from Elizabeth David's innovative cookery book.

5 *Orange Tree* wallpaper was designed by Walter Crane in 1902 and produced by Jeffrey & Co. in London.

6 *Orange Border* paper would have been cut into strips and placed along walls to divide patterns. The designer was possibly J.H. Dearle and it was produced by Morris & Co., London, around 1915.

7 René Lalique's *Oranges* glass vase from around 1926, frosted and decorated with oranges and enamelled leaves, was made at the Lalique glassworks in Wingen-sur-Moder, France.

6

7

1

2

3

4

5

6

1 British designer Nigel Quiney is credited with making gift wrap fashionable and producing the first paper tote bags to be sold in the UK retail market. Quiney's use of psychedelia as well as Art Nouveau and Art Deco influences was an instant success in the 1960s. Shown here is *Field 4*.

2 Nigel Quiney's pattern of strawberries in his *Field 5* wrapping paper design from 1971 recalls Alphonse Mucha's Art Nouveau illustrations.

3 Produced in different colourways, Nigel Quiney's *Blackberry* design dates from the early 1970s. It is a clever mirroring repeat of fruit and leaves, almost a homage to an Arts and Crafts design.

4 This is Nigel Quiney's *Blackberry 2* version (1970) of his wrapping paper design. Quiney's wrapping paper was used for countless different things, including decoration in the home in place of wallpaper.

5 *Strawberry Thief* is one of William Morris's best-known designs. His inspiration was the thrushes that stole strawberries from his garden at Kelmscott Manor in Oxfordshire. First designed in 1883, the pattern is still a firm favourite.

6 From the 1780s, John Turner's Lane End potworks, Staffordshire, became noted for making an almost porcellaneous white to cream-coloured stoneware. The blank earthenware was then exported for decoration at a workshop in the Netherlands.

1

1 The twig trellis from which the bunches of cherries hang forms repeating lozenges in this 1960 wallpaper design for the *Palladio Mondo* collection by Wallpaper Manufacturers, Manchester.

2 The large strawberries on this screen-printed satin fabric are studded with red diamanté pips. It was designed in England in 1972 by John Dove and Molly White for Wonder Workshop's Cut 'N' Sew printed jacket kits.

3 Founded by Jane Wentworth and Susan Saunders, OK Textiles of London produced fashion and furnishing fabrics, such as this 1973 screen-printed synthetic satin, *Raspberry Lips*.

4 Natural forms are ubiquitous in 17th-century English embroidery. This detail from a woman's waistcoat panel is stitched with a pattern of strawberries worked in silk and silver thread.

5 An illustration of a crêpe-de-Chine textile from the French fashion periodical *Art-Goût-Beauté* of the 1920s blends Art Deco style with the traditional use of nature in fabric design.

6 This octagonal bowl from around 1920 is by Alfred and Louise Powell for Wedgwood. The Powells revived the art of freehand painting on pottery at Wedgwood's Etruria Works, one of the most successful marriages of Arts and Crafts ideas with industrial manufacturing.

7 Made in New York by Stehli Silks, this fabric swatch from 1930 displays the clear bold lines and abstraction that were typical of the Art Deco style.

2

3

4

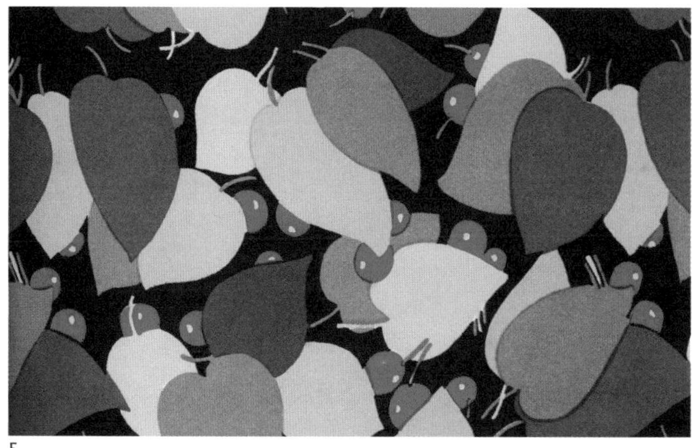

5

6

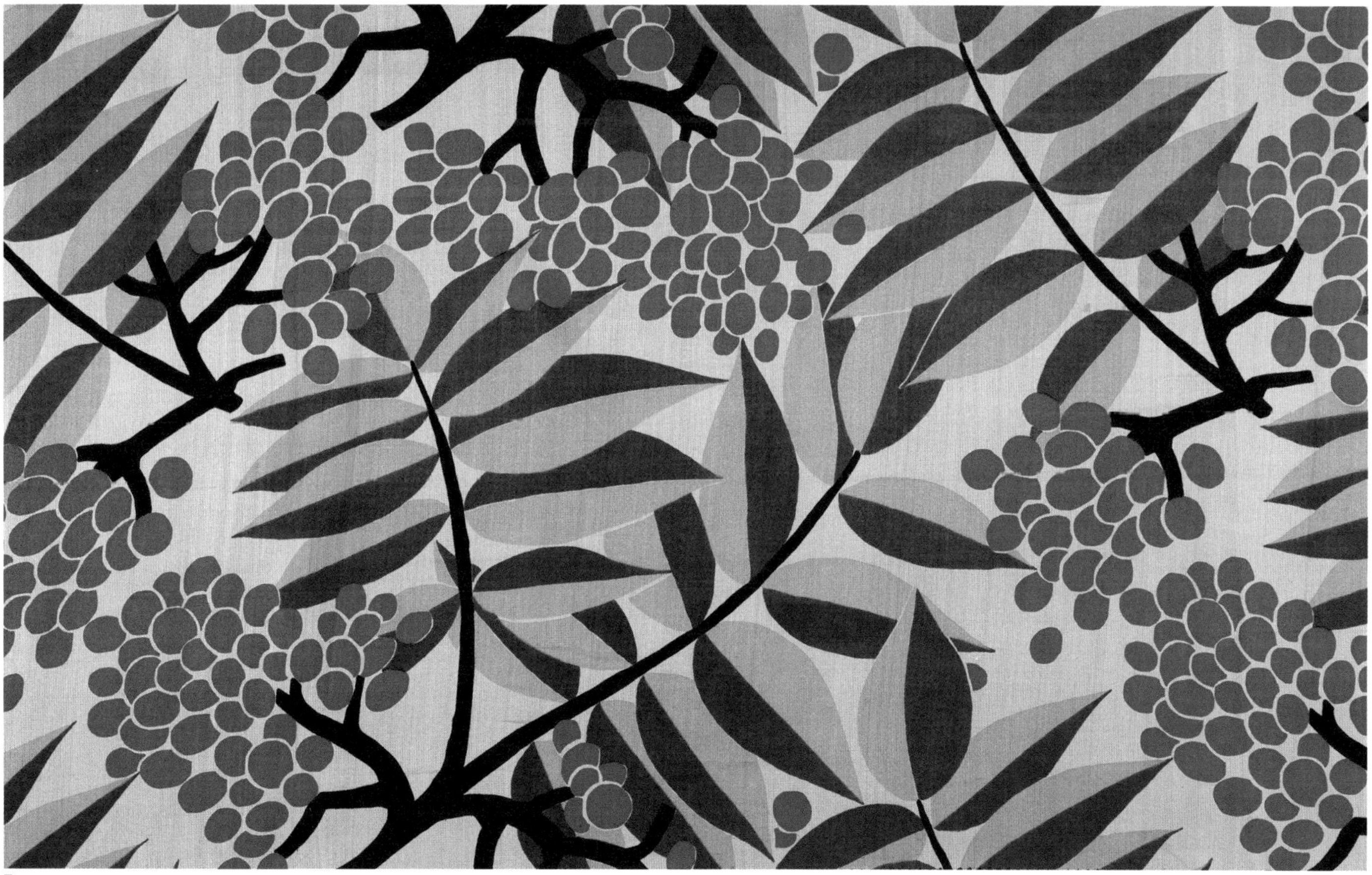

7

1

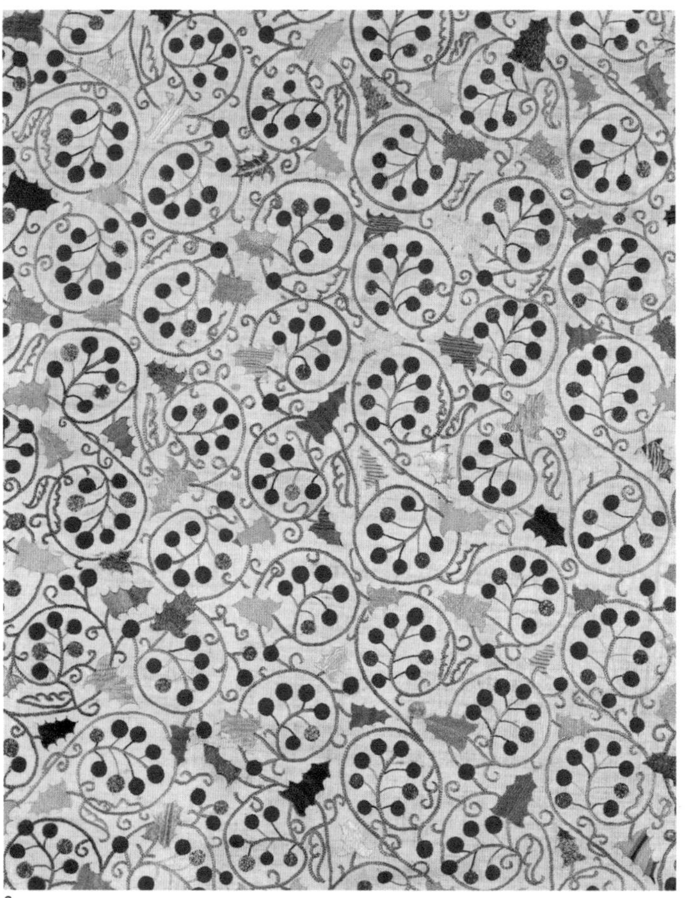

2

1 Each element of this child's tea service, made in Germany in about 1900, is charmingly decorated to look like a strawberry fruit or leaf.

2 The repeating all-over design on this English hanging or cover was worked in the early 17th century using a variety of embroidery stitches in silk on a linen background.

3 Sidney Mawson was a British freelance designer who had considerable success in the early years of the 20th century. He produced finely drawn naturalistic patterns such as this *Chatsworth* roller-printed cotton design made by Turnbull & Stockdale for Liberty, London, in 1909.

4 *Bramble* wallpaper by Kate Faulkner for Morris & Co., London, has been on continuous sale since its design was registered in 1879.

5 In the late 1880s C.F.A. Voysey started designing repeat patterns for carpets, wallpapers and textiles, such as this 1897–98 roller-printed cotton furnishing fabric for Morton Sundour, Carlisle.

3

4

5

1

1 This red silk voided velvet, produced in Italy in the 15th century, is patterned in an all-over repeat of stylized pineapple-like plants, each sprouting blossom.

2 Designed by William Greatbatch, this Staffordshire pottery pineapple-shaped tea canister was moulded from a block made by either Josiah Wedgwood or Thomas Whieldon. The pineapple symbolizes hospitality. The Rococo style in the mid-18th century embraced the imitation of naturalist forms.

3 Wine and fruit in baskets inspire the name of this 1952 printed furnishing fabric, *Bon Viveur,* which was designed in Britain by Mary Harper for Gayonnes.

4 British artist Frank Dobson was well known as a sculptor when he started creating textiles with his wife, Mary, in the 1930s. *Fruits and Glasses* from 1938 is hand-screen printed on linen.

5 Three scenes after paintings by Adam Buck form the pattern repeat on this early 19th-century English roller-printed cotton furnishing fabric. Each vignette is surrounded by garlands of fruit and flowers that suggest abundance and happiness.

6 Brussels lace was highly fashionable from the 1840s onwards. This deep flounce was produced in the 1860s and combines machine-made net with a complex pattern of hand-worked floral and plant forms.

2

3

4

5

6

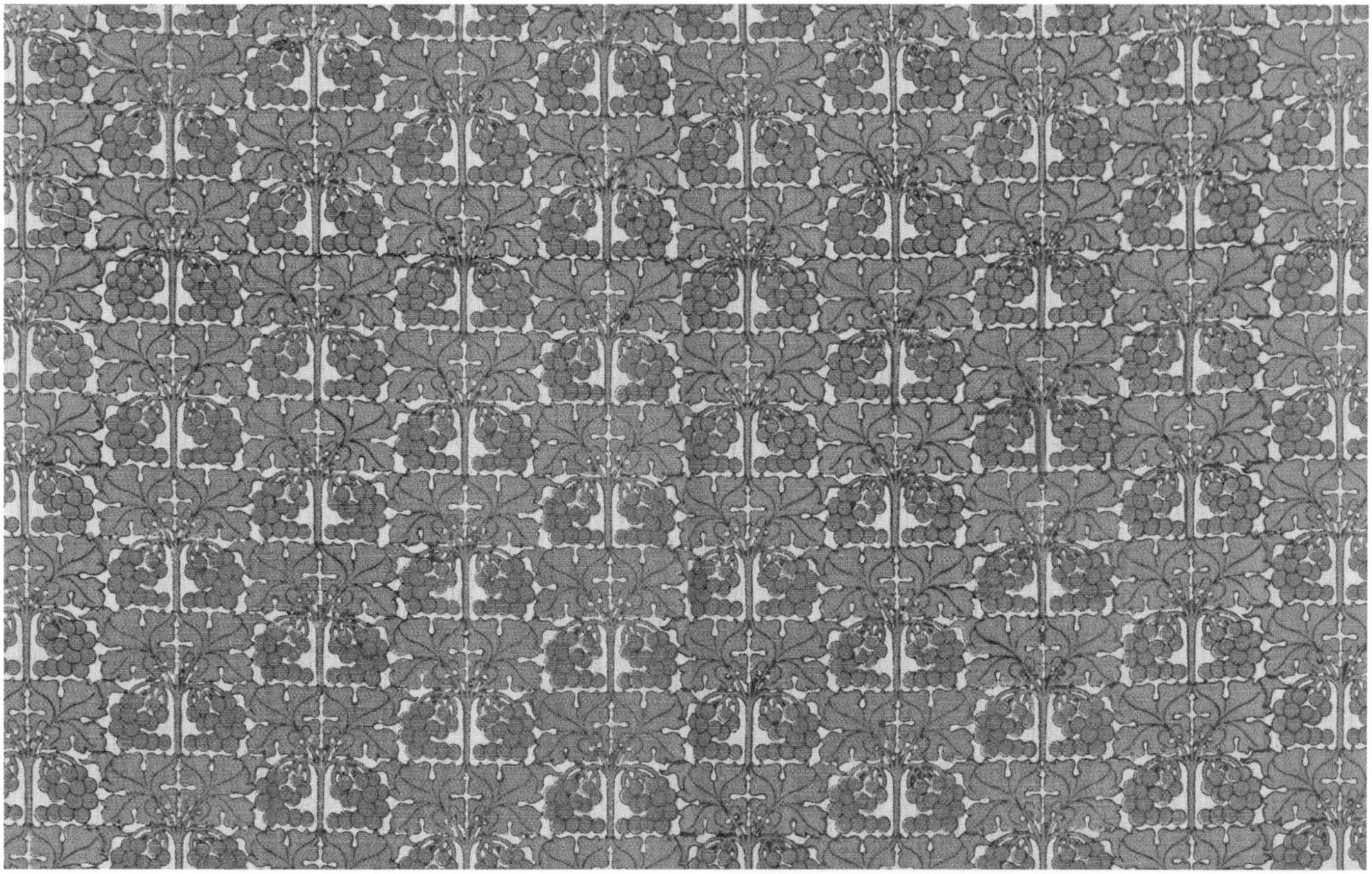

1

1 Ronald Simpson, a designer for Morton Sundour in Carlisle, designed the symmetrical vine and grapes pattern for this fabric in 1909. Simpson was the son of an Arts and Crafts furniture-maker based in Kendal, Cumbria.

2 Supported on a Rococo scrolled base, this Bacchus with a youthful satyr, from the set *The Classical Seasons*, is emblematic of autumn. The figure, made in soft-paste porcelain, was produced in 1765–70 by William Duesbury & Co., Derby.

3 Luxuriant leaves and grapes under the watchful eyes of birds suggest the abundance of harvest and good times to come in C.F.A. Voysey's textile design made in London in 1918.

4 The Spanish artist and textile designer Mariano Fortuny spent his adult life in Venice, where he immersed himself in Renaissance art. The design on this 1927 block-printed silk velvet fabric derives from a 16th-century Italian textile.

5 Natural forms were the main inspiration for decorative textiles in early 17th-century England and Scotland. Resembling a bunch of grapes, this small silk purse was probably intended to hold a special keepsake or gift.

6 Featuring a traditional pattern of birds and vines, this Morton Sundour furnishing fabric from the early 20th century, called *Geltsdale*, was printed on a woven cloth designed to give the appearance of tapestry work.

2

3

4

5

6

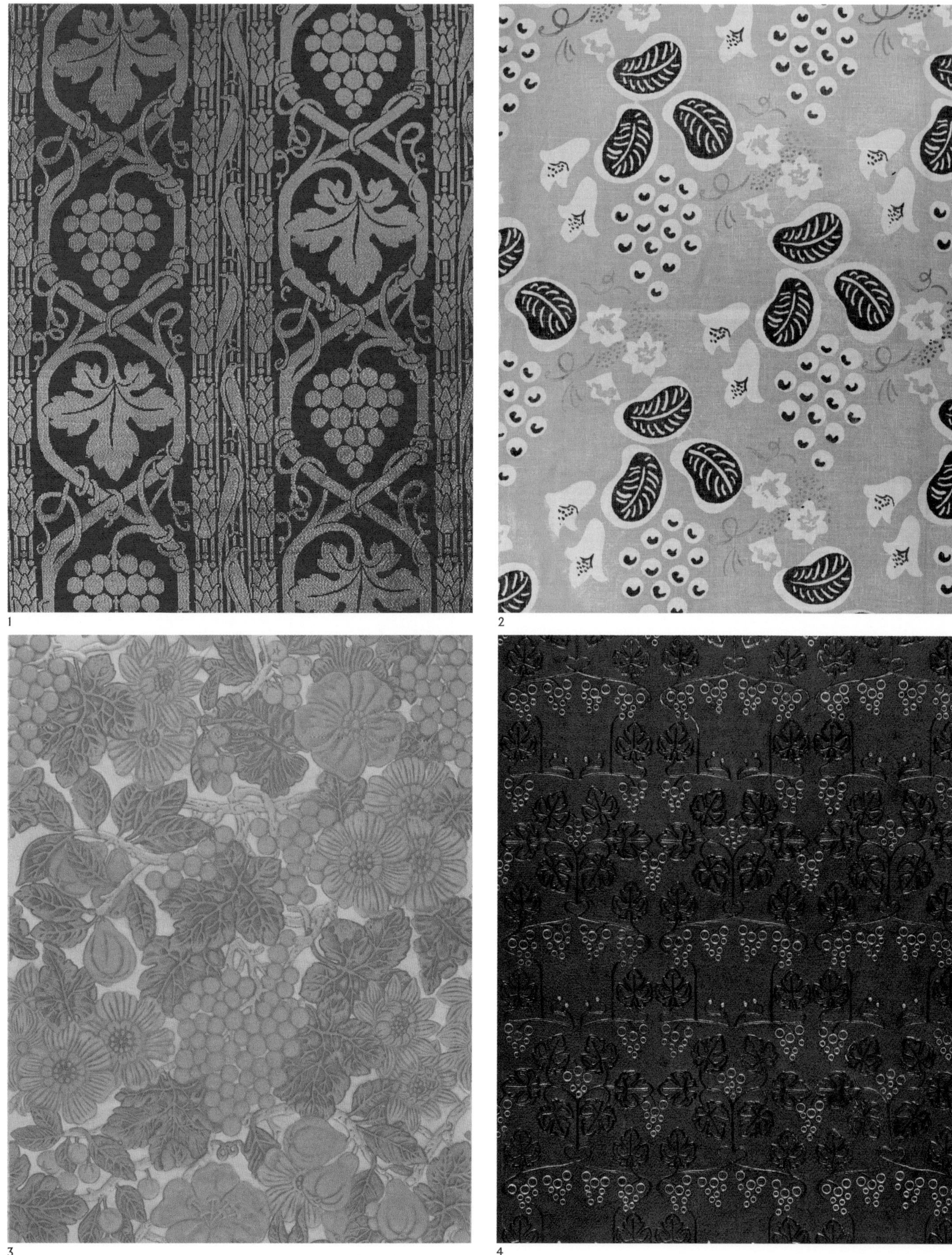

1

2

3

4

1 Arts and Crafts maker Edmund Hunter's satin furnishing fabric *Vineyard* is woven using silk and gold thread. It was made by his firm the St Edmundsbury Weavers in Haslemere, Surrey, in 1904.

2 In 1932 Vanessa Bell and Duncan Grant designed a music room for the Lefevre Galleries in London. The theme was autumn and the walls were decorated with Grant's *Grapes* fabric, made by Allan Walton Textiles.

3 This wallpaper was produced by M.H. Birge & Sons Co. in America in 1900–14, with an embossed design of intermeshed foliage and grapes.

4 This bookbinding for the Pre-Raphaelite journal *The Germ* was made in 1898 by the Guild of Women Binders, London.

5 *Henri II* wallpaper by L.F. Day was manufactured in London by Jeffrey & Co., around 1887–1900. The name and stylized grape vine design pick up on the 'Henry II style', the chief artistic movement of the 16th century in France.

6 The Greek god of grape growing and winemaking, Dionysus, would surely go wild for this Victorian necklace artfully formed of bunches of cultured seed-pearl grapes, possibly made in England, around 1850.

7 Made in England around 1725–1750, this crewelwork hanging is embroidered with vine leaves, bunches of grapes and tendrils. It has a design with an open repeat pattern that is stitched with wool thread into linen.

5

6

7

1 In China the pomegranate is considered a symbol of fertility. This Cizhou ware jar with pomegranate decoration cut through white slip under a clear glaze was produced in China during the Ming dynasty (1368–1644).

2 Dating from 1926 and inspired by the earlier *Fruit* (or *Pomegranate*) wallpaper by William Morris, *Bird and Pomegranate* was designed by Kate Faulkner for Morris & Co., England.

3 Possibly adapted from a design by William Morris, this printed cotton with a bold pattern of repeating pomegranates, leaves and flowers was produced in 1918, more than two decades after his death.

4 Bruce J. Talbert designed this wallpaper frieze showing branches of pomegranates, which was produced in London by Jeffrey & Co. in 1878.

5 This detail is from a tapestry table carpet dating from around 1620–50, with fruit and flowers worked in wool and silk. Such woven furnishings were a speciality of several Dutch tapestry workshops.

6 The *Fruit* (or *Pomegranate*) wallpaper pattern with branches bearing fruit, including limes and pomegranates, was designed by William Morris and produced by Morris & Co. around 1865–66.

7 This 18th-century dress fabric of woven silk has a small-scale pattern of wavy parallel stems bearing pomegranate fruit, split open to reveal the seeds. It was probably made in Chios, Greece.

1

2

3

4

5

6

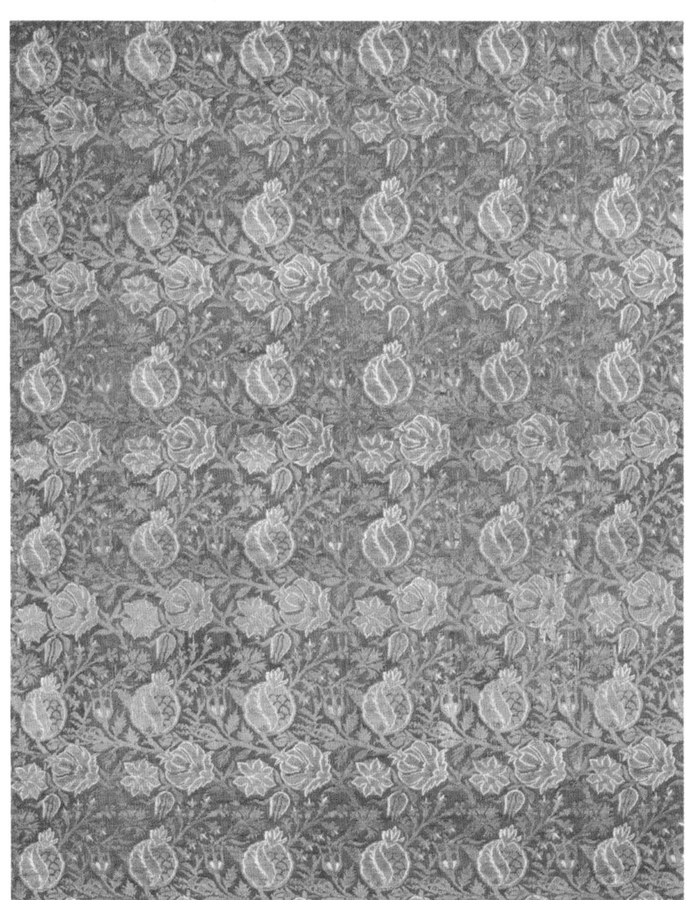

7

1

2

3

4

1 Made by Morton Sundour, Carlisle, this woven and warp-printed cotton cretonne features a design that took inspiration from a variety of historical periods to create a look popular with British consumers in the 1930s.

2 The Aesthetic Movement pattern of this table cover of block-printed velveteen shows circular, curving acanthus leaves filled with pomegranates and bunches of small-scale flowers. It was designed by Thomas Wardle, in Leek, Staffordshire, around 1885.

3 Kate Faulkner designed this *Vine and Pomegranate* woven furnishing or ingrain carpeting fabric for Morris & Co., England, around 1877–80.

4 This is part of a linen hanging or quilt cover embroidered with a pomegranate design in silk in surface darning and split stitch, made in Turkey in the seventeenth century.

5 Produced around 1530–50 in Iznik, Turkey, this fritware dish is painted with stylized tulip flowers and pomegranates.

6 With its floral medallion or pomegranate design, this block-printed and painted cotton textile was made in Ponneri, Chennai, India, around 1855.

5

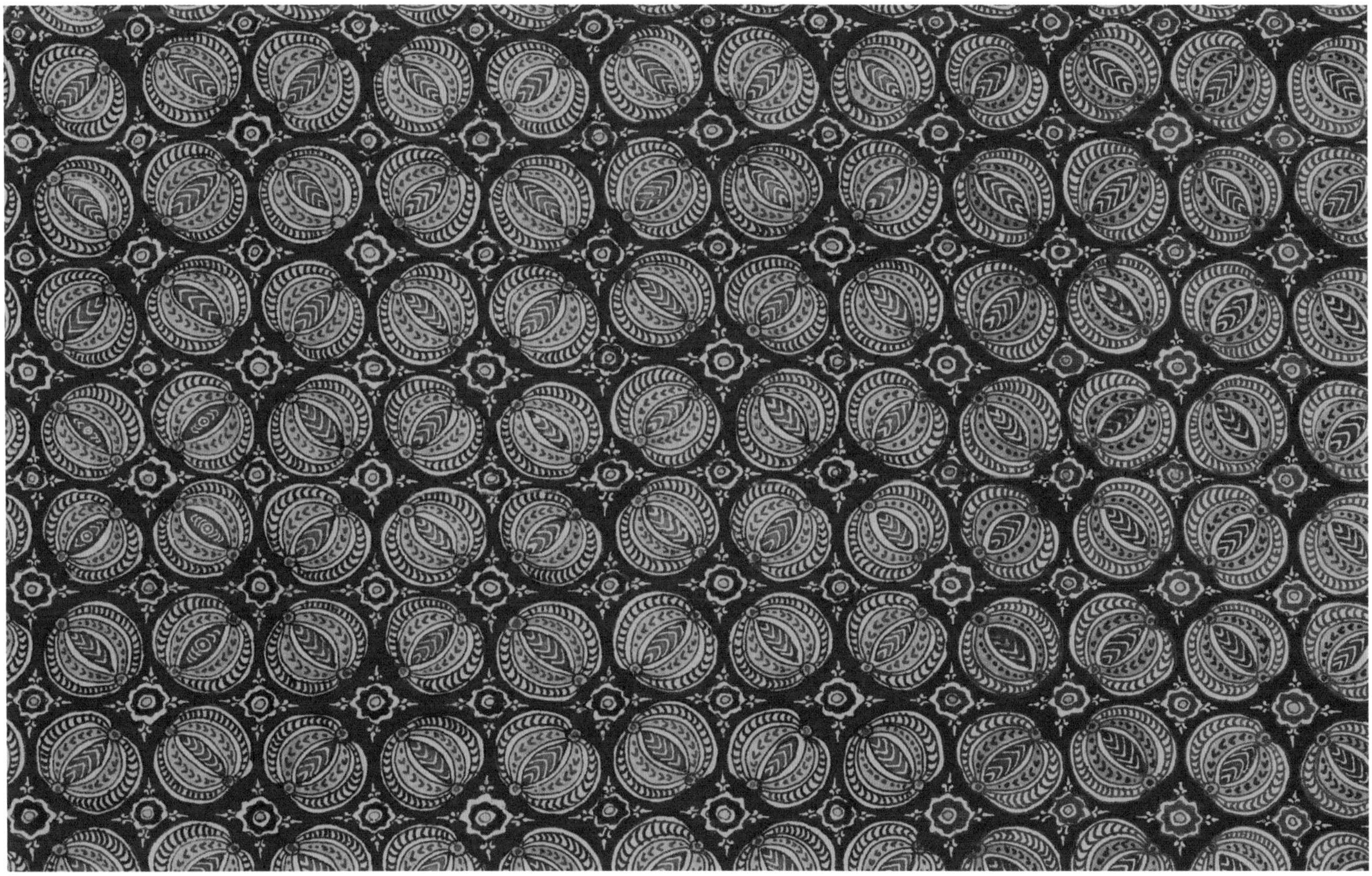

6

1

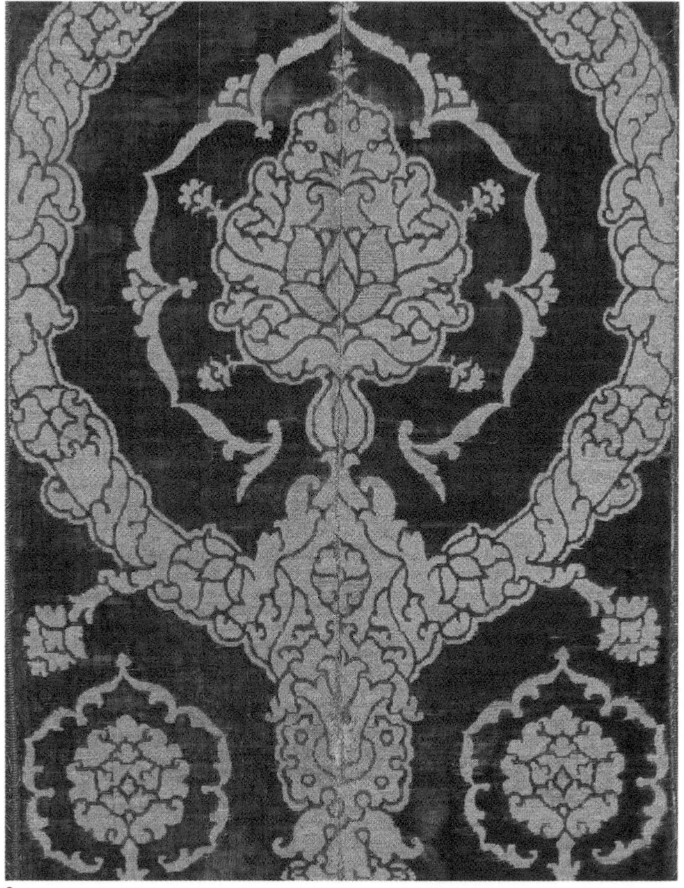

2

1 *Little Chintz*, a linen fabric designed by William Morris, was printed by Thomas Wardle of Leek, Staffordshire, in 1876. Its pomegranates were inspired by Indian block-printed cotton fabrics, or chintzes.

2 Velvets made of silk and gold were among the most highly prized luxury fabrics of the Renaissance. This pomegranate motif is typical of late 15th- or early 16th-century Italian designs.

3 A.W.N. Pugin's design for a wallpaper for the Palace of Westminster, London, from around 1850, composed of pomegranate motifs, is influenced by European textiles from the 15th and 16th centuries.

4 This fragment of sumptuous silk velvet from mid-15th century Italy is patterned with a stylized plant reminiscent of a pomegranate. It once formed part of a chasuble, a ceremonial garment worn by a Roman Catholic priest for the celebration of Mass.

5 *Pomegranate* block-printed cotton furnishing fabric, designed by William Morris and manufactured by Morris & Co., London, in 1877, is based on the medieval and Renaissance Italian velvets and Middle Eastern textiles that Morris studied at the V&A.

3

4

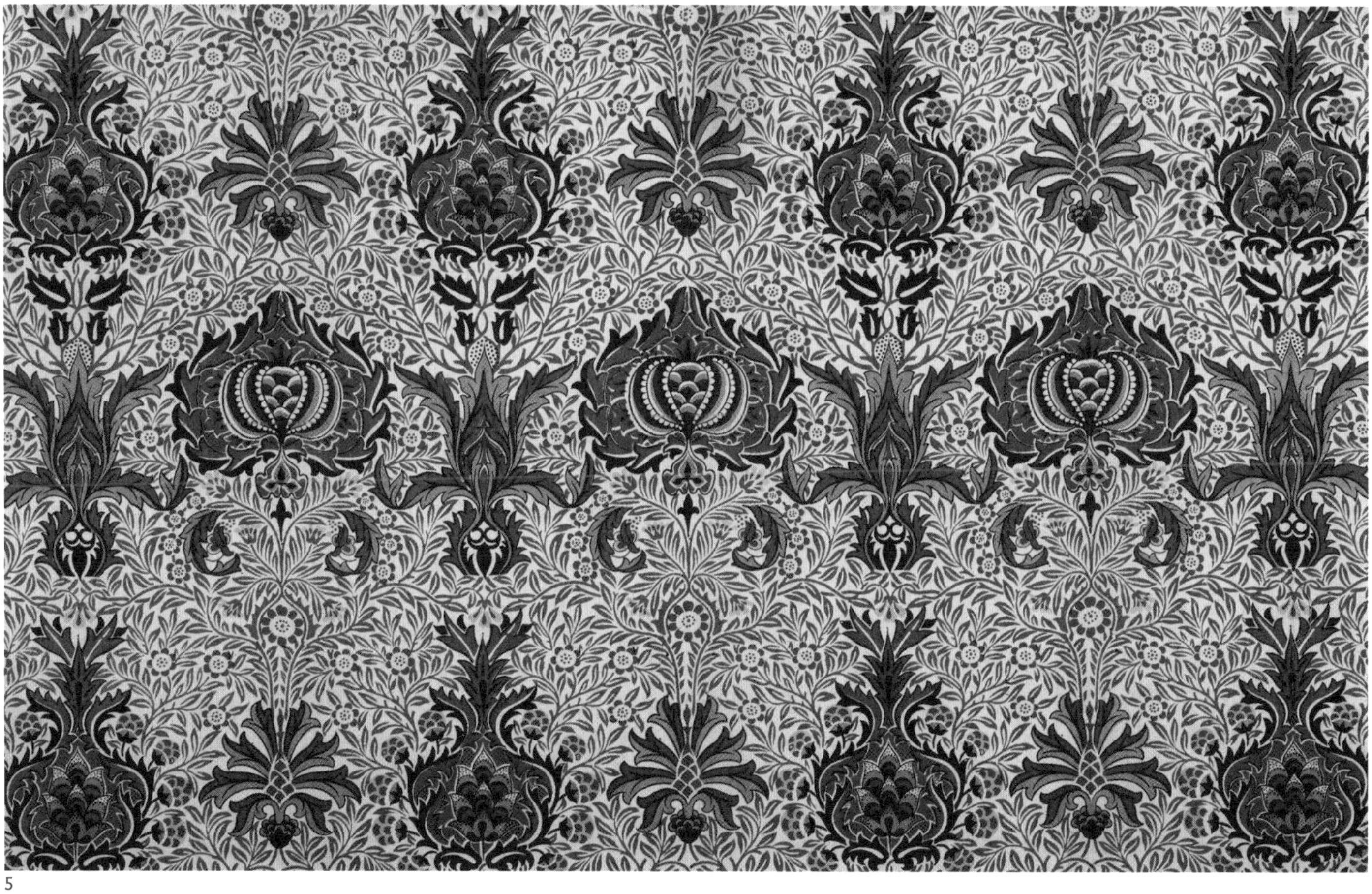

5

1

2

1 The celebrated English artist and craftsman George Heywood Maunoir Sumner, follower of William Morris and the Arts and Crafts Movement, designed *Fig and Vine* wallpaper, which was produced by Jeffrey and Co. in London around 1900.

2 Attributed to Charles-Jacques de Mailly, St Petersburg, this gold and enamel basket-shaped snuffbox from around 1775 is painted on the outside with basketwork and inside with fruit and vegetables.

3 This printed cotton furnishing fabric was produced by F. Steiner & Co. in Lancashire in 1911. The pattern uses fruit, berries, flowers and fir cones in a trellis design.

4 Clusters of fruit, flowers and shell motifs were combined by decorative artist and theatre designer George Sheringham and printed on linen for Sefton Fabrics, Belfast, Northern Ireland, in 1922.

5 Inspired by a study of plant structures, *Harvest* is a printed fabric with graphic depictions of fruit, flower and seed-heads. It was made in England in 1950.

6 This woodblock-printed cotton chintz, made in England around 1790, features alternating stripes of fruit and flower garlands. Printed entirely with natural dyes, the delicate touches of blue were added afterwards by hand with a brush.

3

4

5

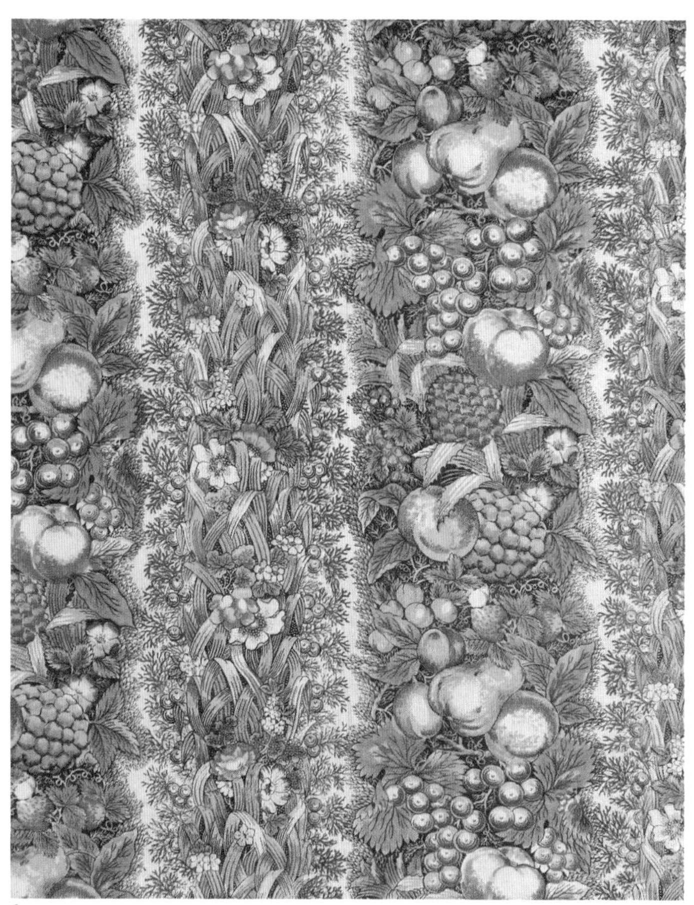

6

1

2

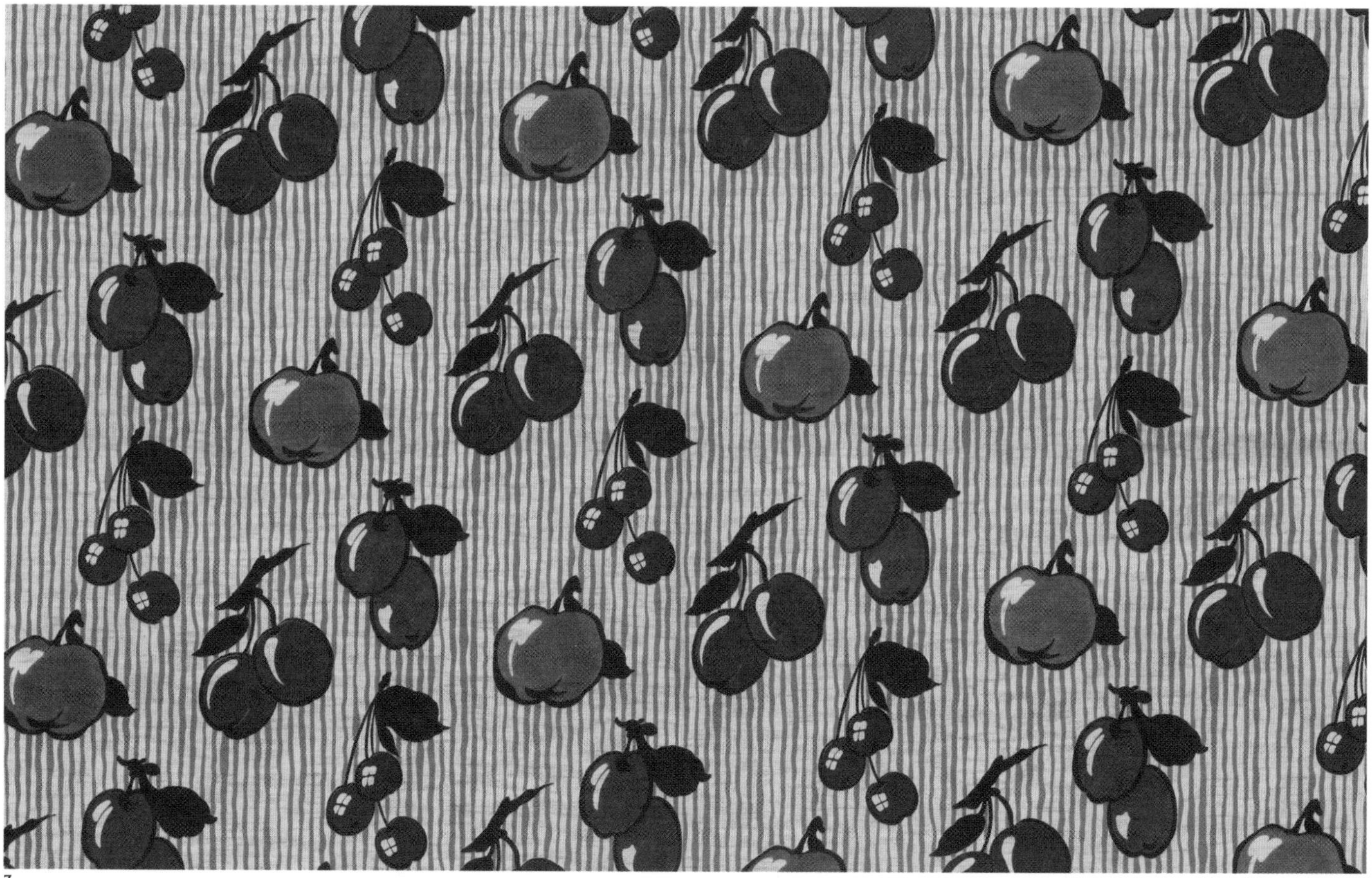

3

4

1 *Pomegranate*, designed by Stuart Watkins for Edinburgh Weavers, Carlisle, in 1958, recalls illustrations on early 20th-century British seed packets or in horticultural manuals, although the fruit illustrated is from warmer climes.

2 This 20th-century wallpaper design of horizontal bands of fruit is called *Juicy Fruit*.

3 Produced by the Calico Printers' Association, Manchester, around 1923, this textile sample has a design featuring fruit with a shiny surface.

4 Textile designer Pat Albeck's skilful banana drawing was one of many imaginative patterns she created in her first professional job at Horrockses Fashions, Lancashire, between 1953 and 1958.

5 Inspired by her parents' garden in Anlaby near Hull, Pat Albeck drew the pattern for this dress fabric, *Wild Fruits*, directly from nature in line and wash while still a student at the Royal College of Art, London, and the design went into production for Horrockses Fashions in 1953.

5

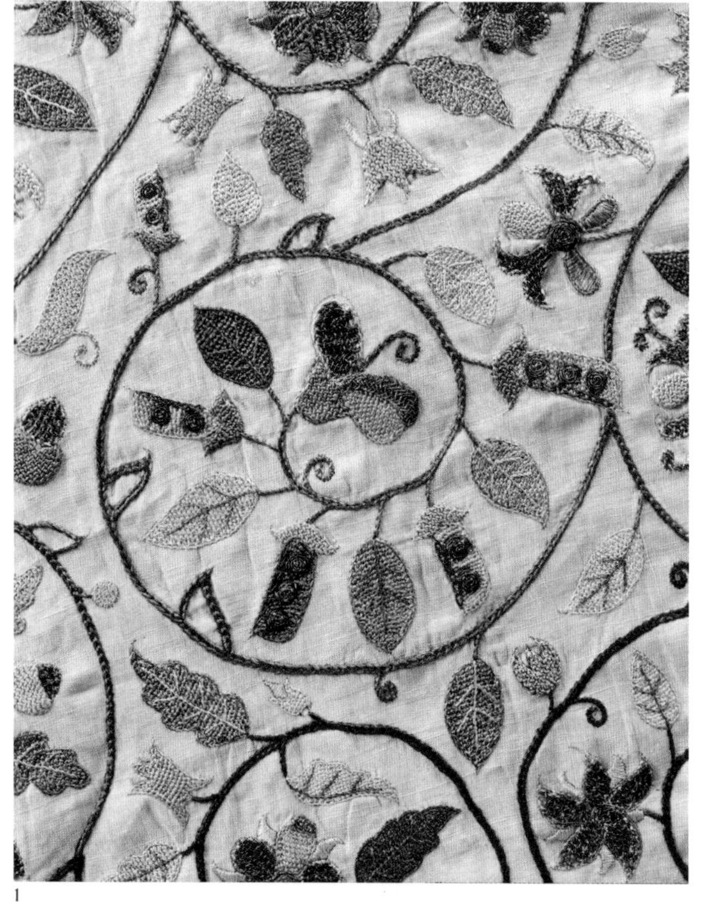
1

2

3

4

5

6

1 A design of coiling peapods comes from a woman's jacket, embroidered in England in the early 17th century with silk and metal threads.

2 This lead-glazed earthenware custard pot with lid is referred to as an 'artichoke cup'. It was produced in Staffordshire around 1780–1800.

3 Walter Crane designed *Artichoke* wallpaper in 1895 and it was produced in London by Jeffrey & Co.

4 Garden visitors feast on freshly harvested peas in *Blackbirds* furnishing fabric from 1956 made at the Ramm, Son & Crocker manufactory in England.

5 Featuring robust stalks and statuesque flower heads growing up the wallpaper, *Artichoke* pattern was designed by J.H. Dearle in 1898 for Morris & Co., England.

6 Marianne Westman designed this ceramic pot in 1956 as part of her *Picknick* series. Coloured by hand, giving it a unique touch, the popular tableware range was made by Rörstrand, Stockholm, until 1969.

7 This is a sample of *Artichoke*, a woven furnishing or ingrain carpeting fabric designed by William Morris and manufactured in Kidderminster, Worcestershire, between 1875 and 1880. The pattern was influenced by Italian, Iranian and Turkish historical silks that Morris had studied at the V&A.

7

2

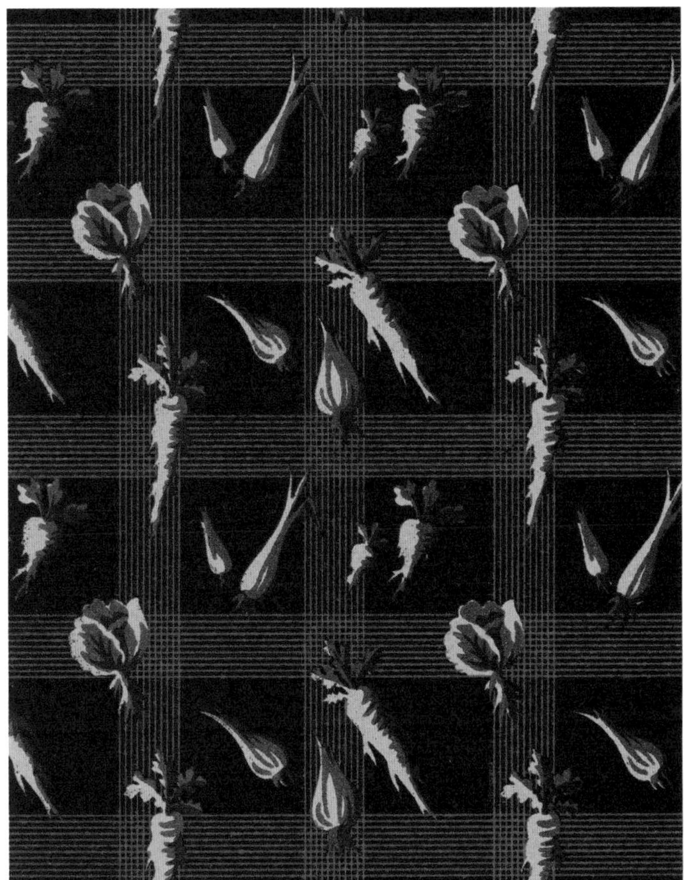

3

1 The traditional floral has had a surprising makeover with a cascade of root vegetables in this textile design published by Lechartier et Paul in 1880.

2 This skirt was made by Horrockses Fashions, Lancashire, in the 1950s. Pat Albeck, one of Horrockses' most gifted textile designers, was responsible for the printed fabric design of peppers and sweetcorn.

3 Integrating vegetables into a check, this crop of allotment staples designed by French publishers Lechartier et Paul was included in the monthly journal *Dessins Nouveautés*, published between April 1880 and April 1881.

4 Dating from the 1970s to 1980s, this clay teapot from Yixing, China, is exquisitely modelled in the form of a pumpkin. The pot body is divided into lobes continuing to the base.

4

1 *Picknick*, an earthenware cheese board, has a printed decoration of vegetables and herbs. It was designed by Marianne Westman and produced by Rörstrand, Stockholm, from 1956 to 1969.

2 *Herb Anthony* curtain fabric of stylized plant motifs was designed by Lucienne Day and manufactured for Heal's, England, in 1956.

3 After equipping himself with books about flora and fauna, Swedish-based Austrian designer Josef Frank created exceptional print compositions. One of these is *Söndagsmorgon* (Sunday morning) wallpaper, made by the Norma Tapetfabrik, Fredrikstad, Norway, in 1956.

4 *Zephyr* furnishing fabric from 1953, by Anne Loosely for Story Fabrics, England, takes its inspiration from the delicate shapes of wild plants and flowers found in hedgerows and fields.

5 Designed by Bernard Rudofsky for the *Stimulus* collection, and made by Schiffer Prints in New York in 1950, *Herbal* furnishing fabric is a feast for the senses.

6 *Florae Americanae* furnishing fabric from 1930 is beautifully illustrated with botanical specimens of North America by Ruth Reeves for W. & J. Sloane, New York.

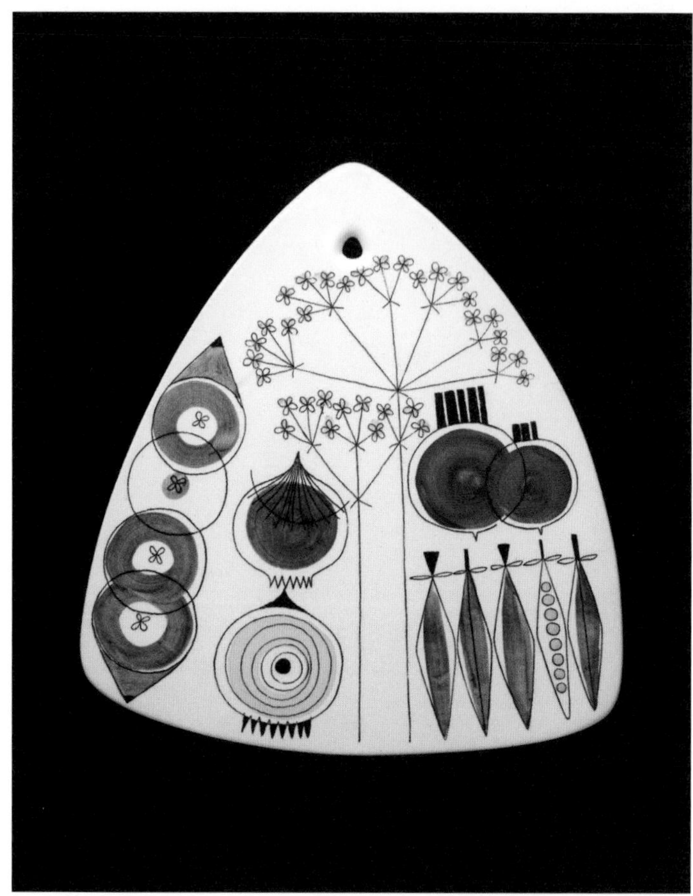

1

2

3

4

5

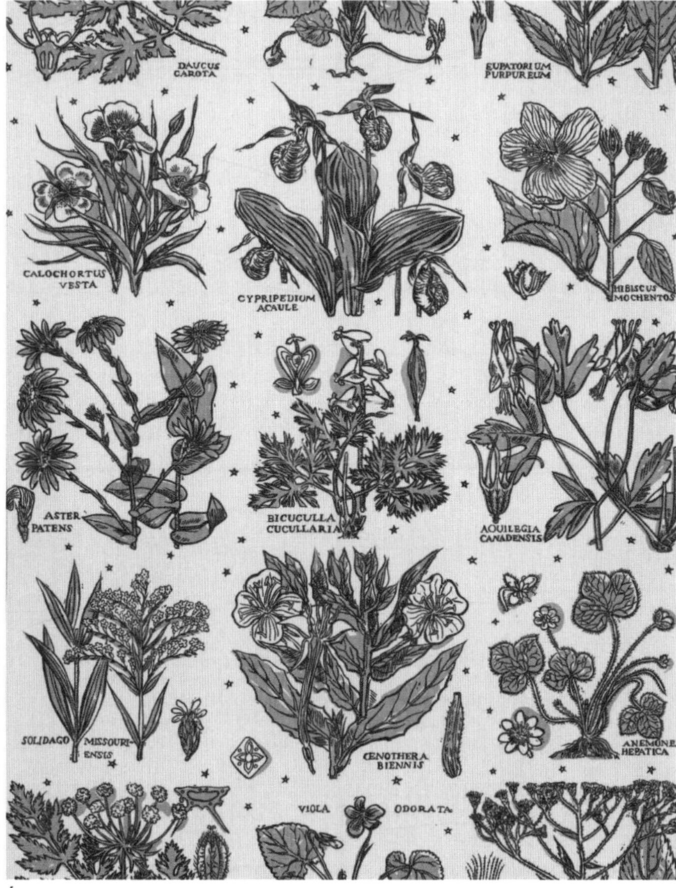
DAUCUS CAROTA
EUPATORIUM PURPUREUM
CALOCHORTUS VESTA
CYPRIPEDIUM ACAULE
HIBISCUS MOCHENTOS
ASTER PATENS
BICUCULLA CUCULLARIA
AQUILEGIA CANADENSIS
SOLIDAGO MISSOURI-ENSIS
CENOTHERA BIENNIS
ANEMONE HEPATICA
VIOLA ODORATA

6

1 This silk dupion horse chestnut shaped bag, with details in copper wire, was created by Emily Jo Gibbs, Britain, in 1996.

2 Made from a coquilla nut, this 19th-century English nutmeg grater is turned and carved in the form of an acorn, the screw-off cover revealing a removable metal grating plate.

3 Designed by Stuart Proverbs, this furnishing fabric of woven and machine-printed cotton was manufactured by Morton Sundour, Carlisle, in the early 20th century.

4 *Acorn* woodblock-printed wallpaper border was designed by Owen Jones and produced by Jeffrey & Co., London, *c.*1872.

5 Walter Crane designed this oak leaves and acorn woodblock-printed wallpaper border, produced by Jeffrey & Co., London, in 1875–1910.

6 Ice pails, also known as iced cream or fruit coolers, became popular for serving ice cream during the dessert course in the 18th century. This example from around 1810 is made of pearlware painted in enamels by Davenport & Co., Staffordshire.

7 This Huntley & Palmers *Nuts* biscuit tin from 1908 is made of offset litho-printed tinplate with embossed hazelnuts, by Barringer, Wallis & Manners, Nottinghamshire.

8 Alternating squirrels, acorns, birds and oak leaves form C.F.A. Voysey's autumnal wallpaper pattern, produced by Lightbown Aspinall in England in 1924.

1

2

3

4

5

6

7

8

1

2

3

4

5

1 Printed with a design of stylized mushrooms, this silk crêpe-de-Chine was produced by Stehli Silks in New York around 1930. The company had commissioned designs from contemporary American artists and illustrators since 1925.

2 Dating from 1750 to 1850, this netsuke from Japan is made of boxwood and carved in the shape of a bunch of *honshimeji* mushrooms.

3 This brooch of enamelled foliage with a bulrush and toadstools set in gold and platinum with precious stones and a pear-shaped pearl, resting on a line of diamonds, was made in Britain around 1920–30.

4 This pattern comes from an 18th-century album of textile designs from Mulhouse, Alsace, France.

5 *Woods Delight* is a furnishing fabric fungarium manufactured in 1951 by Grautex Fabrics, Copenhagen.

6 C.F.A. Voysey's signature stylized birds fly through a forest with toadstools in his *Fairyland* wallpaper produced by Essex & Co., England, in 1896.

6

1

2

3

1 Combining bamboo branches with yellow and white tigers and an all-over fretwork pattern, this printed cotton dress or furnishing fabric was manufactured by Beith, Stevenson & Co., Manchester, in 1911.

2 *Bamboo Grove* furnishing fabric of screen-printed cotton, designed by Clarence Wilson for Edinburgh Weavers, Carlisle, in 1957, uses bamboo plants to create a simple, elegant design.

3 This Wedgwood 'bamboo vase' from around 1790 is modelled as four upright canes of varying heights applied with bamboo leaves painted with enamels. It was manufactured by Josiah Wedgwood & Sons, Stoke-on-Trent, Staffordshire.

4 A kimono for a young woman (*furisode*) has an overall design of embroidered flowering plums and *shibori* (tie-dyed) bamboo. It was made in Japan between 1910 and 1930.

5 This printed cotton dress or furnishing fabric, manufactured by Beith, Stevenson & Co., in 1911, features freely drawn stems of bamboo foliage on clouds.

6 The same year, Beith, Stevenson & Co. produced another design based on bamboo motifs for dress or furnishing fabric. This example shows delicate leaves against a background of brown and black stems.

7 Made in France in 1950–60, this woodblock-printed wallpaper with a bamboo trellis design was used to decorate a residence in Canonbury Place in London.

4

5

6

7

1

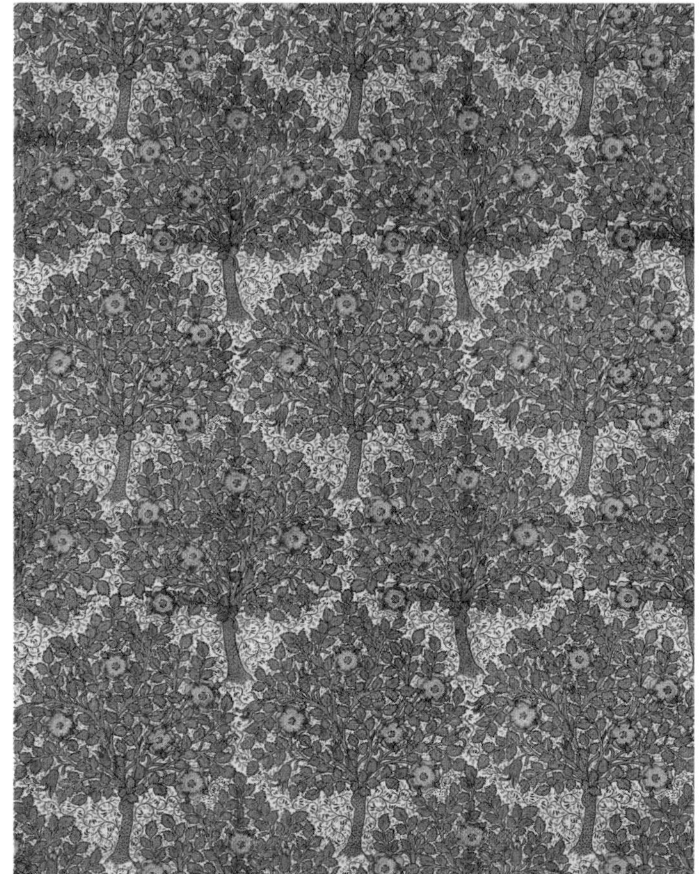
2

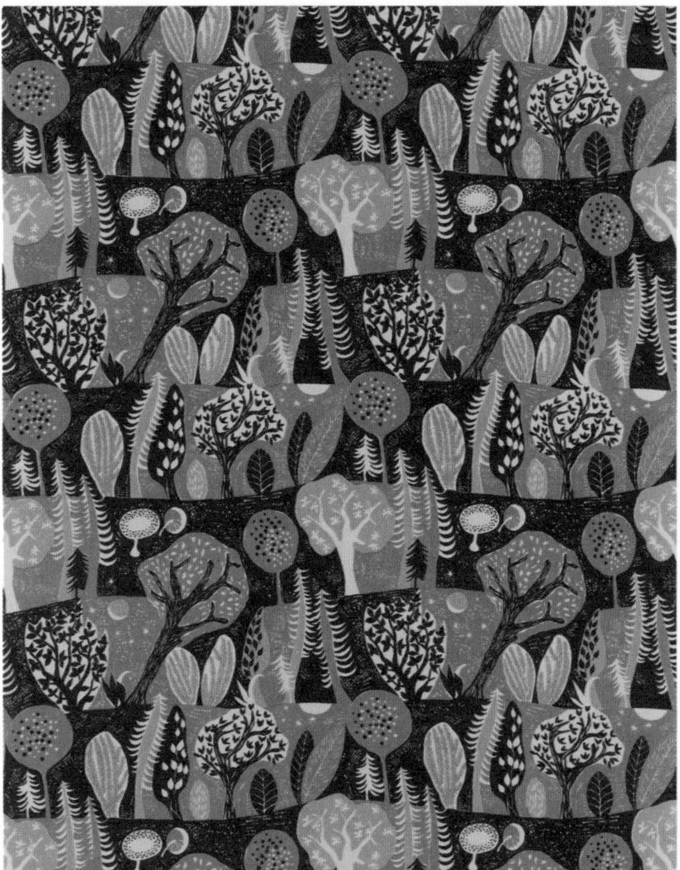
3

4

1 Striking pale branches form a perfect contrast to the dark background in this 1955 *Louisiana* wallpaper, designed by the artist Shinkichi Tajiri for Rasch & Co., Bramsche, Germany.

2 Featuring stylized flowering rose trees, this Arts and Crafts furnishing fabric of block-printed cotton was designed by Ronald Simpson for Morton Sundour, Carlisle, in 1909.

3 This printed furnishing fabric by Frank Studios for Simpson & Godlee, made in 1952 in Manchester, brings the woodland indoors with a playful mix of trees in different shapes.

4 On this roller-printed cotton furnishing fabric, made by the Calico Printers' Association, Manchester, in 1921, silhouettes of palm trees against sunny skies or stylized flowers create a semi-abstract pattern.

5 *The Savaric* wallpaper by C.F.A. Voysey, produced by Essex & Co., England, around 1897, features his characteristic stylized birds flying through a woodland scene.

6 In these hand-chased and polished brass candle sconces made by Ernest Gimson in Gloucestershire, England, around 1910, the motifs of acorns and oak leaves reflect the Arts and Crafts nostalgia for the English countryside.

5

6

1 This traditional lacquer stationery box made by Kwang-Woong Lee in South Korea in 2014–15 is decorated with a plum blossom design with fine inlaid mother-of-pearl.

2 Paul Nash's *Cherry Orchard* design, printed by Cresta Silks in Welwyn Garden City, Hertfordshire, in 1932, illustrates the artist's facility for producing abstracted motifs suitable for repeating patterns.

3 In 1920 Alec Walker established his Cornwall-based firm Crysède to manufacture dress silks. Many of his productions, such as this 1930 example, were based on his own landscape sketches and paintings and were produced in strong, contrasting colours.

4 An elegant design of clouds and pine trees decorates this crêpe silk kimono for a woman, made in Japan between 1880 and 1910. Pine trees are an auspicious motif in Japan. Remaining green even in the harshest winter, they are symbolic of longevity and resilience.

5 *Fractal Table II*, created by Platform in conjunction with the 3D-printing company Materialise for their MGX collection in 2007–9, mimics growth patterns found in nature and features trunk-like legs that divide into branches and form a patterned top surface. The table was built of epoxy resin using an additive manufacturing technique called stereolithography.

1

2

3

4

5

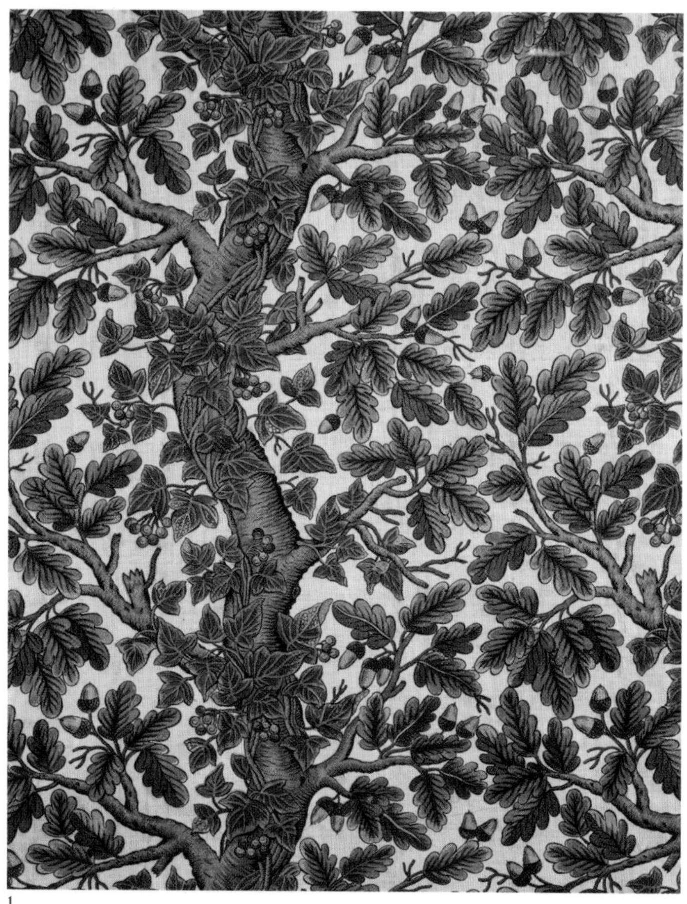
1

2

1 *Royal Oak and Ivy* furnishing fabric of cotton in then fashionable drab colours of brown, green and yellow was block printed in Lancashire for the London retailer Richard Ovey of Covent Garden in 1799.

2 *Boys in Trees* furnishing fabric of printed cotton was designed by Dujardin for the Château of Wesserling, Alsace, France, around 1775.

3 This sample of printed furnishing fabric made in Britain in the 1920s features a fantasy landscape of mountains, waterfalls and large canes of bamboo.

4 *Duleek* by C.F.A. Voysey features a woodland scene of swans, stags and songbirds created in the architect's distinctive style. Here the pattern is on a muslin curtain. It was also produced on different weights of furnishing fabric.

5 These hard-paste porcelain palm-tree ornaments were produced by Meissen, Germany, in 1740–80 as decorative accents for a table setting. They are finished with a shiny glaze and sculptural elements such as coconuts and bark texture.

6 *Girl in a Tree* furnishing fabric of screen-printed glazed cotton, designed by Olive Sullivan for Edinburgh Weavers, Carlisle, in 1956, has an ethereal quality, with two girls unexpectedly appearing in clearings in dense foliage.

3

4

5

6

1

2

3

4

5

1 Dating to about 1734, this exquisite brocaded silk has a tree and island design. It was woven in Spitalfields, London, which flourished as a centre of silk production from the late 17th century onwards.

2 Retailed by Lacloche Frères of Paris, this pin from around 1927–30 in the form of a cypress tree in a tub is made of white gold, platinum, emeralds, brilliant-cut diamonds and stained chalcedony.

3 This silk damask was produced in Spitalfields, London, around 1734. The scale of the tree motifs made the design versatile enough to be used for furnishings or dress.

4 *The Formal Garden* is a wallpaper design by Walter Crane from 1904, produced in London by Jeffrey & Co.

5 British designer Nigel Quiney's wrapping paper *Pastoral 3* from 1975 depicts an idyllic countryside scene studded with details of copses and hedgerows, with a clean, modern styling.

6 *The Heron* is an elegant textile design by C.F.A. Voysey from 1919, which shows long-legged birds fishing in a sinuous and sedate river by tall trees perfect for heronries.

6

1

2

3

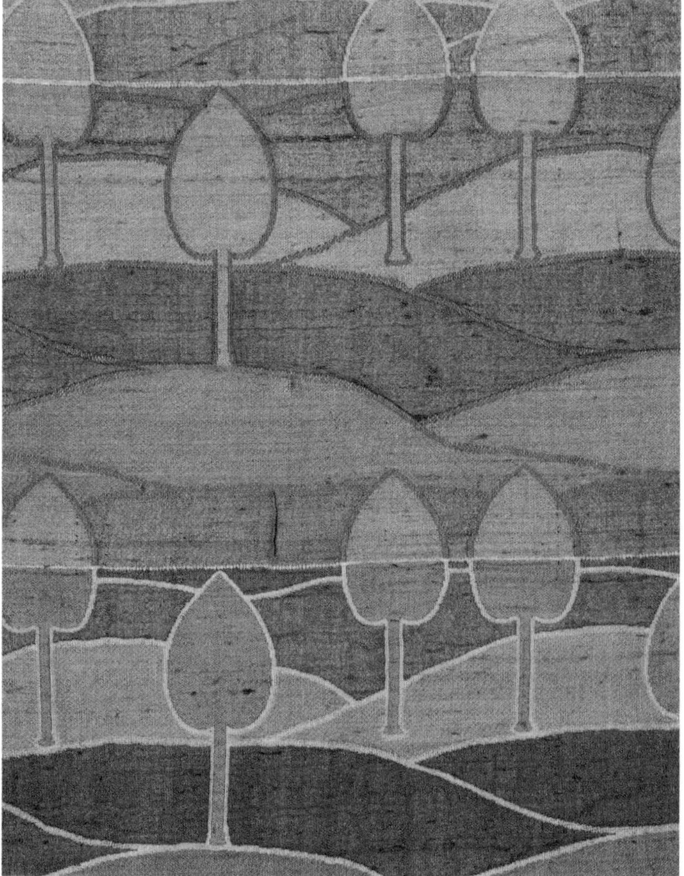
4

1 This rayon and linen furnishing fabric is decorated with an Art Deco pattern of rhythmic tree branches. It was designed for and produced by the Old Bleach Linen Co. in Randalstown, Northern Ireland around 1935.

2 Produced by F. Steiner & Co., Lancashire, in 1922, this fabric sample is a fanciful mix of Western-style topiary trees with East Asian-influenced cherry blossom branches.

3 John Pearson designed and made this Arts and Crafts copper charger in London, in 1890. It is decorated with the Tree of Knowledge and entwined serpent with Greek characters beneath.

4 Dating from 1895 to 1900, this wool and silk double cloth designed by C.F.A. Voysey for Morton Sundour, Carlisle, has a design of trees and hills. The detail shown here is from a pattern 'blanket' used to show different colourways to potential retailers.

5 On this roller-printed cotton furnishing fabric, manufactured by F. Steiner & Co. in 1923, palm and fruit trees alternate with stylized motifs from Arabian architecture, reimagined for an Art Deco interior.

1
2
3
4
5

6

1 Willow leaves were one of William Morris's favourite motifs. This block-printed wallpaper, *Willow Bough*, with its pattern of intertwined leaves and stems, dates from 1887 and is a naturalistic version of an earlier design.

2 *Laybourne* furnishing fabric of printed linen, was designed by Hans Tisdall in 1938 for Donald Brothers, Dundee. Tisdall's flair as an illustrator and mural painter is apparent in his textile designs.

3 The crisp pattern of oak leaves with their distinctive outline colour on this block-printed cotton of 1910 is typical of fabrics used in early 20th-century Arts and Crafts-style interiors.

4 English artist Richard Redgrave was commissioned by museum director Henry Cole (trading as Felix Summerly's Art Manufactures) to design this *Well-Spring* carafe in 1847, with plant motifs painted in enamels.

5 This delicately worked piece of English crewelwork from 1650 to 1699 displays motifs influenced by exotic flora and fauna found on imported Indian chintzes.

6 Each leaf has been given a pale aura, created by cutting into the ground pattern, on this printed furnishing fabric, *Chestnut*, designed by Mary Bryan for Edinburgh Weavers in 1949.

7 This watercolour was composed by Julius H. Frank around 1965 as a design for a printed textile. Metallic pigment has been used to draw in detail on a tumbling plethora of leaves.

7

1

1 Medieval life and art was the model for much of the ecclesiastical pattern work of the 19th century. This German design imitates woven textiles from the Middle Ages.

2 *Elvas* wallpaper, with its all-over foliate design, was designed by Lewis Foreman Day, and manufactured by Jeffrey & Co., London, in the 1890s.

3 This 1880s design for a textile is from the journal *Dessins Nouveautés*, published monthly by Lechartier et Paul in France. Its principal likely audience was textile designers and those in the fabric industry.

4 A detail from a beret-shaped hat is decorated with leaves and berries of glossy golden straw. It was made for Balenciaga, Paris, around 1950.

5 Donald Brothers of Dundee, Scotland, employed many talented artists, including André Bicât, a painter and highly skilled printmaker. Here he adapts his knowledge of printing to inform a design for a 1938 linen furnishing fabric, *Rustic*.

6 Crash is a rough fabric made from thick, uneven yarns. *Killearn*, a 1938 printed crash furnishing linen, was designed by Barbara Pile for Donald Brothers of Dundee. Her naturalistic motifs complement the fabric's texture.

7 *Clematis and Jasmine* was designed by Mary White for Liberty, London, in 1954. Her textile designs often featured flowers from gardens and the countryside, used here as silhouettes to create a colourful repeating pattern.

2

3

4

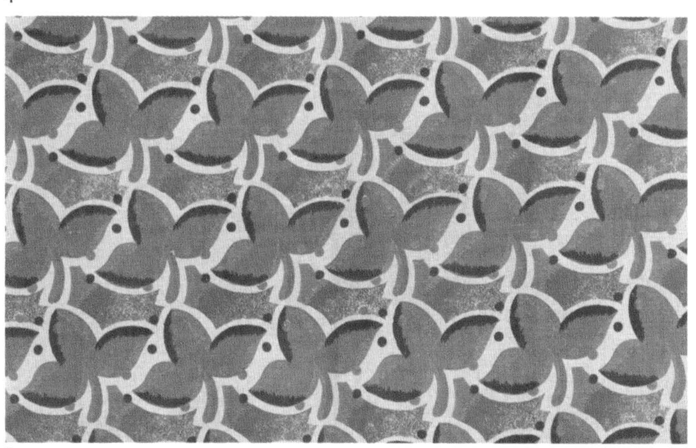

5

6

7

1

2

3

4

5

6

1 There is no disputing the charm of this mid-19th-century life-size rendition of a cabbage – a tureen from Spode Ceramic Works in England or Jacob Petit's porcelain factory in France.

2 Mary White's versatile approach to floral motifs can be seen in her 1954 abstract design *Coppice*, a printed cotton she designed for Heal's range of contemporary furnishing fabrics.

3 Vera Neumann's design *Happy Leaves* was printed as a wallpaper by F. Schumacher & Co., New York, in the early 1950s. The design features the silhouettes and shadows of leaves and flowers.

4 *Folia* by Edward Veevers was a wallpaper in the *Palladio 4* series of 1960 by Wallpaper Manufacturers, Manchester. The graphic impact of the leaf veins and the dark background gives a feel of strength and modernity.

5 The *Palladio* wallpaper series, was a mid-century bid to improve British interior design and was intended for use in large spaces. *Forest*, with its strongly vertical elements suggesting bark, was included in 1955.

6 This striking block-printed linen from 1925 to 1930 was designed in Germany by Josef Hillerbrand, who later became a professor at the Academy of Fine Arts in Munich.

7 Robert Nicholson's refreshingly contemporary abstracted leaf design *Avenue* is one of a series of works commissioned by Wallpaper Manufacturers for the 1955 *Palladio* wallpaper series.

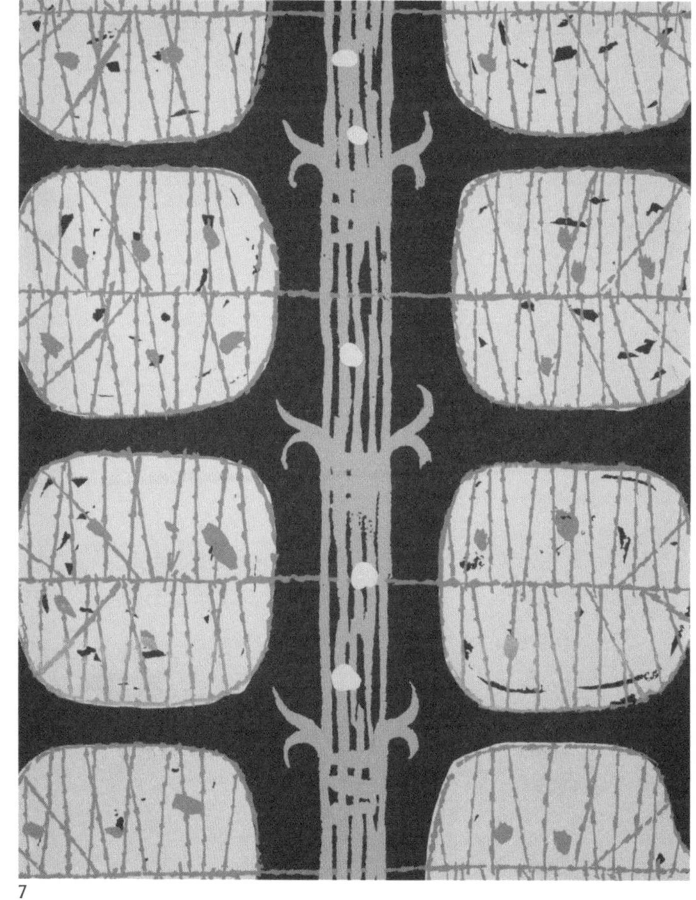

7

2

3

4

1 William Morris's 1875 design *Acanthus* was the first in a group of large-scale, heavily patterned and deep-coloured wallpapers. It required 30 separate woodblocks to complete the pattern, which made for an expensive product.

2 The 1950s saw a flourishing of new design in Britain, born out of the demand for exciting new patterns after wartime austerity. This printed fabric, *Palamos*, was designed by the Scottish designer Sylvia Chalmers in 1953 for Elizabeth Eaton, London.

3 The type of embroidery worked on a linen ground, as shown here, was typical of decorated coverlets and pillows from the early years of the Jacobean period in England (1603–25). The scrolling foliage is embellished with spangles.

4 This woodblock wallpaper frieze was designed by Bruce J. Talbert, considered to have been one of the most influential figures of the British Aesthetic Movement, and was made in England between 1875 and 1910.

5 Delicate wild flowers, along with the nettles from which this colour-woodblock wallpaper takes its title, *Naelderne,* were clearly appreciated by its designer, Bent Karlby, and manufacturer, Dahls Tapetfabrik. It was produced in Copenhagen in 1951.

5

1

2

3

4

1 The London firm of Hindley & Wilkinson supplied this sample of chintz furnishing fabric in about 1890. The company's stamp on the back is just visible through the glazed cotton and stripes of laurel and ribbon.

2 Dating from around 1810, this porcelain 'Roman Emperor' plate by Darte Frères, Paris, is a typical production of the Napoleonic Empire. It depicts Emperor Vespasian as an imitation cameo encircled by a laurel wreath.

3 *Wreath* wallpaper dating from 1887 to 1900 was designed by Lewis Foreman Day and manufactured in London by Jeffrey & Co.

4 Walter Crane's 1911 *Laurel* wallpaper, produced in London by Jeffrey & Co., has a classical revival design typical of the first decade of the 20th century.

5 Edwardian wallpapers incorporated an eclectic mix of design styles. *Myrtle Wreath*, designed by Walter Crane, was produced in London by Jeffrey & Co. in 1904.

6 Printed with a repeating pattern of laurel wreaths against a simple stripe, this cotton furnishing fabric was designed by Margaret Simeon for Edinburgh Weavers, Carlisle, around 1950. Its title, *Homage*, reflects the use of wreaths as a symbol of triumph or honour.

5

6

1

1 The oldest and simplest designs can sometimes look the newest and best. This watercolour design for a printed cotton is from an English textile manufacturer's pattern book from the early 19th century.

2 Seen here is a detail of the puff of a *gigot*, or leg-of-mutton, sleeve from an 1830s day dress. The woollen fabric is printed in a complicated design of shamrocks on a lilac and brown chequered ground.

3 An early 19th-century design for a printed cotton from an English textile manufacturer's pattern book has a dainty all-over pattern of tiny florals and small petal-shaped dashes.

4 This is an early 19th-century design for a printed cotton with ditsy scattered florals, from an English textile manufacturer's pattern book. These textiles were popular as patchwork quilt squares as the patterns paired well with other designs.

5 This unfussy design for a printed cotton comes from an English textile manufacturer's pattern book. The small no-nonsense floral pattern would have been ideal for everyday dress fabrics in the early 19th century.

6 Looking just as fresh now, this is an early 19th-century design for a printed cotton from an English textile manufacturer's pattern book.

7 This particularly fine floral design is also from an early 19th-century English textile manufacturer's pattern book.

2

3

4

5

6

7

1

2

3

1 This is a design for a printed cotton from the 1820s produced on India's southern shores for the European market. Ateliers would sew the cloth into dresses, robes, undergarments, jackets, pillow covers and bed curtains.

2 Produced by artisans in southern India who evolved their patterns to meet European tastes, this is one of a set of textile designs for printed cotton from the 1820s.

3 From an album produced in Mulhouse, Alsace, in the late 18th to early 19th century, this design for a French printed textile has a calligraphic flourish.

4 This design for a printed cotton comes from an English textile manufacturer's pattern book from the early 19th century.

5 Seen here is one of a set of textile designs from the 1820s with floral motifs designed to fill the cotton ground when printed. The cottons were produced in southern India for the European market, which had become intoxicated with 'Indienne' fabric.

4

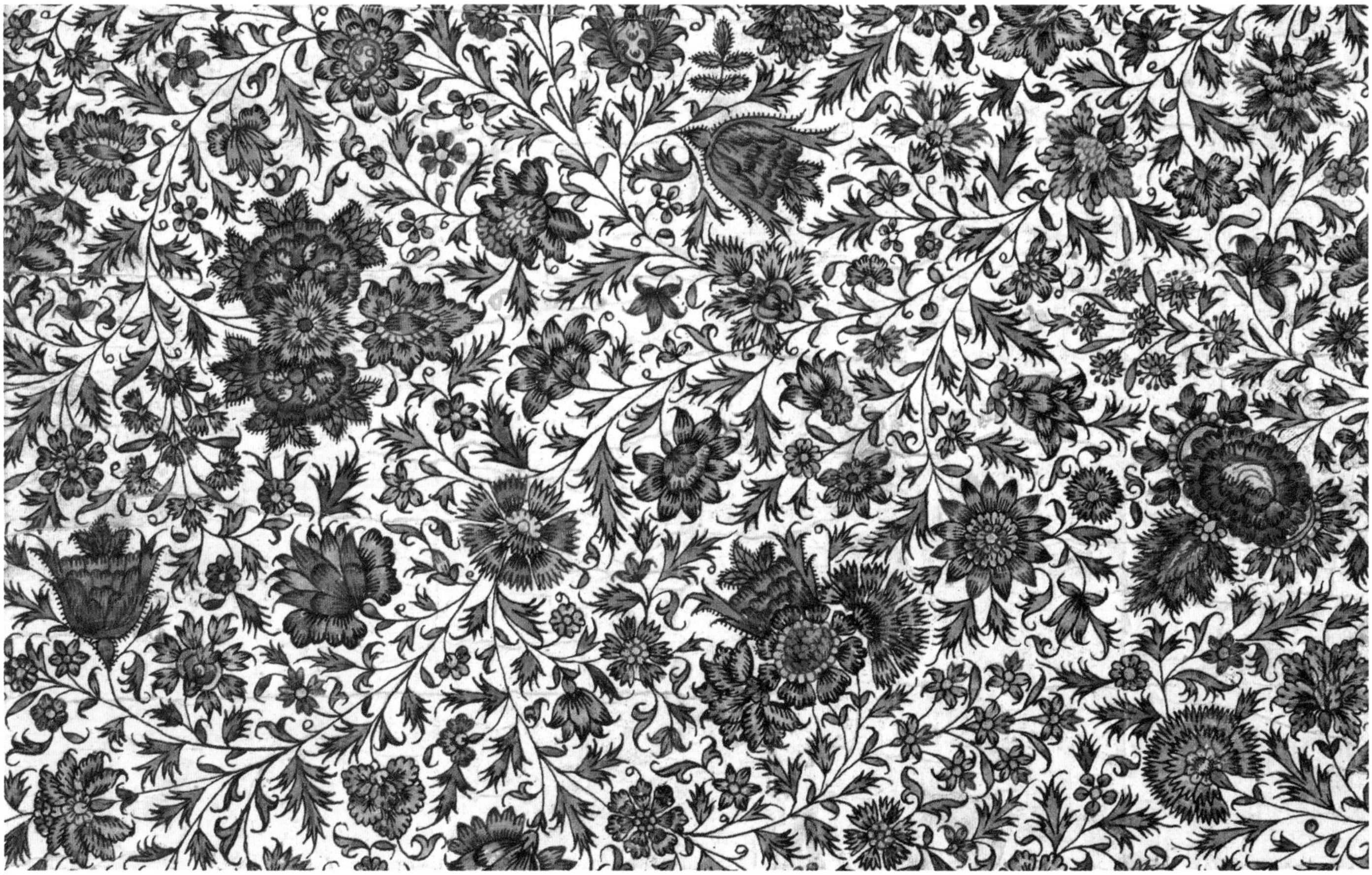

5

1

1 Lewis Foreman Day created fine wallpaper designs that could be cheaply made by machine printing. *Lettice* (1887–1900) was one such, a foliate design of acanthus leaves produced in London by Jeffrey & Co.

2 *Acanthus*, a printed cotton velvet furnishing fabric from 1875, was designed by William Morris and printed by Thomas Wardle for Morris at the Hencroft Works in Leek, Staffordshire.

3 *The Atmy* wallpaper frieze uses a bold pattern of large stylized acanthus leaves designed by William Shand Kydd for Shand Kydd, London, in the 1890s.

4 This silver-gilt garniture consists of two flasks and a vase, chased and embossed, featuring foliate scrolls and acanthus leaf ornamentation. The set was made in England and has London hallmarks for 1675–6.

5 Intended to cover a chair seat, this velvet furnishing fabric was probably made in Genoa around 1680–1710. Its symmetrically arranged pattern features large flowers and scrolling leaves.

6 This silk damask came from an anteroom to the State Apartments at Hampton Court Palace, London, which were furnished by King William III and Queen Mary II in the 1680s. The material was almost certainly woven in Genoa.

7 *Stanhope* woven silk furnishing fabric was designed by Owen Jones in 1872 to emulate 16th- and 17th-century Florentine silks, and manufactured by the London firm of Warner, Sillett & Ramm.

2

3

4

5

6

7

1

2

3

1 Densely arranged, rich leaf ornament was a commonly used type of decoration in northern Europe around 1500. *Ornament with Acanthus*, an etching of interwoven leaves and stems made by Daniel Hopfer in Germany around 1500–1520, is also known as *Bear's Breeches*.

2 The scrolling foliage of this monumental mirror frame in the Baroque style was carved using many small sections of wood and then gilded in Italy towards the end of the 17th century.

3 Made by Federico Lancetti in Rome, this marquetry panel was bought by the V&A at the 1855 Exposition Universelle in Paris. It elaborates on 16th-century Italian arabesque patterns, with slices of contrasting materials against an ebony ground.

4 This wallpaper border combines classical motifs with *trompe l'oeil* moulding in a scrolling acanthus pattern, or *rinceau*, supplied by Sanderson, England, in 1840–50.

5 Acanthus-like foliage decorates a high-rising broken pediment from the top section of a magnificent Rococo writing cabinet from 1750 to 1755, veneered in kingwood with gilded brass. It is attributed to the Dresden *Cabinett-Tischler* (cabinetmaker) Michael Kimmel.

6 *Single Stem* wallpaper by John Henry Dearle was produced for Morris & Co., the decorative arts company of William Morris, England, around 1905.

4

5

6

1

2

3

4

1 A range of classical references appears in this printed cotton furnishing fabric, including olive branches and two types of anthemion or stylized flower forms. It was printed with brightly coloured dyes for London retailer Charles Hindley & Sons in 1870.

2 The anthemion, from the Greek for 'flower', was a motif fashionable in the Greek Revival style of the Regency era in Britain (1795–1837). It is seen in the back of this 'Trafalgar' chair, named after Nelson's victory at the Battle of Trafalgar, and made in England around 1810.

3 With its anthemion motif based on honeysuckle petals, this cast-iron balcony front designed by Robert and James Adam and made by Carron Company, Stirlingshire, Scotland, around 1773, shows a Greek influence.

4 This engraving of Grecian ornament taken from the Temple of Apollo at Didymaion, the fourth largest temple in the Ancient Greek world, is from Peter Nicholson's influential book *The Principles of Architecture*, published in London in 1809.

5 A sheet of uncut wallpaper borders has a quasi-Greek anthemion–Egyptian palmette design reinvented by the Georgians for British domestic interiors of the early 19th century.

1

2

3

4

1 A ceramic ewer probably made in Iznik, Turkey, around 1520–5, is decorated in cobalt blue with arabesque designs on a diamond-shaped field. It was restored in the 19th century with silver mounts, including a dragon's-head spout.

2 This late 19th-century photograph by Isabel Agnes Cowper, the V&A's first female Official Museum Photographer, shows the geometric wooden panel with stars and arabesques of the *minbar* (mosque pulpit) made for Mamluk Sultan Lajin, Cairo, in 1296.

3 Made in Germany between 1550 and 1600, this blackwork design of foliated arabesques in the style of leading 16th-century German sculptor and printmaker Peter Flötner, was intended as designs for goldsmiths.

4 Glazed fritware tiles from Damascus, Syria, dating from around 1570 to 1580, are painted in underglaze with a design of floral medallions filled with small flower-heads in interlacing geometrical compartments.

5 Walter Crane's *Peacocks and Amorini* wallpaper features arabesques, peacocks, parrots, putti and cornucopia. It was produced by Jeffrey & Co., London, in 1877.

5

1 This wallpaper fragment with a pattern of thistle arabesques was probably made in London around 1850–5 by Woollams & Co., an English manufacturer famous for its handmade and flocked paper hangings.

2 This woodblock-print wallpaper from around 1840–50 was hung at Stubbers, a stately home in North Ockendon, Essex.

3 *Arabesque* furnishing fabric, woven in silk by Warner & Sons, London, in 1870, is a symmetrical design of scrolls, ribbons and floral motifs.

4 French wallpaper manufacturer Paul Balin, Paris, made this flock wallpaper. The gold arabesque design was based on the background of a 15th-century picture.

5 A Moorish decoration in the Alhambra palace in Granada, Spain, is depicted in *Plans, Elevations, Sections and Details of the Alhambra* (1842–5) by Owen Jones and Jules Goury.

6 This wallpaper fragment with floral arabesques by Thomas Willement originally hung in Charlecote Park, Warwickshire, England, in around 1832.

7 A blackwork design of foliated arabesques in the style of Peter Flötner, made in Germany (1550–1600), was intended as designs for goldsmiths.

8 Designed by Heather Brown for Heal's, this 1971 black and white furnishing fabric, *Alhambra*, recalls tile mosaic panels of the Alhambra palace in Spain, or Middle Eastern carpet designs.

1

2

3

4
5
6
7
8

1

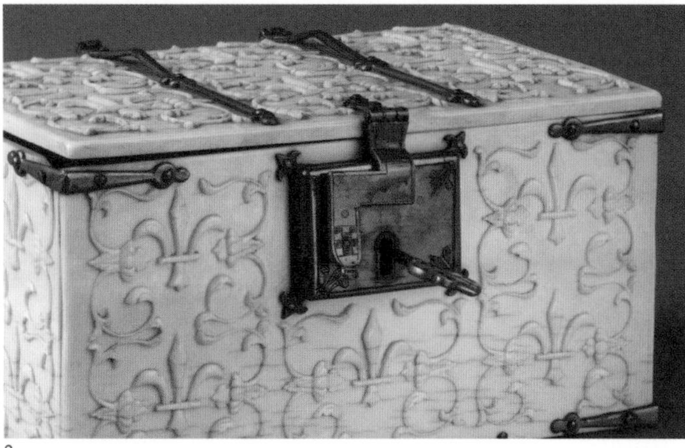
2

3

4

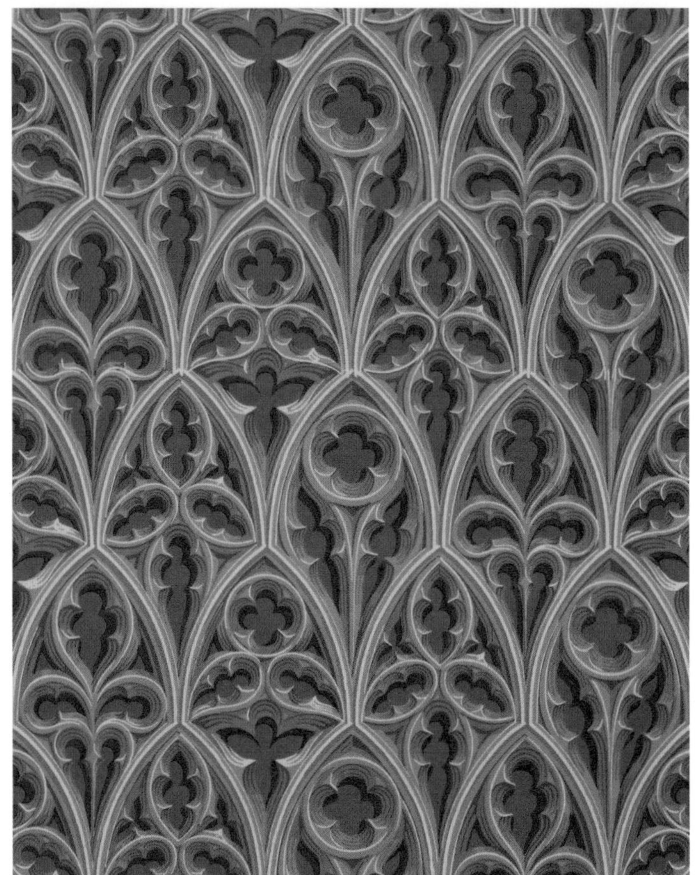
5

6

1 Owen Jones's work sits somewhere between A.W.N. Pugin's and William Morris's, with his wallpaper designs capturing a high Victorian Gothic style as well as moving into the Arts and Crafts era.

2 In late medieval France, luxurious *objets d'art* served as tangible records of wealth and social status. This trinket-sized ivory casket decorated with fleur-de-lis was made in the middle of the 19th century in France, imitating those earlier cherished objects.

3 This wallpaper with a design of alternating crowned fleur-de-lis and Tudor roses set within ogival borders is by A.W.N. Pugin and was used in the decoration of the new Palace of Westminster, London, around 1848–50.

4 The fleur-de-lis was incorporated into 100 designs for wallpaper by A.W.N. Pugin for the interior design of London's Palace of Westminster around 1848–50.

5 *Nowton Court* wallpaper by Cole & Son is a 1975 reprint of an earlier paper by Cowtan & Sons, London, from around 1840.

6 A stylized lily was a common feature of Victorian decorative schemes. Miles & Edwards specialized in fabrics for curtains and furnishings and produced this printed cotton fleur-de-lis lattice in the 1840s.

7 This panel of flock wallpaper with a fleur-de-lis pattern from around 1850–60 was supplied by the London firm of decorators W.B. Simpson.

7

1

2

1 A.W.N. Pugin rejected the busy naturalism of Victorian floral patterns in favour of strong, stylized motifs adapted from medieval patterns, often in two tones, as seen in this wool–cotton damask from 1845.

2 Owen Jones designed this specimen of wallpaper with a pattern of formalized floral motifs, suggestive of floriated fleur-de-lis. It was produced by Townsend, Parker & Co., England, around 1852–74.

3 Designed by A.W.N. Pugin in 1847, this enamelled gold brooch set with garnets and pearls was made by John Hardman & Co., Birmingham, in 1848. It formed part of a set of jewellery shown in the Medieval Court at the Great Exhibition in London in 1851.

4 With inlaid decoration in the Gothic Revival style, this luncheon tray was designed by A.W.N. Pugin in 1859 and made by Minton, England.

5 This is another specimen of wallpaper designed by Owen Jones with a pattern of formalized foliage, produced by Townsend, Parker & Co., England, around 1852–74.

6 *Seed and Flower* wallpaper was designed by Walter Crane and produced in London by Jeffrey & Co. in 1893.

3

4

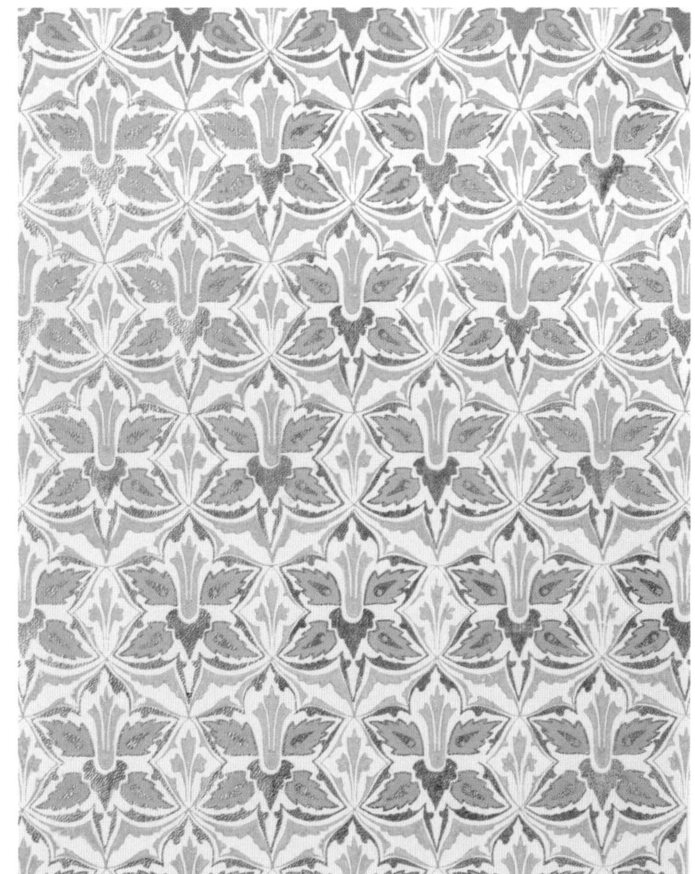
5

6

1 The curving 'paisley' motif originates in the *boteh* or *kolka* shape, a stylized floral form from India and Islamic cultures, often woven into the luxurious woven shawls from Kashmir that became popular in Britain in the 19th century. This design for a British printed shawl is by George Haité.

2 British manufacturers emulating Kashmir shawls commissioned designs for printed versions, often incorporating motifs with jagged outlines and hatched areas replicating the hallmarks of a more expensive woven shawl from India, as seen in this George Haité design from the 1850s.

3 Booth & Fox, London, feather merchants and manufacturers of underskirts, made this feather-filled cotton petticoat. It offered support for the dome-shaped skirts fashionable in the 1860s and provided warmth without too much additional weight.

4 George Haité's work gives us an indication of the great range of intricate patterns and colourways that were designed for shawls in the 1850s, all variations of the original teardrop-shaped *boteh* stylized plant motif.

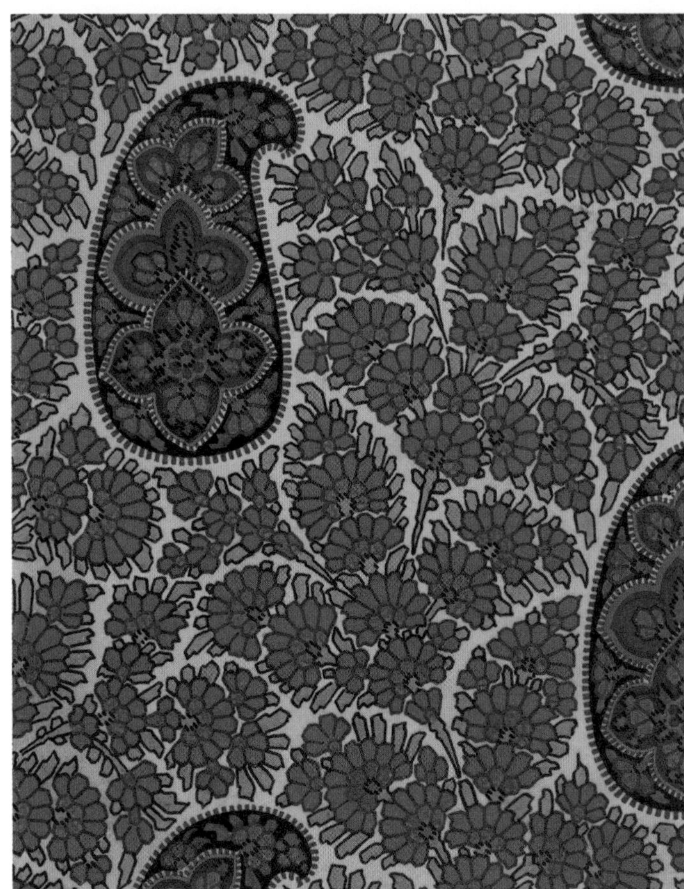

1

2

3

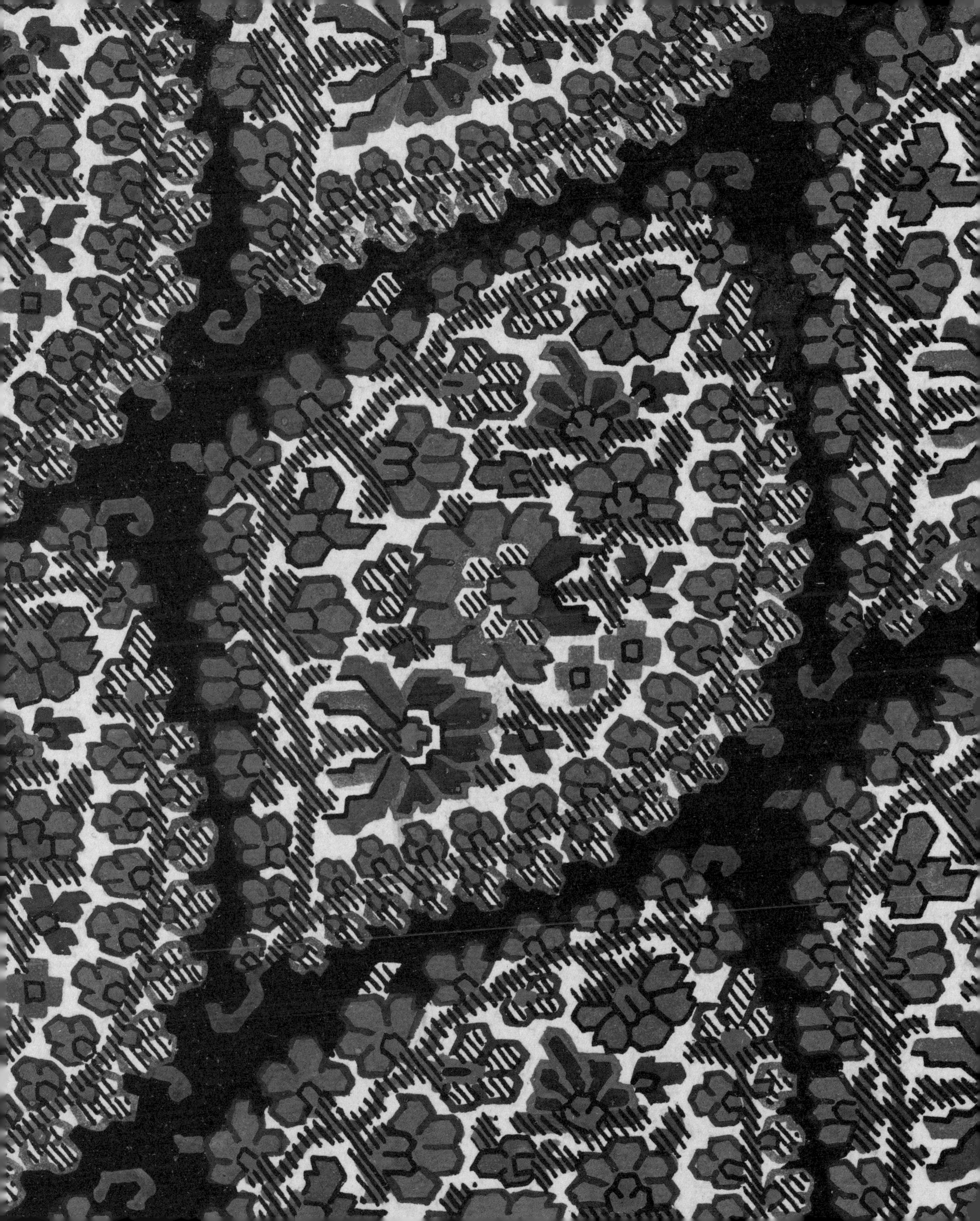

1

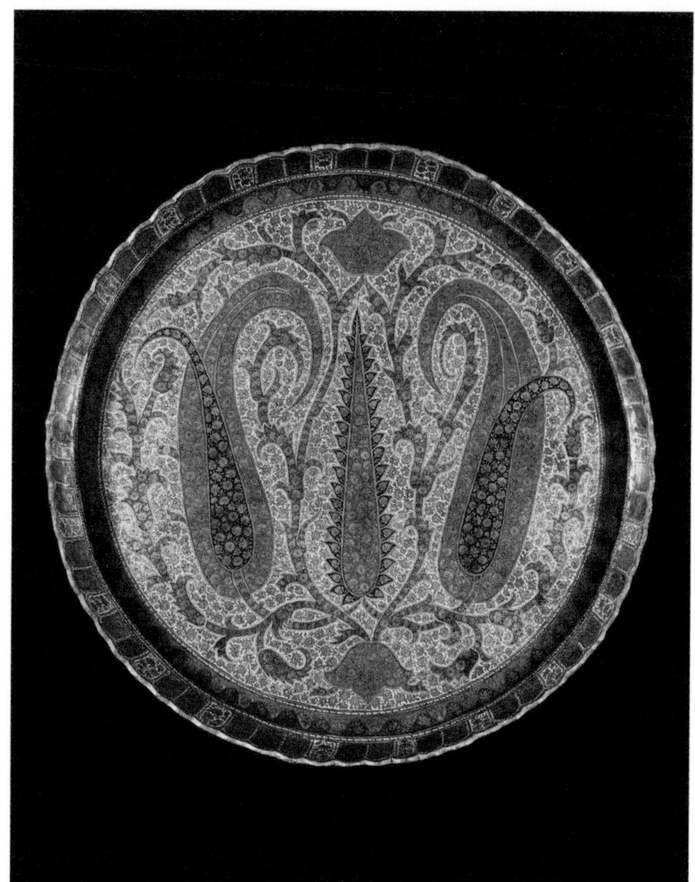

2

3

4

5

1 Textile manufacturers in 19th-century Britain exploited the demand for Kashmir shawls by producing their own versions, both woven and printed. One centre of textile printing was Wandsworth, London, where this design was made by Garratt Print Works.

2 Papier-mâché trays of this kind (c.1850) were made in India predominantly for the European market and produced in enormous quantities, especially in Srinagar. The hand-painted motifs relate closely to those on Kashmir shawls of the period.

3 This very stylized paisley design was produced at the Garratt Print Works in Wandsworth, London, in 1850. Around this time, widely circulated photographs of Queen Victoria in shawls helped to make them an indispensable accessory for fashionable Victorians.

4 Patterned Kashmir shawls, such as this wool fragment with handwork made using the twill-tapestry technique, were a popular fashion item in 19th-century Britain.

5 This is a design for an 1850s shawl produced at the Garratt Print Works in Wandsworth, London.

6 Repeating rows of *boteh* are seen in this 19th-century Iranian dress fabric.

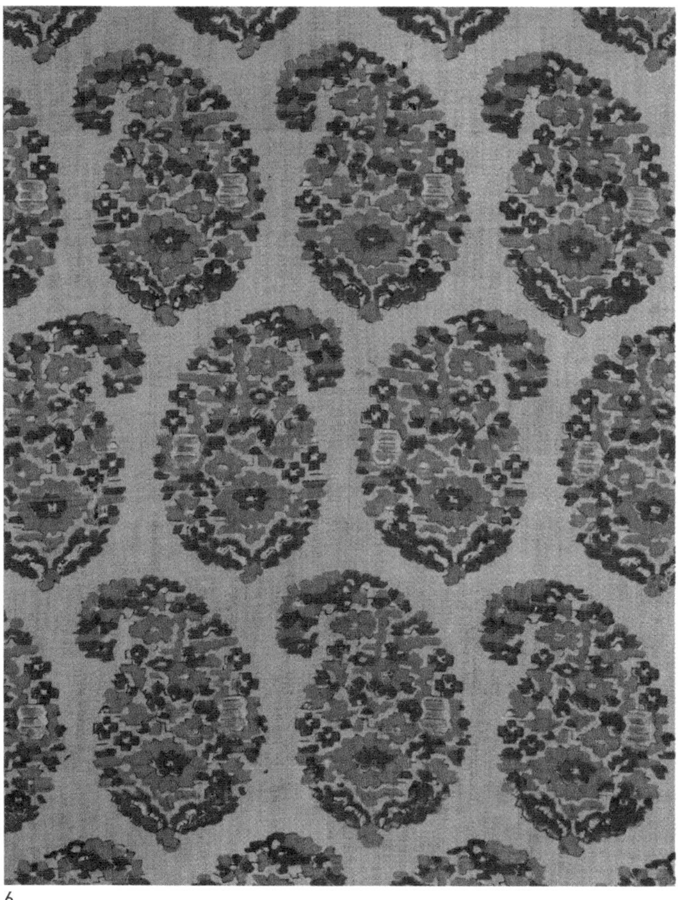

6

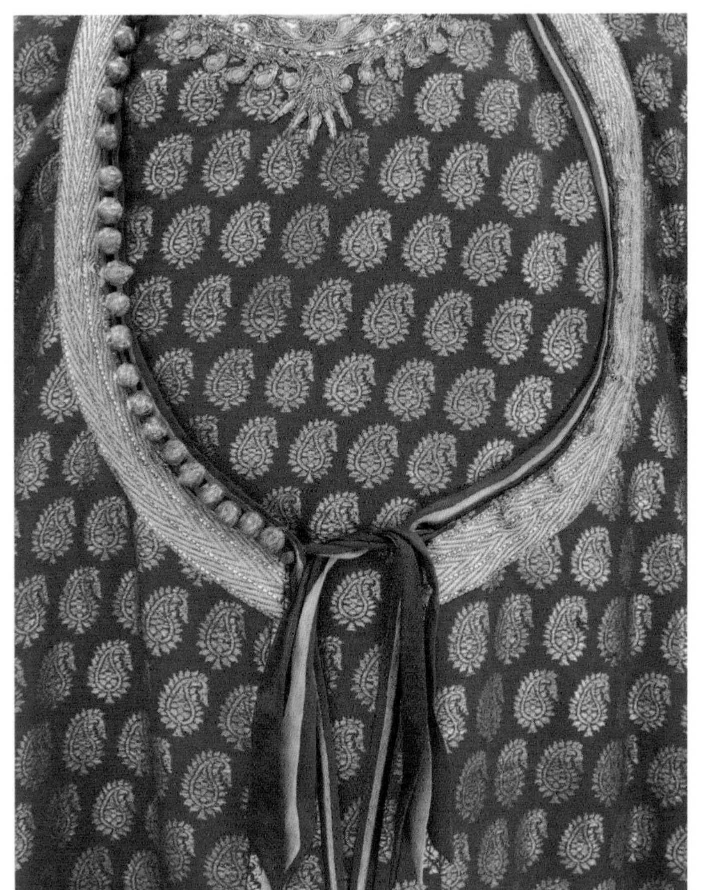
1

2

3

4

5

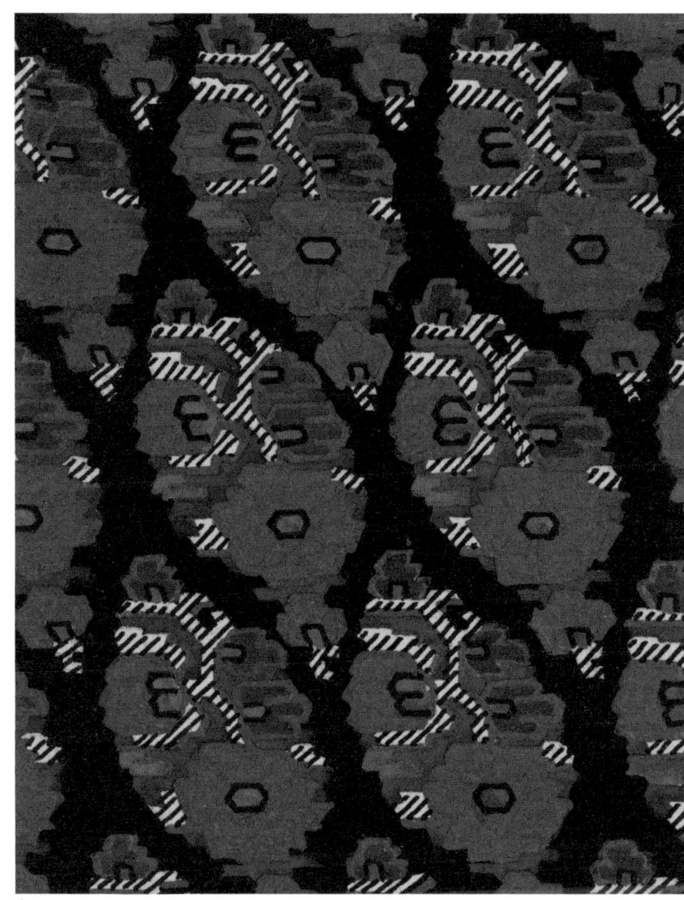
6

1 This 19th-century courtly robe (*angarkha*), once worn by a young man in Sindh, Pakistan, is of red silk woven with silver-gilt-wrapped thread.

2 A detail from a mid-19th-century *choga*, a loose-fitting, open-fronted robe worn as an outer garment on the Indian subcontinent, is seen here. It was made in Amritsar, northern India, with heavy embellishment of couched metal-wrapped thread in *boteh*, floral and scrolling designs.

3 This is another detail from the *choga* described above.

4 A pattern of crossing *boteh* motifs on a plain ground adorns this fresh glazed cotton furnishing fabric retailed by Hindley & Wilkinson, London, around 1892.

5 Shown here is a detail from a square muslin textile dating from around 1880, possibly a scarf, embroidered in white cotton thread, from Sultanpur near Lucknow, India.

6 George Haité's designs for shawls from the 1850s included large-scale borders as well as tiny all-over patterns such as this example. We can enjoy his work today because his son donated 60 of them to the V&A in 1911.

7 A decorative design of *boteh* motifs surrounded by a stylized foliate pattern in blue and turquoise adorns this glazed earthenware dish made in Turkestan in the 19th century.

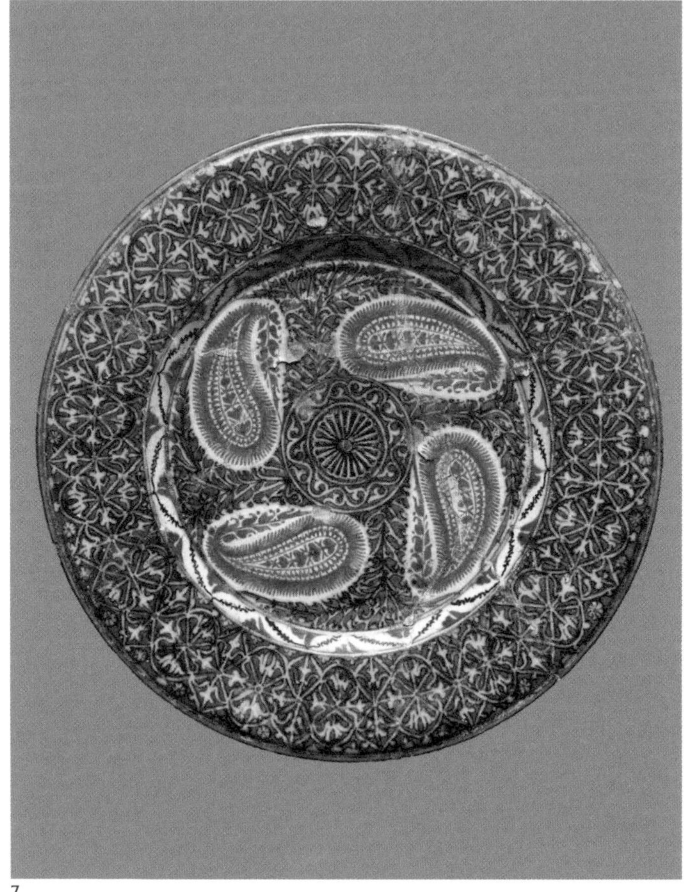
7

1 *The Lure of the Pipes of Pan*, (1932–3) is a decorative relief bronze panel made by Gilbert Bayes in London, with a stylized treatment of reeds and water that recalls Ancient Egyptian or Mesopotamian art.

2 With a pattern of lotus and palmette motifs, this mid-19th-century British chintz furnishing fabric was retailed by Miles & Edwards of London. Designs inspired by Greek and Roman archaeological finds became popular in Britain from the 18th century onwards.

3 *Athens*, a silk textile woven by the English firm of Warner & Sons in the early 1870s, reveals Owen Jones's skill in creating formal, repeating patterns inspired by his survey of decorative motifs from many periods, countries and cultures.

4 A formalized palmette motif is seen on this sheet of uncut, machine-printed wallpaper borders, American or English, from around 1850–75.

5 This is one of a series of colourful decorations and ornamental motifs documented by the British architect Richard Phené Spiers on his travels through the Near East in the 19th century.

6 Silk velvets, such as this Iranian textile from the 17th century, would have been used as hangings and often featured highly stylized blossoms, like the large woven palmettes in this design.

1

2

3

4

5

6

1

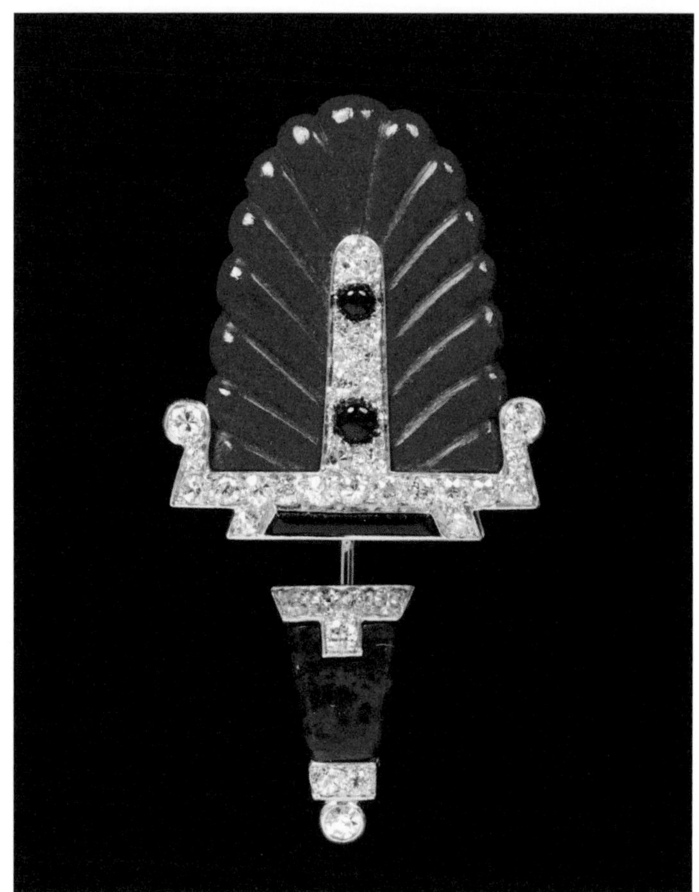

2

3

4

5

1 This 1923 evening jacket, probably made in Paris, is a good example of 1920s Egyptian-inspired design. The figures, hieroglyphics, lotus and palmette motifs are embroidered with glass beads in a fashion sparked by the discovery of Tutankhamun's tomb in 1922.

2 Modelled as a palmette or stylized feather and worn attached to a cloche hat, this Cartier lapis lazuli and diamond brooch draws on the archaeological discoveries of the 1920s and the European appetite for the imagery of ancient cultures.

3 This ornamental design for a frieze for the South Kensington Museum (now the V&A) by Godfrey Sykes, dating from the 1860s, features flowers and foliage in the form of a palmette.

4 A dress fabric produced by French manufacturer Alfred Wallach in 1922 showcases the imaginative artistry of its anonymous designer, its falcons, lotus flowers and palmettes influenced by recent archaeological finds in Egypt.

5 Lionesses walk through a cover of palms and grasses in this design for a textile and wallpaper by C.F.A. Voysey, made in London in 1918.

1

2

3

4

5

1 This is a design dating from 1847 for one of A.W.N. Pugin's Gothic furnishing decorations for London's new Palace of Westminster.

2 Queen Victoria's sapphire and diamond coronet was designed by Prince Albert in 1840. The cresting of trefoils comes from the coronet on his Saxon coat of arms.

3 Inspired by medieval ecclesiastical decoration, this enamelled gold headband was designed by A.W.N. Pugin and made by John Hardman & Co. of Birmingham in 1848.

4 Designed by A.W.N. Pugin for the Great Exhibition in London in 1851, this wallpaper pattern incorporates the national flower emblems of the British Isles, in the Gothic Revival style.

5 This wallpaper specimen shows conventionalized foliage designed by Owen Jones. Produced by Townsend, Parker & Co. in 1850, it was supplied by the London firm of decorators W.B. Simpson.

6 Seen here is another example of wallpaper with 'conventional' foliage in a lozenge pattern, dating to about 1850–60, from the stock of the decorating firm W.B. Simpson of London.

7 These earthenware tiles, possibly by L.A.C. Macé, Paris, around 1867, have a printed quatrefoil pattern.

6

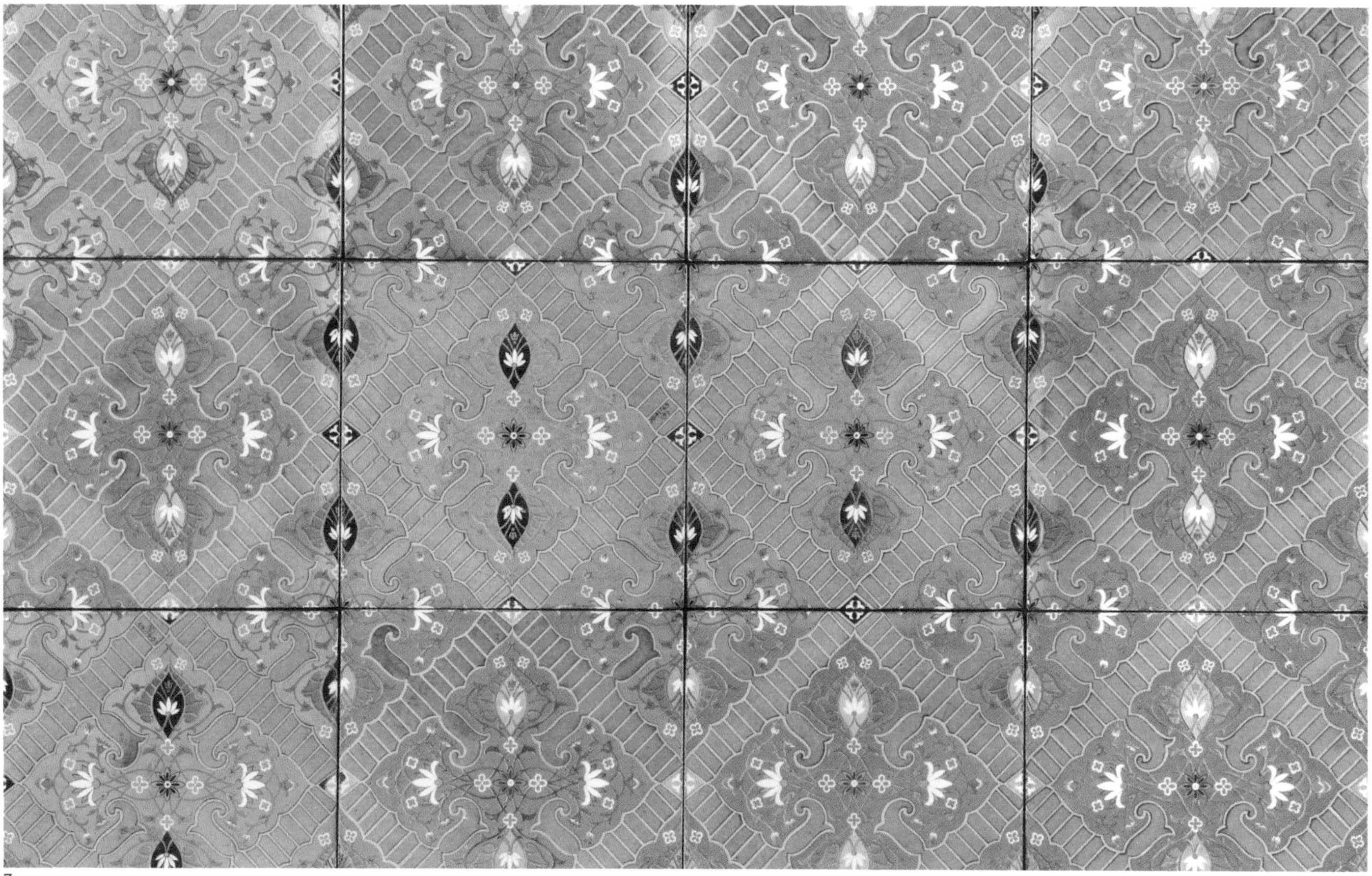

7

1

2

1 This is one of a series of wallpapers from the stock of the London decorating firm W.B. Simpson, showing a pattern of quatrefoils in flock, dating to around 1850–60.

2 Shown at the 1862 International Exhibition in London, this ruby glass flagon, mounted in silver-gilt and set with cabochon gemstones and enamels, was made by John Hardman Powell, chief designer for John Hardman & Co. of Birmingham.

3 Another panel of flock wallpaper with quatrefoils is seen here from the stock of W.B. Simpson of London, dating to around 1850–60.

4 Skilled craftsmen made this extravagant but functional washstand to William Burges's design in London in 1880. Although for a domestic s etting, like much of his work it reflected the ideals of medieval church architecture.

3

# ANIMALS

**Opposite.** Detail from a linen cover, embroidered in silk, silver and gilt thread, England, 1600–29

1

1 Probably made in the early 18th century, this Mughal nephrite jade horsehead dagger hilt is realistically carved, and embellished with gold and precious stones.

2 Anne Morgan and Karin Warming ran their textile workshop from 1937/8 until they became active in World War II. The foals on this charming hand-block-printed linen, *Fenn* (1938), gently disrupt the regularity of the diagonal motifs.

3 Founded in 1929, the fabric house of Scalamandré has become synonymous with the manufacture of the finest quality furnishings in the USA. Their commitment to art and craft yielded this design of prancing show horses in 1949.

4 *Cavallo*, based on a painting called *Horse* by the Italian sculptor Marino Marini, was translated into this jacquard-woven rayon and cotton furnishing cloth by Alistair Morton for his firm Edinburgh Weavers, Carlisle, in 1958.

5 The association between French artist Raoul Dufy and silk-weaving manufacturer Bianchini-Férier, Lyon, from about 1911 to 1928 resulted in many jacquard-woven fabrics. Subjects depicting scenes based on Greek mythology, such as *Pegasus*, were fashionable for dress at this time.

6 This deceptively simple design, full of movement, energy and grace, is a cotton dress fabric first printed in 1936 by British firm Dilkusha.

2

3

4

5

6

1

2

1 The agricultural theme of Marion Dorn's furnishing fabric *Farmer's Arms*, produced by Gordon Russell in 1939, recalls the two-handled mugs used extensively in the cider-drinking areas of the West of England.

2 *Essex Hunt* furnishing fabric by Ruth Reeves for W. & J. Sloane, New York, made in 1930, shows various scenes from a hunt, from the meet to galloping in full cry across the countryside.

3 The central micromosaic image of Benedetto Boschetti's table top, made in Rome around 1820–70, depicts Cupid in his chariot. The composition follows one of Michelangelo Barberi's most successful works, *The Triumph of Cupid*.

4 Designed by John Drummond under the direction of Dora Batty at the Central School of Arts and Crafts, London, this screen-printed equine-themed furnishing fabric dates from around 1947–8.

5 *Horse's Head* curtain fabric was created by Lucienne Day for her Royal College of Art diploma show in London and screen printed by hand in 1939.

6 It was Daoist belief that jade could preserve the body of the deceased. This carved nephrite jade horse's head, made in China in 206 BCE–220 CE, was intended to carry the tomb's occupant into the heavens.

3

4

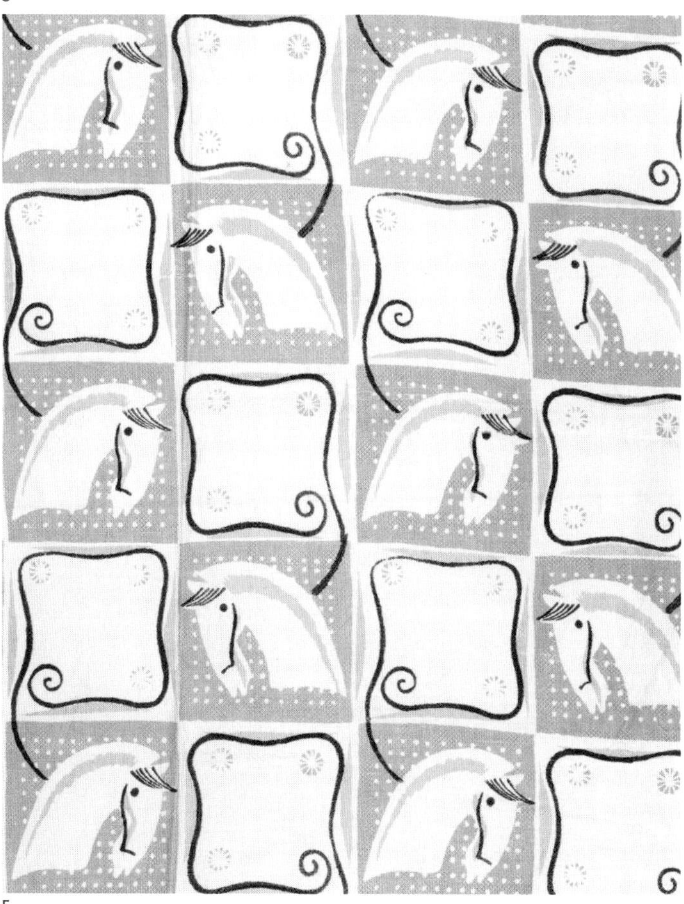
5

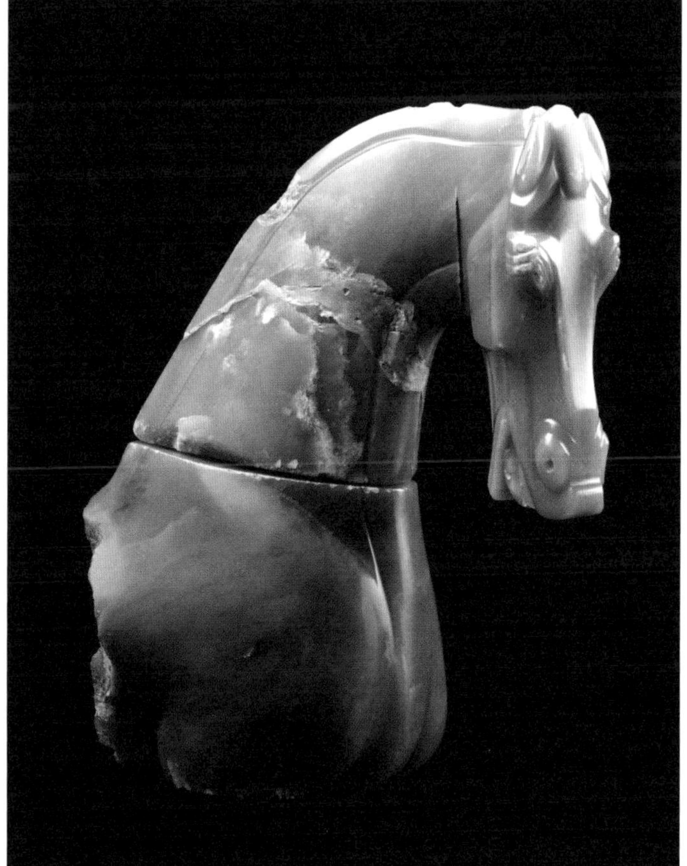
6

1

2

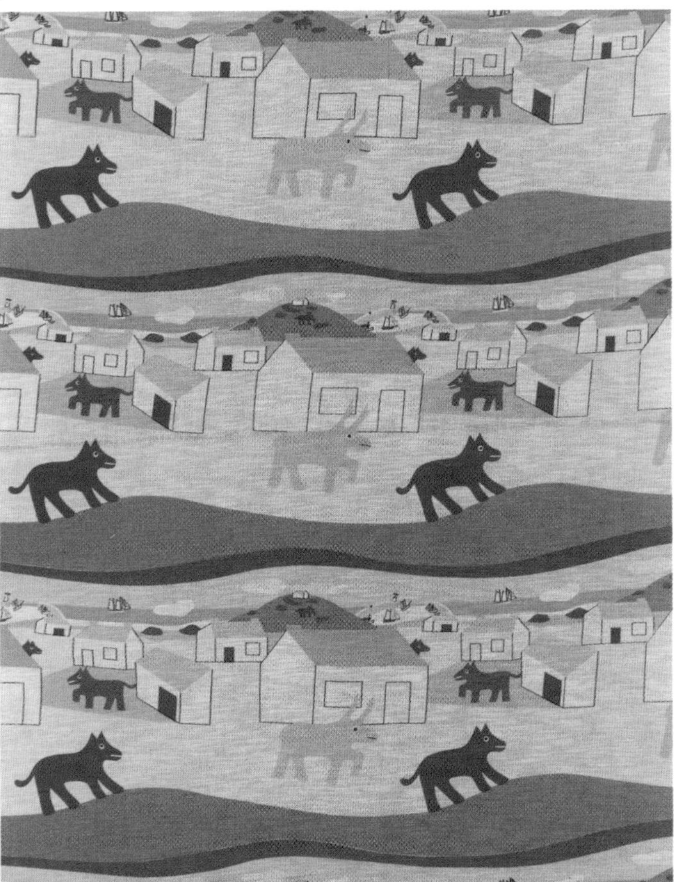

3

1 British company Sanderson's *Triad* collection from 1974 introduced a variety of mainstream patterns for wallpaper and textiles, including this luxuriant floral with cute animals for the young Sanderson customer.

2 This tin-glazed and lustre-painted earthenware serving platter, or charger, made in Reus, Spain, around 1600–25, is decorated at the centre with a hound.

3 Designed by Ben Nicholson and printed in collaboration with Alastair Morton, founder of Edinburgh Weavers, Carlisle, *George and Rufus* nursery fabric from 1938 was based on a series of naive drawings and paintings intended for a children's book.

4 This Japonisme-style printed cotton dress fabric with a pattern of playful, tumbling puppies was produced in Manchester by Beith, Stevenson & Co. in 1909.

5 *La Chasse* by Marian Mahler, with its two-colour vignettes of huntsmen, hounds and castles, produced by Edinburgh Weavers around 1951, chimes with the upbeat mood of the post-war era.

6 Miriam Wornum designed this whimsical figurative print called *Dalmatian* in 1937 for Edinburgh Weavers. More spaniel than dalmatian, the dogs depicted on the rayon fabric resemble 'Staffordshire dog' figurines standing guard on the mantelpiece.

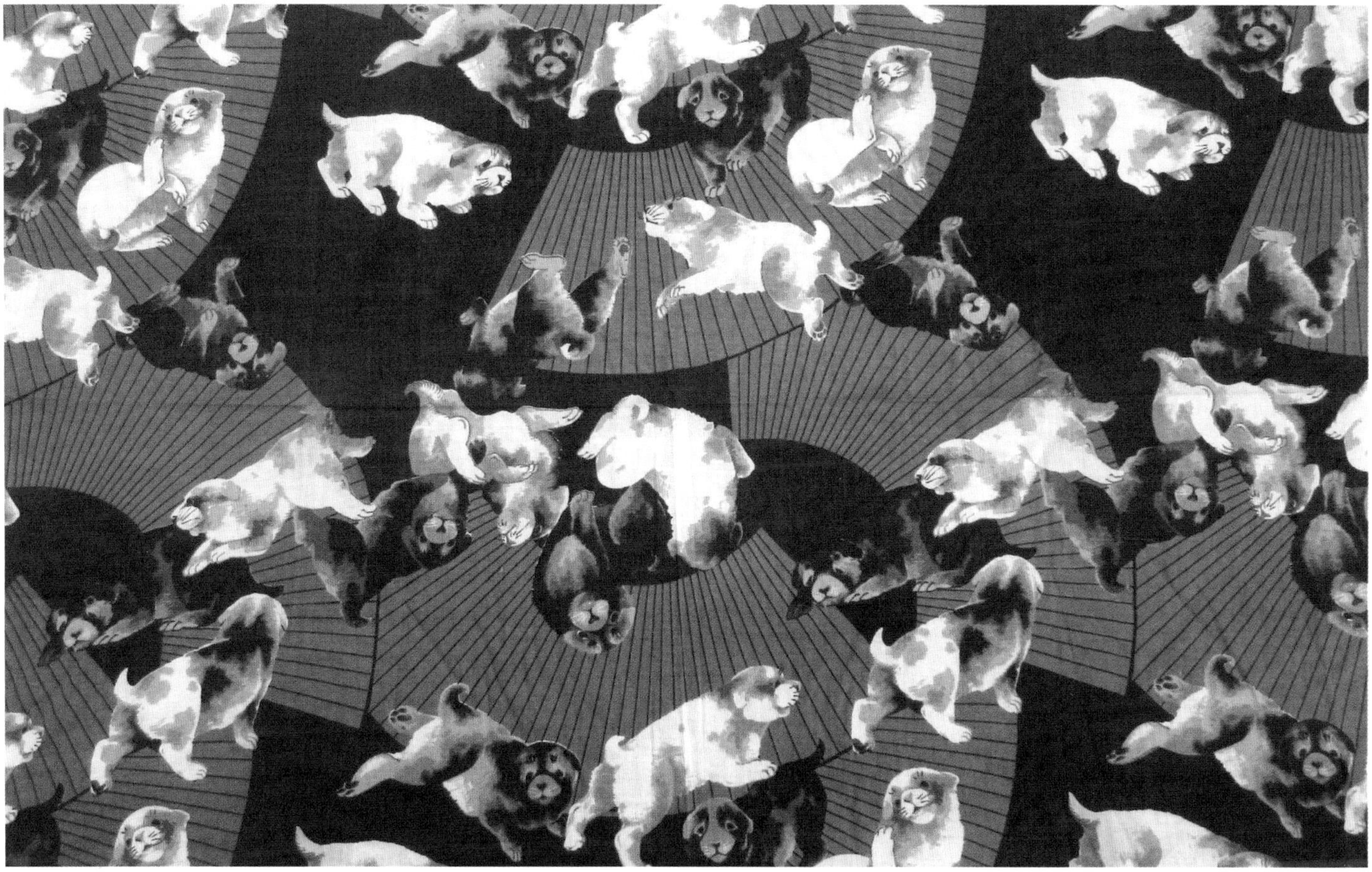

4

5

6

1 In 1875 the British decorative artist Walter Crane was commissioned by Jeffrey & Co. to design a series of nursery wallpapers based on his children's book illustrations. Here is the cat and fiddle from the rhyme 'Hey Diddle Diddle'.

2 Joyce Badrocke designed this small print pattern of anthropomorphized animals for one of Horrockses Fashions' younger clothes ranges between 1958 and 1964.

3 *Homage to Emily Dickinson*, a furnishing fabric designed in 1930 by Ruth Reeves for the New York retailer W. & J. Sloane, features a repeat pattern inspired by the American poet.

4 C.F.A. Voysey's textile design from 1909 shows a repeat pattern of a cat watching a canary, the canary watching a worm, etc. The grim humour of the title, *Let Us Prey*, is clear.

5 Felix the Cat, the cartoon character created by Otto Messner, debuted in 1919 during the silent film era in the USA. This dress fabric by the Calico Printers' Association, was one of the first items of merchandise to appear – unofficially – in Britain in 1924.

6 A gold ring with a layered onyx cameo depicts a crouching cat in a 'Roman' setting, possibly made in England, around 1825.

7 This dress fabric of block-printed rayon featuring cats is by designer-craftswoman Joyce Clissold and was produced at Footprints Textile Printing Workshop in Hammersmith, London, in 1925–39.

1

2

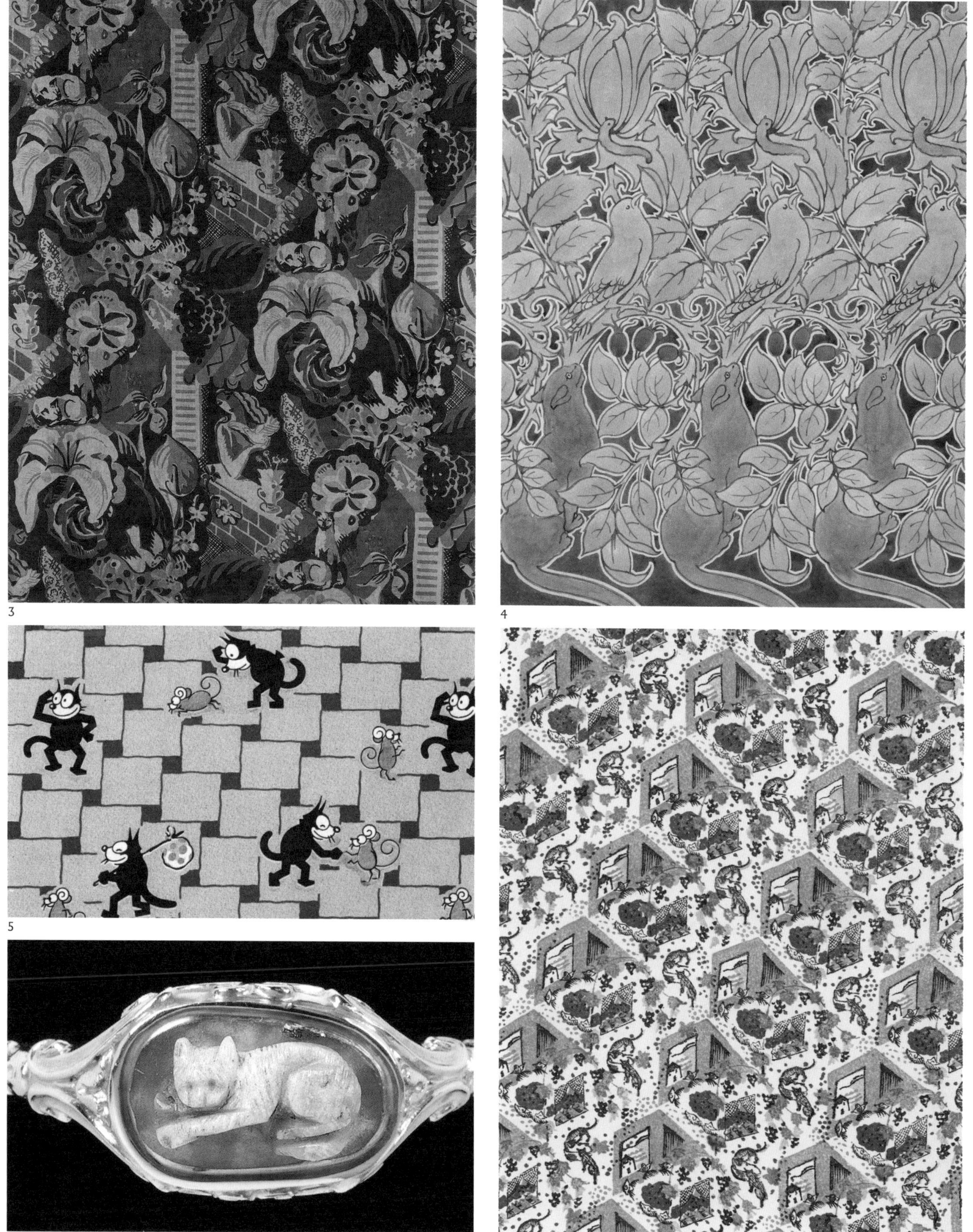

3

4

5

6

7

1

1 Patterns of creatures with flowers and insects were extremely popular in England in the late 16th and early 17th centuries. This rabbit was embroidered in red wool on a woman's linen jacket in the 1640s, and is surrounded by butterflies, caterpillars and imaginary birds and animals.

2 This cotton fabric, printed from stipple-engraved rollers in chrome colours, was produced in Mulhouse, Alsace, around 1830–90.

3 The innovative English Arts and Crafts potter William De Morgan famously experimented with the reduction-fired lustre technique, inspired by Iranian lustreware, in order to produce tiles such as these boxing hares, made in 1872–6.

4 This is a detail from an English embroidered linen cover from 1600 to 1629. It is crowded with fauna, such as birds, snails, a camel and butterflies, and a variety of fantastic flora in the form of flowering and fruiting branches and scrolls in silk, silver and silver-gilt thread.

5 William Morris designed *Brer Rabbit*, sometimes known as *Brother Rabbit*, in 1881 specifically for indigo discharge block printing on textiles, a method he revived at his Merton Abbey workshops in south London. His use here of paired animals among fantastic foliage illustrates his interest in medieval European textiles.

2

3

4

5

1

2

1 A historical textile in the V&A known as the Abigail Pett bed hangings provided Morton Sundour's designers with inspiration for this furnishing fabric of the 1920s–30s, with its flowers, foliage and deer.

2 This furnishing fabric sample made by Green & Abbot of Marylebone, London, in 1930, was possibly intended for nursery curtains.

3 In *Huntsmen*, C.F.A. Voysey evokes a medieval scene of a huntsman, his dog and a majestic stag. This detailed design was produced as a wallpaper in 1919.

4 Deer among autumn flowers in gold on black lacquer decorate this tobacco set from Japan, dating from 1775 to 1825.

5 *Woodnotes* wallpaper, designed by the book illustrator Walter Crane in 1886 and printed by Jeffrey & Co., London, depicts a hunting scene among large foliage.

6 *Enara*, depicting deer in a wood, was designed by Karin Williger in 1951 for Edinburgh Weavers, Carlisle, as a jacquard-woven cotton. Williger's vocabulary is highly distinctive, drawing on her European background and redolent of fairy tales.

3

4

5

6

1

2

3

4

1 The deer motif was a popular form in Art Deco design, their sleek appearance connoting speed. This furnishing fabric was produced by the Calico Printers' Association, Manchester, in 1934.

2 Block-printed fabrics such as this German example dating from 1750 to 1774 were popular in 18th-century Europe. The stag was an important symbol of hunting culture.

3 Medieval art was the model for much of the ecclesiastical pattern work that emerged in the 19th century. This anonymous design imitates luxury woven textiles and originates from Cologne, Germany.

4 Such printed linen cloths with characteristic bands of inscriptions and motifs were used in the home. Attractive and utilitarian, this Swiss fabric dates from 1766. The motto translates as 'pray and work'.

5 This sample length of woven wool showing five different colourways for *The Duleek* was designed by C.F.A. Voysey in 1899 and woven by Morton Sundour, Carlisle, for Liberty, London.

6 *The Forest* was designed by Edmund Arthur Hunter in 1910. This handloom-woven fabric was produced by the St Edmundsbury Weaving Works, established by Hunter at Haslemere in Surrey.

5

6

1

2

1 A design for an upholstery fabric from 1918 created by C.F.A. Voysey depicts deer leaping through forest trees and woodland flowers.

2 Made for export in Lancashire in the 1850s, this roller-printed furnishing fabric has bright colours and a bold design that suggest it was intended for Spain, Portugal or South America.

3 This mid-20th-century furnishing fabric was designed by Czech textile artist Jan Hladik for Centrotex in Czechoslovakia.

4 Designed in a strong Art Deco style, this figure group, *Axis Deer*, by John Rattenbury Skeaping in cream-coloured earthenware was produced by Wedgwood in 1927.

5 Possibly a furnishing fabric, this printed cotton, with a lattice-work design featuring a long-horned creature, probably an ibex or gazelle, was made by the Calico Printers' Association, Manchester, in 1913.

6 This 1860 German mirror made by H.F.C. Rampendahl is framed with antlers, goat horns and boar tusks.

7 This is a detail from an English embroidered linen cover from around 1600–30, crowded with fauna, including birds, snails, butterflies and a camel, and a variety of fantastic flora, in silk, silver and silver-gilt thread.

8 F. Gregory Brown designed the leaping deer silhouettes for this printed linen fabric by William Foxton, London. It is typical of 1930s Art Deco motifs.

3

4

5

6

7

8

1 This cotton furnishing fabric depicts squirrels encircled by briars. It was designed by English architect and designer Arthur Heygate Mackmurdo around 1882.

2 English architect-designer William Burges's style was influenced by medieval art, as seen in this 1872 wallpaper frieze of squirrels, which recalls medieval encaustic tiles.

3 This black basalt bulb pot in the form of a hedgehog, dating from 1820, would have been planted with crocuses. Wedgwood has made these pots since at least 1783.

4 Owen Jones's *Examples of Chinese Ornament* (1867) presents 100 plates of designs taken from a wide range of decorative and applied arts, including this chromolithograph of squirrels and grapes.

5 Like most Arts and Crafts designers, William De Morgan was inspired by nature, and he created beautiful tiles, such as this 1880s panel design.

6 Yorkshire craftsman Robert Thompson's furniture bore a carved mouse, giving rise to his nickname, Mouseman. This mouse sits on the arm of his *Ampleforth* chair from 1932.

7 *Woodland Notes* by C.F.A. Voysey was designed for a nursery textile or wallpaper in 1929.

8 This English wallpaper from around 1700 imitates the Chinese style, but shows a poor understanding of the conventions of the originals, with figures dwarfed by squirrels.

1

2

3

4

5

6

7

8

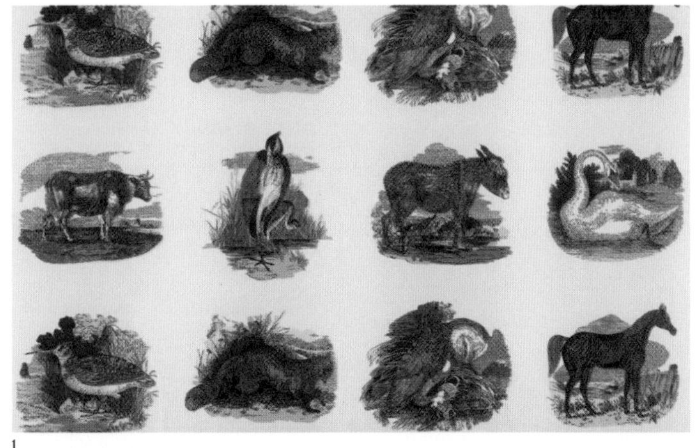
1

2

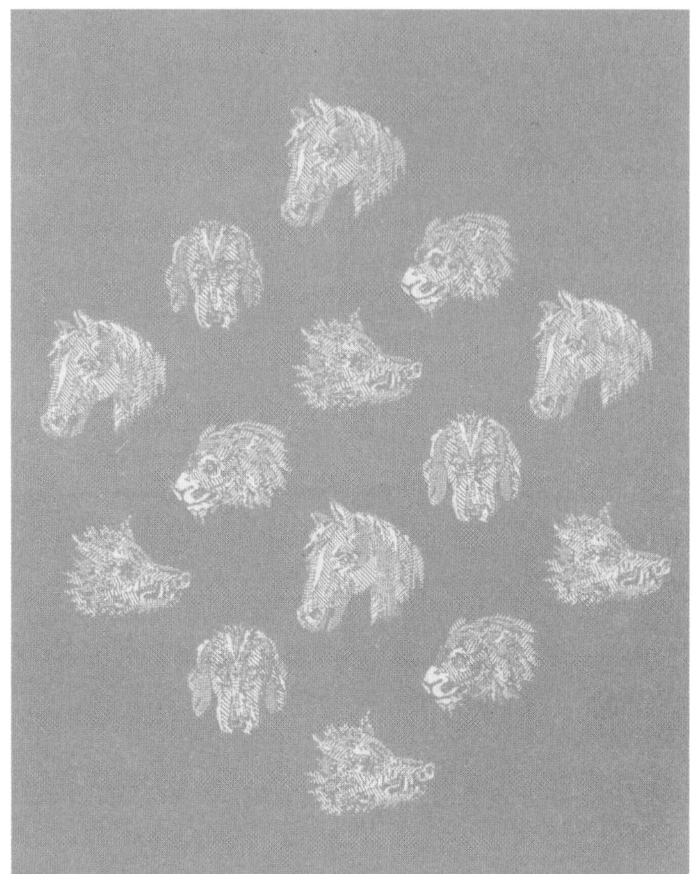
3

4

5

1 *Rustica*, designed by Charles Raymond in 1962 for Edinburgh Weavers, Carlisle, draws on natural history as well as referencing the ever popular wood engravings of Thomas Bewick (1753–1828).

2 Made in Kutch, Gujarat, in the late 19th century, this fragment of a shrine hanging (*pichhwai*) is made of woven cotton embroidered in silk with a design of cows in three colours.

3 Published in 1880–1, the monthly illustrated journal *Dessins Nouveautés* by Lechartier et Paul included textile designs that covered all aspects of country living, wildlife, rural pursuits and hunting.

4 *The Farmer's Boy*, a printed linen cretonne by Manchester-based Tootal Broadhurst Lee from 1926, recalls traditional English folk ballads about ploughing as well as late 18th- and early 19th-century furnishing fabrics depicting a range of pastoral scenes.

5 This printed linen called *Pastoral* was designed by Tootal Broadhurst Lee in 1925. It features bucolic fields with dairy cows and a milkmaid, suggesting an earlier era. The British textile merchant was drawn to an idealized pastoral past in the 1920s.

6 The printed cotton furnishing fabric *The House that Jack Built* was designed by the great Arts and Crafts architect C.F.A. Voysey and manufactured around 1929 by Morton Sundour, Carlisle.

6

1

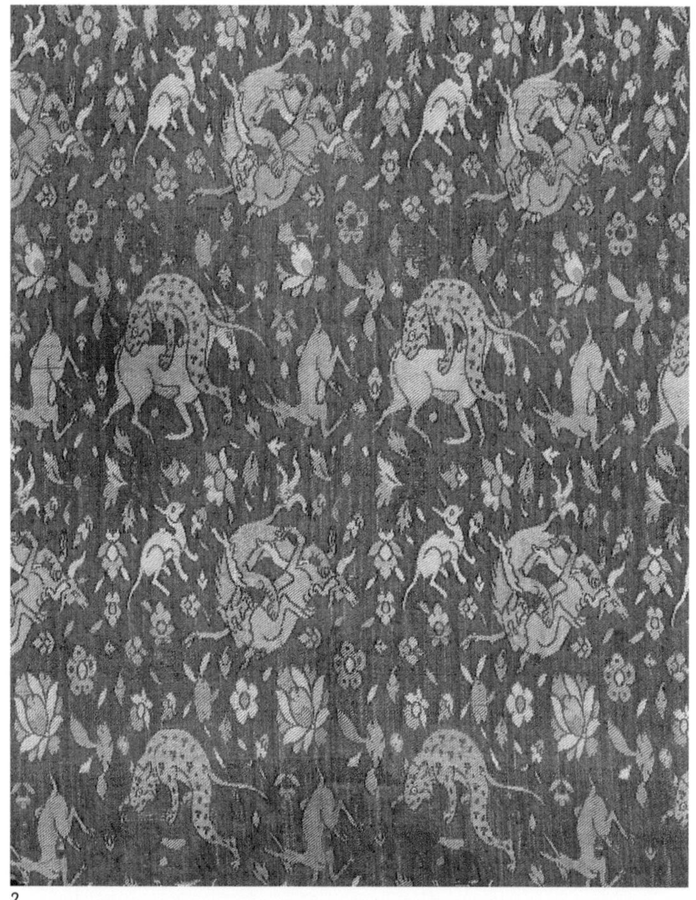
2

1 This is one of a series of designs for textiles for London's new Houses of Parliament by the Gothic genius A.W.N. Pugin, from around 1847.

2 This silk lampas-woven dress fabric from 16th-century Iran depicts scenes of animals in combat on a deep green ground. Similar imagery appears on Iranian works in other media of the same time, including painting and bookbinding.

3 The playful and vibrant *Puma* printed furnishing fabric was designed by Michèle Catala in 1950–2 for Carl Eschke, Zurich.

4 A detail of a Mughal coat shows silk chain-stitch embroidery of a landscape with lions, ducks and flowers. Made in 1620–5, it is one of the finest surviving examples of Indian court dress.

3

1 The Sapozhnikov factory in Russia was internationally renowned for producing different types of high-quality woven silks, some used to decorate the interiors of Russian palaces. This example from 1870–2 shows a pair of stylized big cats.

2 This printed textile featuring diagonally placed pink tigers was produced by the Calico Printers' Association, Manchester, in 1911.

3 By the early 17th century, print sellers provided simplified patterns and outlines for embroidery. Many of these designs, such as this English block-printed linen, were inspired by the illustrations in natural history and botanical books.

4 This snuffbox has the mark of Mouliné, Bautte & Cie and was made in Geneva in 1804–9. The recumbent lion is painted in enamel and set with pearls.

5 A finely woven 16th-century Iranian carpet fragment is decorated with medallions and pairs of lions, cheetahs, antelope and, more unusually, wolves and jackals, which are distributed across a field of fantastic blossoms and arabesques.

6 Dating from 800 to 1000, this silk fragment is ornamented with pairs of lions facing each other. Variants of this pattern, depicting slightly different animals or plant forms, have been made in Central Asia since around the 9th century.

1

2

3

4

5

6

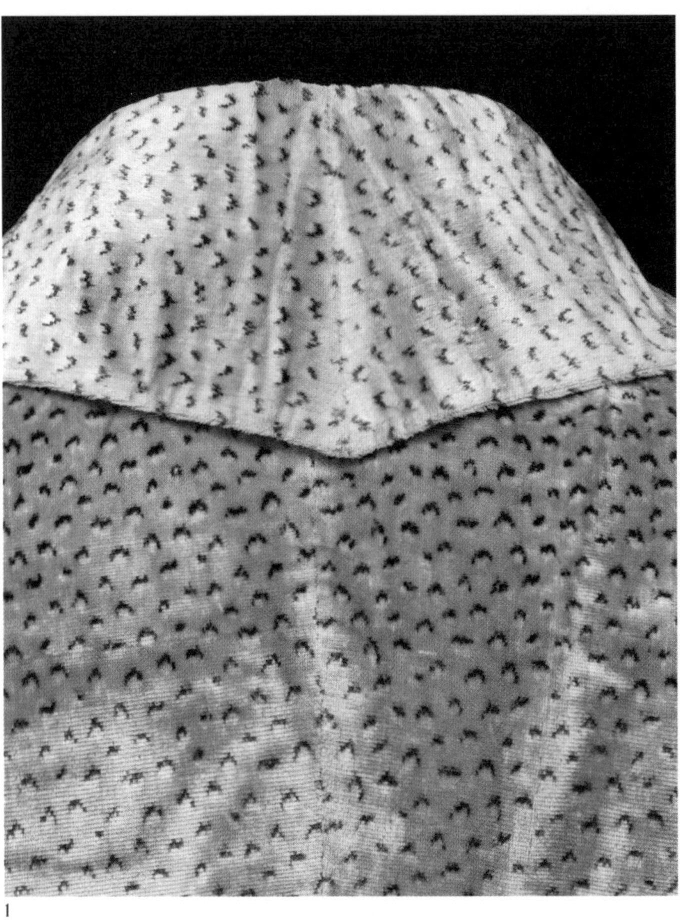
1

1 The imitation leopard spot was woven into the turquoise silk velvet of this French frock coat. Such a whimsical pattern was common in men's fashions in the 1770s and 1780s.

2 A silk dress fabric from around 1760 with a meandering leopard-skin brocaded pattern epitomizes fashionable woven designs of the 1750s and 1760s that simulated undulating trimmings such as fur, lace and ribbons.

3 Made in Britain in 1825–30, this fabric swatch of glazed, roller-printed cotton furnishing fabric has a pattern of bold leopard spots.

4 This dress fabric sample of a leopard spot and check is from a pattern book, *Fancy Vestings and Handkerchief Goods*, by Maze & Steer, London, in 1786–91.

5 The pattern of this tile panel made in Turkey or Syria around 1550 to 1600 is inspired by tiger stripes and leopard spots, connoting strength and courage.

6 Probably from Ottoman Turkey around 1550 to 1600, this silk damask fragment has an ogival lattice pattern of medallions with stylized representations of leopard and tiger skins.

7 This graphic animal print, from a set of designs for shawls by F. Toraud, working in Norwich in the 19th century, is not the usual paisley or floral of the period.

8 A luxurious 15th-century Ottoman Turkish silk velvet incorporates three circles (representing the leopard) alternating with two wavy bands (the tiger), designs with powerful associations.

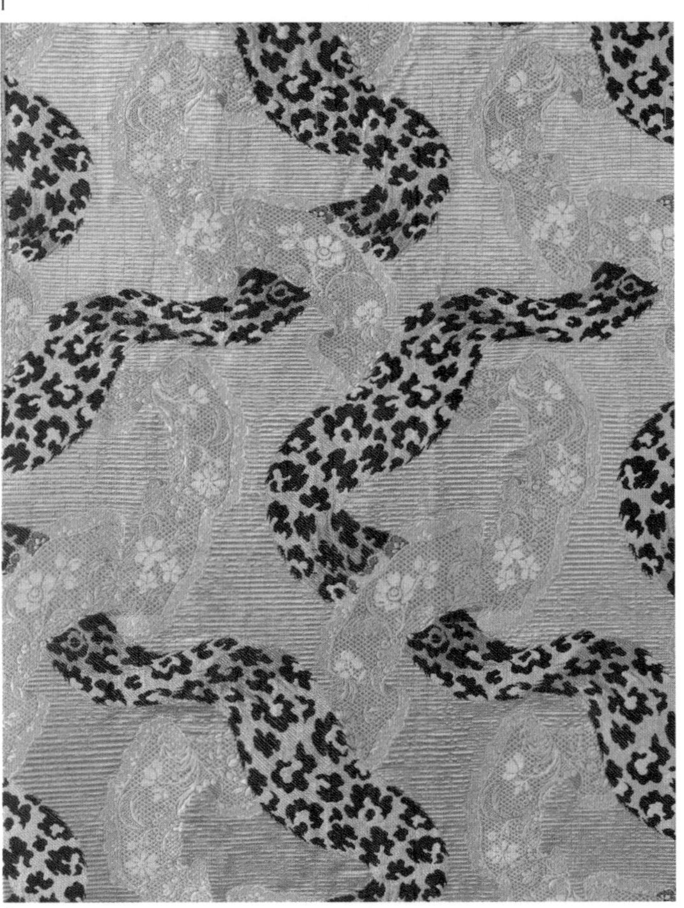
2

3

4

5

6

7

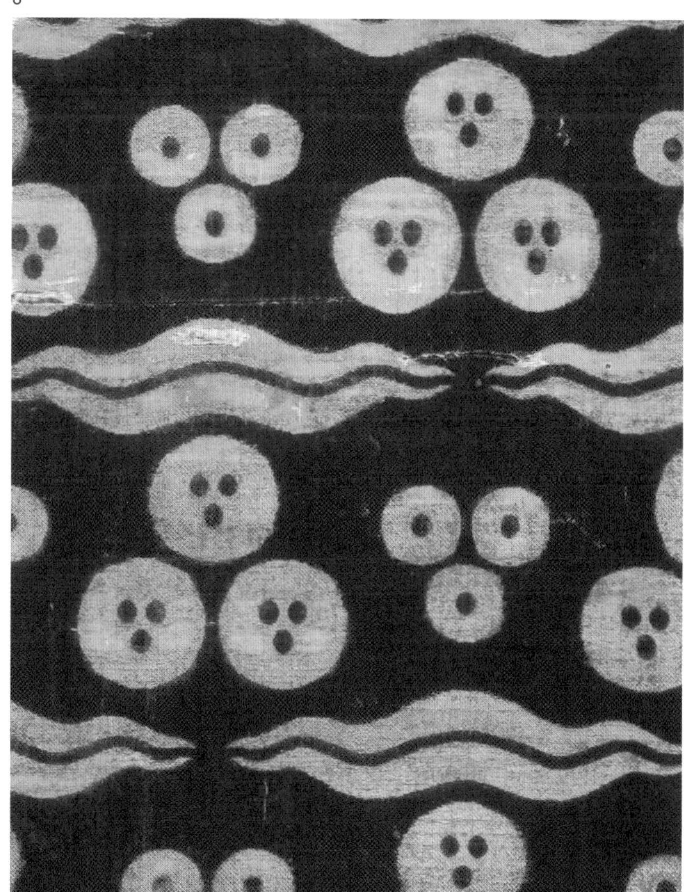
8

1

2

1 This camel is a detail from an English embroidered linen cover dating from 1600 to 1630, which is crowded with fauna, including birds, snails and butterflies, flora in the form of flowering and fruiting branches, and scrolls, in silk, silver and silver-gilt thread.

2 This Moore Brothers novelty teapot retailed by Thomas Goode & Co., London, dates from 1876. The handle is formed by the driver, who is trying to get the stubborn, laden camel up onto its feet.

3 Woven in Italy in the early 15th century, this brocaded silk was made into an ecclesiastical garment. In the Bible, the Magi on their camels brought gifts to the infant Jesus from distant lands.

4 *The Zoo* was designed by George Day for Tootal Broadhurst Lee, Manchester, in 1925. Such subjects – children enjoying themselves among animals at the zoo – were favoured by fabric manufacturers for nursery prints.

3

4

1

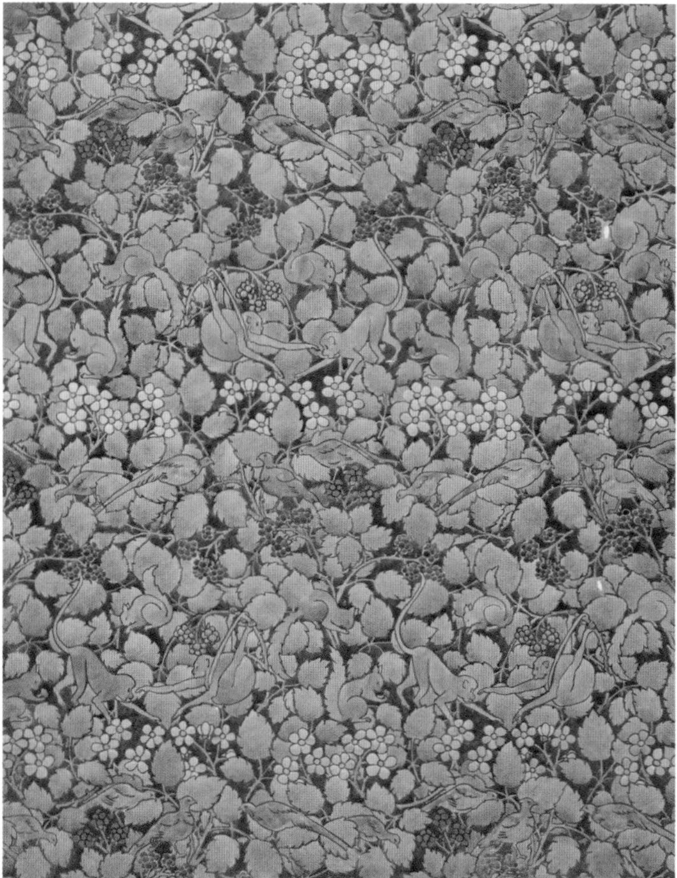

2

3

1 Made in southern India, probably Machilipatnam, this palampore (large bed or wall cover or hanging) of around 1855–79 is block printed, dyed and painted with designs of birds and flowers. This detail shows a monkey sitting in a fruit-laden tree.

2 This design for a woven tapestry hanging by Kathleen Kersey was entered by the designer as a student work for the National Art Competition in 1911. Kersey went on to become a member of the Morris & Co. design studio.

3 Manufacturer J.H. Birtwhistle in Manchester included playing yellow monkeys in *Noah's Ark*, a 1948 furnishing fabric probably designed for a nursery.

4 This graphic print with a joyful design of monkeys swinging from garden flowers is from an 1881 issue of the journal *Dessins Nouveautés* published in France by Lechartier et Paul.

5 On this waistcoat, two playful monkeys sit below the pocket, with a pile of hoarded fruit. They were embroidered in coloured silks on the ivory ribbed silk in France in the 1780s.

4

5

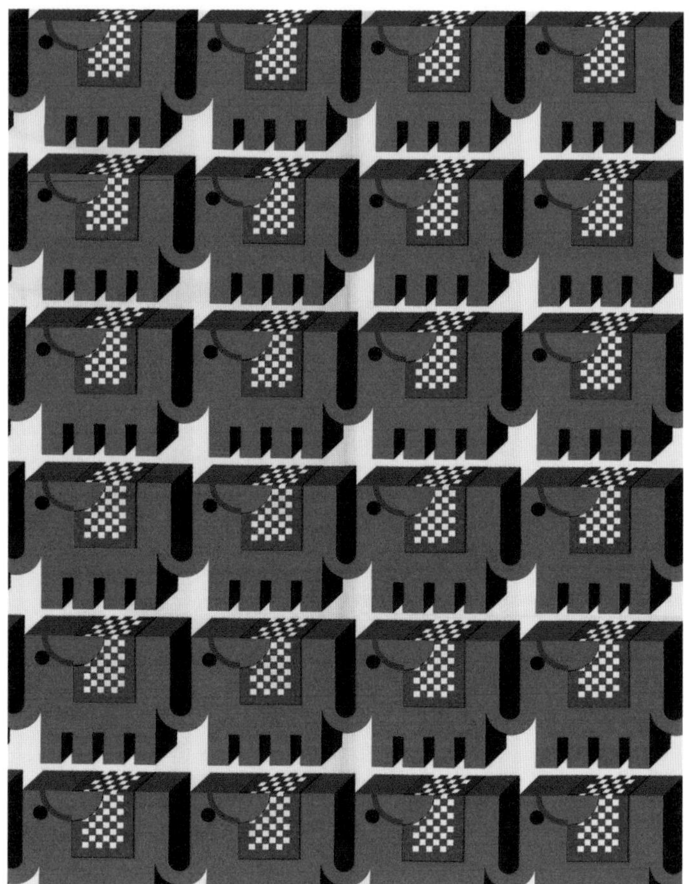

1

2

3

4

5

1 Heal's geometric *Small Elephants* was designed by Neil Bradburn in 1974 to coordinate with the firm's large-scale *Elephants* furnishing fabric and to be retailed as a design for children.

2 This 19th-century Indian cover was made in Kutch in Gujarat. Of satin silk, it is embroidered entirely in chain stitch with a design of elephants and floral and leafy stems.

3 German-born French manufacturer Christophe-Philippe Oberkampf commissioned successful painters to create the monochrome designs for the cottons he printed in Jouy, near Paris. Made in 1792–4, this fabric, designed by Jean-Baptiste Huet, depicts the four parts of the world and their associated animals.

4 The coffee pot in the form of an elephant head was created by the designer and decorator Marc-Louis Solon for Sèvres, France, in 1862, and constructed of porcelain with *pâte-sur-pâte* decoration and gilt.

5 This elephant trunks lithographic print was created for an 1880 issue of *Dessins Nouveautés* published in France by Lechartier et Paul.

6 Finnish textile printing company Printex (later Marimekko) hired Maija Isola in 1949 as its first full-time designer. For nearly four decades, Isola generated designs inspired by nature, her travels around the world, folk art and modern visual art. She created *Circus* in 1956.

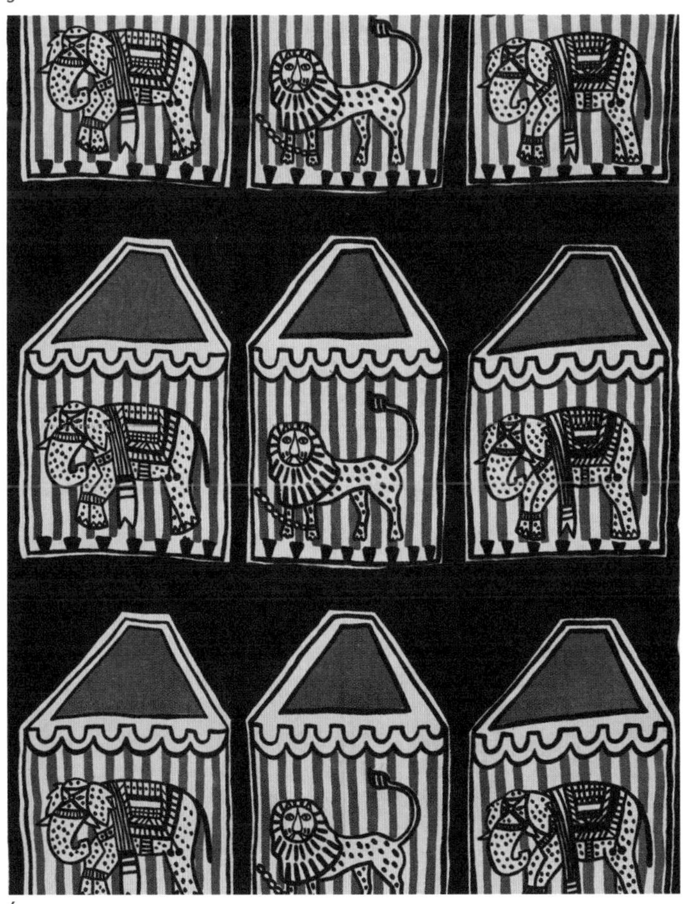

6

1

2

1 A textile design depicting elephants in a decorative floral setting is seen in an 1881 issue of *Dessins Nouveautés* by French publishers Lechartier et Paul.

2 This printed cotton nursery or dress fabric featuring Asiatic elephants was made by the Calico Printers' Association, Manchester, in 1912.

3 The complex and ambitious agate-panelled and gold-mounted *nécessaire* standing on four elephants was made in the workshop of London-based watchmaker James Cox around 1770.

4 Well known for her poster designs for London Transport between 1922 and 1954, Dorothy Hutton also collaborated with William Foxton to create furnishing fabrics. This 1929 design is based on a cottagey Noah's Ark filled with carved animals.

5 This printed cotton nursery or dress fabric featuring a a jumble of handsomely bedecked elephants was made by the Calico Printers' Association, Manchester, in 1911.

3

4

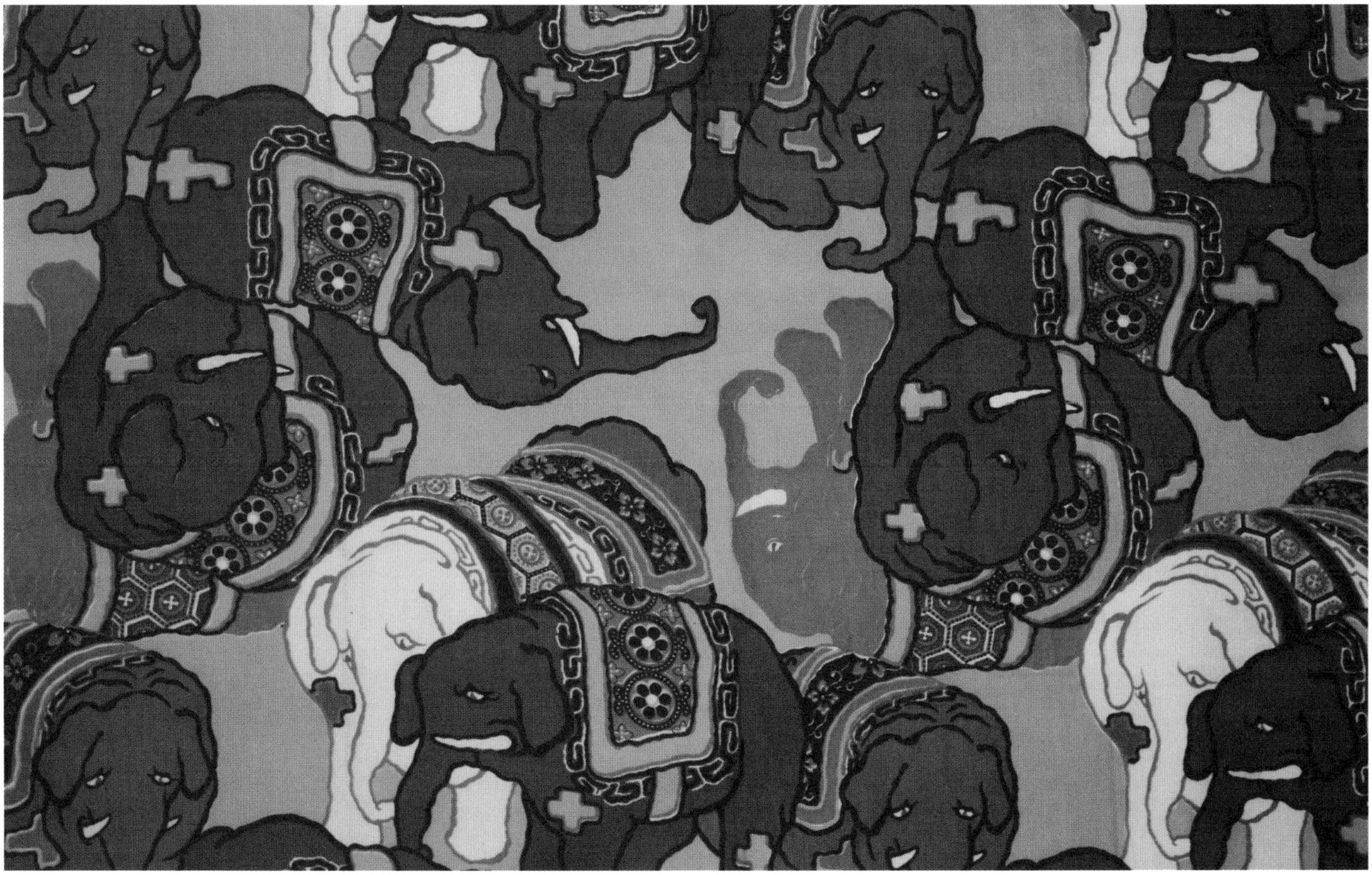

5

1

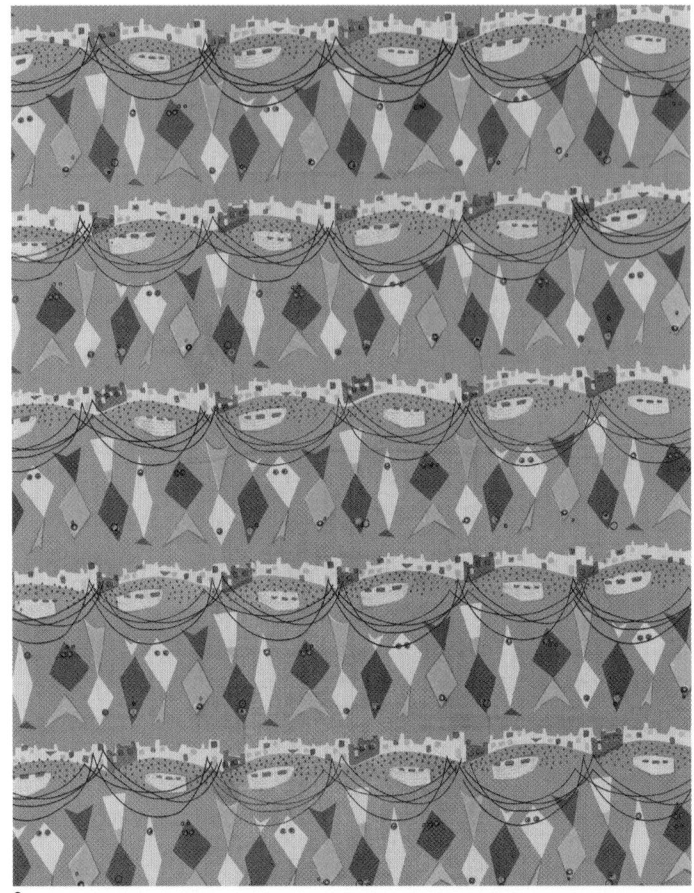
2

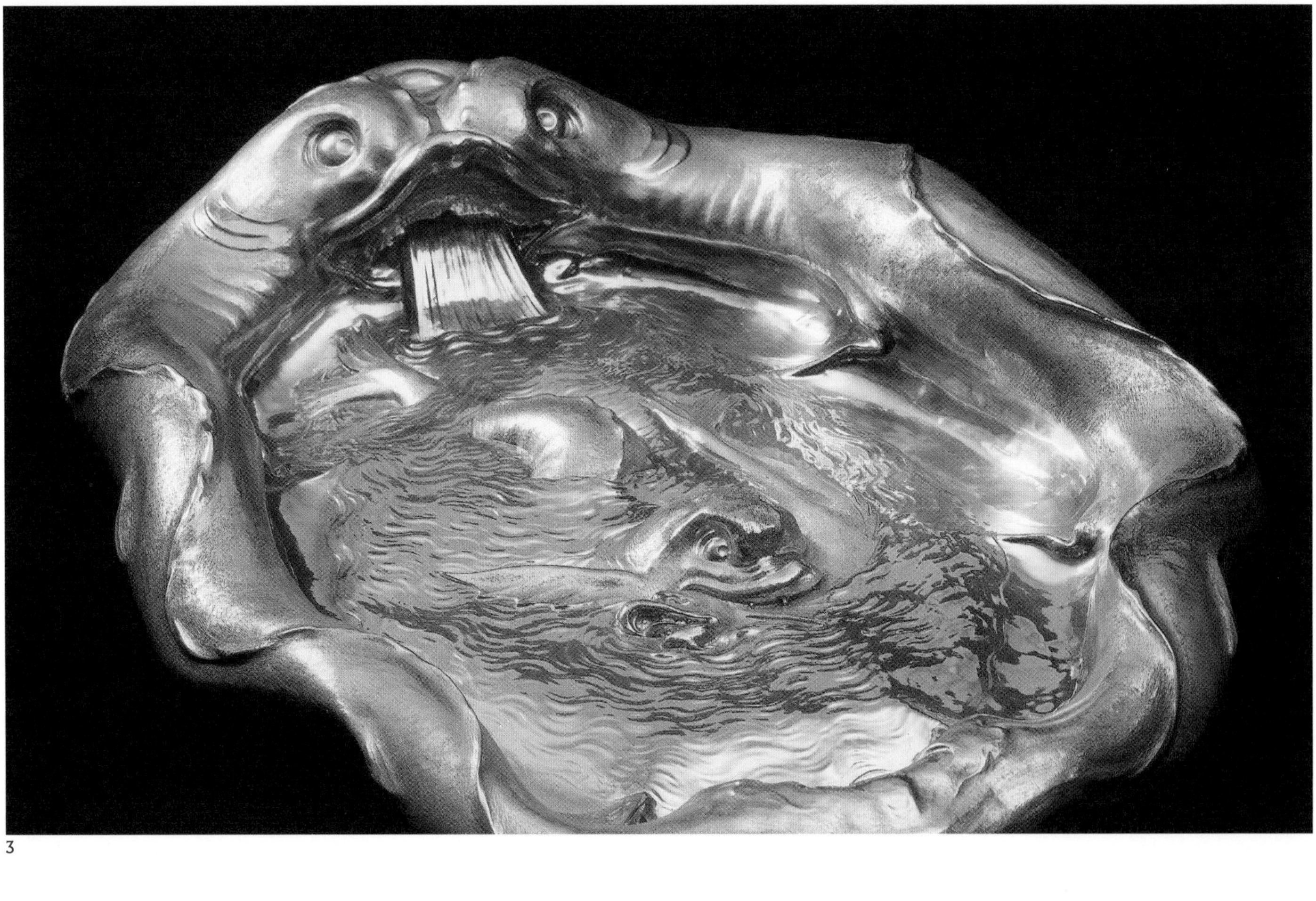

3

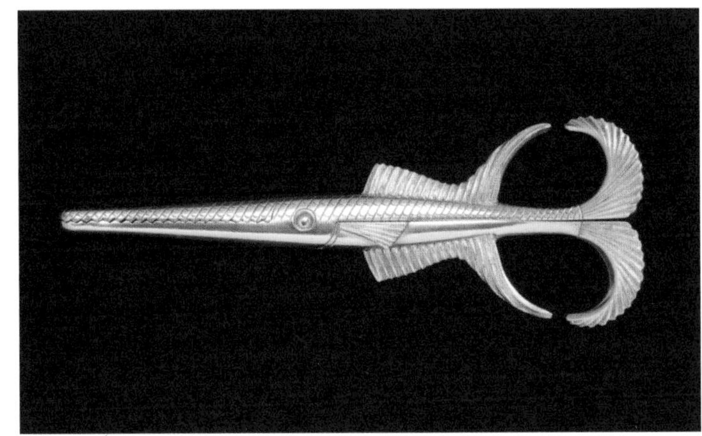

4

5

6

1 *Mandalay* furnishing fabric is a witty design by Felix C. Gotto for the Old Bleach Linen Co. of Randalstown, Northern Ireland, dating to about 1935. Shoaling fish with air bubbles are printed on a linen ground.

2 Rhona Park designed this fishing-themed furnishing fabric under the design direction of the Central School of Arts and Crafts in London in 1951.

3 This remarkable silver basin, designed to hold rosewater, was created in London by Dutch silversmith Christiaen van Vianen in 1635. Two sinuous dolphins frame a pool of water, their eyes and mouths creating the illusion of a grotesque mask.

4 These sugar tongs in the form of a stylized fish belong to the Festival of Britain tea service designed by Robert Goodden and made by Leslie Durbin in London in 1950–1951, which was used to serve tea during the royal visit to the festival.

5 *Frobisher* furnishing fabric was designed by C.B. Costin-Nian for Donald Brothers, Dundee, in 1938. It is perhaps named after the 16th-century English seaman who made three voyages to North America.

6 This dress fabric printed by the Calico Printers' Association, Manchester, in 1940, displays a range of nautical themes.

7 Furnishing fabrics printed by Simpson & Godlee in the 1950s appealed to British consumers with a taste for patterns with food or holiday motifs. They were often used in kitchens and dining areas.

7

1

2

3

1 Made in Japan in the first half of the 20th century, this woman's informal summer kimono displays a dynamic design of flying fish on silk.

2 Produced in 1941, *Sea Maidens*, by Tootal Broadhurst Lee, Manchester, epitomized modern design of its decade, in its lively rendition of abstracted seaweed, fish and swimmers in arresting colours.

3 A series of avant-garde and modern prints by the Calico Printers' Association, Manchester, celebrated leisure activities. This printed jellyfish dress fabric of 1945 was inspired by the British craze for seaside-influenced textiles.

4 Paul Simmons designed *Large Eel* for his degree show at the Glasgow School of Art in 1988. This version, a screen-printed velvet furnishing fabric, was produced by Timorous Beasties, the Glasgow-based firm that he went on to establish with Alistair McAuley.

1 This 19th-century fabric from Japan has been preserved as a hanging scroll. Curved neatly into a circle, the bent form of the crayfish suggests an old man, and as such represents longevity.

2 A silver hair ornament from 1900 by Arts and Crafts architect-designer Henry Wilson is decorated with a pierced medallion of a crab and set with cabochon garnets.

3 By the early 20th century, the Japonisme trend in Britain had been incorporated into mass-produced items, such as this dress fabric by Beith, Stevenson & Co., Manchester, with its crowded pattern of crayfish and ferns.

4 A mid-19th-century sample book from Japan, containing swatches of textiles, has been covered in a brocaded silk fabric featuring sea creatures on a scallop-pattern framework.

5 Painted and dyed cottons produced by Indian craftsmen were identified as lucrative goods for export to Europe in the 1700s. This hanging, with madder-red crab detail, was made on the Coromandel Coast in south-east India.

1

2

3

4

5

1

2

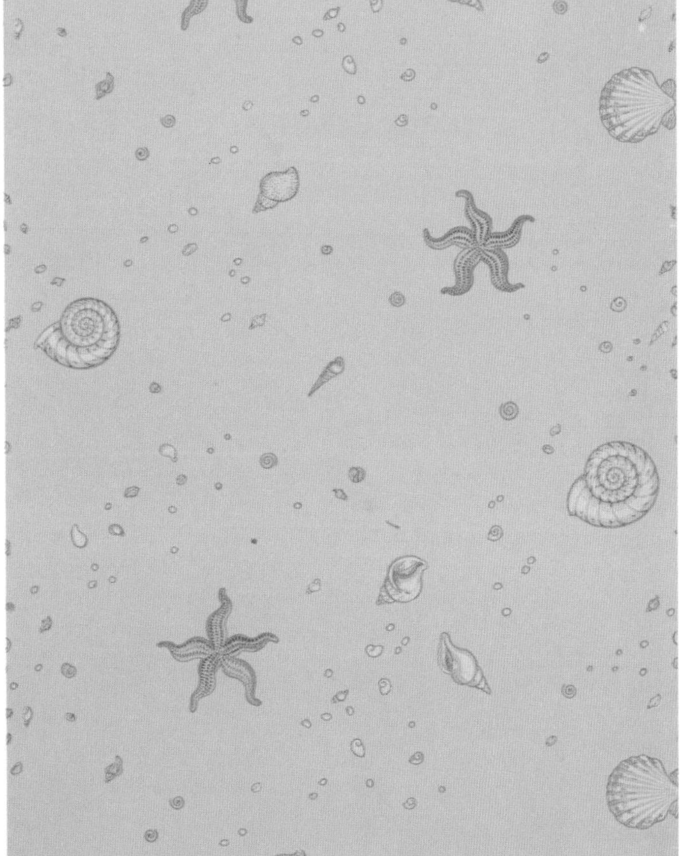
3

4

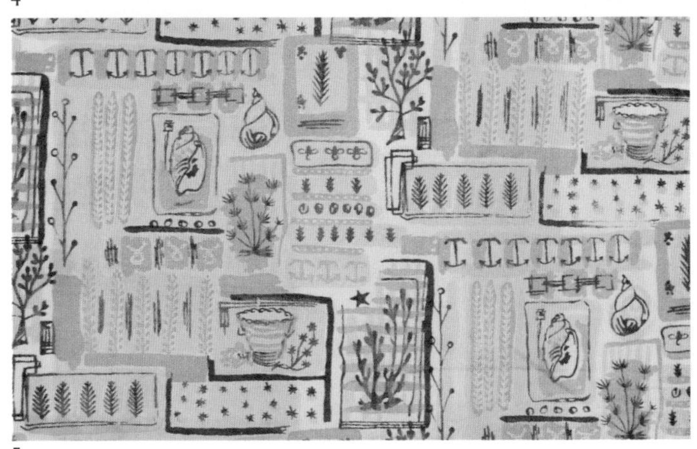
5

1 This brocaded silk, *Conchus*, has a pattern of seashells and foliage. It was designed by William Folliot in 1873 for the manufacturer Daniel Walters & Son, London.

2 Raoul Dufy designed *Les Conques* furnishing fabric for the Lyonnais silk manufacturer Bianchini-Férier around 1925. The bold, graphic motifs are close in mood to textiles of the Wiener Werkstätte in Vienna, which Dufy had visited in 1909.

3 A wallpaper designed by Walter Crane in 1879 shows shells and starfish at low tide.

4 This seashell-shaped fruit plate or comportier by Wedgwood from the early 1800s is made of a type of creamware called pearlware.

5 Constance Howarth designed this cotton textile in 1947, under the direction of the Manchester School of Art. Patterns such as this were popular in the post-war years.

6 Made in Japan in the 1860s, this tiered box is decorated with shells in gold and silver lacquer.

7 Norman Hartnell designed this ballgown for Lady Zia Wernher in 1953, possibly for the coronation of Queen Elizabeth II. Embroidered with silk thread, delicate crystals and seed pearls, this detail depicts elements of an underwater world.

8 Manchester based Nahums Fabrics' playful design from 1947 brings marine life of the deep blue sea to this printed cotton textile.

6

7

8

1

2

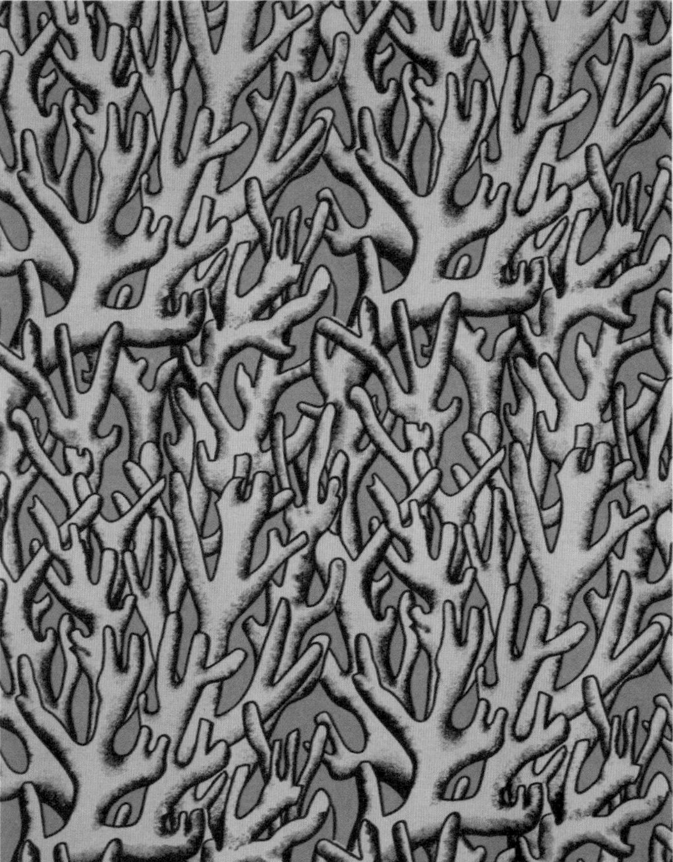
3

1 William Kilburn's most original and delicate designs are those that use seaweed and coral motifs, such as the one shown here (*c.*1788–92). He presented one of his seaweed-patterned fabrics to Queen Charlotte, wife of Britain's George III.

2 This seaweed-patterned fabric, *Wayfarer*, was produced by Edinburgh Weavers in Carlisle in the 1960s.

3 *Symphony* furnishing fabric was designed by Russian avant-garde artist Paul Mansouroff for the Old Bleach Linen Co., Randalstown, Northern Ireland, in 1938. The design features coral-shaped branches.

4 Featuring stylized coral, this printed and glazed cotton fabric was made by Miles & Edwards, London, in the 1830s and 1840s.

5 This 1919 design of fish in a kelpy seascape was created by C.F.A. Voysey in London to be produced as both a woven textile and a wallpaper.

6 Dating from around 1820, this porcelain coffee cup and saucer made by the Coalport porcelain factory, Shropshire, features a stunning 'seaweed pattern number 859' in gilt.

7 William Kilburn was celebrated in his day for his talent for drawing patterns for block printing. This Rococo coral-patterned design made in England between 1788 and 1792 shows his mastery in representing botanicals.

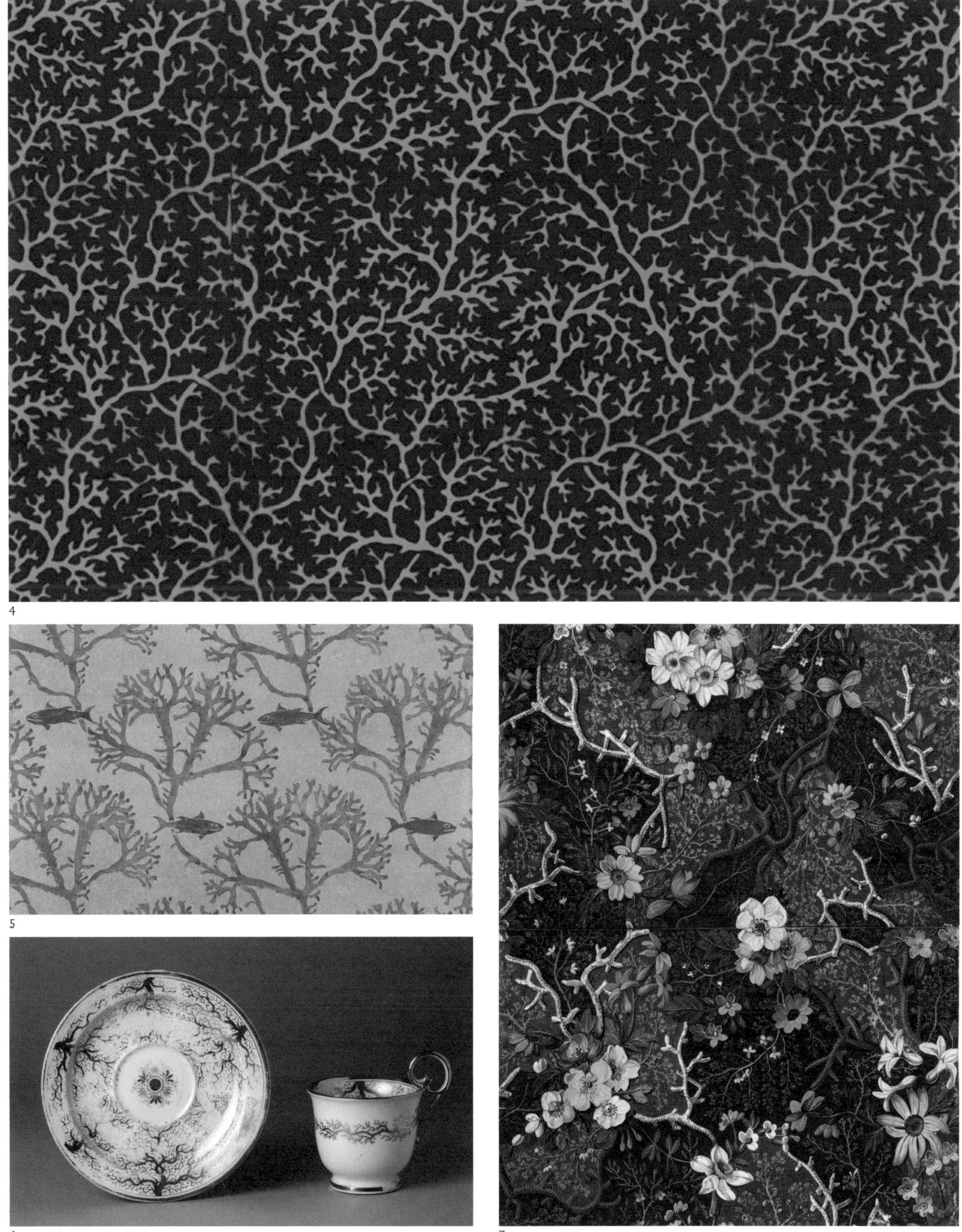

4

5

6

7

1

2

3

4

5

6

1 Made in Muel, Aragon, Spain, around 1550 to 1600, this is part of a tin-glazed earthenware tile panel. Large scrolls spring from symmetrical floral devices and end in eagles' heads, arranged facing one another.

2 Possibly produced in India between 1800 and 1975, this block-printed cotton features offset rows of double-headed birds – known in Hindu mythology as Gandaberunda.

3 This repeating pattern of birds of prey perched in stylized trees by C.F.A. Voysey was created in London in 1926 for a wallpaper and textile design.

4 A giltwood pier or console table is supported by the figure of a carved eagle with outstretched wings; such tables seem to have been at the height of fashion in the later 1730s in England.

5 This is a sample of printed cotton from 1921 produced by the Ramsden Wood Print Works of Todmorden in Lancashire.

6 An ornamental band of vases of carnations, interspersed with snakes, birds and double-headed eagles, is embroidered on linen. The fabric was produced as a dress or skirt border in Crete, Greece, in the 18th century.

7 Featuring a collared leopard and an eagle with outspread wings, this 14th-century brocaded silk lampas was woven in Italy for ecclesiastical or secular use.

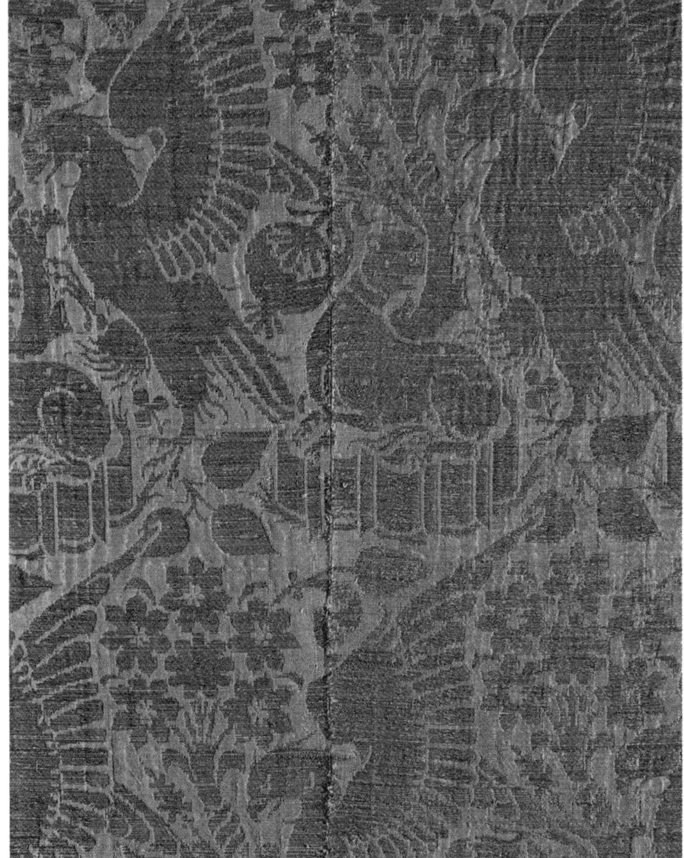
7

1

2

3

1 Produced by Essex & Co. in England in 1897, this is a portion of *The Owl* wallpaper frieze designed by C.F.A. Voysey.

2 Also called *The Owl*, this design by C.F.A. Voysey plays with owls and owlets, foliage and nests. This furnishing fabric of woven wool was made by Morton Sundour, Carlisle, in 1898.

3 This William De Morgan gourd-shaped earthenware vase from 1888 to 1898 was produced in Fulham, London, and decorated in red lustre with a pattern of owls on the hunt for mice.

4 *The Owl*, a wall hanging worked in silks on a background of woven silk damask, was embroidered by Frances Battye around 1898–1900 from a kit designed by J.H. Dearle for Morris & Co., England.

5 Hand screens were used to shield the face from the heat of the fire. This one is decorated with an illustration from Christopher Dresser's 1875 book *Studies in Design*. The owl and owlet enact a scene from Shakespeare's *Hamlet*.

6 Small owls are perched on the border of this French-style handkerchief in painted and dyed cotton (chintz) made in India on the Coromandel Coast, around 1710 to 1720.

7 Mrs Archibald Christie, the first teacher of embroidery at the Royal College of Art, London, embroidered this panel with birds, butterflies and flowers in 1914. One of the most striking characteristics of her work is the use of contrasting textures, epitomized by those in the owl motif.

4

5

6

7

1

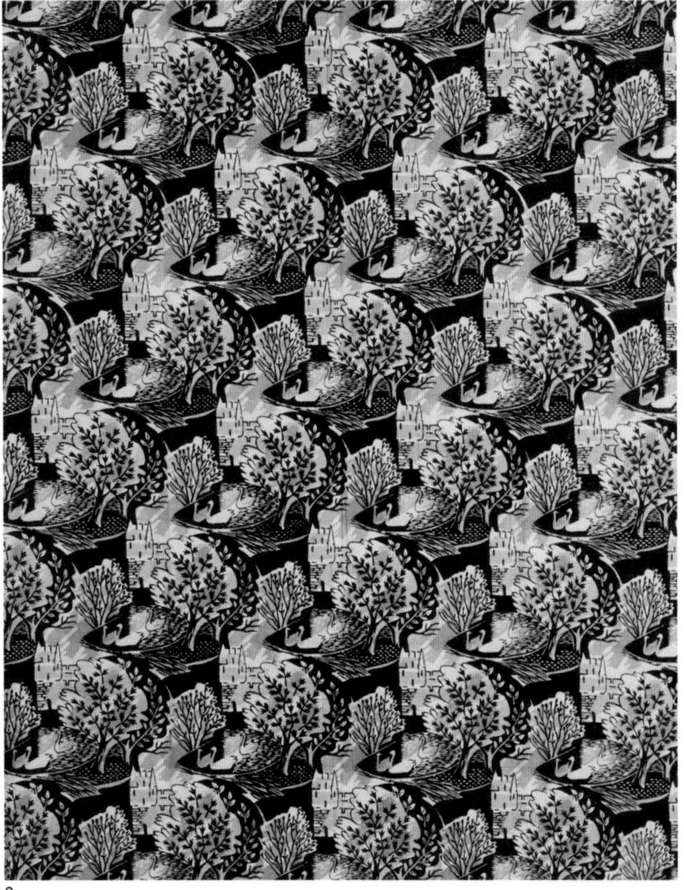

2

1 One of Walter Crane's earliest wallpaper designs, *Swan, Rush and Iris* was created in 1875. The silhouetted swans on a stylized background of bulrushes and irises suggest the influence of Greek vase paintings.

2 British designer Alexander H. Williamson designed both textiles and glass. *Swan and Castle* is a furnishing fabric made in 1948.

3 More a sculpture than a practical flower holder, this vase by Walter Crane dating from 1889 is decorated with scenes from Homer's *Odyssey* in ruby lustre. It was made by Maw & Co. in Jackfield, Shropshire.

4 This is an H. & R. Daniel swan-lipped ewer dating from around 1825–30. It is painted with enamels and gilded, with the swan's neck forming the handle and its wings the spout.

5 Seen here is a detail of a large square carpet tapestry woven in Aubusson, France. Its scrolling floral motifs and beautifully blended colours are characteristic of that important centre of production in the 1820s.

6 This lidded sugar basin was made by the Coalport porcelain factory, Shropshire, around 1830, during the Rococo Revival era. The sugar basin is composed of shells and bulrushes with a swan on top.

7 Designed by Jean-Baptiste Huet for Oberkampf & Cie, France, this fabric, made around 1792 to 1794, represents the four parts of the globe and their associated animals.

3

4

5

6

7

1

2

3

1 Made in 19th-century Okinawa, this dazzling robe was created with two lengths of stencil-dyed fabric that run over the shoulder, resulting in an inverted pattern on one side of the garment, in this case the back.

2 A *fukusa* (textile cover) was traditionally an important element of the gift-giving ritual in Japan. This gift cloth with a design of cranes, a symbol of longevity, was woven in the 19th century.

3 Cranes and pines decorate this futon cover. The pattern has been created using a stencil-dyeing technique called *katazome*.

4 Circular tables with decorative supports, such as this elaborate example by the firm of George J. Morant, London, were very fashionable in the mid-1800s and display the Victorian taste for naturalistic ornament.

5 This satin *fukusa* is embroidered in silk and metallic threads with an image of cranes. These birds represent long life, for they are believed to live for 1,000 years.

6 By the 1920s Selfridges was one of the most glamorous department stores in London, with fittings such as this bronze lift panel designed by Edgar Brandt in 1928. The storks associate the elevator with flight.

7 *Feather Birds* was produced by the American company Stroheim & Romann in the 1950s. The mid-century textile captures the essence of wading birds in just a few visual elements.

4

5

6

7

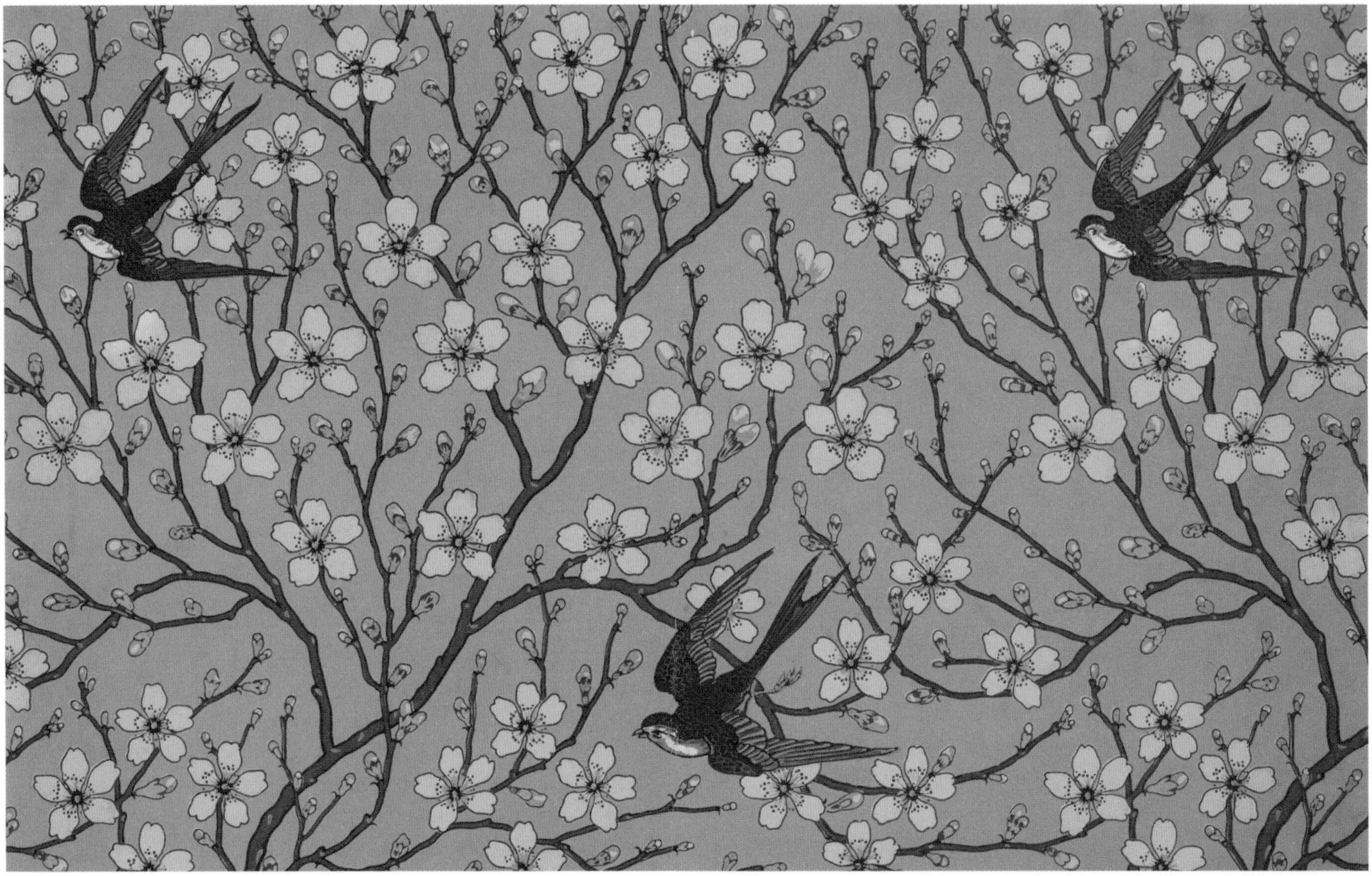

1

2

3

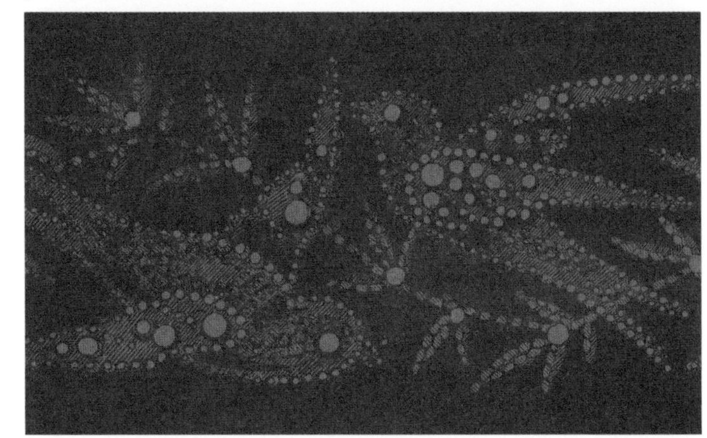

4

5

6

1 *Almond Blossom and Swallow* wallpaper frieze by Walter Crane was produced in London by Jeffrey & Co. in 1878.

2 This hanging was made in 1896 at the Haslemere Peasant Industries workshop, Surrey. Designed by Godfrey Blount, a member of this community of artist-craftspeople, it was created using the simple method of applying linen on linen with embroidery in linen thread.

3 Produced at the Bromsgrove Guild, Birmingham, in 1933, and designed by Walter Gilbert, this aluminium Art Deco panel was part of a decorative frieze over a lift entrance in the Derry & Toms department store in Kensington, London.

4 Designed as a textile motif or border in 1880, this machine-printed paper, published in *Dessins Nouveautés* by Lechartier et Paul, Paris, is decorated with bejewelled birds rendered in shiny gems or pearls.

5 *The Lerena* is a spectacular wallpaper pattern of trees and birds in the Art Nouveau style by C.F.A. Voysey, produced in London by Jeffrey & Co. in 1897.

6 *Aircraft* by Marion Dorn was chosen for the lounge of an ocean liner, *Orcades*. Stylized birds in flight were printed on a linen and rayon background by the Old Bleach Linen Co., Randalstown, Northern Ireland, in 1938.

7 As seen in his *The New Silk Cloth* textile design from 1901, C.F.A. Voysey's birds frequently look like doves or swallows and are often paired as lovebirds.

7

1

2

3

1 Designed by William Morris in 1879, the *Dove and Rose* pattern was woven in Scotland by Morton Sundour for Morris & Co. The complex design was suitable for curtains and hangings and available in different scales and colourways.

2 A French diamond, emerald, ruby and silver brooch, dating from around 1755, is designed in the form of a dove holding an olive branch, a symbol of peace.

3 The Calico Printers' Association, Manchester, screen printed this striking graphic bird repeat on cotton in 1935.

4 Aspects of this dove and fig design, commissioned by London textile manufacturer William Foxton in 1920, resemble the book covers its designer, Charles Shannon, and his partner, Charles Ricketts, created for their publishing company, the Vale Press.

5 This cotton and rayon furnishing fabric called *Avis* was designed by Marion Dorn for Edinburgh Weavers, Carlisle, around 1939. The pattern is made up of tessellating birds in flight.

6 *Dove* dado, or frieze, was designed by Walter Crane to accompany *La Margarete* wallpaper, made in London by Jeffrey & Co. in 1876.

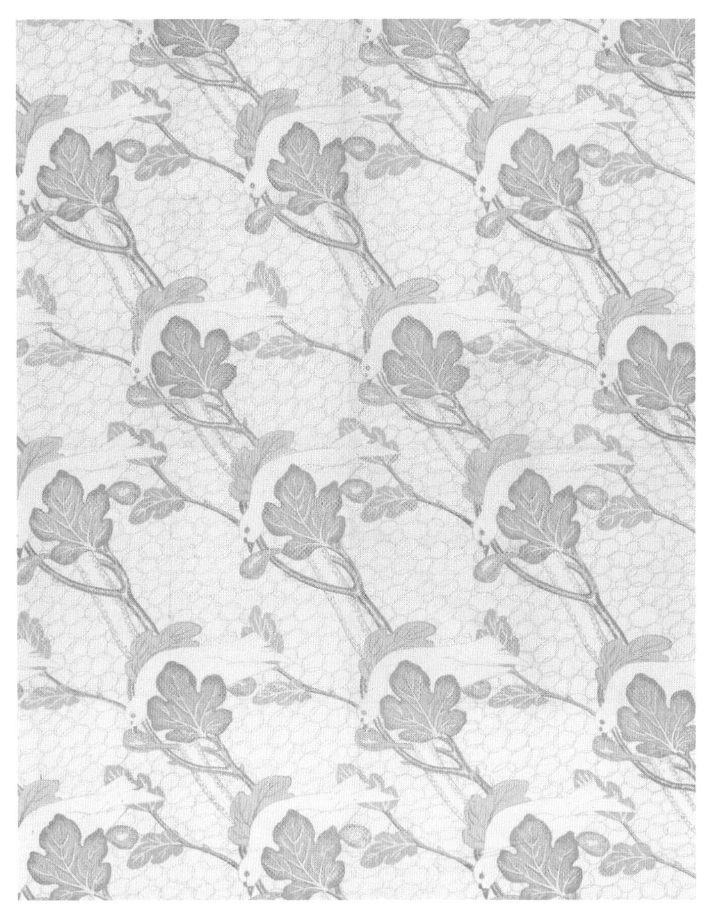

4

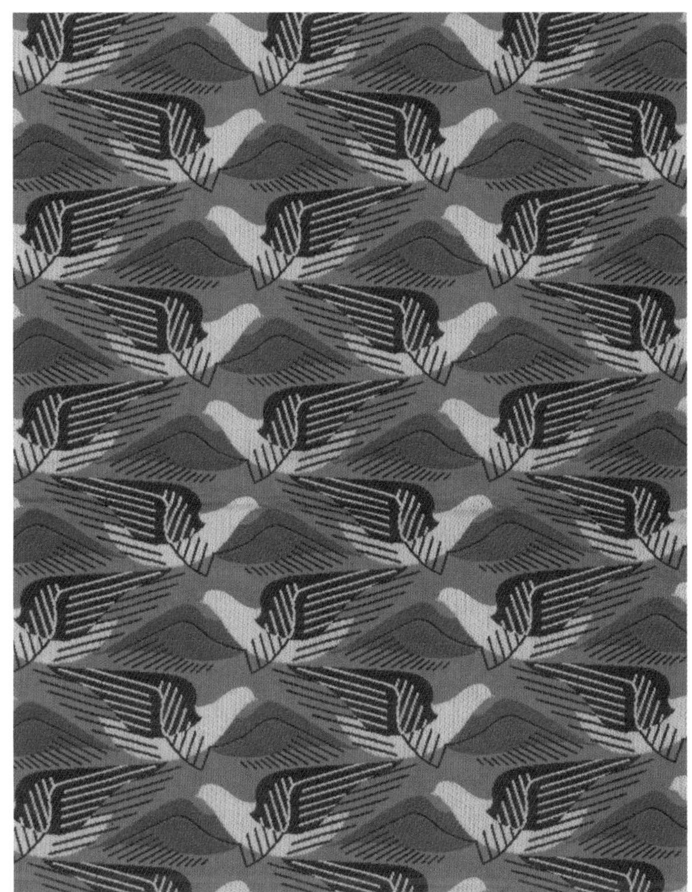

5

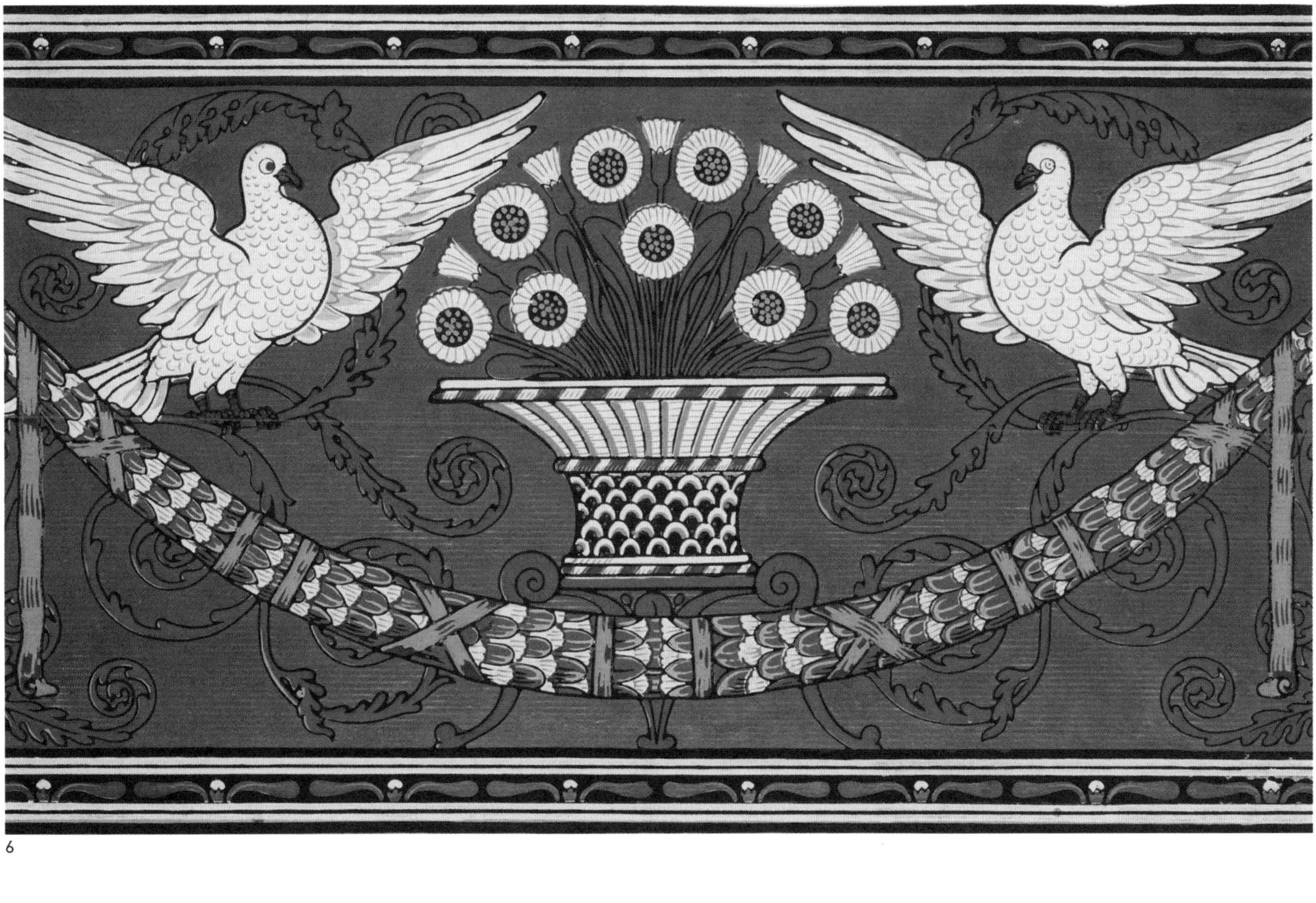

6

1

1 The peacocks in this furnishing fabric by F. Steiner & Co. reflect the taste for exoticism during both the Art Nouveau era at the turn of the 20th century and the Art Deco period of the 1920s.

2 The peacock was a favourite among the animals René Lalique chose to represent in both his jewellery and his glass creations. The majestic *Deux Paons* (Two Peacocks) night light was designed in 1920.

3 This portion of a wallpaper frieze by Walter Crane was produced in 1878 by Jeffrey & Co. The manufacturer also adopted a peacock with outspread tail as its logo to emphasize its association with the highest artistic standards in design.

4 One of the earliest surviving examples of copper-plate printing on cotton, this idealized landscape was produced in 1761 by Robert Jones & Co., of the Old Ford factory, Middlesex.

5 The peacock was an established symbol of the Aesthetic Movement of the 1890s. Walter Crane's *Peacock Garden* wallpaper was designed in 1889 and produced by Jeffrey & Co.

6 Manufactured for Liberty to be sold in their Regent Street store in London, this lightweight silk dress fabric from 1900 to 1905 has been block printed with rows of small, stylized peacocks in profile.

2

3

4

5

6

1

2

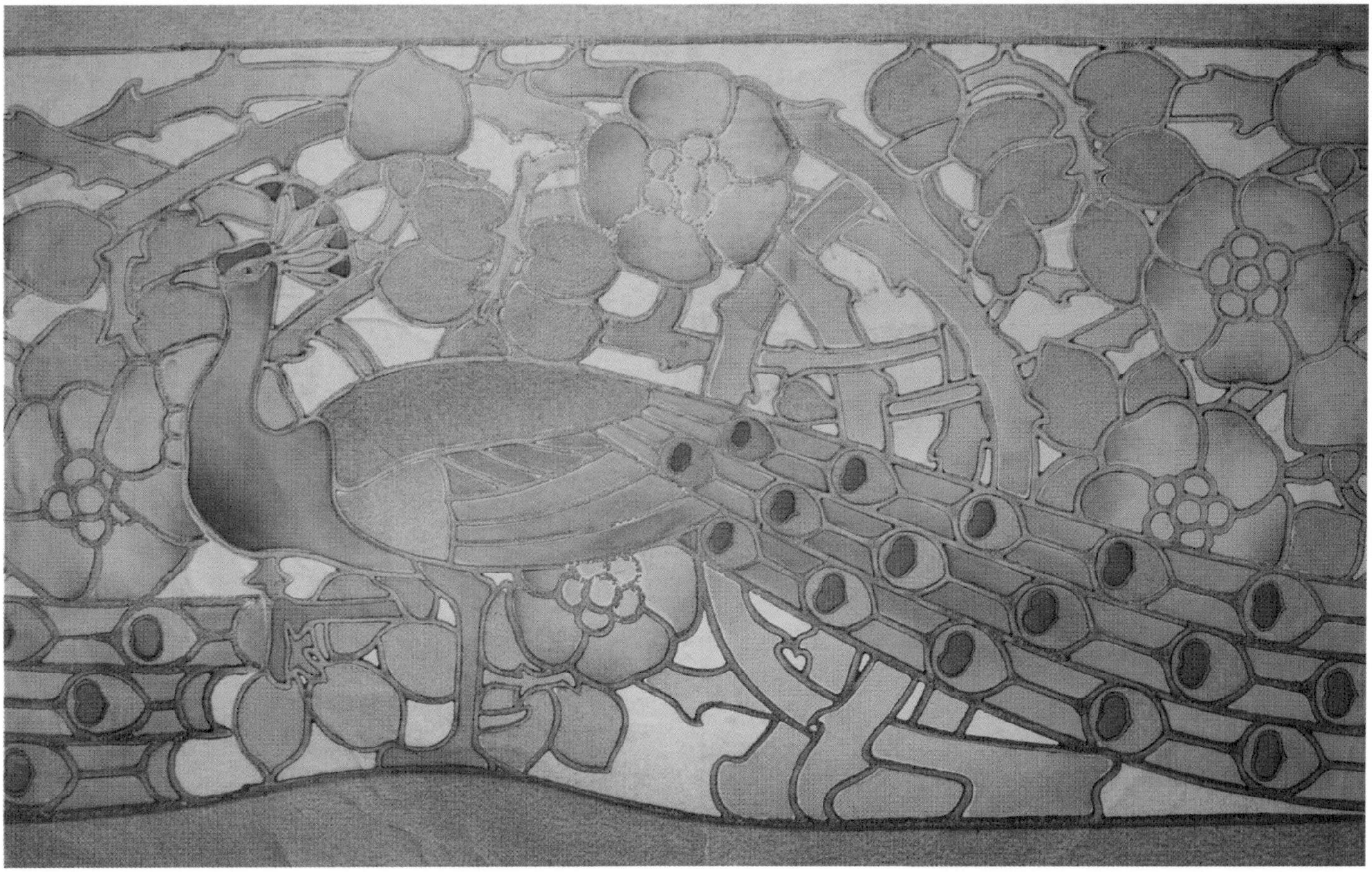

3

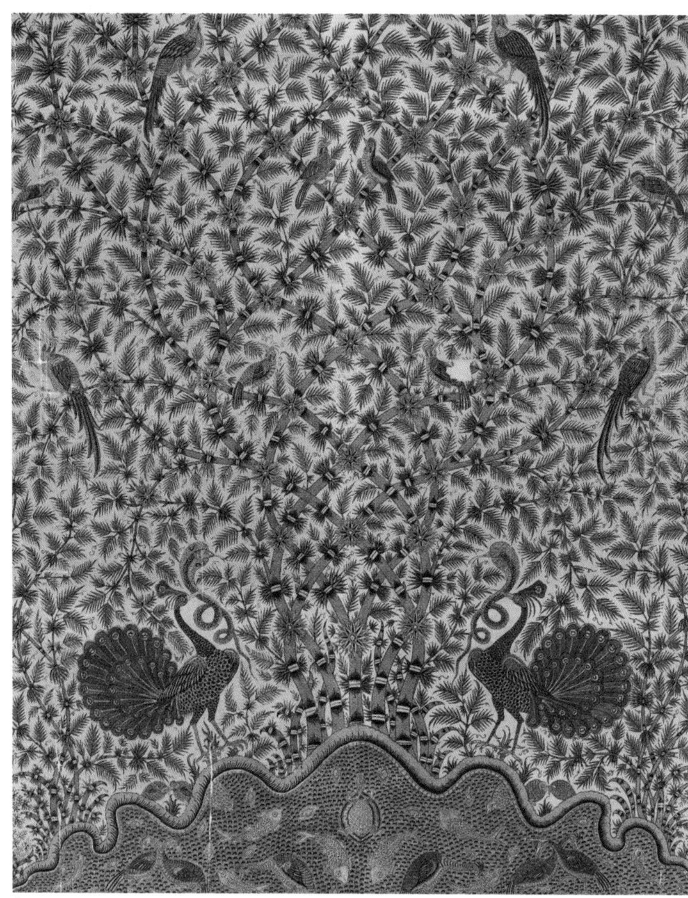

4

5

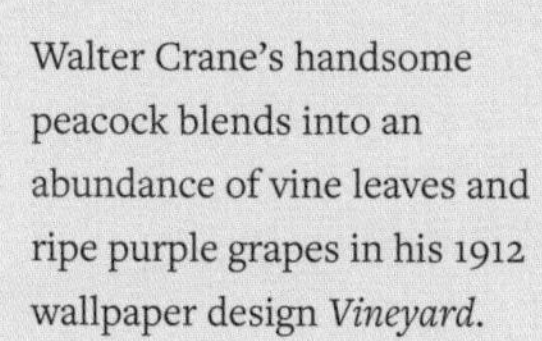

1 Walter Crane's handsome peacock blends into an abundance of vine leaves and ripe purple grapes in his 1912 wallpaper design *Vineyard*.

2 This gold pendant in the form of a displaying male peacock is decorated with *plique-à-jour* enamel and set with rose- and brilliant-cut diamonds, emeralds and opals. It was made in France by Lucien Gautrait, around 1900.

3 *Peacock* wallpaper frieze was designed in 1900 by W. Dennington and produced by Shand Kydd, London. Founded in 1891, Shand Kydd had already established a reputation for attractive, original wallpapers with beautiful colouring.

4 This resist-dyed cotton palampore (large bed or wall cover or hanging) was made on the Coromandel Coast of India in 1855 for the export market.

5 C.R. Ashbee was an Arts and Crafts architect-designer, and the peacock was one of his favourite and most distinctive motifs. This peacock pendant is from the early 1900s and made of silver or silver gilt mainly set with blister pearls.

6 This peacock design is from a series of impressions on paper in an album known as the Bromley Hall Pattern Book, from Middlesex, dating to around 1765 to 1800. The illustrator is thought to be Charles Fenn.

6

1

2

3

4

1 Adored for their bright feathers and their ability to talk, parrots are often considered the most intelligent of birds. This parrot and macaw tile panel design by English potter William De Morgan dates from the late 1800s.

2 Featuring a scene of parrots against the moon, this furnishing fabric was manufactured by the Calico Printers' Association, Manchester, around 1922.

3 This is a portion of *Macaw* wallpaper designed by Walter Crane in 1908 and printed by Jeffrey & Co. in London.

4 Walter Crane designed this *Cockatoo and Pomegranate* wallpaper in 1899 and it was printed by Jeffrey & Co. in London.

5 This 19th-century Indian panel was possibly made for a skirt border. It is from Kutch, a district in Gujarat famed for its embroidery. Motifs typically relate to daily life and feature animals, birds and flowers.

6 Dating from around 1835, this furnishing fabric of roller-printed cotton from England has a design of parrots and hoopoes on flowering branches.

7 Produced in England around 1910, this ladies' umbrella features a parrot head made from carved and moulded horn with glass eyes.

5

6

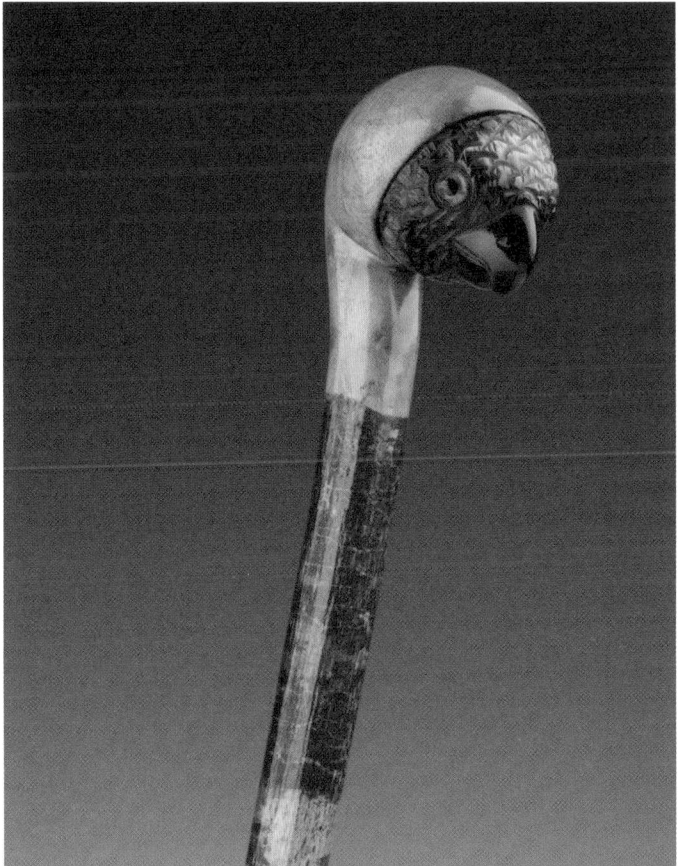
7

1 With its depictions of birds of paradise and parrots with fabulous plumage, this chintz furnishing fabric made around 1860 to 1875 probably comes from France.

2 This roller-printed cotton produced in Mulhouse, Alsace, around 1830 to 1840, for home furnishings features greedy cockatoos perched on bunches of flowers and fruit.

3 The title of *Tropicana* sums up perfectly the vibrant colour range, tropical birds, butterflies and luscious flowers of this 1977 printed cotton furnishing textile designed by Natalie Gibson for British textile manufacturer and retailer Heal's.

1

2

1

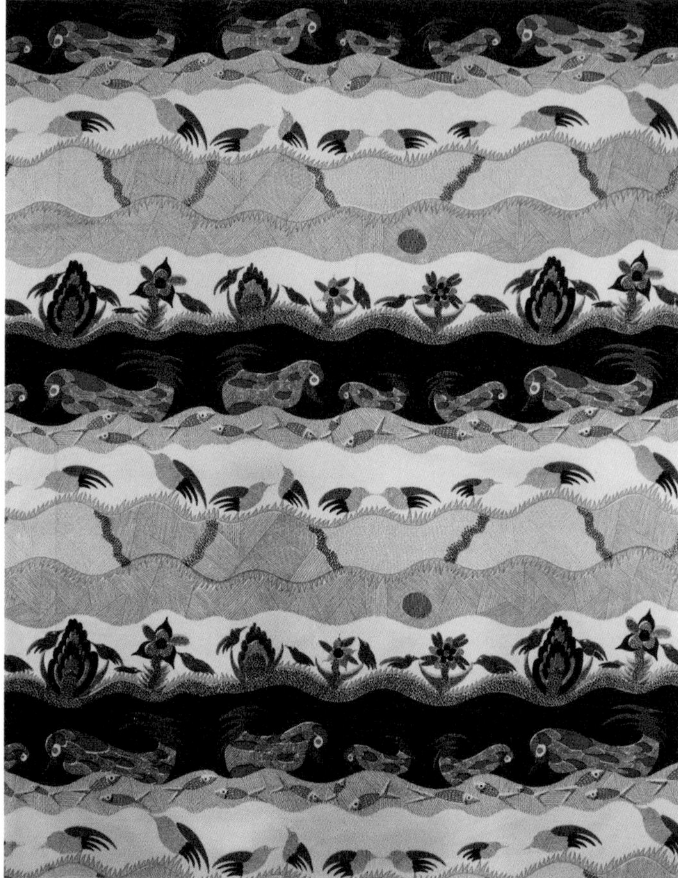

2

3

4

1 A design of mandarin ducks on rippling satin water is seen in this detail from a kimono made in Japan between 1840 and 1870. Paired ducks are a symbol of marital harmony, so this robe may have been made for a bride.

2 *Scottie Stripe* is a wavy banded pattern with rows of fish and pecking birds by Scottie Wilson, an idiosyncratic self-taught artist. It was produced by Edinburgh Weavers, Carlisle, in 1953.

3 This is a detail from a tapestry commissioned by Elizabeth I's favourite courtier, Robert Dudley, 1st Earl of Leicester. Produced by the Sheldon workshop in the 1580s, it includes birds based on contemporary engravings.

4 The skilfully composed design of this porcelain dish from China shows a pair of mandarin ducks and peonies framed with a painted and gilded border. The dish is painted in shades of pink known as *famille rose*. It dates from 1730 to 1740 (Qing dynasty).

5 This simple design of ducks produced in 1911 by the Calico Printers' Association, Manchester, would have been popular for nursery textiles.

6 These two communing ducks, from a mid-19th-century Japanese kimono, have been embroidered in lustrous silk on a satin ground.

5

6

1

1 Modern British fabrics after World War II often featured stylized animals, such as *Feathered Friends* designed by Sylvia Chalmers for Eaton Fabrics in 1953.

2 Edward Bawden designed *Farming* in 1950. It was woven into a tapestry at the Dovecot Studios in Edinburgh by Ronald Cruickshank and his apprentices.

3 *Cockerels* by Hans Tisdall, from 1957, is characteristic of Edinburgh Weavers' designs, which often featured large-scale abstract motifs derived from history or nature.

4 Embroidered with silk on linen, this bolster cover was made on the Greek island of Skyros in the 1800s. The motif of the cockerel was a symbol of independence and resistance to Ottoman rule.

5 The hinged lid of this 17th-century Hungarian silver-gilt flagon is decorated with a cockerel either to create an attention-grabbing table ornament or as a symbol of Christ and the Eucharist.

6 The Gallic rooster has long been a symbol of France. This 19th-century dress fabric reveals the virtuosity of French silk manufacturing, in which there was much national pride.

7 This fabric with drum-heads and cocks, emblematic of good government, was woven in silk and gold thread in Japan, probably in the 18th century.

8 Adorned with embroidered cockerels, these red silk trousers were made in the early 20th century in Mumbai for the Parsee community.

2

3

4

5

6

7

8

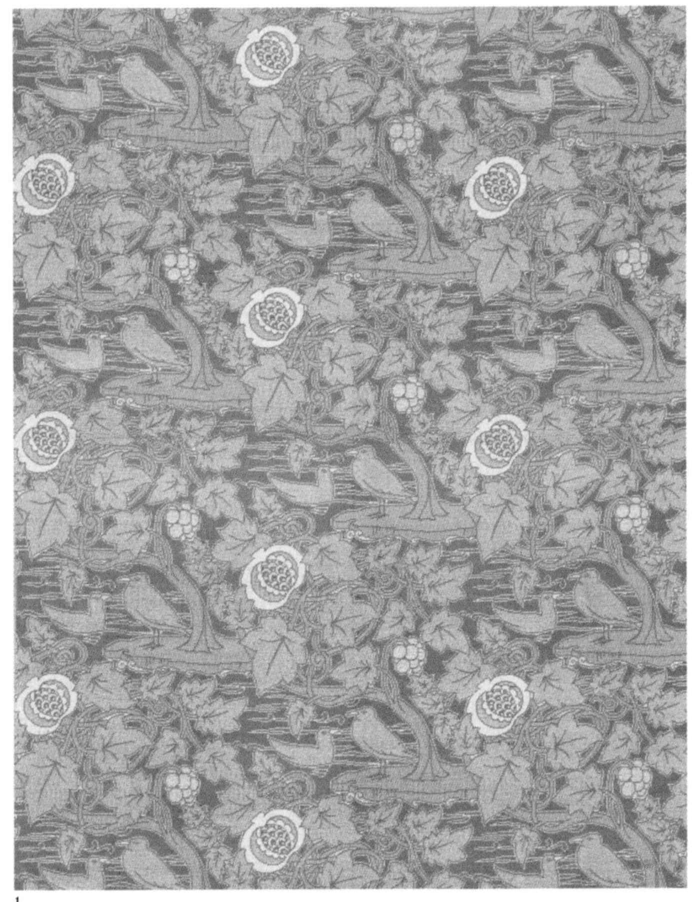
1

2

3

4

1 Produced as a woven double cloth in 1897, this pattern by C.F.A. Voysey of gulls afloat or perched on small islands with assorted foliage and pomegranates was manufactured by Morton Sundour, Carlisle.

2 *Albion* wallpaper frieze designed by T.W. Sharp and made in London by Jeffrey & Co. in 1882 is a celebration of the British coast and its seabird colonies.

3 Seagulls and lifebuoys give a nautical flavour to this dress fabric of printed cotton, made by the Calico Printers' Association, Manchester, in 1938.

4 This design of gulls on a rolling sea by C.F.A. Voysey for A.H. Lee & Sons, England, in 1891 was produced as both a woven textile and a wallpaper.

5 Designed in 1901 by C.F.A. Voysey and named for the type of small boat it depicts, *The Shallop* is a sublime sea scene, produced as a wallpaper by Essex & Co, England.

6 This flock of seagulls on the lookout for chips is on a printed cotton Sanderson fabric made in England in 1936.

5

6

1

2

3

4

5

6

1 This British furnishing fabric of pheasants on flowering branches is in chinoiserie taste, a European interpretation of design motifs from different parts of Asia. It was manufactured by Morton Sundour, Carlisle, in fashionable 1930s colours.

2 Designed by Louise Dellfant and made by Dewtex of Germany in 1955, this furnishing fabric features birds perched on delicate grasses and bulrushes.

3 Meant for when the fireplace was not in use, this carved and gilded firescreen is is a veritable aviary of dozens of real, exotic stuffed birds, including hummingbirds. Such pieces were often made in London in the mid-19th century.

4 Sylvia Priestley's *Britomart*, a design of teeming game birds in a flowery meadow for Edinburgh Weavers, Carlisle, 1951, was named after a character in Edmund Spenser's poem *The Faerie Queene*.

5 Grace Peat's 1938 *Fantasie* fabric print for Donald Brothers, Dundee, repeats a large stylized bird printed on a coarse linen that became a speciality of the company.

6 This is a late 18th- to early 19th-century cotton tent hanging from western India. Embroidered in chain stitch with coloured silk, it depicts long-tailed birds in a flowering tree.

1

2

3

4

1 The plumes on this silver comb made by Henry Adcock of Birmingham in 1809–10 are reminiscent of the feathers of an aigrette (headdress), which were popular in aristocratic circles of the Regency period in Britain (early 19th century).

2 Throughout history, the pheasant has been prized for its tail feathers. Nigel Quiney, of Nigel Quiney Designs, created this wrapping paper pattern in 1977, entitled *Tweed 1*.

3 In Europe, peacock feathers were considered an appropriate symbol for a queen, since the bird was sacred to Juno, the queen of the gods in Roman mythology. Woven in Italy in the early 17th century, this dress fabric was also high status because of its silk and silver threads.

4 This jug and cover in the form of an eagle is made of tin-glazed earthenware painted with a blue stylized feather design. It was probably made by Lorenz Speckner in the Georg Vest workshop, Germany, around 1615–20.

5 Designed by Arthur Silver of the Silver Studio in 1880 for Liberty, London, *Peacock Feathers* furnishing fabric epitomizes the popularity of the motif in the British Aesthetic Movement.

6 *Small Feather* furnishing linen with a quill motif by the English textile design partnership Phyllis Barron and Dorothy Larcher exemplifies fine hand-block printing with indigo. It dates to the 1930s.

5

6

1

1 Made from silk crêpe, this scarf is printed with a border design of Liberty's characteristic peacock feathers. It was sold at the London store in the early 1930s.

2 This late 1830s pair of earrings is made from gold, turquoises, rubies and pearls, beautifully set in the shape of twisted peacock feathers.

3 This length of brocaded silk was woven in Spitalfields, London. These peacock feathers are typical of the 1760s fashion for weaving imitation trimmings into silks. Here they are skilfully placed as if floating over the surface of the silk.

4 The design of this English roller-printed cotton combines baskets of fruit with foliage, drapery, ribbons and ostrich feathers in an extravagant repeat pattern. It offers an impression of abundance for the relatively modest consumers who could afford such textiles by the 1820s.

5 Probably intended for use as a furnishing fabric, this roller-printed cotton presents columns of flowers and feathers – a style that enjoyed great popularity in Britain in the early 19th century.

6 This waistcoat of jacquard-woven silk satin was made in Britain around 1845–50. Peacock feathers were a popular motif for fabrics in the 19th century. Sometimes symbolizing vanity or luxury, the peacock also represented gracious demeanour.

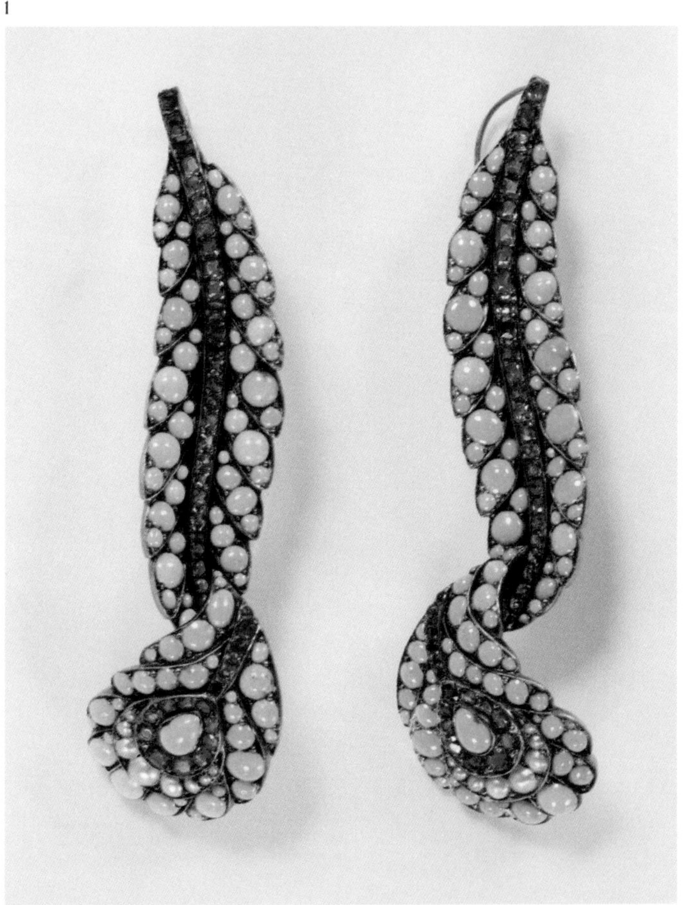

2

3

4

5

6

1

2

3

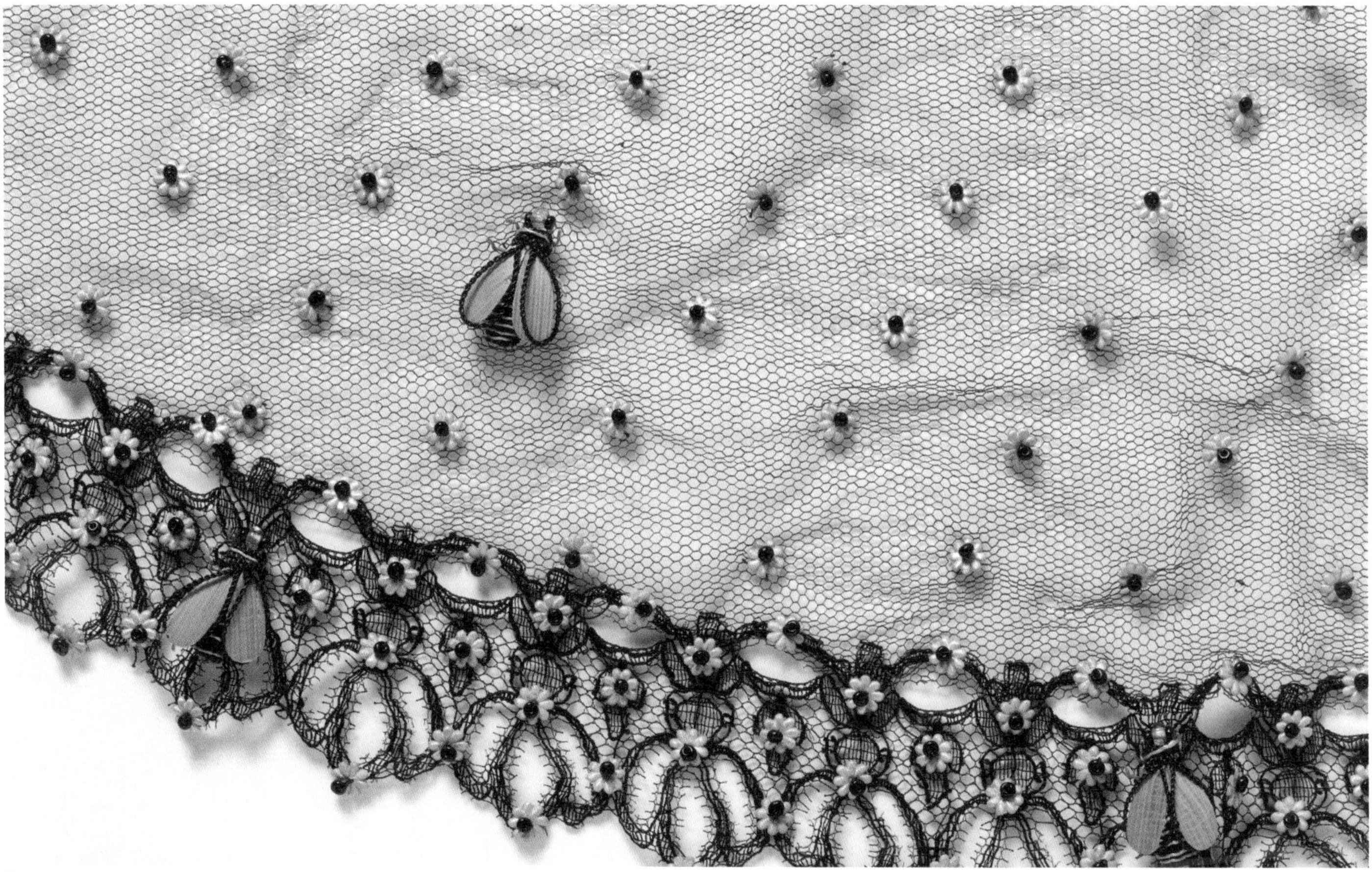

4

1 A bejewelled detail from the *Flowers of the Fields of France* state gown made by Norman Hartnell for Queen Elizabeth II's visit to Paris in 1957 shows a Napoleonic bee, diplomatically included to compliment the host nation.

2 A fichu was a small triangular shawl worn draped over or tucked into the bodice of a woman's gown for warmth, modesty or fashion. This detail of a fichu with bee motifs, from around 1805–10, was cut from a larger piece of needle lace made in Alençon, France, a centre supported by Napoleon.

3 This detail is from a screen-printed leather coat by Scottish fashion designer Bill Gibb. It was made in London for his first solo collection, for Autumn/Winter 1972. The bee was Gibb's signature motif and often appeared in his designs.

4 Made in France in the 1860s, this bonnet veil of net and lace is decorated with three-dimensional bees made of straw veneer, black silk and glass beads.

5 Engraved with grapevines and bees, this wine glass was made in England and dates to 1850–2.

5

1

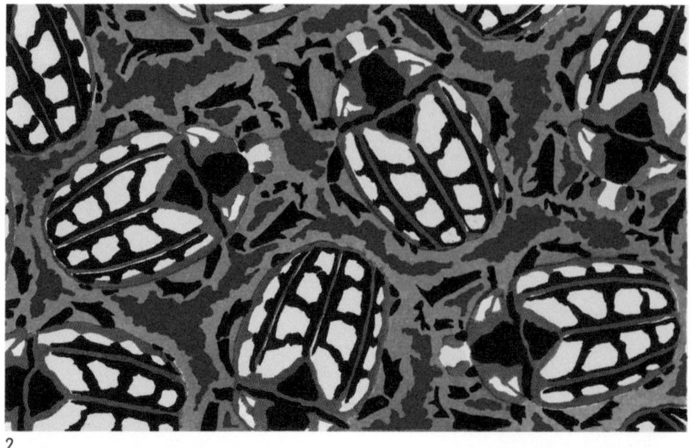

2

3

4

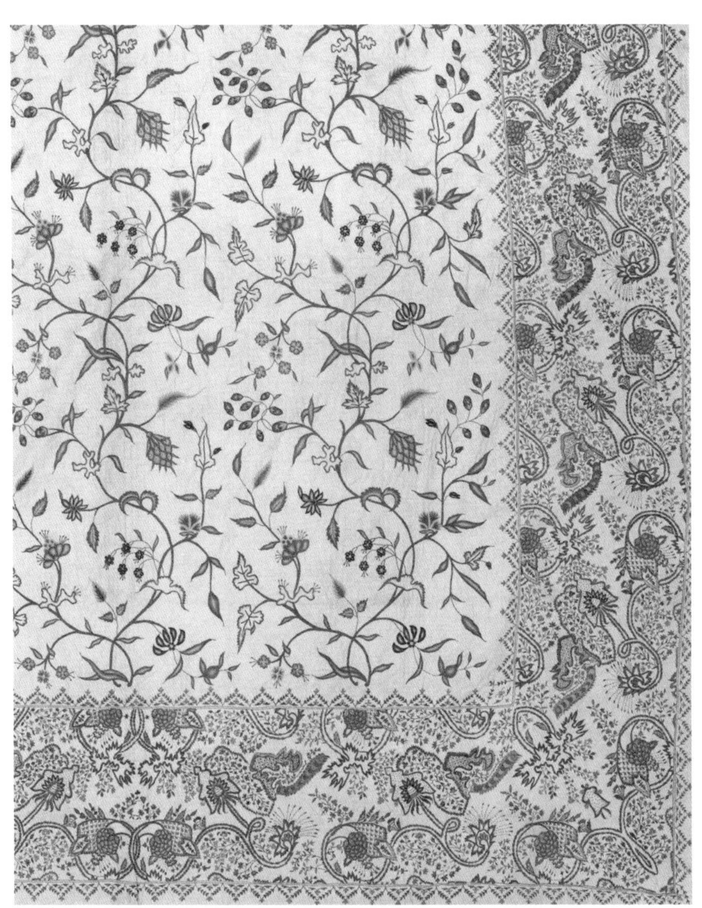

5

1 Made in England around 1880, this brooch is a superb example of the Victorian taste for insects in jewellery. Here a scarab beetle is decorated with translucent enamels and set with diamond chips.

2 This is a detail from a composition by E.A. Séguy, an influential French designer of decorative art. The original appears in Séguy's portfolio *Insectes*, published in Paris in 1924.

3 Made of woven sea-grass and adorned with metallic insects, this Elsa Schiaparelli hat, designed in Paris, was part of her Surrealist-influenced *Pagan Collection* of Autumn 1938.

4 Joy Jarvis combined flowers and insects to create this modern British textile under the direction of London's Royal College of Art in 1948. The college was restructured in that year, with the aim of training innovative designers to revitalize bleak post-war production.

5 What appears to be a caterpillar is repeated in the border of this trade fabric, possibly for a curtain, embroidered with silks in India around 1700.

6 The linen ground of this 17th-century curtain is crowded with a variety of fantastic flora, fruiting branches, animals and insects, including caterpillars. It is embroidered in polychrome silk threads in a range of stitches.

6

1

2

1 Fascinating or frightening, insects have adorned British textiles since the 1500s. On this early 20th-century cretonne by Morton Sundour, Carlisle, dragonflies make a graceful design element.

2 This is a five-case *inrō* (tiered container used by Japanese men, worn hung from the waist sash) decorated with dragonflies and butterflies in flight in gold, red and silver *takamaki-e* (high-relief) lacquer. It was created in Japan between about 1775–1850.

3 Blackwork, monochrome silk embroidery on linen, was a fashionable embellishment for dress in the 16th and 17th centuries. This example made in Britain around 1610–20 depicts dragonflies and vines on a sleeve panel for a woman's jacket.

4 This gold bracelet comprised of a moonstone and a pair of dragonflies was made in London in 1979. The goldsmith was Roger Doyle and the enameller Jane Short.

5 Featuring cherry blossom and a dragonfly in the Aesthetic style, this decorative design for a wallpaper or textile by Bruce J. Talbert dates from the 1870s.

6 Dating from around 1800, this six-lobed incense burner from Japan is decorated with *maki-e* and *mura nashiji* techniques (types of lacquer decoration using gold or silver sprinkled powder) in a design of dragonflies. It is signed by its maker, Yamamoto Shunsho.

3

4

5

6

2

3

4

1 *Butterfly*, a 1974 design for a wrapping paper by English designer Nigel Quiney, celebrates the profusion and warmth of summer.

2 Bruce J. Talbert, a Scottish architect and furniture designer interested in Oriental art, designed this wallpaper featuring butterflies. It was produced by Jeffrey & Co., London, around 1875.

3 This is one of 616 prints of textile designs published and distributed under the title *Dessins Nouveautés* between April 1880 and April 1881 by French publishers Lechartier et Paul.

4 Originally created as a tiara crest by an unknown jeweller in France, this tortoiseshell piece, set with diamonds and pearls, was adapted in 1900 to be worn as a comb head (its teeth are now missing).

5 A British roller-printed cotton chintz furnishing fabric dating from around 1830 shows birds of paradise and butterflies, referencing historical chintzes imported from India since the 17th century.

5

1

1 The Anglo-Japanese design craze of the late Victorian era introduced stylized butterflies in fabric and wallpaper designs, such as this 1877 Aesthetic butterfly and apple frieze by Bruce J. Talbert.

2 Produced by William Foxton, London, in 1923, this furnishing fabric depicts large-scale flowers in a hand-painted style by British designer Minnie McLeish, showing the influence of early English textiles.

3 Lilian Ethel Rowarth embroidered this cotton nightdress yoke with butterflies and various flora in London in 1905.

4 This design features a lively butterfly print, from *Dessins Nouveautés* (1880–1) by French publishers Lechartier et Paul.

5 The Wiener Werkstätte textile department in Vienna designed this printed silk dress fabric around 1925.

6 This is a page from a sample book of fabric swatches. The specimens, made in Japan in 1939, are grouped by month. The black butterfly against the bright flowers and foliage would make for a striking summer kimono.

7 French Art Deco designer E.A. Séguy was known for decorative albums inspired by natural forms. This composition from *Papillons* (1920) is a marriage of art, technique and nature.

8 Exotic and decorative butterfly specimens feature in this vibrant pattern, produced in the 1930s as one of Morton Sundour's *Cumberland Prints* series of furnishing fabrics.

2

3

4

5

6

7

8

1

1 The natural world is central to Japanese aesthetics. The maker of this piece, Yoshitomi, drew inspiration from a large variety of insects in the creation of this inlaid ivory *inrō* (tiered container used by Japanese men, worn hung from the waist sash) between about 1850 and 1900.

2 This imitation batik dress fabric was made by the Calico Printers' Association, Manchester, in 1914 for export to West Africa. The spider-web print is very different from the conventional patterns made for the Edwardian home market.

3 Made in Britain around 1875, this cabinet is brightly painted in the Gothic Revival style, with elements from nature in the Anglo-Japanese style, such as the spider and insects on the door panel seen here.

4 Simple, charming motifs of ladybirds, worked in red floss silk and black chenille, decorate this machine-made net overskirt. Each ladybird is decorated with an iridescent grain-shaped glass bead that adds a little sparkle. It was made in Britain around 1870.

5 Made around 1620, this is a Dutch gold-mounted nautilus cup. The shell is engraved with various insects, among the earliest attempts to depict moths, flies and beetles accurately.

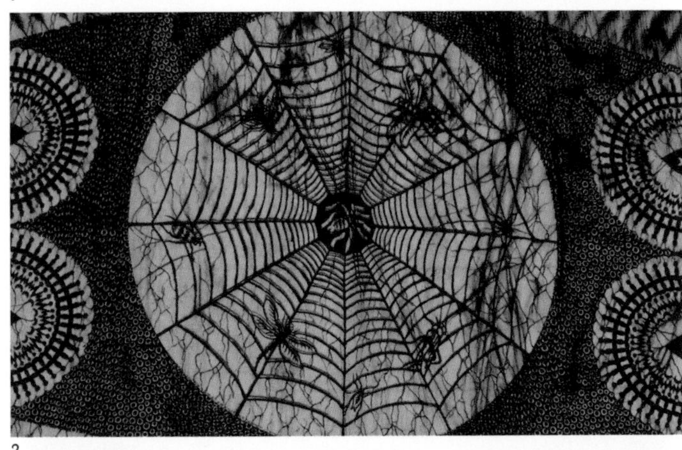

2

3

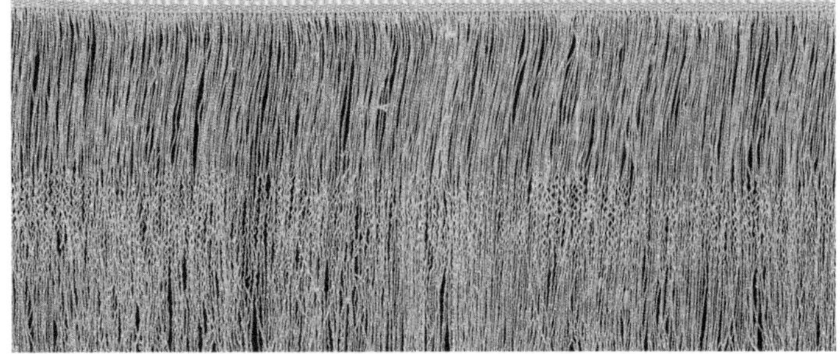

4

1

1 *Corona Vitae* (crown of life) wallpaper was designed by Walter Crane and produced by Jeffrey & Co., London, in 1890. The symbolism of the arrangement may be understood as emblematic of a full, rich and ample life, while the serpent indicates the Tree of Knowledge in the Christian narrative.

2 The salamander is a symbol of passionate love and was once thought to have the ability to withstand fire. This late 16th-century salamander pendant from western Europe is made in enamelled gold set with pearls.

3 This is a textile design of faceted turtles from *Dessins Nouveautés*, published by Lechartier et Paul, France, in 1880–1.

4 This is another textile design from *Dessins Nouveautés*, published by Lechartier et Paul, this one featuring stylized snakes.

5 At Caldas da Rainha, Portugal, around 1870 to 1880, Manuel Mafra pioneered a style of Palissy ware that featured a distinctive usage of moss as a decorative bed for fish, amphibians and reptiles, as seen in this glazed earthenware dish.

6 A pair of knitted silk stockings is embroidered with sequins and beads. They were made in France and exhibited at the 1900 Exposition Universelle in Paris.

7 Leslee Wills's *Zeme* print from 1981, commissioned by Heal's was inspired by one of the oldest and most widespread mythological symbols, the snake.

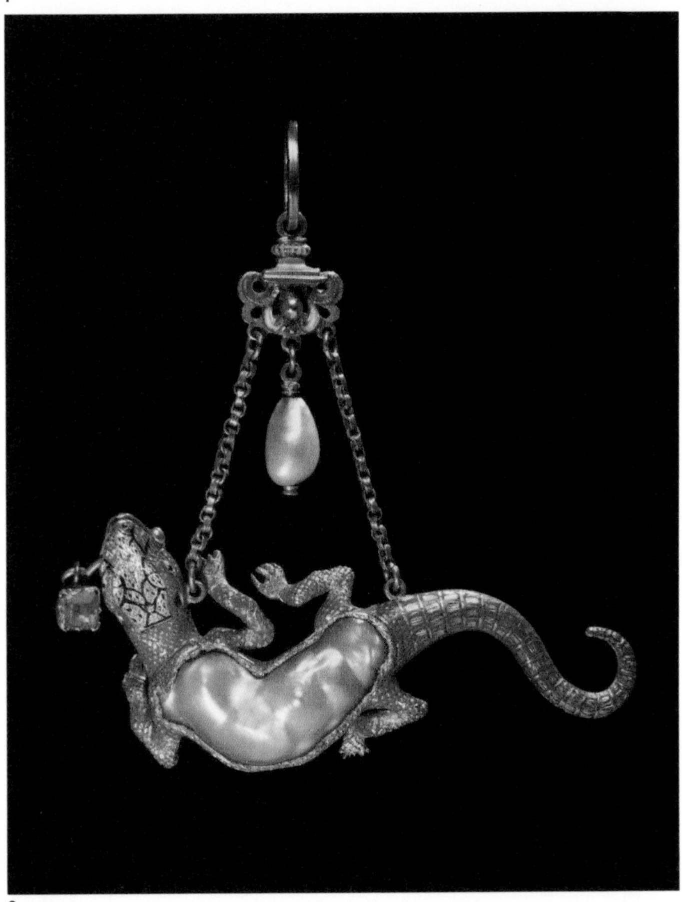
2

3

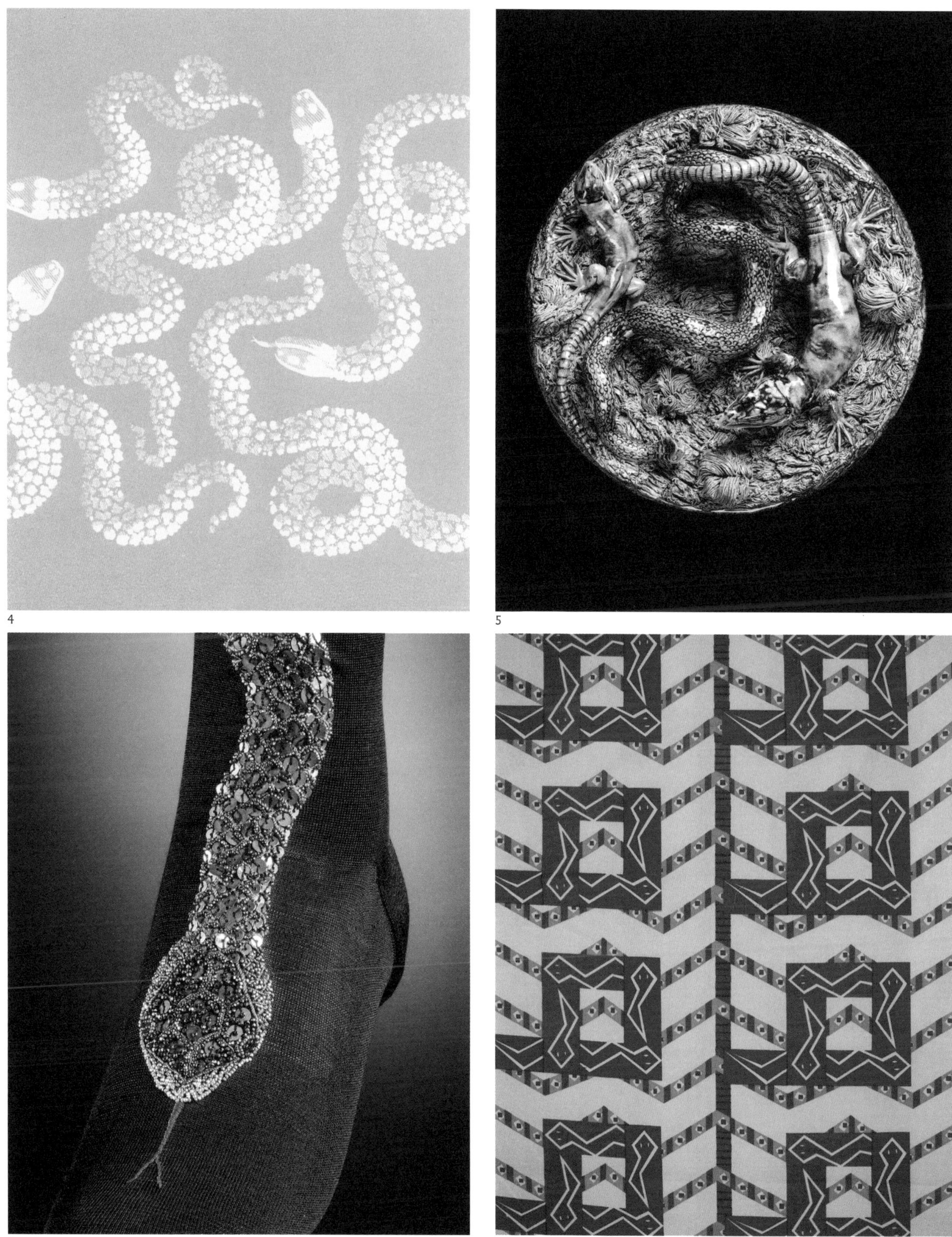

4

5

6

7

1

2

3

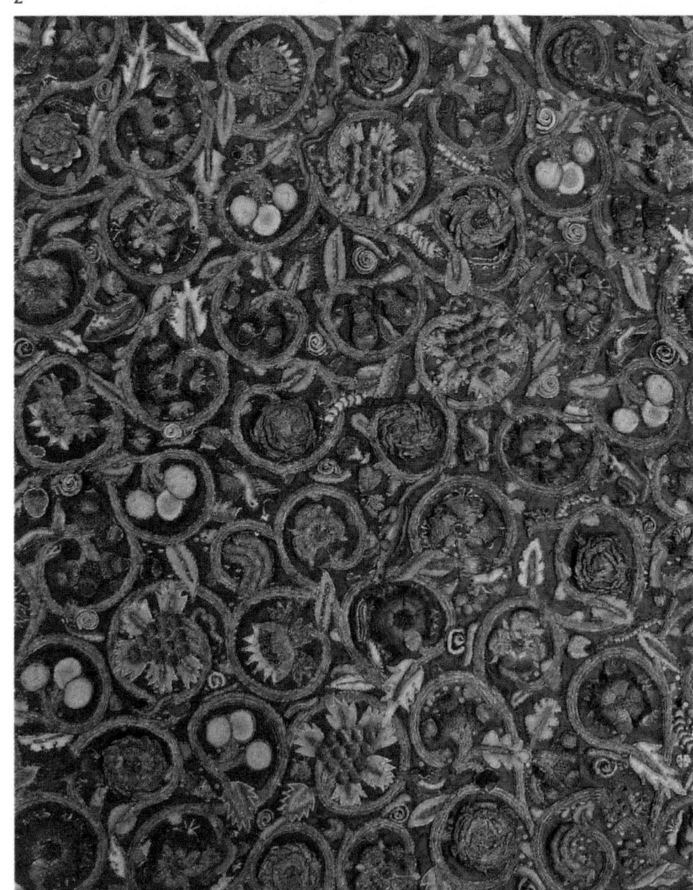
4

1 Dating to around 1765–75, this painted enamel bonbonnière modelled as a coiled snake was probably made in Bilston in England's West Midlands, a major centre for the production of these popular novelties.

2 The textile design *Garden of Eden* from 1923 by C.F.A. Voysey, possibly for a wall hanging, features Adam and Eve with the serpent in the English countryside.

3 Made in Jingdezhen, China, this porcelain mythical toad ornament dates from the early 18th century. The toad is beautifully modelled with a characterful expression and raised detail to its deep-green glazed back.

4 Embroidered with coloured silks and metal threads in England between about 1650 and 1700, this cushion cover has a pattern of scrolling vines with lizards, birds, snails, caterpillars, toads and flies.

5 This is a detail from an ebonized door panel, designed by Christopher Dresser for a wardrobe for Bushloe House, Leicestershire, around 1876. The flatly treated stencilled frogs typify Dresser's design theories.

6 The artist-plantsman Sir Cedric Lockwood Morris, founder of the East Anglia School of Art, Dedham, Essex, designed this furnishing fabric of screen-printed linen for Allan Walton Textiles, London, in 1940.

5

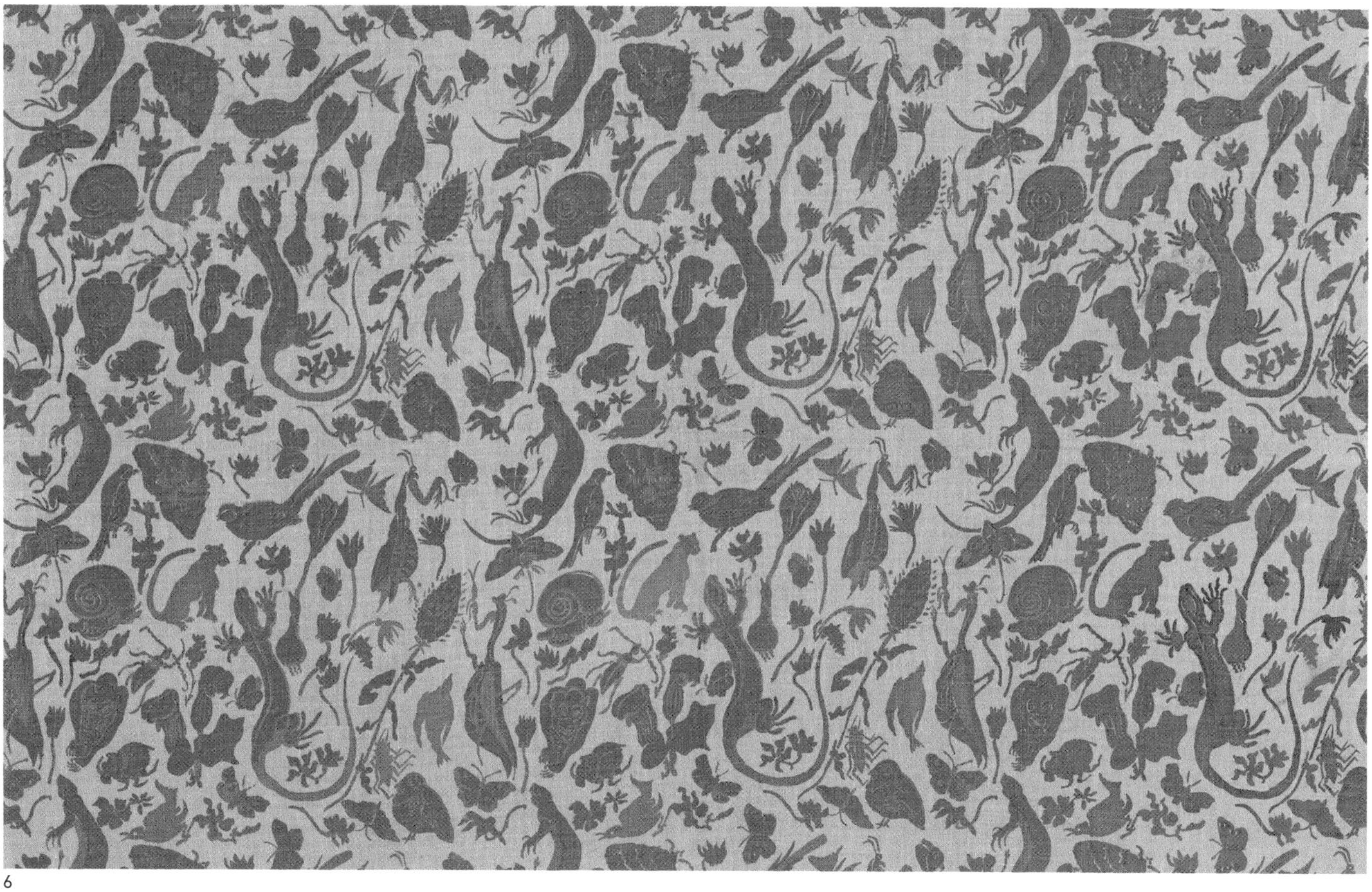

6

1

2

1 This is a detail from a lacquer coffer, made in Japan for the export market between about 1680 and 1720. The inside of the lid is decorated with phoenixes in flight in gold on black lacquer.

2 A dragon, the most powerful of all mythical beasts, flies in sight of Mount Fuji on this striking kimono made in Japan between 1850 and 1880.

3 Designed by Robert Jones and produced by Frederick Crace & Son, this wallpaper based on dragon mythology was intended for rooms on the upper floor of the Royal Pavilion, Brighton.

4 A mythical cockatrice is embroidered in red wool on a linen woman's jacket made in England in the 1640s.

5 Two dragons' heads form this tau-head (the T-shaped top of a staff). Possibly made in Constantinople (Istanbul), between about 1650 and 1700, they are carved in ivory with gold inlay and eyes formed by cabochon rubies.

6 Made in Jingdezhen, China, between 1736 and 1795, this bowl is decorated with dragons and waves in overglaze red and yellow. One of the Twelve Symbols of Sovereignty, dragons are symbols of nature, adaptability and transmutation.

7 Woven in Peru between 1680 and 1720, this tapestry fuses local techniques and colours with motifs and imagery imported from Europe and Spain's East Asian colonies.

3

4

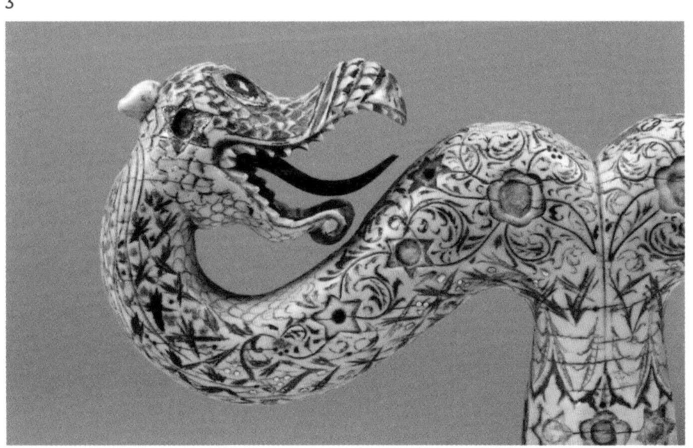
5

7

6

1

2

3

4

1 This dish moulded in relief was probably made in Venice between 1520 and 1540. The grotesque design incorporating winged horses, foliated dragons and lions whose tails end in floral volutes and cornucopias is adapted from a Florentine print.

2 Known as a 'Perugia towel', this textile was woven with wyverns (bipedal winged dragons) in 15th-century Italy. It may have served as a napkin, table cover, altar cloth or towel.

3 *Grotesque*, a dragon entwined in acanthus leaves, was designed by Lewis Foreman Day and printed on cotton in Lancashire by Turnbull & Stockdale in 1886.

4 William Morris designed this medieval-inspired textile featuring pairs of peacocks and dragons in 1878 as a wool fabric for heavyweight curtains or wall coverings.

5 A mix of legendary creatures – part chimera, part hippogriff – is seen in this patern published in *Dessins Nouveautés* by Lechartier et Paul, France, in 1880.

6 This is a detail from a Daoist robe from an imperial temple, made in China between 1800 and 1911 (latter part of Qing dynasty). The borders are embroidered with dragons and the Eight Trigrams, symbols used in Daoist divination, each carried by a human figure.

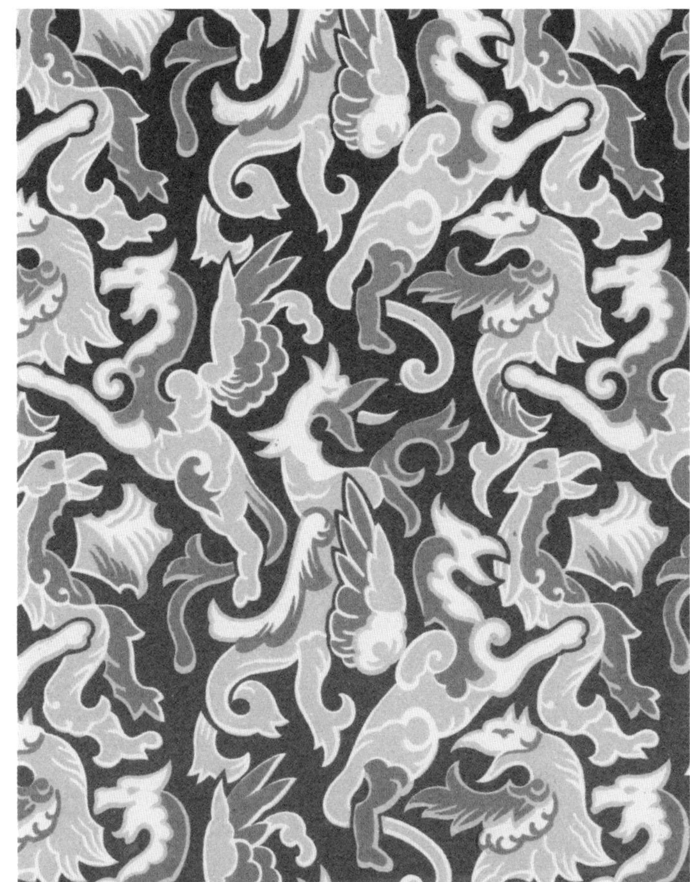

5

6

1 Luxuriously woven in fine wool and silk, this millefleurs (thousand flowers) tapestry with a unicorn was made in Flanders around 1500. The unicorn was associated in legend with chastity and invulnerability, since only a virgin might catch and tame it.

2 Bipedal winged dragons, or wyverns, pattern this 1880 textile design from *Dessins Nouveautés*, published by Lechartier et Paul, France.

3 The front half of an eagle and the hind half of a horse – known as a hippogriff – is reimagined into a repeat for a textile by Lechartier et Paul, France, 1880.

4 This printed cotton with dragons' heads and cloud motifs was produced by the Calico Printers' Association, Manchester, 1911.

5 This loosely fitting gown, or banyan, was tailored in Italy between 1800 and 1810 out of a silk woven for the Chinese imperial court. Dragons for the emperor always had five toes; here they have only four, indicating that the silk was intended for one of his relatives.

1

2

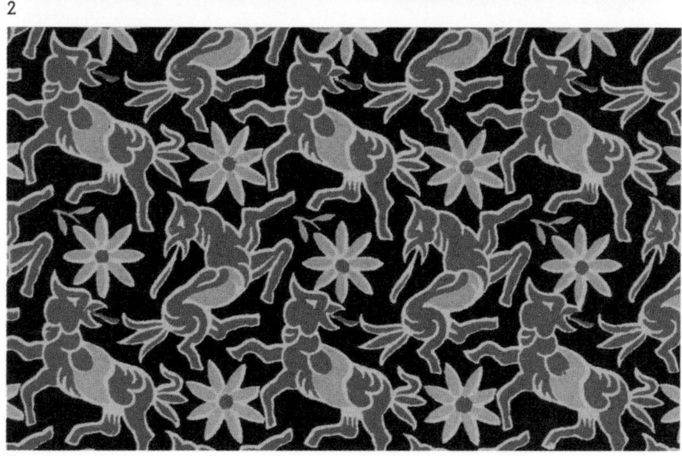

3

4

# EARTH AND THE UNIVERSE

**Opposite.** Printed cotton handkerchief manufactured in the USA, around 1970

1

1 Made in Paris between 1783 and 1784, this gold pocket watch has a movement signed by Le Coeur L'ainé. The image shows the royal-blue enamelled guilloché back decorated with a star pattern.

2 NASA's Apollo programme landed men on the moon from 1969 to 1972. The colourful rockets and astronauts on this dress cotton, possibly screen printed in the USA, reflect this exciting development.

3 Dating from around 1870, this jelly glass is wheel-engraved with stars. Jelly could be given at dinner before dessert in England and was often served in individual glasses. The more expensive jelly glasses had engraved decoration.

4 This patterned paper came from the Gothic Bathroom at Haseley Court in Oxfordshire. Woodblock printed in France around 1830, it is of a very high quality.

5 Designed by Henry Skeen and produced by John Line & Sons, England, this wallpaper pattern, *Derswell*, is from a pattern book of wallpaper specimens manufactured from 1936 to 1959.

6 *Whirling Waves*, a printed cotton furnishing fabric by English designer Thomas Acland Fennemore for Heal's in the 1950s, juxtaposes undulating waves with bright stars.

7 The bright starbursts of *Astra* furnishing fabric, produced by Morton Sundour, epitomize the vibrant Pop Art of 'Swinging London' in the 1960s.

2

3

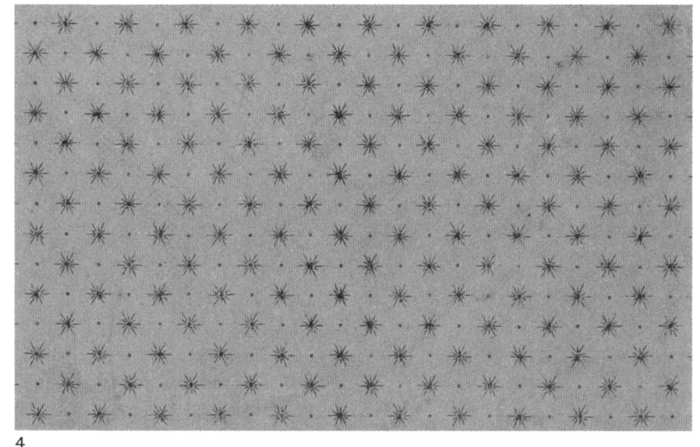
4

5

6

7

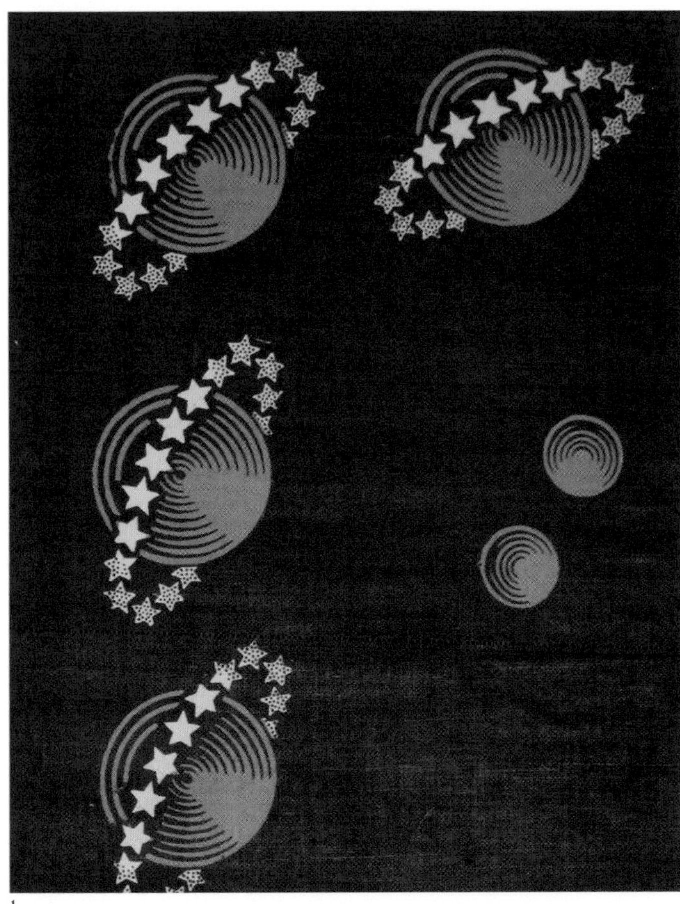

1

2

1 This swatch shows part of a printed pattern, probably intended to be produced as a large kerchief. The simple abstract design incorporates stars and motifs resembling planets, and comes from a large Swiss pattern book of printed and resist-dyed cottons produced from the 1860s to the 1890s.

2 John Wilkinson's *Main Street* wallpaper design from the *Palladio 9* collection was manufactured by Sanderson, London, in 1971. The design ingeniously combines two painting styles – Op Art and Pop Art.

3 The moon and stars may represent night in this exceptional late 17th-century French needle-lace furnishing flounce, whose wider composition incorporates many symbols associated with the court of the Sun King, Louis XIV.

4 A printed cotton swatch made for Naj-Oleari of Milan in 1979 presents a rather chic planetary system in gold and black.

5 Tennis champion and artist Helen Wills Moody plays with the American flag in her design for the 1927 printed silk crêpe *Stars and Stripes*, which was part of the manufacturer Stehli Silks' series celebrating American life in the 1920s.

6 *Stellar*, a printed cotton furnishing fabric with colourful pop culture details of stars, was designed for Heal's, London, by Anne Fehlow in 1965.

3

4

5

6

1

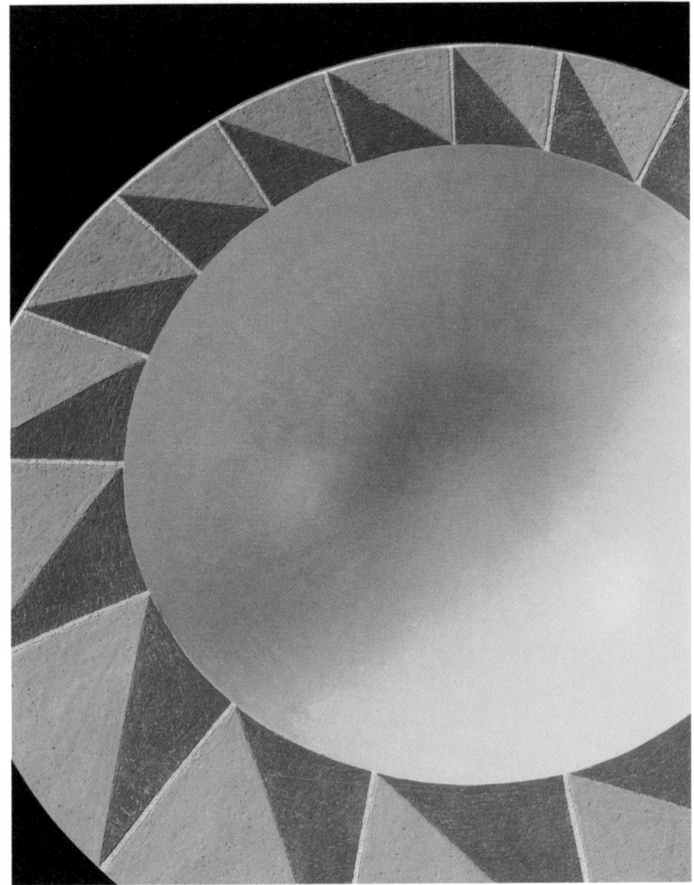

2

1 In the late 1960s, Lucienne Day's designs favoured large patterns in bold colours, such as *Sunrise*, a geometric pattern for a screen-printed cotton curtain fabric for Heal's, London, from 1969.

2 British studio potter Judy Trim's richly coloured and celebratory *Sun Bowl* from 1985 makes bold and striking use of primary colours.

3 A sunray pattern, with its evocation of joy and nature, decorates Nigel Quiney's *Sun* tote bag from around 1966. The sunburst was a popular Art Deco motif, featuring everywhere from windows to hotel foyers.

4 Glowing orbs feature on *Corona*, a screen-printed furnishing cotton, designed by Fay Hillier for Heal's, London, in 1961.

5 This eccentric Martinware ceramic jug with large sun face was made by the four Martin brothers, who lived in London in the late 19th century.

6 Created by British architect Sir William Chambers in the 1750s–60s, this meticulously composed design for a plasterwork ceiling features sun and star motifs.

7 Designed by Robert Stewart, *Sunman* was printed as a furnishing fabric for Liberty in 1954. Stewart's hallmark trefoil devices and dotted and solid lines frame a smiling sun face.

8 *Seasons*, a 1955 monochrome printed cotton designed by Olive Sullivan for Edinburgh Weavers, features finely drawn suns, moons and supernatural figures with seasonal plants.

3

4

5

6

7

8

1

1 Photographs taken on the Apollo 9 flight inspired Eddie Squires's design for *Lunar Rocket*. The manufacturers, Warner & Sons, displayed a sample in their London showroom on the morning of the first walk on the moon, in 1969.

2 The form of the *Videosphere* television, manufactured by JVC in Japan in 1970, alludes to an astronaut's helmet. In the late 1960s space travel was influential in many areas of design.

3 Sue Thatcher Palmer's *Space Walk*, produced by Warner & Sons, depicts astronauts bounding weightlessly in zero gravity. The design was commissioned three months before the 1969 moon landing.

4 This contemporary *Moon* sari in beautiful indigo hues was created by Aziz and Suleman Khatri in Gujarat in 2012. The halo effect is achieved by a clamp dyeing process that uses circular wooden discs.

5 Inspired by space exploration and based on photographs of the moon's surface, *Lunar* wallpaper, by Michael Clarke and produced by British manufacturer Cole & Son in 1964, is printed in vivid purple and reflects graphic designs of the period.

2

3

4

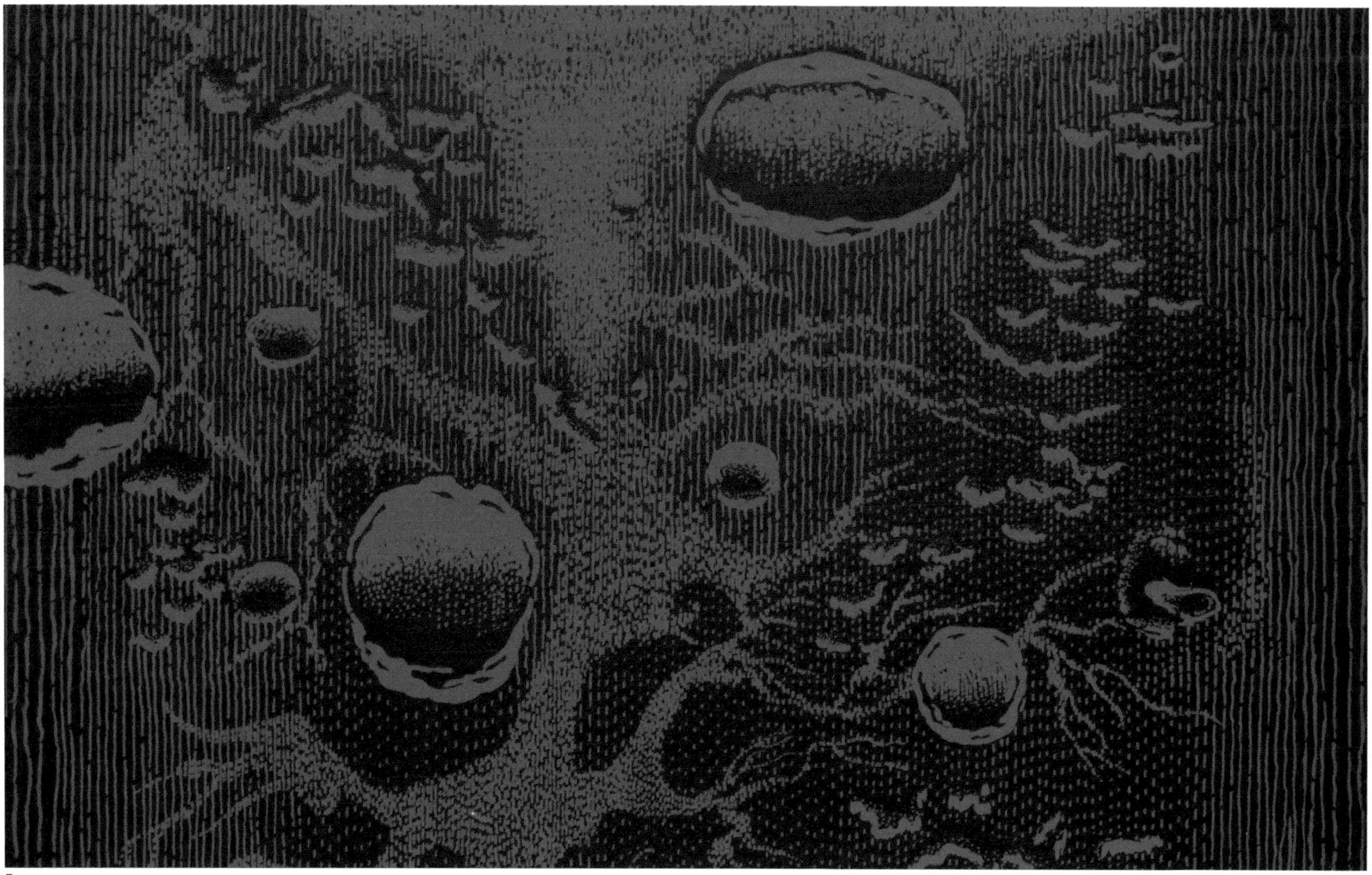

5

1 A jasperware plaque depicting the signs of the zodiac and made in the Josiah Wedgwood factory between 1780 and 1800 is set (possibly by Matthew Boulton) in a cut steel frame to form this button.

2 Constructed of loops of ribbon on a canvas back, this carpet was designed by British artist William Nicholson around 1925. The zodiac signs of Gemini, Virgo, Aquarius and Sagittarius rest on a central globe surrounded by the other signs.

3 *Zodiac* is a screen-printed fabric designed around 1939 by Marion Dorn with a bold depiction of astrological signs and symbols for the Old Bleach Linen Co..

4 This Gothic Revival oak cradle from 1861, with gilded and painted signs of the zodiac, was designed by British architect Richard Norman Shaw.

5 Edmund Hunter's designs for his firm St Edmundsbury Weavers, Haslemere, Surrey, drew on his interest in early Christian iconography, Celtic mysticism and astrology. *Zodiac* was hand-loom woven in silk with metallic threads in 1905–10.

6 Arnold Machin designed *Taurus the Bull* around 1946, when examples were shown in the *Britain Can Make It* exhibition at the V&A. This example was made around 1950.

7 This late 17th-century wool and silk needlework hanging is one of a series commissioned by Mme de Montespan, mistress of Louis XIV. Three zodiac signs represent autumn, including Scorpio, seen here.

1

2

3

4

5

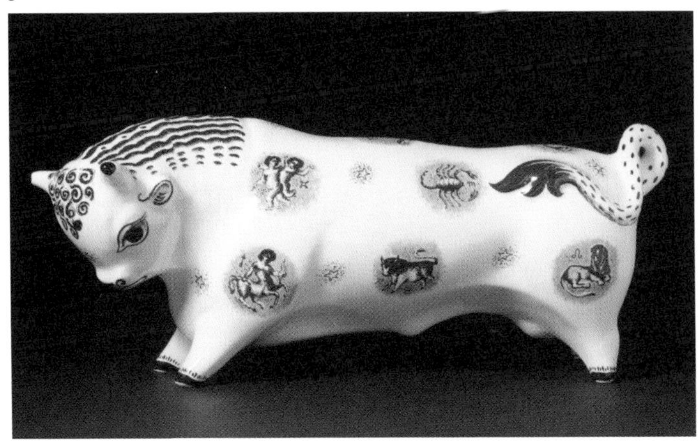

6

7

1

1 The *Cipriani* cocktail cabinet with atom-styled ball feet and 'antennae' was designed by Alessandro Mendini for newly established Memphis, Milan, in 1981.

2 This wallpaper is based on the mineral afwillite, from a collection of samples designed for the 1951 Festival of Britain. William J. Odell worked with X-ray crystallographer Helen Megaw to design the pattern.

3 *Insulin 8.25*, designed by Robert Sevant and made by the wallpaper firm John Line & Sons for the 1951 Festival of Britain Crystal Design Project, was inspired by the crystalline structure of insulin.

4 Marianne Straub, head designer at Warner & Sons, London, designed *Helmsley*, a woven cotton furnishing fabric, in 1951. The different circles represent atoms at separate levels in the nylon structure.

5 The motif on this *haori* (kimono jacket), made in Japan around 1957–8, is a rendition of Sputnik, the first artificial satellite, launched by the Soviet Union in 1957.

6 Made by Italian jewellery artist Giovanni Corvaja in 2000, this gold and platinum brooch is a three-dimensional hexagonal frame intertwined with fine wire on to which granules of gold have been fused.

7 This wallpaper pattern by William J. Odell is based on the chemical structure of boric acid. It is another of the patterns designed for the 1951 Festival of Britain.

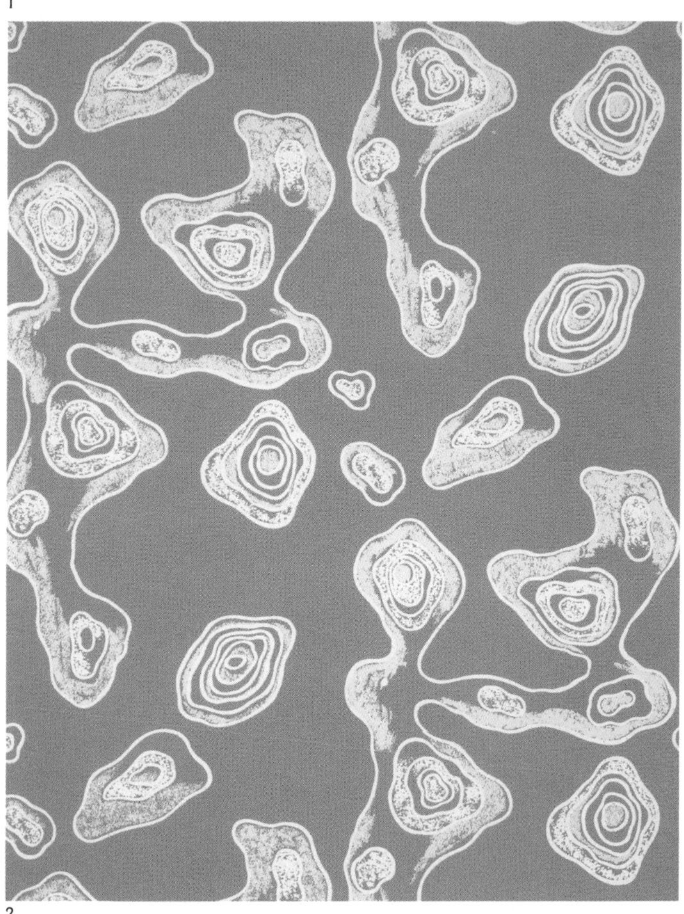

2

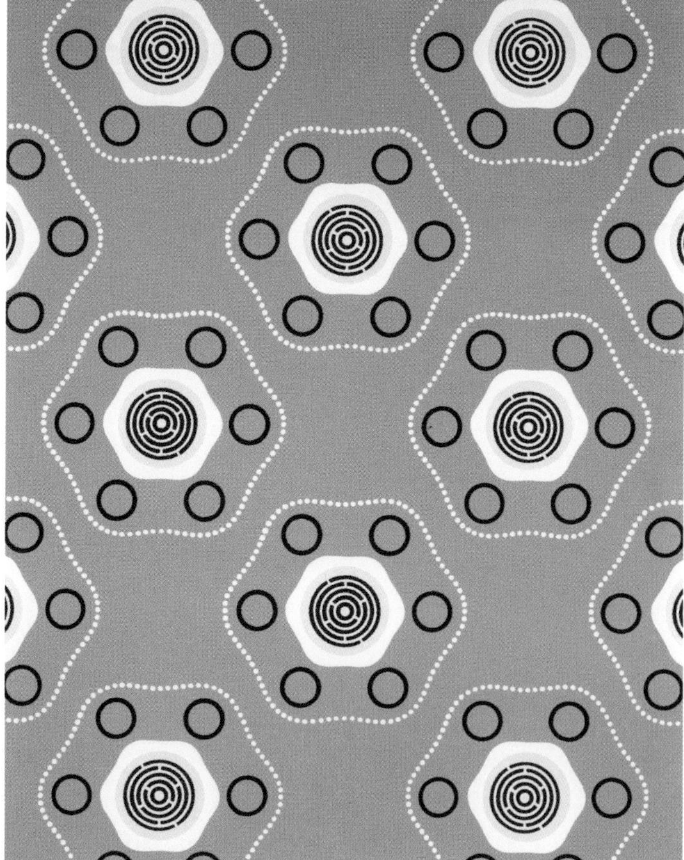

3

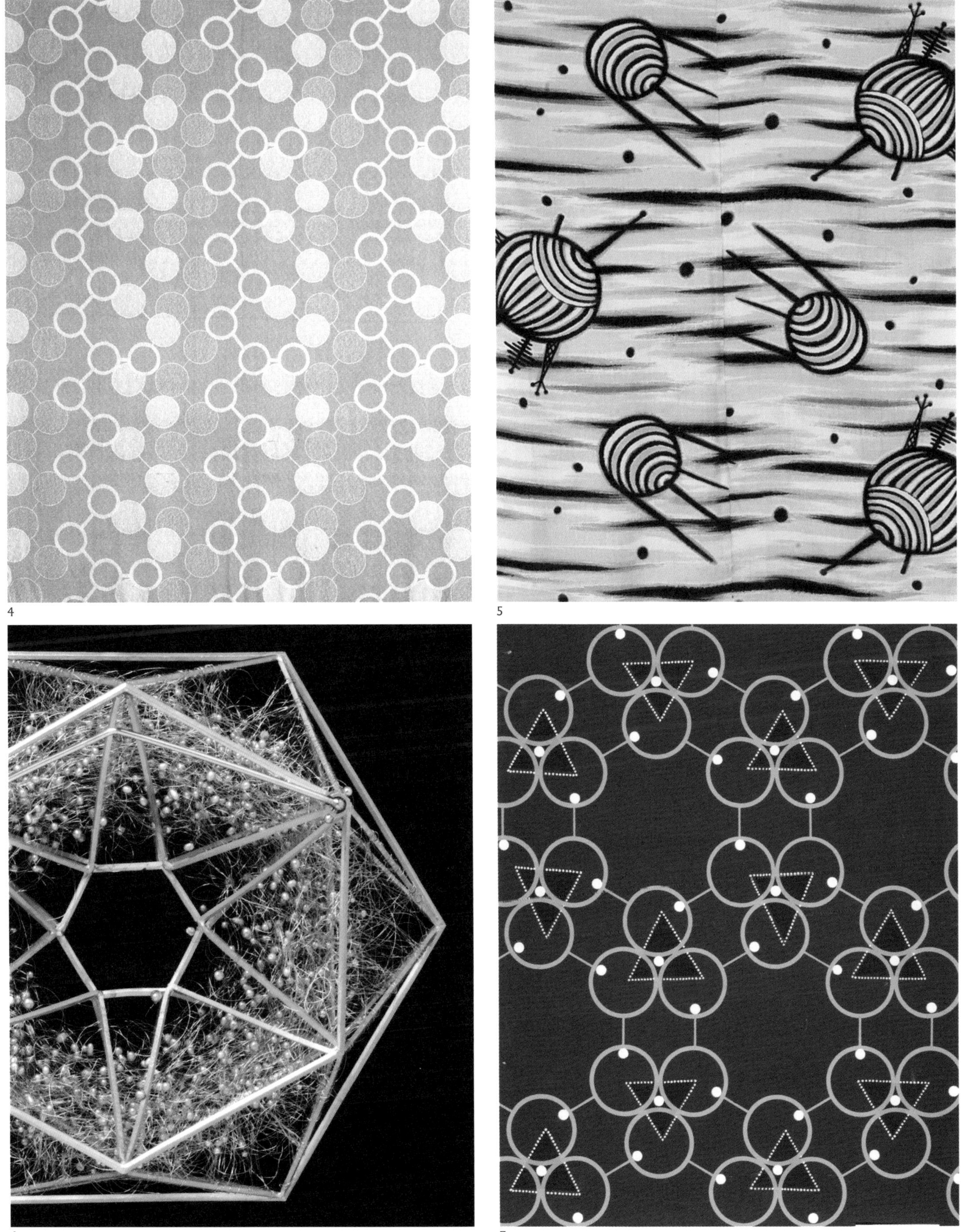

4

5

6

7

1

2

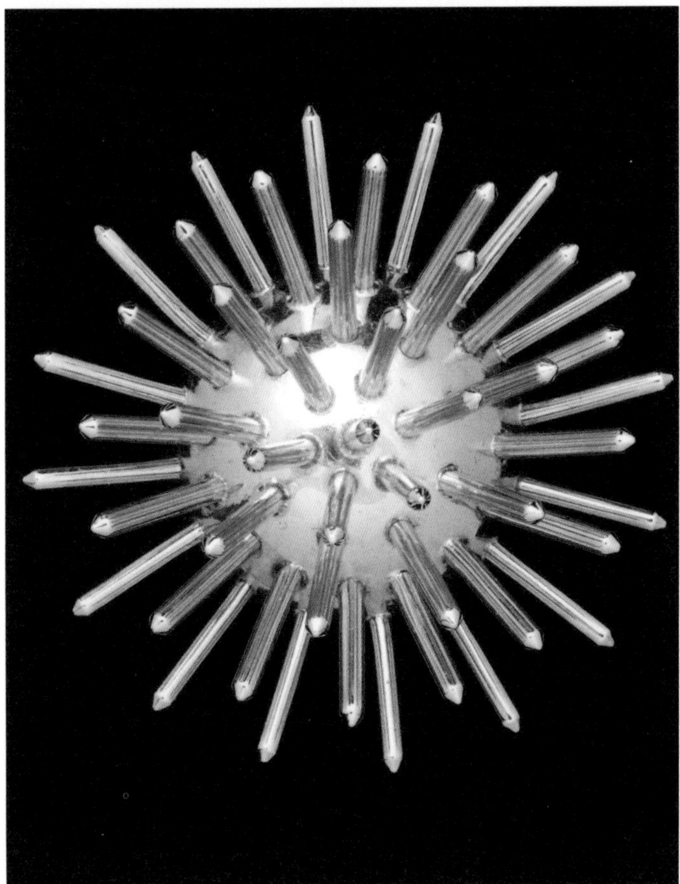
3

4

5

1 This geometric Art Deco design is part of a *pochoir* (stencil-based printing) pattern book titled *Prismes*, created by Émile-Allain Séguy and published in Paris by Éditions d'Art Charles Moreau around 1930.

2 Tom Dixon's 1997 *Jack Light* is inspired by a polyhedron and is one of the British designer's first works in plastic. Made of rotary-moulded polyethylene, it is a multipurpose stacking floor lamp/stool/trestle.

3 This gold brooch made by Cartier, New York, illustrates the far-reaching influence of the space age. The launch of the Soviet Union's Sputnik satellite triggered the space race, along with the audacious jewellery designs that appeared from the late 1950s to the 1960s.

4 French pattern designer E.A. Séguy spans the Art Nouveau and Deco movements. He was known for decorative albums inspired by natural forms. *Prismes*, from around 1930, contains a variety of abstract and semi-abstract motifs.

5 *Eleanor*, a roller-printed cotton fabric, designed by Alastair Morton in England for his Sundour prints collection around 1954, features cartouche and rosette patterns resembling observations made by high-speed cameras of the crown shape formed during a water splash.

6 Gerald Holtom's *Plankton* magnifies microscopic organisms to dramatic effect. Screen printed on cotton, it was a wall covering in the Dome of Discovery at the Festival of Britain in 1951.

6

1

2

3

4

5

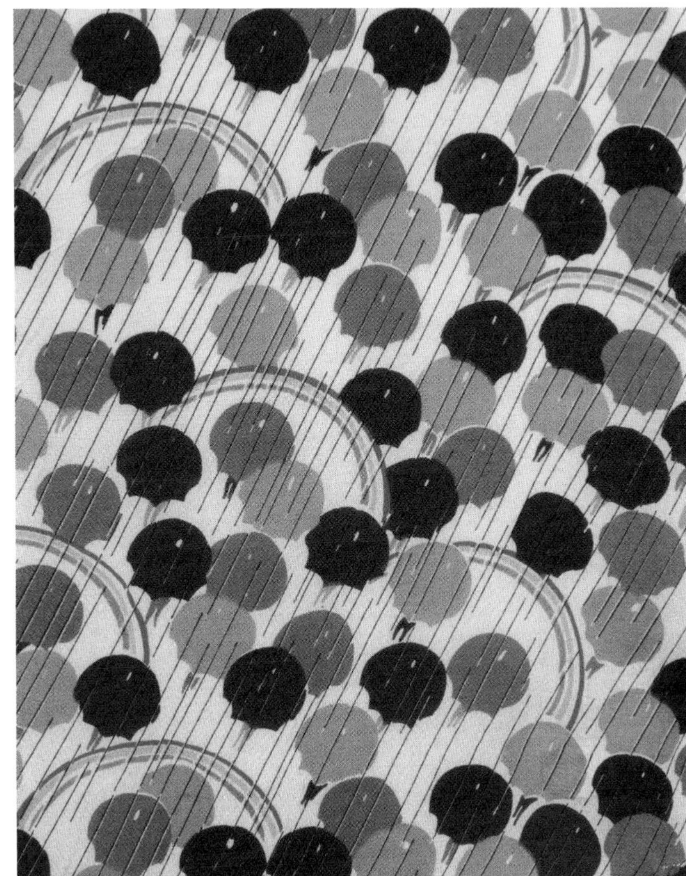

6

1 *Summer Storm*, designed by Jeanine and Michael Fieldsend for Heal's around 1970, is a bold, graphically styled printed cotton furnishing fabric echoing comic strip cartoons and paintings by Roy Lichtenstein.

2 After graduating as a fashion student in the 1980s, Julie Verhoeven worked with John Galliano for four years in London, where she created this design of stars and thunderbolts for a T-shirt for his diffusion line, Galliano Genes.

3 The title *Birds, Clouds, Sun, Rain* sums up the repeating motifs on this block-printed linen furnishing fabric, designed by British painter and sculptor Frank Dobson in 1938.

4 *Froth*, designed by British abstract artist Paule Vézelay for Heal's in the early 1960s, is a printed furnishing textile with organic forms that are typical of her bold patterns.

5 *Rain*, a cut-crystal champagne flute, was designed by the artist Paul Nash for Stuart & Sons, Stourbridge, England, and shown at the Harrods *Modern Art for the Table* exhibition, 1934.

6 *April*, designed by Clayton Knight for Stehli Silks' *Americana Prints* series, was printed on silk crêpe in the USA in 1927. The bird's-eye view of umbrellas evokes the showers associated with that month.

7 This atmospheric wheel-thrown Bizen vessel *Kuro Fusetsu* (*fusetsu* means 'wind-driven snow') was sculpted by Isezaki Jun in 2013. Bizen ware is a type of unglazed Japanese stoneware.

7

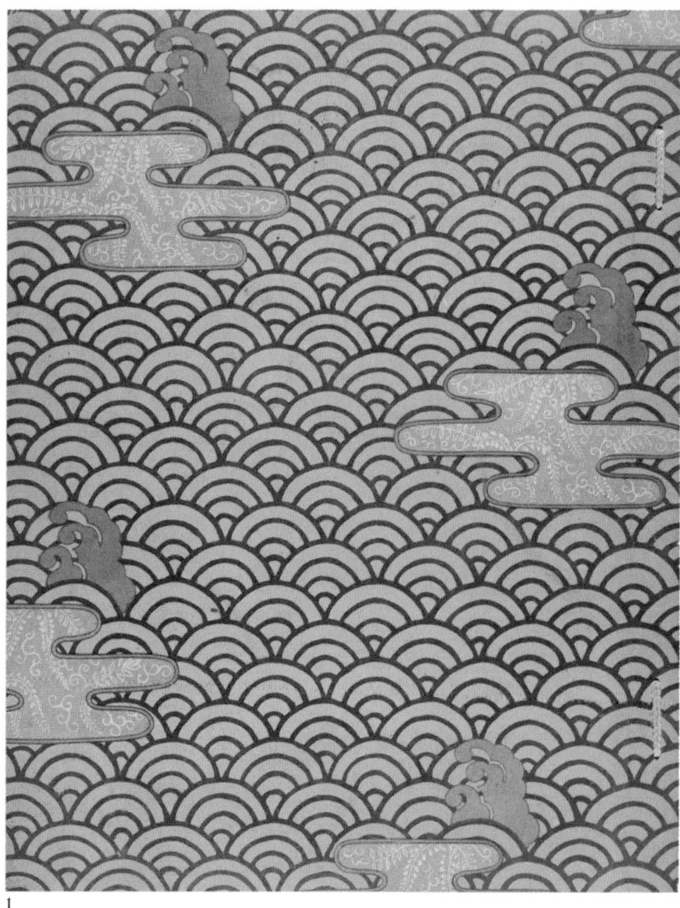

1

2

1 This cover from Kazumasa Ogawa's *Some Japanese Flowers* from around 1894 depicts stylized clouds patterned with leaves on a repeating design of concentric overlapping half-circles representing waves, and breaking silver waves.

2 In *Cloudy Sky at Sunset*, the changing colours conjure up a day ending on America's West Coast. Marijke Koger's design was screen printed on synthetic jersey for Astrobeams of Los Angeles in the 1970s.

3 A motif of scrolling clouds woven in silk and gold threads graces this Nō theatre robe made in 19th-century Japan.

4 The all-over cloud motif of this Iznik earthenware jug, made in Ottoman Turkey around 1585, is Chinese in origin.

5 The British firm Eton Rural Fabrics (later Sanderson) produced this colourful printed cotton in 1933, with clouds in a warm colour palette set off against a blue sky.

6 This detail of floating clouds, with bamboo and plum blossom, comes from a silk crêpe *juban* (under-kimono) for a woman, made in Japan in the 1940s.

7 These multicoloured stylized clouds are from a Chinese dragon robe of tapestry-weave silk (*kesi*) dating from the late 18th or early 19th century.

3

4

5

6

7

1

2

3

1 The geometric motif of *Green Waves*, made in Japan in 1973, is Living National Treasure Kunihiko Moriguchi's unique interpretation of waves. The tonal grading was created with the technique of freehand resist dyeing (*yuzen*) on pongee silk.

2 Made in 1860–80, this Japanese kimono of silk crêpe (*chirimen*) is decorated with an auspicious motif of carp and swirling water, deriving from a Chinese legend.

3 This is a mid-19th-century Japanese paper for a *shōji* (screen, sliding door or room divider), with a rhythmical repeated pattern made by stencil printing.

4 The delicate white forms of waves and chrysanthemum flowers on the deep-blue background of this indigo futon cover, made in Japan in the late 19th century, were made using a technique called *tsutsugaki* (tube drawing).

5 The shape of this porcelain pot was designed by Grethe Meyer, with decoration by Ole Kortzau. It is part of the tableware range *Picnic*, which was manufactured by Royal Copenhagen in Denmark in 1984.

6 This printed furnishing fabric sample, with its pattern of abstract waves and seabirds, was produced by Donald Brothers, Dundee, in 1936.

7 Rosalind Wong's *The Swimmer* was bleed and discharge printed on cotton in 1975 – possibly at the Chelsea School of Art, London – giving rise to the blurred line effect, often seen in Chinese paintings.

4

5

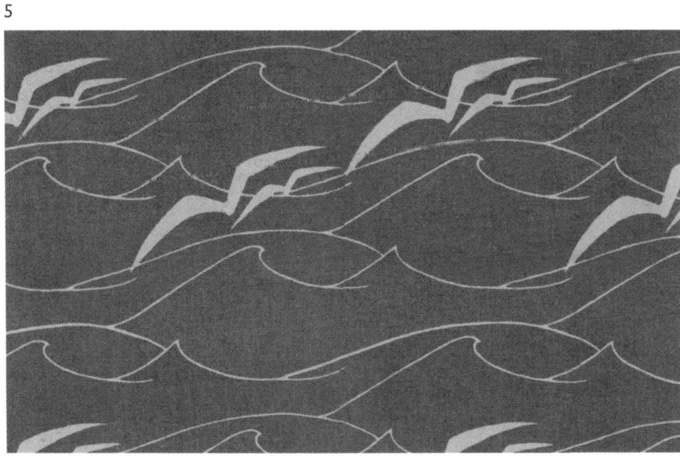

6

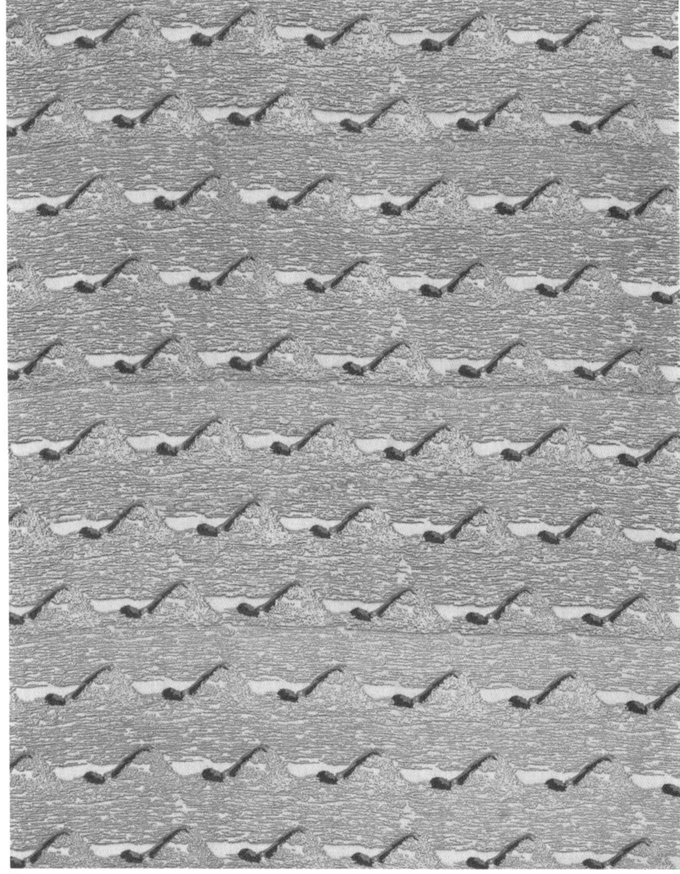

7

1

2

3

4

5

6

1 *Shipyard*, designed by Anthony Harrison for Edinburgh Weavers in 1956, is screen printed on cotton. It depicts small boats at low tide on the quayside.

2 The Kon-Tiki expedition of 1947, a three-month voyage from South America to the Polynesian Islands by raft, inspired Mary Harper's design *Kon-Tiki* for the British manufacturer Gayonnes in 1951.

3 Artist David Faithfull presents a secluded bay among rocks in his 2011 wallpaper *Perpetual Landscape* for the landscape-themed *cabin:codex* exhibition at the Centre for Artists' Books, Dundee Contemporary Arts, Scotland.

4 A block-printed linen furnishing fabric designed by Alec Hunter for Edinburgh Weavers in 1930 features a galleon or sailing ship of the late 16th century.

5 This wallpaper is evocative of woodblock prints by 17th- to 19th-century Japanese *ukiyo-e* artists, but is a romanticized British view of East Asia from the 1920s.

6 John Clappison's *Summit* range was designed in 1960 for Hornsea Pottery, Yorkshire; these examples were produced around 1962 to 1965. This cruet set and oil bottle resemble snow-peaked mountains.

7 Various views of Munster, Alsace, are depicted on this 1818 printed cotton panel designed by 'Casimir', or J.J. Karpff, and manufactured by Hartmann et Fils, including the Rhine and the ruins of Schwarzenbourg and Pflixbourg castles.

7

1

2

3

4

1 Alec Walker used his own sketches and paintings to create designs for his St Ives-based company Cryséde Silks, such as this block-printed silk, *Cornish Farm*, from 1930.

2 Designed by Jennie Foley for Heal's in 1976, *Country Walk* evokes the stillness and beauty of the land on screen-printed cotton, at a time of growing environmental awareness.

3 This footed stoneware bowl decorated with an undulating landscape in inlaid porcelain on a ground of dry ash glaze was made by studio potter Michael Casson at Wobage Farm, Herefordshire, in 1977.

4 A block-printed scarf by designer-craftswoman Joyce Clissold for Footprints commemorates the 1951 Festival of Britain, especially through its depiction of the futuristic Dome of Discovery and Skylon.

5 Probably copper-plate printed in England around 1780, this cotton presents an idealized rural scene, with country people going about their everyday duties and a group of strolling players.

6 Designed by Edward Bawden and hand-printed around 1931 by Cole & Son from lino blocks, *Knole Park* wallpaper was probably named after Knole Park in Kent, England, with its historic country house and deer park.

7 Countryside scenes of dancers, haycarts, windmills and half-timbered houses are plate printed on this English cotton of around 1790.

5

6

7

1 A trellis with roses frames the view of a formal garden on this printed furnishing fabric produced for the *Cumberland Prints* series by Morton Sundour, Carlisle, in the 1930s or 1950s.

2 This screen-printed furnishing fabric, made by Feinweberei Elsaesser of Switzerland in 1956, captures a verdant garden in bloom, with birds and bees among snowdrops, lilies of the valley, roses and peonies.

3 The Calico Printers' Association, Manchester, roller printed this design of a peaceful garden with vistas of graceful trees, Italianate columns and pool on a cotton furnishing fabric in 1924.

4 Made by the Manchester-based firm Tootal Broadhurst Lee, this printed linen furnishing fabric entitled *An Old Garden* is overflowing with details of planting, architectural features and birds flying off with fruit.

5 Silk embroidery adorns the interior and exterior of this English casket from around 1660–1685. Its lid opens to reveal a removable tray with a miniature garden of fruit trees interspersed with ivory figures.

6 This block-printed linen manufactured by Morton Sundour, Carlisle, in the 1920s bears a pictorial hunting and hawking scene with orange trees and blossom, of the type found in historical Iranian art.

1

2

3

4

5

6

1

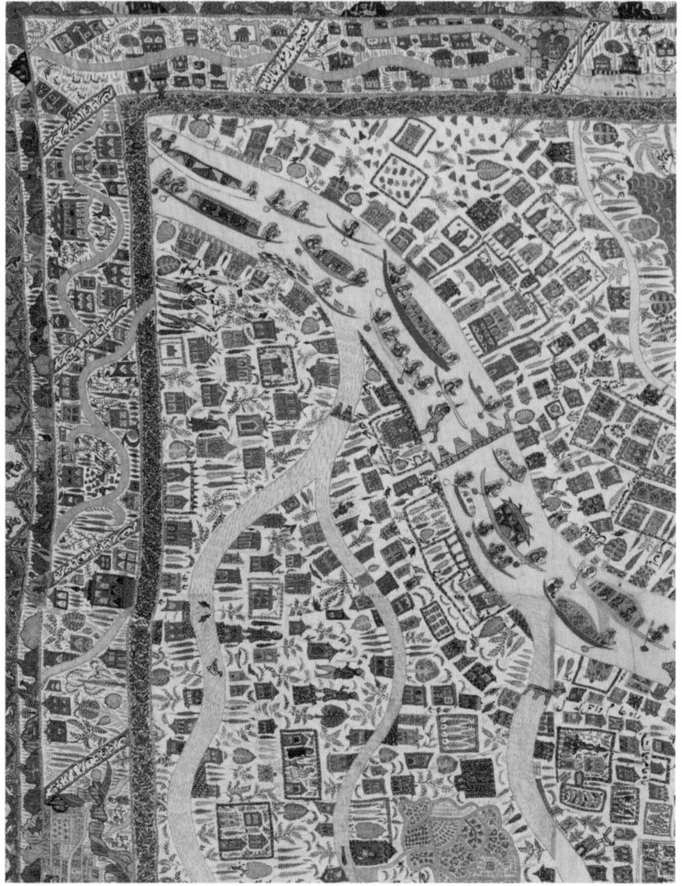

2

1 Freelance designer Hilda Durkin made this design of linear and geometric buildings entitled *Isola Bella* for Liberty, London, to print as a furnishing fabric in 1954.

2 This is a detail from a large wool map shawl with the streets, waterways and landmarks of Srinagar, the capital of Kashmir, embroidered in fine coloured wool. The shawl was produced in Kashmir in the third quarter of the 19th century.

3 *Pride o' London*, a printed linen fabric by Tootal Broadhurst Lee, Manchester, from 1927, features contemporary and historical people and buildings, such as the Beefeaters in front of the Tower of London.

4 *Shop Fronts & Hot Air Balloons*, a 1950s printed cotton dress fabric produced by Zika Ascher's company Bourec, London, features stripes of brightly coloured shop fronts and houses. Cheerfully decorated hot air balloons, recalling the designs of 18th-century French balloon pioneers the Montgolfier brothers, hover overhead.

3

RESTAURANT
1857 TAVERN
CAFEWAY

1 This wallpaper, attributed to Heywood, Higginbotham & Smith, Manchester, commemorates London's International Exhibition of 1862. It is block printed with framed views of the exhibition site.

2 David Faithfull's 2011 wallpaper *Bricks/Urban Landscape*, made for the *cabin:codex* exhibition at the Centre for Artists' Books at Dundee Contemporary Arts, Scotland, represents the UK's history of brick manufacturing.

3 *Manhattan*, a printed cotton designed by Ruth Reeves for W. & J. Sloane of New York in 1930, captures modern buildings and activities, such as the recently inaugurated Empire State Building and telephone switchboard operators at work.

4 Schiffer Prints of New York worked with furniture designer Edward J. Wormley to produce fabrics for the American market. *Our Town* from 1954 features a lively printed pattern of brownstones and tenements.

5 Sanderson commissioned John Piper in 1959 to produce a screen print for its centenary in 1961. The artist based his design, *Northern Cathedral*, on his studies of townscapes and ecclesiastical buildings.

6 *Crowded Skies* footed vase in clear glass is a classic shape from the Swedish Orrefors glassworks, designed by Vicke Lindstrand and engraved by Karl Rössler. Depicting industry and technology, the vase was possibly intended for inclusion in the 1930 Stockholm Exhibition.

1

2

3

4

5

6

1

2

3

4

1 This enamelled cover of a copper-gilt beaker looks like a fairy-tale city imagined by the Brothers Grimm, but it dates from around 1475–1500 and was probably made by a German goldsmith inspired by the towers of medieval Nuremberg.

2 *Medioevo* was designed by G. Cipriani for Manifattura in northern Italy in 1957. Medieval castles or towers have been screen printed on cotton with painterly fluidity and marks.

3 The design of this linen furnishing fabric, possibly printed in 19th-century Germany, imitates Delft tiles with simple vignettes of palaces, castles and windmills.

4 Decorated with a painting of the popular tourist attraction Warwick Castle, this mid-19th-century papier-mâché chair was made by Jennens and Bettridge of Birmingham, England.

5 On this late 18th-century English plate-printed cotton, the Prince of Wales (later George IV) is one of the huntsmen disporting himself in the vicinity of the royal residence Windsor Castle, which he subsequently renovated.

6 *Scottish Castles*, a printed cotton furnishing fabric made by Tootal Broadhurst Lee in Manchester between 1926 and 1935, features the bastions of Edinburgh and Stirling alongside smaller medieval tower-houses and castles.

5

6

1

2

3

4

5

6

1 John Piper designed this architectural repeat pattern, *Tombs*, in 1956 for David Whitehead, Lancashire. The screen printing on rayon achieves a fluid, painterly effect.

2 Inside an ebony-veneered cabinet made in the Neapolitan workshop of Jacopo Fiamengo around 1600, Corinthian columns made of ivory and engraved by Giovanni Battista Fontana create a miniature architectural set with tiny drawers for valuable possessions.

3 *Architettura*, a ceramic lidded jar with a monochromatic Palladian façade decoration, was designed in Milan in the 1960s by Pietro Fornasetti.

4 This is a sheet of uncut dado wallpaper borders with a design of plaster cornices with classical mountings, made in England, around 1825–50.

5 Block printed with Corinthian capitals surrounded by naturalistically rendered flowers and foliage, this glazed cotton furnishing fabric was made in England around 1805.

6 Alternating stripes of fluted columns and roses adorn this block-printed furnishing cotton made in England around 1791.

7 Repeating rows of Corinthian-style columns make a striking wallpaper design by Robert Nicholson for the Manchester-based Wallpaper Manufacturers' 1955 *Palladio* range.

7

1

2

3

4

1 William Burges based this 1858 cabinet on medieval cupboards he had seen in northern France. It was made by Harland & Fisher, London, and painted by Edward Poynter.

2 This block-printed cotton was made in England between 1830 and 1840 during the Gothic Revival, one of the important architectural and design movements of the 19th century.

3 A picturesque Gothic arch frames a landscape view on this block-printed cotton, made in England in the 1830s and probably intended for use as a window blind.

4 *Village Church*, designed by Hilda Durkin and printed on cotton for Heal's in 1954, delineates features of traditional English church buildings.

5 This printed wallpaper shows the interior of a ruined abbey. It may have been produced by Heywood, Higginbotham & Smith, Manchester, 1870–80.

6 Made by Deroche, Paris, around 1830, this spill vase in the Gothic Revival style was intended to hold splints, spills and tapers.

7 This repeat pattern of Gothic windows, complete with tracery and leaded glass, was printed on cotton before being glazed, in England, around 1830–5.

8 *Nowton Court* wallpaper made by Cole & Son in 1975 was based on London decorating firm Cowtan & Sons' order books containing fragments from the 1830s held in the V&A's national collection of historic wallpapers.

5

6

7

8

1

2

3

4

5

1 *Willow Pattern Plate* wallpaper is based on the chinoiserie pattern used on ceramics in Britain from 1780. It was produced by John Perry & Co. (now Cole & Son), London, in 1909.

2 Produced in France between 1850 and 1899, this printed cotton has a chinoiserie design in purple on a sepia ground, depicting a scene of musicians and boats.

3 This detail is from the lid of a sewing table, made in Canton (now Guangzhou) between about 1830 and 1850 especially for export to the West. The scene, in black and gold lacquer, shows pagodas, pavilions and boats.

4 This Meiji-era pagoda-style porcelain winepot with dragon handle and spout was made by Japanese potter Makuzu Kōzan in Kyoto between about 1890 and 1900.

5 Probably made in England around 1805, this block-printed cotton represents a landscape with pagodas, characteristic of the chinoiserie that was popular in the 18th and 19th centuries.

6 Dating from 1768 to 1778, this painted pine corner cupboard in the Chinese style was supplied by the cabinet-maker Thomas Chippendale to the celebrated actor David Garrick for his bedroom in his London villa.

6

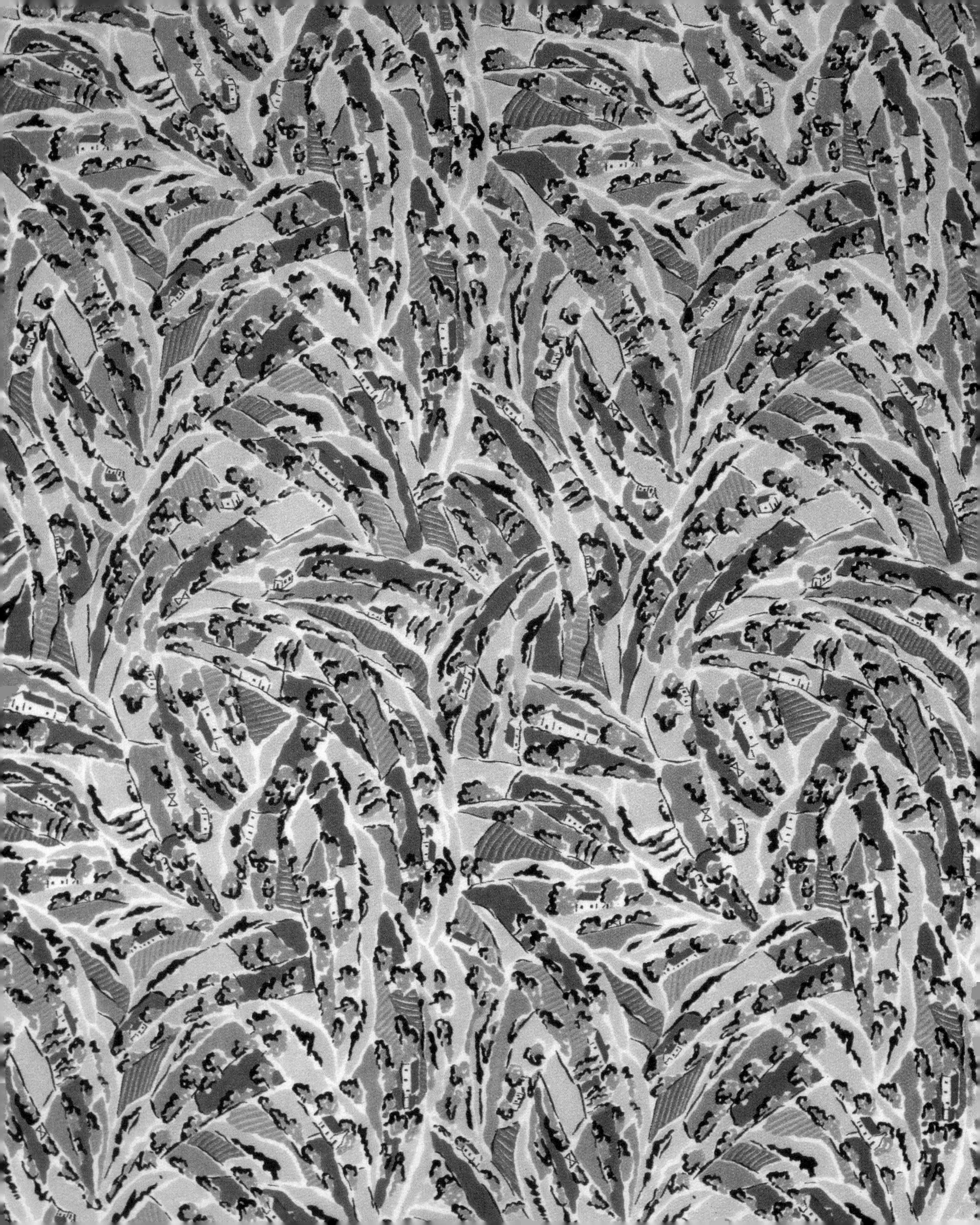

2

3

1 Seen from a distance, *Aerial View* looks like floral sprays, but on closer inspection, the rayon crêpe reveals details of the countryside. It was printed in 1936 by the Calico Printers' Association, Manchester.

2 Stripes of houses and trees alternate in *Riverside*, a dress fabric of screen-printed rayon crêpe made by the Calico Printers' Association, Manchester, in 1946.

3 Made in New York in the 1950s, Morton Sundour's furnishing fabric sample of *Rustic Americana* is printed with vignettes of historical American furniture and household objects.

1

1 *Houses*, a printed furnishing fabric designed by Joy Jarvis for Gerald Holtom in 1950, creates stripes from colourful terraced buildings.

2 Lulu Guinness designed *The House*, a box-shaped handbag that was crafted from embroidered satin and suede in England in 1998.

3 The pattern for *Red House* was designed by Claud Lovat Fraser in 1914, and then reissued by Liberty of London in 1973, printed on silk.

4 *Homemaker* was launched in 1957 by Ridgway Potteries, Staffordshire, for sale exclusively in Woolworth stores, and was in production until 1970. The surface design was created by Enid Seeney and the form by Tom Arnold.

5 *Soup Can* was designed by Lloyd Johnson for Patrick Lloyd, Britain, in 1973. Screen printed on shantung silk, it probably took inspiration from Andy Warhol's Pop Art images.

6 Entitled *The Old Furniture Shop*, this printed cotton furnishing fabric was designed by Lilo Hörstadius for Borås Wäfveri in Sweden in 1992.

7 This wallpaper specimen titled *Gustave* is from a John Line & Sons pattern book. The colour screen print was designed by Walter Krauer, and produced in Reading, Berkshire, between 1936 and 1959.

8 Produced by Wallpaper Manufacturers in 1955, *Malaga*, from the *Palladio* series, reflected the new British interest in foreign holidays, food and wine.

2

3

4

5

6

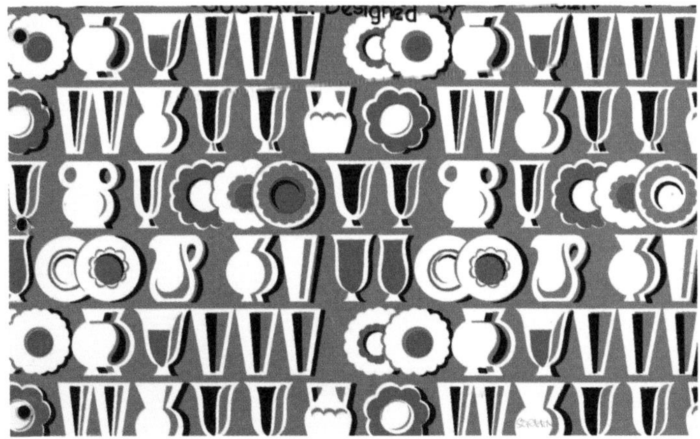


7

8

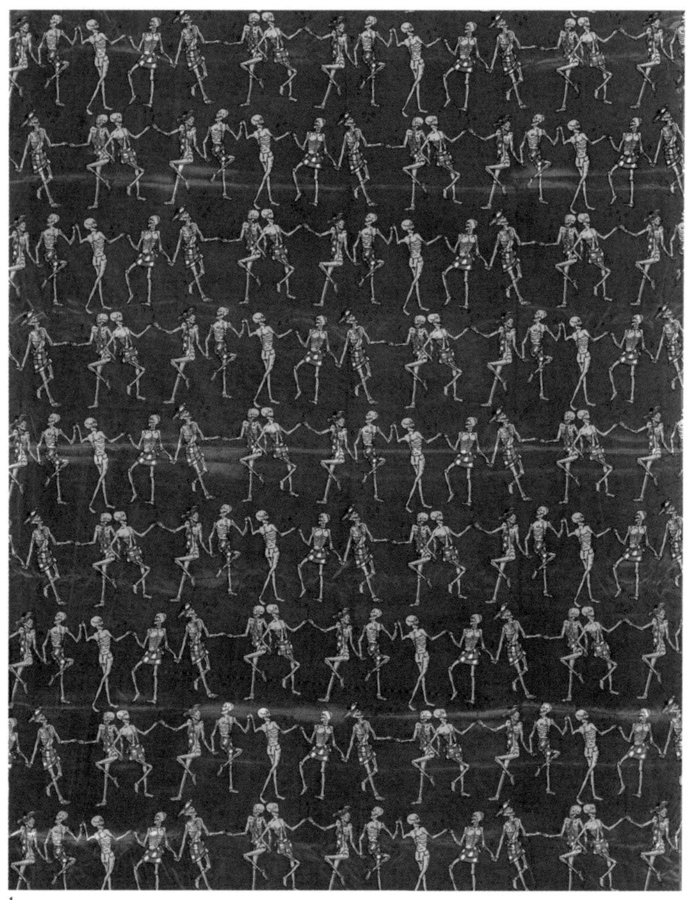
1

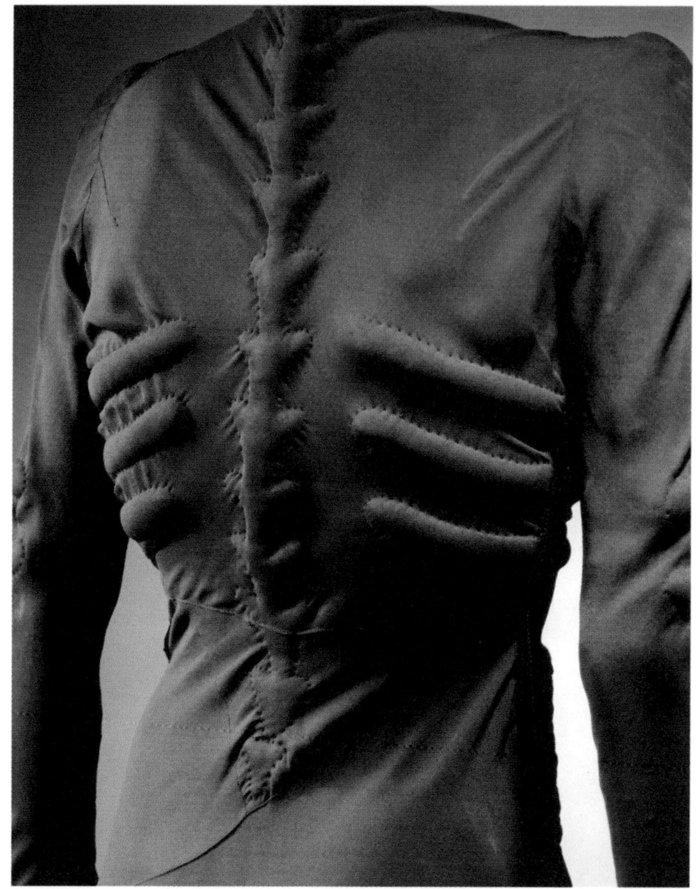
2

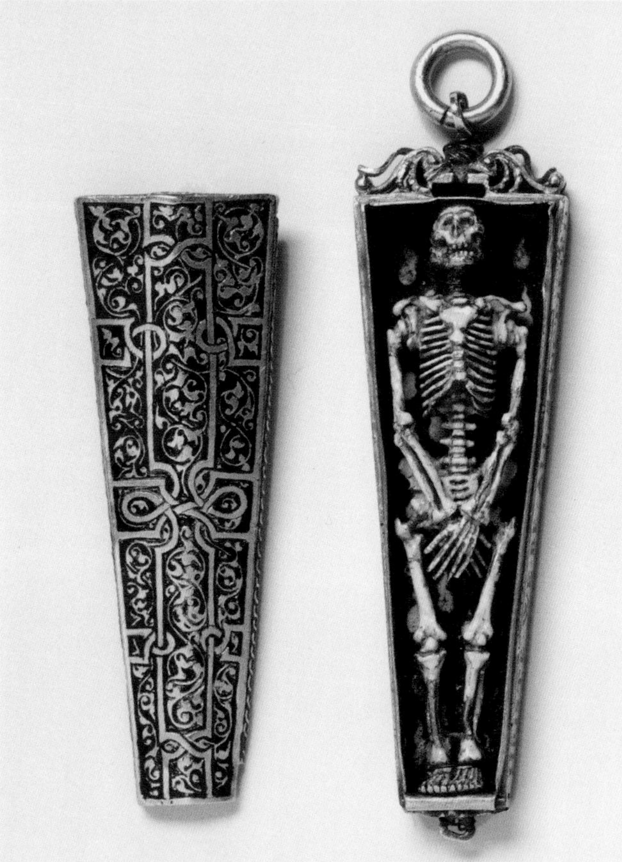
3

1 *Skeleton* is a printed synthetic satin, designed by the British label Red or Dead in 1993. It features singing and dancing skeletons wearing tartan skirts, ties and tam o' shanters.

2 Padded ribs and vertebrae stand out in profile from Elsa Schiaparelli's silk crêpe *Skeleton Dress*, from the designer's collaboration with Surrealist Salvador Dalí for her sensational *Circus Collection* in 1938.

3 Found in the grounds of Torre Abbey in Devon, this enamelled gold pendant from the 1540s in the form of a skeleton in a coffin is a memento mori – Latin for 'remember you will die'.

4 This *Salon* wallpaper specimen from a John Line & Sons pattern book was designed by Willy Hermann, with a design of stylized female figures wearing dresses. It was produced in Berkshire, England, between 1936 and 1959.

5 *Hammada*, the title given to this cotton furnishing fabric printed by Liberty of London in 1992, may refer to the single figures possibly drawn from the shadow puppet tradition of the Middle East.

6 Continuing on the theme above, *Saadian* depicts recognizably European theatrical types as shadow puppets, such as Puss in Boots.

7 *The Bough*, designed by Keith Vaughan for this screen-printed cotton crêpe manufactured by Edinburgh Weavers, Carlisle, in 1956, bears a nude male figure typical of the painter's work.

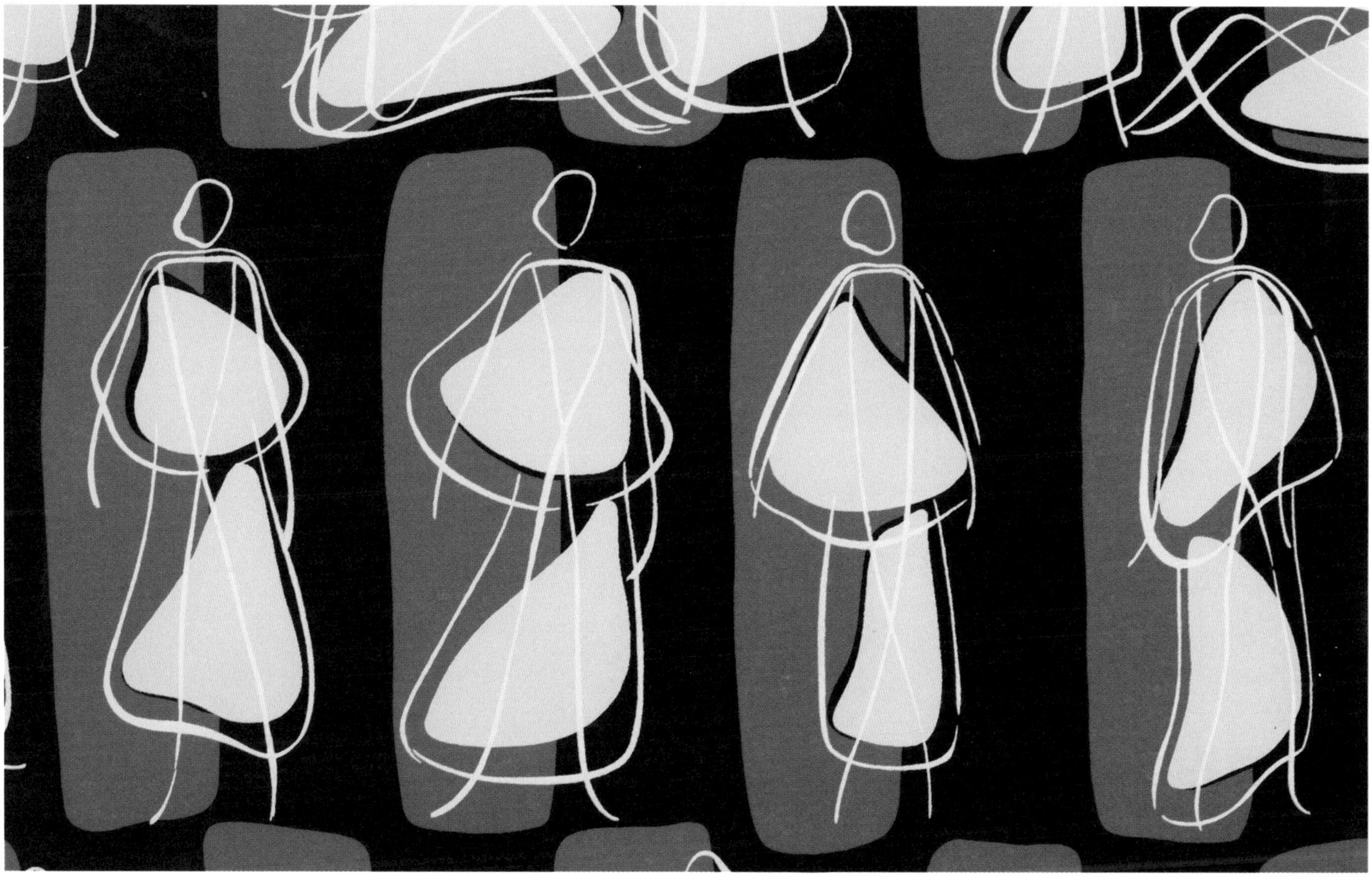

4

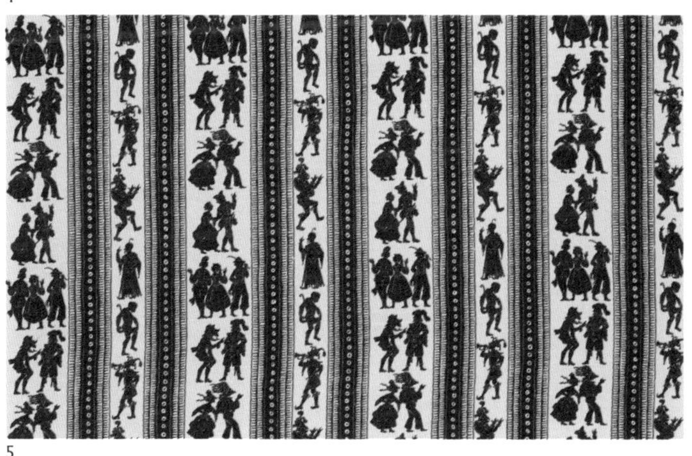

5

6

7

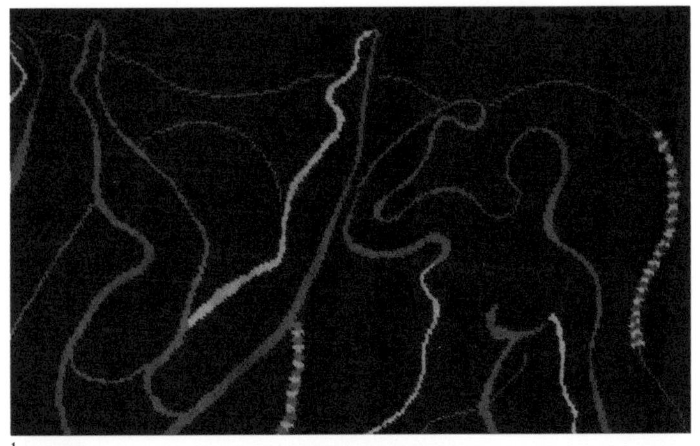
1

2

3

4

5

6

7

1 This is a detail of a hand-knotted carpet designed by Victor Boberman for the avant-garde French association of furniture designers DIM (Décoration Intérieure Moderne) between 1928 and 1929. The abstract composition features acrobats.

2 These lead-glazed earthenware tiles are part of a frieze in the Gamble Room, part of the V&A Café, made by Minton, England, from a design by Godfrey Sykes, London (1867–9).

3 Elenhank Designers, established in New York in 1946 by artist Eleanor Kluck and her architect husband, Henry, had *Open House* screen printed on linen in 1954.

4 The printed cotton silhouettes appliquéd to this cotton coverlet, made in England after 1851, include a figure based on a celebrated sculpture of a girl captured during the Greek War of Independence and sold as a slave (see fig. 5).

5 American sculptor Hiram Powers's greatly admired marble statue *The Greek Slave* was first exhibited in London in 1845. Minton, England. issued this smaller-scale Parian porcelain version in 1862.

6 Inspired by 17th-century French illustrations, Gary Page designed this printed cotton, *Improper*, for British fashion label Red or Dead in 1996. It was used for pyjamas and bedlinen.

7 *Dancing Women*, a linen furnishing fabric, was designed by British sculptor Frank Dobson and hand-block printed by his wife, Mary, in 1938.

1

2

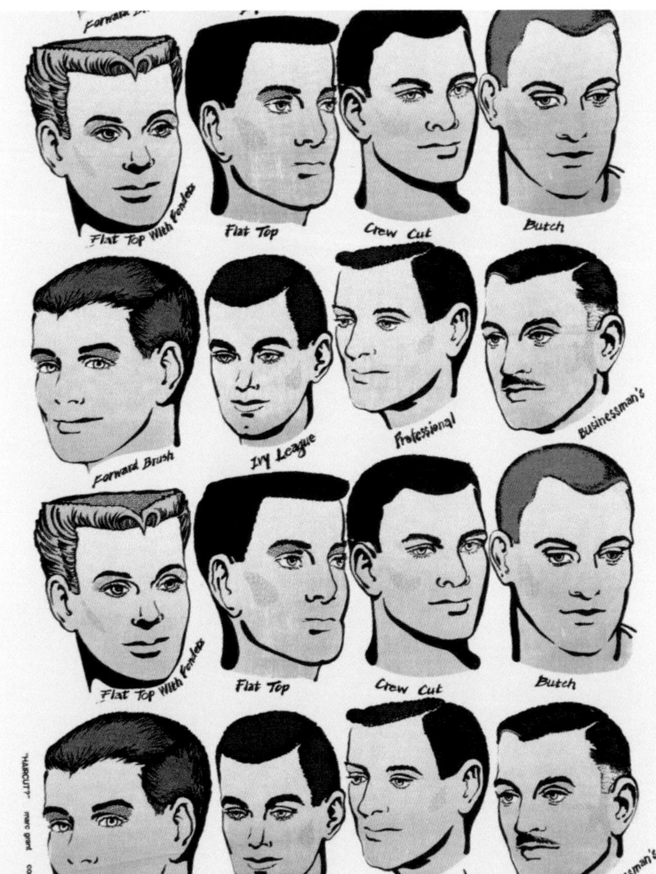
Flat Top With Fenders
Flat Top
Crew Cut
Butch
Forward Brush
Ivy League
Professional
Businessman's
Flat Top With Fenders
Flat Top
Crew Cut
Butch

3

4

5

1 *Clapping Hands* wallpaper was designed by Sonia Boyce and printed by the London Printworks Trust, for an installation in the group exhibition, *Wish You Were Here* (London and Newcastle, 1994).

2 The 1998 *Crosby* child's chair, designed by Gaetano Pesce, was manufactured in moulded resin and metal by Fish Design, New York. The back has a smiling face and the seat a profile.

3 This dress fabric of screen-printed cotton sateen is titled *Haircut? Yes Please!* It was designed by Marc Foster Grant and made by Michael Yates in Britain in 1973.

4 Eye miniatures came into fashion in Britain at the end of the 18th century. An attempt to capture 'a window into the soul', they were often striking pieces of jewellery. This brooch, made in England in the early 19th century, has a diamond tear.

5 *Cefalu*, a screen-printed furnishing fabric by John Drummond for Story Fabrics, was made in England in 1953. Its imagery references its namesake Sicilian coastal village.

6 This screen-printed rayon crêpe takes its name, *Lipsticks*, from its pattern. It was designed by British fashion designer Zandra Rhodes in 1968 for use in her fashion collections.

7 Salvador Dalí's famous *Mae West Lips* sofa derived from an idea of his British patron, Edward James. Made in London in 1937–8, this version has felted-wool upholstery and larvae-shaped appliqués.

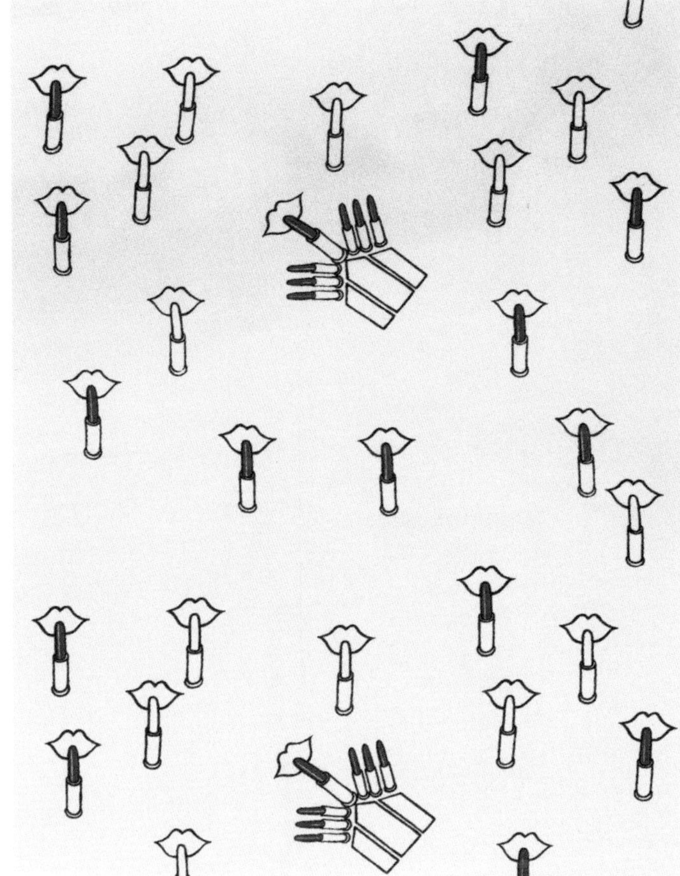

6

7

1 This porcelain plate from the series *Tema e Variazioni* was designed in Italy in the 1950s by Piero Fornasetti and transfer printed in black enamel on to blanks.

2 Sonia Boyce designed this screen-printed umbrella for the exhibition *Portable Fabric Shelters* at the London Printworks Trust, Brixton, in 1995.

3 *Westray*, an ornate textile design of stylized leaves, some shaped like eyes, was produced by Morton Sundour, Carlisle, in the 1960s.

4 This silk crêpe, designed by the French avant-garde writer and artist Jean Cocteau, was made into an evening dress by the Anglo-American couturier Charles James in Paris in 1938–9. The masks in the print may be portraits of Cocteau and his lover, the actor Jean Marais.

5 This silk jersey evening coat is one of the best examples of Elsa Schiaparelli's collaboration with Jean Cocteau. The embroidery is based on two of Cocteau's drawings, and was executed by the Paris firm Lesage in 1937.

6 This pair of gold and ruby brooches was designed by Paul Flato and made in the USA between 1940 and 1950. The pair would have been worn on either side of an open bodice.

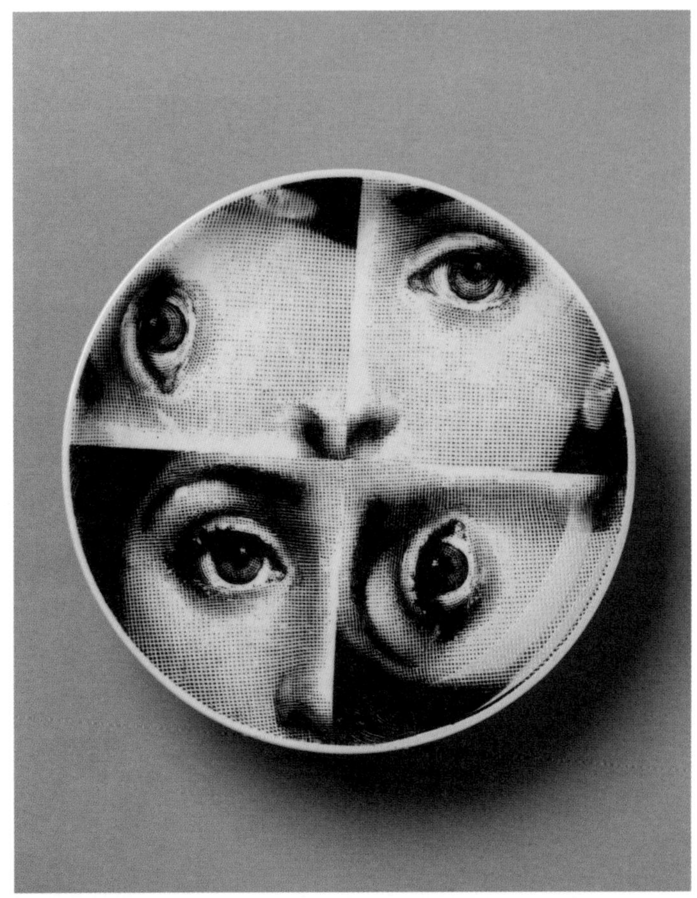

1

2

3

4

5

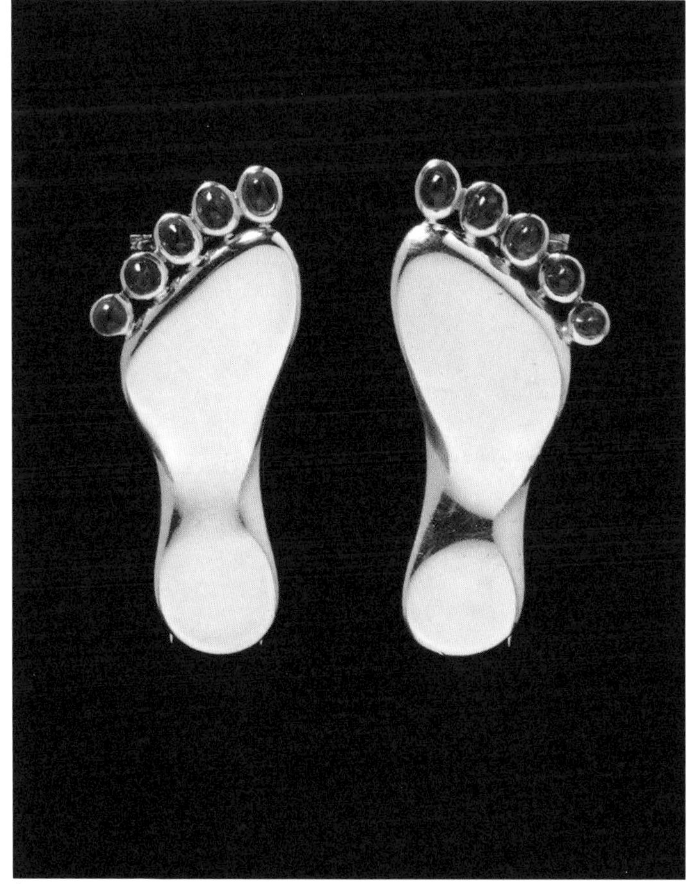

6

1

1 This wallpaper frieze has a design reproducing part of the Parthenon marbles, probably produced by Jeffrey & Co., London, in about 1851.

2 These porcelain figurines depicting dancing classical muses are one of a pair that were probably designed to stand together as a mantelpiece decoration. Painted with gold enamel, they were made in Europe in the 19th century.

3 The *Alcestis* wallpaper frieze depicts the figure of Alcestis, a princess from Greek mythology, as a caryatid standing alongside the winged personification of Love. Designed by Walter Crane, the paper was produced by Jeffrey & Co., London, in 1876.

4 French silk manufacturer Bianchini-Ferier produced this fabric with a pattern of Roman coins, some with figures in profile, for interior furnishings, in Lyon in 1920–1.

5 On *Statues*, an elegant printed linen furnishing fabric designed by Frank Dobson for Allan Walton Textiles, London, in 1938, goddesses morph into columns with Ionic capitals.

6 *Etruscan Head* is a screen-printed silk furnishing fabric designed by Marion Dorn, England, around 1939.

7 This Attic terracotta *lekythos* (oil flask) painted with four warriors in combat, dates to 6th-century BCE Greece.

2

3

4

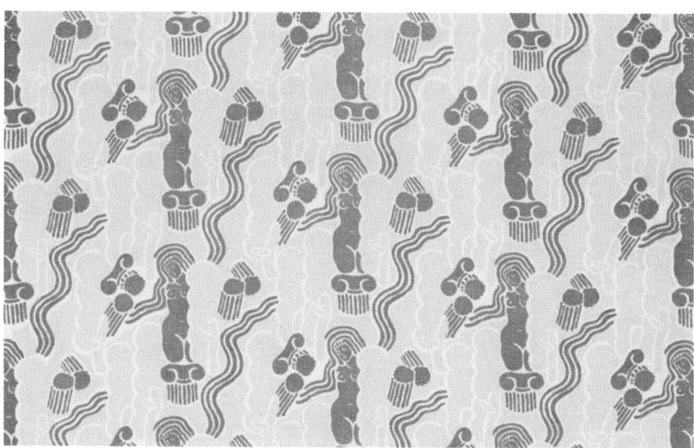
5

6

7

1

2

3

4

5

6

1 This cotton dress fabric, printed by Tootal Broadhurst Lee of Lancashire in 1938, depicts a woman dancing in a style of traditional European folk dress.

2 These cast-metal acrobat buttons, attributed to Jean Clément, adorn a silk twill jacket with a woven pattern repeat of horses. Elsa Schiaparelli designed the jacket as part of her *Circus Collection*, Paris, in 1938.

3 *Derby Day* cotton furnishing fabric, printed in Lancashire in 1925, depicts crowds of people enjoying the spectacle of the races.

4 Designed by George Sheringham for Tootal Broadhurst Lee around 1925, this roller-printed cotton takes inspiration from the scenes of fanciful country festivities on 18th-century printed toiles.

5 *Rhapsody*, made by Stehli Silks to American cartoonist John Held Jr's design in 1927, is a humorous take on polka dots. In this composition, the jazz musicians' faces and instruments printed in white on blue silk crêpe are the dots.

6 This is a diamond-point-engraved glass beaker by Willem Mooleyser of Rotterdam, the Netherlands, dating to 1685, with figures probably based on engravings by an Amsterdam artist.

7 Helen Wills Moody, American artist and top-ranked women's tennis player, designed *A Game of Tennis* for a printed dress silk by Stehli Silks, New York, in 1927.

7

1

1 *Indoor Sports* is a dinner or hostess dress of hand-painted synthetic fabric, probably made in London in 1937. The pattern depicts the outdoor sport of skiing.

2 A bird's-eye view of rows of seated spectators is printed on this crêpe de Chine, entitled *Stadium*. It was designed by René Clarke for Stehli Silks, New York, around 1928.

3 This furnishing silk has a woven pattern showing a game of polo, the world's oldest known competitive team sport. Made before 1964, possibly in Europe, the figures and their dress evoke the origins of the sport in the Middle East.

4 Designed by Rae Spencer-Cullen, *Paints and Palettes* was roller printed on satin for Squeekers, England, in 1974.

5 *Orpheus* wallpaper featuring stringed instruments, drums and French horns was designed by Arnold Lever and produced by John Line & Sons, England, for their series *Limited Editions* in 1951.

6 Screen printed with stylized book spines on linen, *Books* was designed by Jacqueline Groag for Liberty, London, in 1954.

7 This printed cotton dress fabric with a design of people playing on the beach was made in 1929 by the Calico Printers' Association, Manchester.

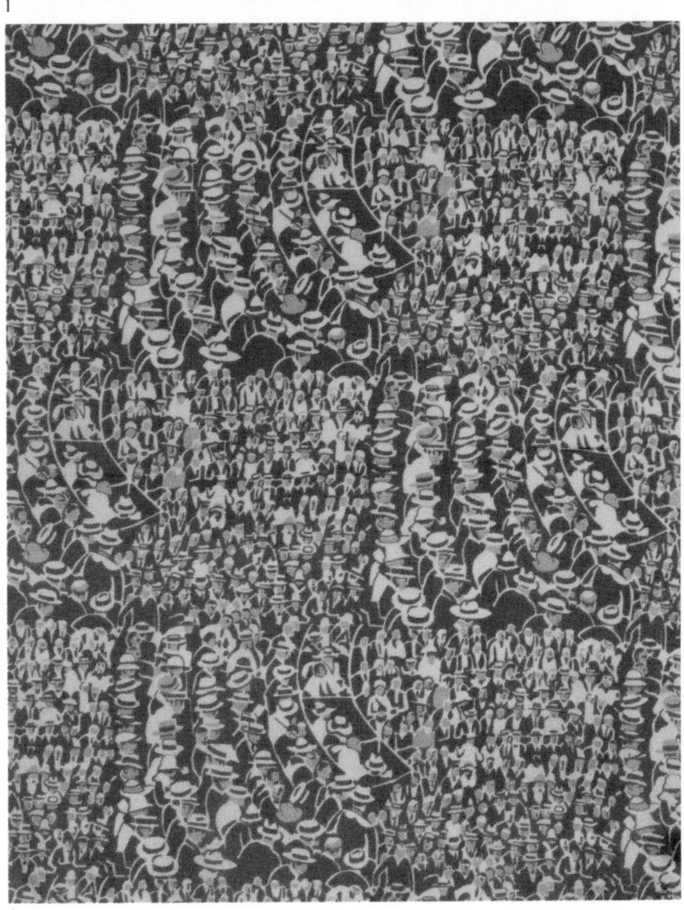
2

3

4

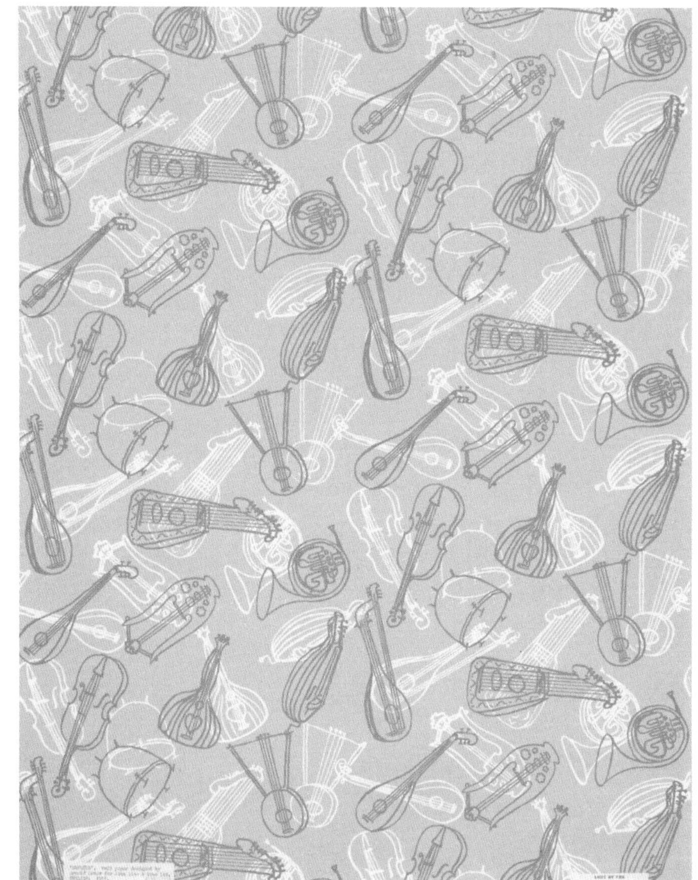
5

6

7

1

2

1 *Grand Prix*, designed by Rex Hays and Erwin Meayers for Heal's, London, around 1970, is a furnishing cotton printed with cars and race tracks, each labelled by name and date.

2 Roger Nicholson's *Locomotion* wallpaper design from the *Palladio* series depicts antiquated modes of transport; it was produced by Wallpaper Manufacturers, Manchester, in 1955.

3 *Puffing Billy* screen-printed cotton furnishing fabric with a train on a track, designed for a children's room, was created by Doreen Dyall for Heal's in 1962.

4 *The Pioneer Days*, a furnishing fabric from Morton Sundour's *Cumberland Prints* series, made in New York in the 1950s, features silhouettes of waggons, carriages, trains and houses in horizontal stripes.

5 This monoplane aircraft pattern was designed by architect and interior designer Raymond McGrath in London in the early 1930s for a house for a woman aviator, which unfortunately was never built.

6 This sample comes from a pattern book of silks manufactured by Bianchini-Férier, Lyon, France, around 1920. The biplane flying through a sunset is jacquard-woven.

7 Omnibuses, horse-drawn caravans, traction engines and cars fill the countryside on this printed furnishing fabric, *The Open Road*, designed by George Day for Tootal Broadhurst Lee, Lancashire, in 1925.

3

4

5

6

7

2

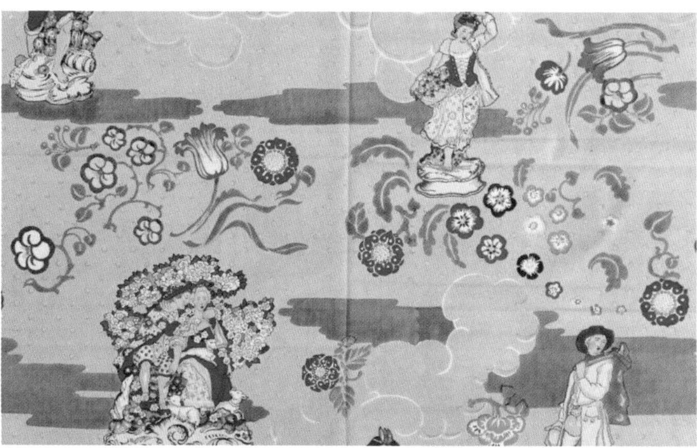

3

4

1 *Last Waltz*, a cotton dress fabric printed in 1942 for Tootal Broadhurst Lee, Lancashire, captures romance with couples dancing amid a joyous abundance or balloons and streamers.

2 This fustian – a linen and cotton fabric – has been dyed with madder and block printed with figures enjoying themselves around a country inn. It was made in the Netherlands in the mid-18th century.

3 *The Music Lesson*, with its printed design of bucolic ceramic figurines, comes from the Carlisle firm Morton Sundour's series *Cumberland Prints* from 1926 to 1928, and surely appealed to porcelain lovers.

4 Modelled by Joseph Willems after a painting by François Boucher, this porcelain group of a shepherd and shepherdess titled *The Music Lesson* (or *The Agreeable Lesson*) was made by the Chelsea porcelain factory in London around 1765.

5 This detail of *The Art of Loving*, a copper-plate-printed cotton furnishing fabric, possibly made by Favre, Petitpierre, Nantes, France, around 1785–90, is based on an engraving after a painting by the French painter François Boucher.

5

1 This cobalt-blue glass beaker (detail) made in Spain in the late 18th century has the inscription 'DA CLAUDIA BAQUERO' on one side and a heart pierced with an arrow on the opposite side.

2 Hungarian-born Tibor Reich, a pioneering textile designer, established his company in Stratford-upon-Avon in 1946. In *Anna*, a screen-printed cotton produced in 1969, he drew on Hungarian folk art, combining tradition with modernity.

3 This calf-leather handbag with brass trumpet handle comes from Irina Laski's witty *Fanfare* range of accessories made in England in 1992. It was inspired by John Tenniel's illustrations in Lewis Carroll's *Alice's Adventures in Wonderland* (1865).

4 This heart-shaped ring brooch made of gold has a romantic inscription engraved on the reverse; it was made in England or France around 1400.

5 *Carol* furnishing fabric, with a stylized floral and heart pattern with bold outlines, was produced by Morton Sundour, Carlisle, in the 1960s.

6 *Happy Dreams* screen-printed cotton, designed by Natalie Gibson for Conran Fabrics, England, in 1967, is a furnishing fabric that captures the exuberant mood of the times.

7 *Bird* furnishing fabric of jacquard-woven silk was designed by architect-designer E.W. Godwin with a formalized repeat of berried branches and birds for Daniel Walters & Son, London, in 1876.

1

2

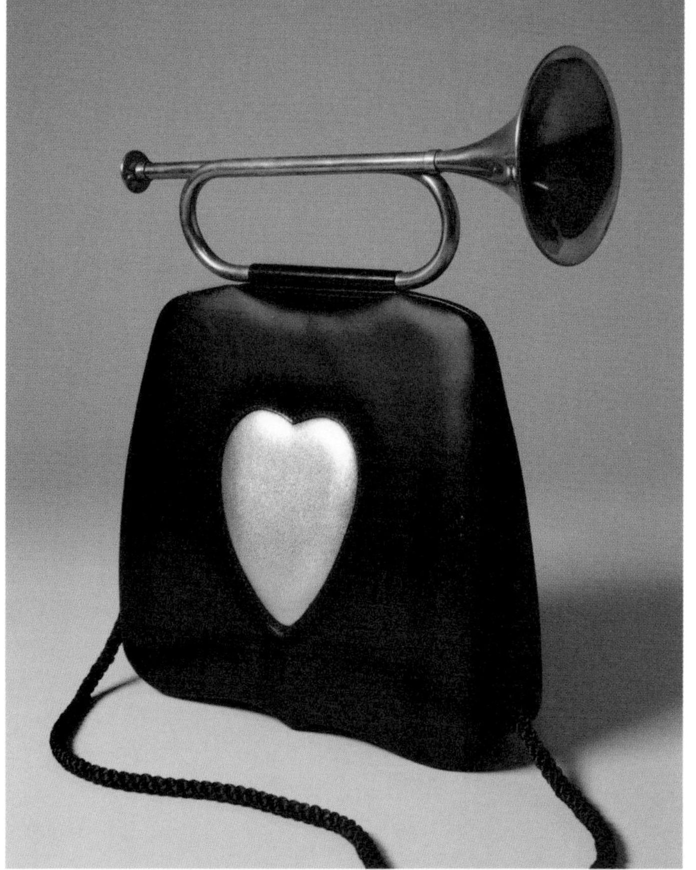

3

4

5

6

7

1

2

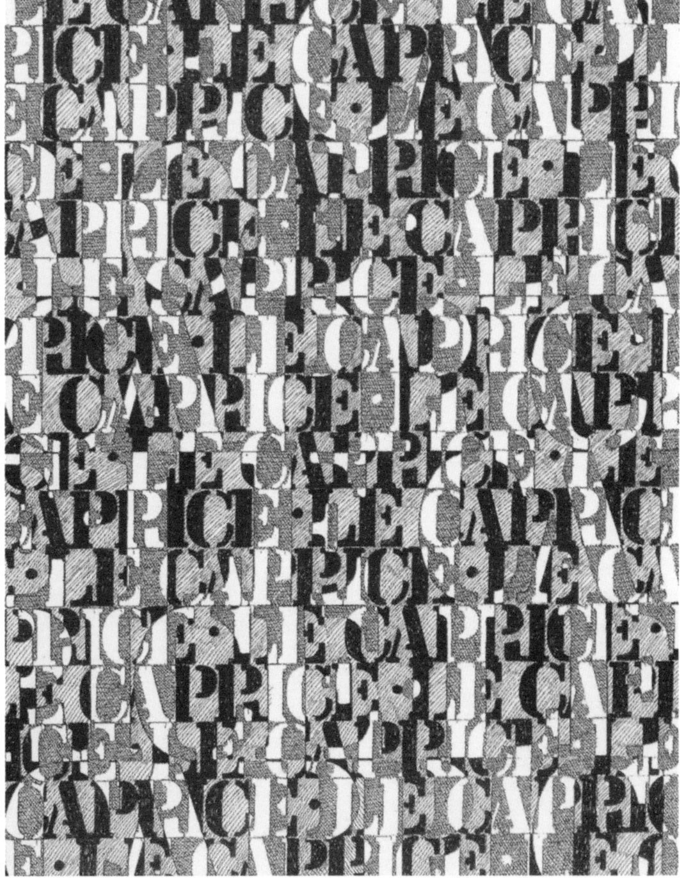

3

4

5

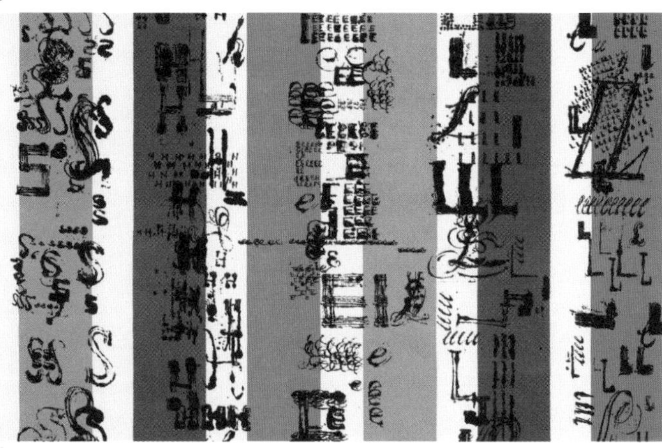
6

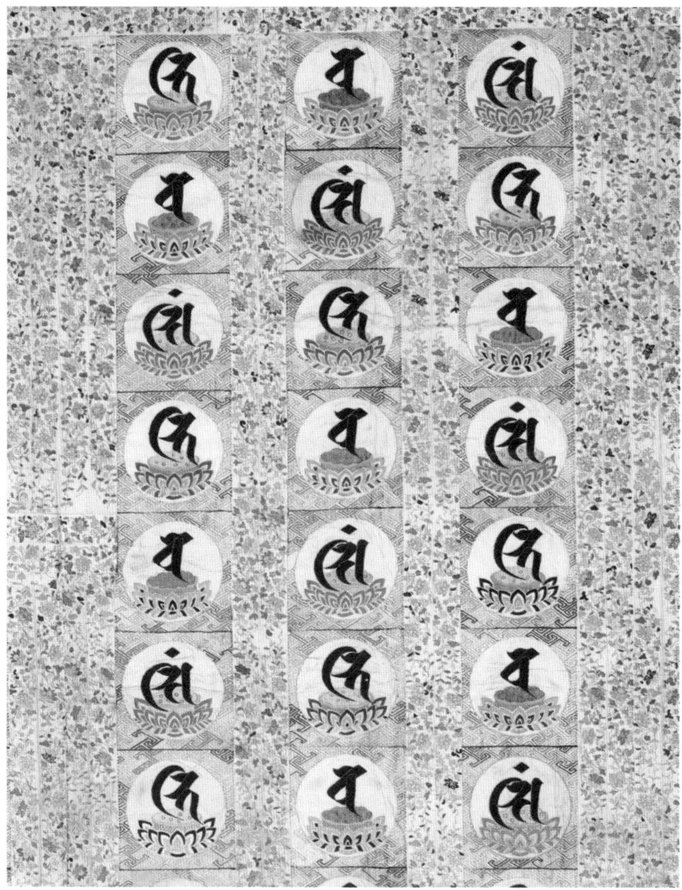
7

8

1 This furnishing fabric from a 1923 sample book compiled by Lyon-based silk manufacturer Bianchini Férier, has a jacquard-woven design of numbers.

2 *Chair Thing*, a child's chair made from a single piece of folded card, was designed by Peter Murdoch for Perspective Designs, London, in 1968.

3 Le Caprice restaurant, London, was a celebrity hotspot in the 1980s and 1990s. Its menu features a design of letters in a military-style stencil font.

4 This paper dress printed with a Persian-style script was produced by Diane Meyersohn and Joanne Silverstein for Dispo in London in 1967.

5 Letters and associated motifs arranged in coloured bands are transfer-printed onto this 1939 Wedgwood creamware mug, designed by Eric Ravilious.

6 In 1963 Shell Chemical Company commissioned Lucienne Day to design this screen-printed cotton curtain fabric, which was produced by Heal's, London. *Shell* is spelled out on a background of stripes.

7 This is a panel of a Buddhist silk textile embroidered with roundels framing characters in the Siddham script, made in Japan in the late 18th or early 19th century.

8 English abstract painter Ben Nicholson designed *Numbers* around 1933, a block-printed cotton with linocut numbers and letters that recall the influence of Cubism on newsprint and typography.

# ABSTRACT PATTERNS

**Opposite.** *Haydon* furnishing fabric, machine screen printed on cotton, designed by Haydon Williams for Heal's, London, in 1967.

1

2

3

1 *Bullseye 3* is a gift wrap design from 1967 by Nigel Quiney. It deploys a target motif, which will forever be associated with mod subculture in Britain.

2 Shown here is plate 3 from *Relais* by Édouard Bénédictus, a design folio published in Paris in 1930 using the *pochoir* technique, a printing process that uses stencils to create clean lines.

3 This design by Heussner & Co., England, dates from the 1700s. The watercolour, small in scale, was intended as a wallpaper and looks more like the work of mid-20th-century designers.

4 The colour palette and Op Art aesthetic of this printed furnishing fabric made by SICO, Germany, in the late 1960s, complement the modernity of its synthetic material.

5 British designer Mary Yonge's artwork for a printed textile from the 1960s to 1970s with overlapping discs could be mimicking oversized sequins.

6 Simple circles, possibly inspired by a slice of lemon or a metal washer, are screen printed on this cotton furnishing fabric, *Rondelle*, designed by Paul Augener for Heal's in 1956.

7 Henrietta Coster's 1966 *Perspective* pattern for Heal's creates an optical illusion, in which circles within circles increase and decrease in size.

8 Screen-printed furnishing fabric *Equilibrium*, designed by Gabrielle Fountain for Heal's in 1972, consists of a pattern resembling an abacus, with concentric 'beads' disposed in a balanced triangular formation.

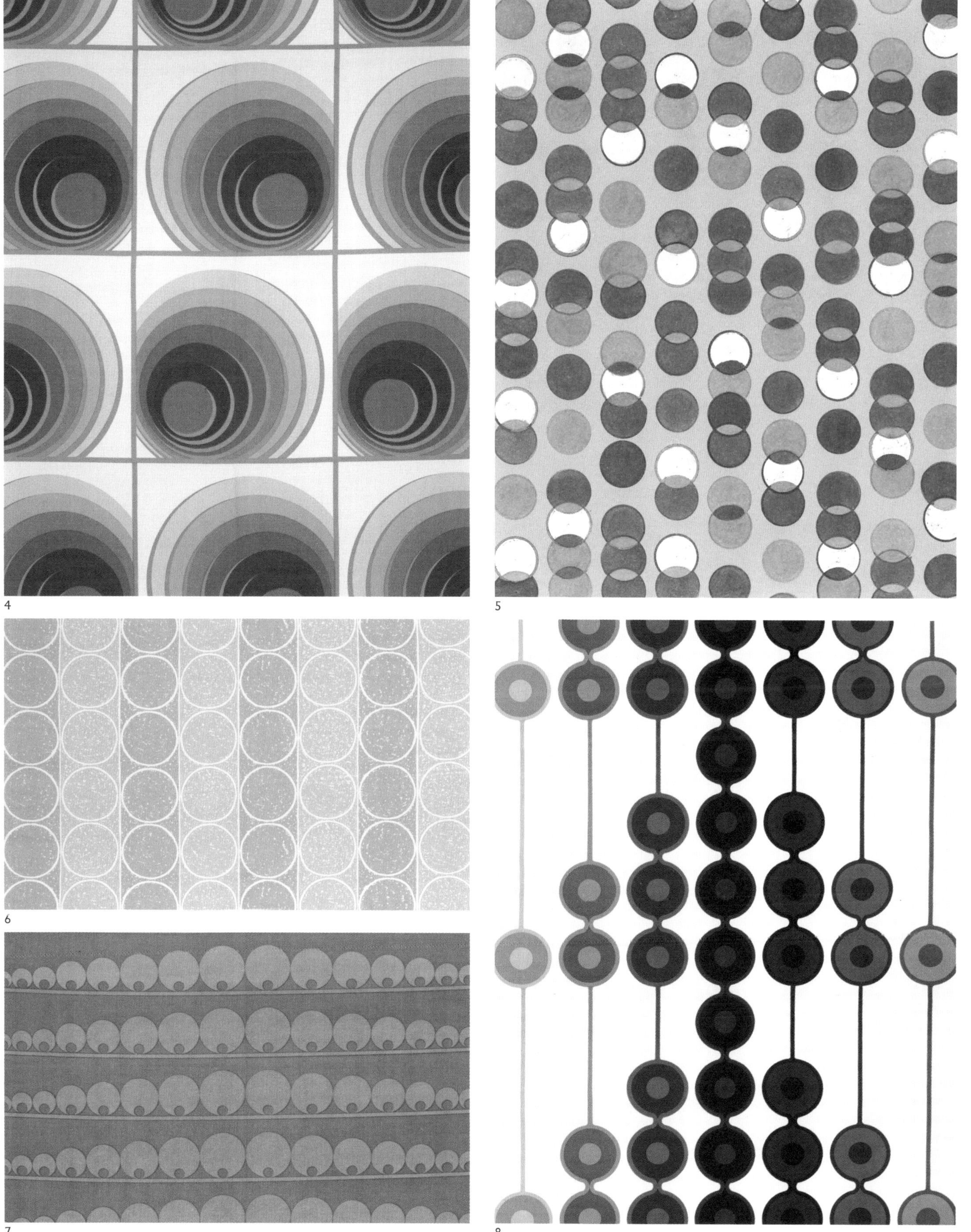

4

5

6

7

8

1 This brocaded velvet textile with roundels was made in Turkey between 1550 and 1600. Metal-wrapped threads create the pale rings of each circle.

2 Pearl-like beads line this pattern by Mary Yonge created around 1970 as part of her work as a freelance designer in London during the 1960s and 1970s.

3 This roller-printed cotton furnishing fabric in Art Deco style was manufactured for Sanderson, England, in 1930. The tonally segmented circles are superimposed upon each other to dynamic effect.

4 Designed by Minnie McLeish for William Foxton, London, in 1921, this roller-printed cotton furnishing fabric has geometric motifs typical of much European design of the decade.

5 The asymmetrical *Bel Air* armchair was designed by American artist Peter Shire in 1982 for Memphis and made in Milan in 1984.

6 A highly imaginative textile design from 1880 by Lechartier et Paul, France, evokes nuclear energy, predating the Atomic Age by about 65 years.

7 Mary Yonge's bold exploration of shape and colour was designed for a printed fabric for one of Britain's leading textile firms in the 1960s and 1970s.

8 Karin Heath Warming's 1960s to 1970s design for a printed tie fabric is an alternative to the usual spot and dot patterns.

9 This is another printed tie fabric design by Karin Heath Warming from the 1960s to 1970s.

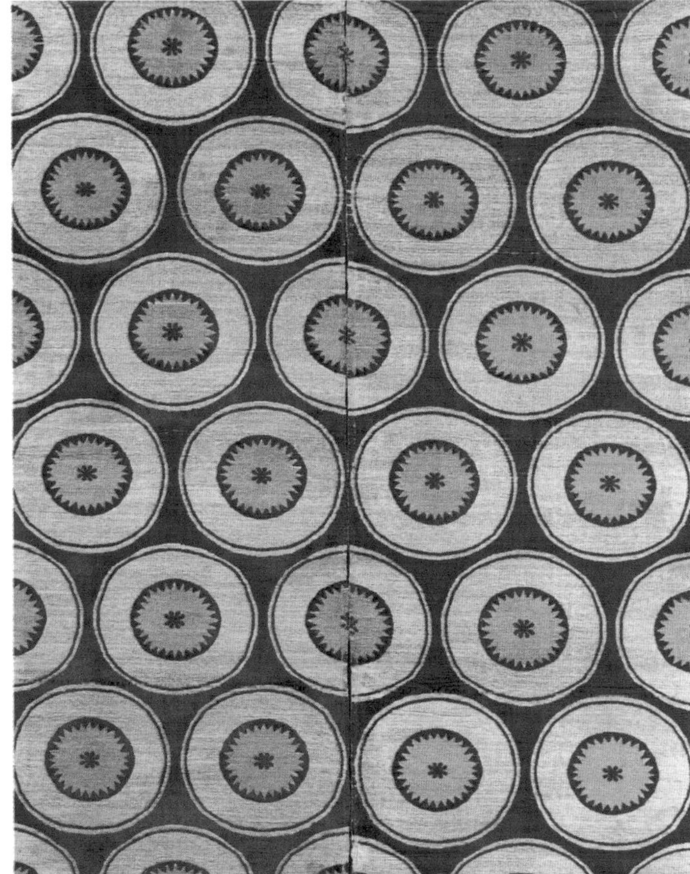

1

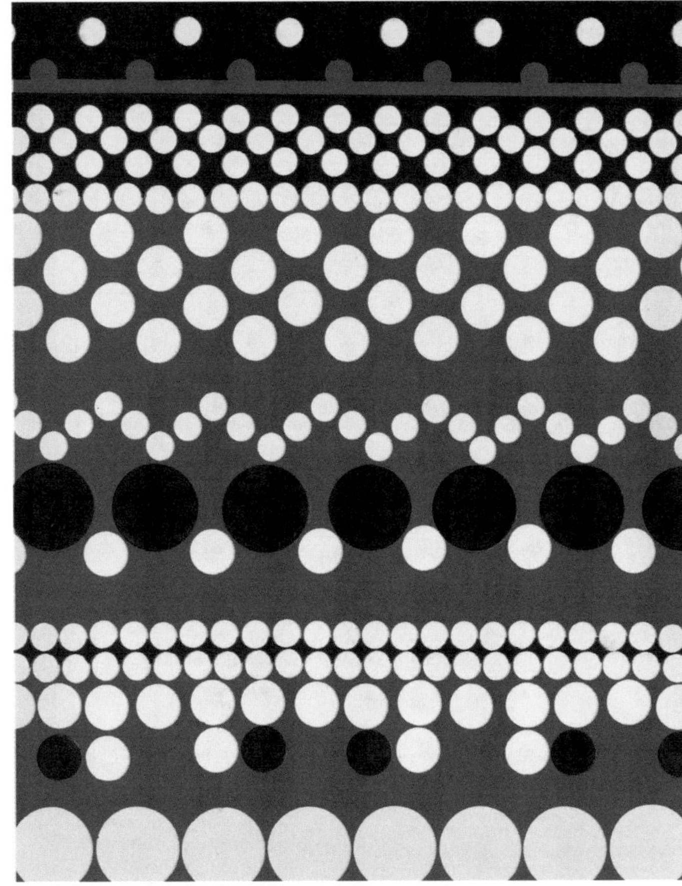

2

3

4

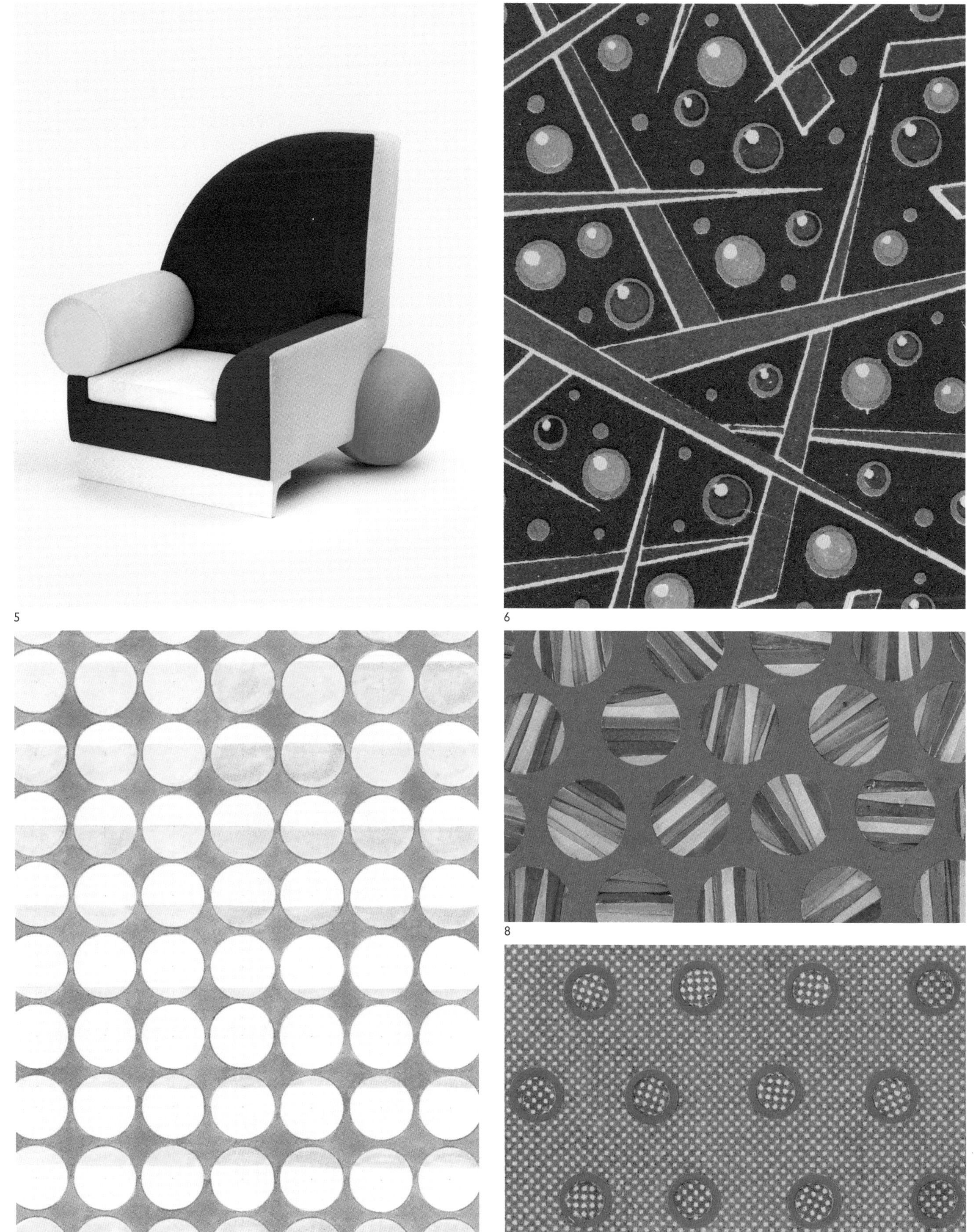

5

6

7

8

9

1

2

1 This example of indigo resist-dyed cloth, known as *adire*, was made by the Yoruba people of south-western Nigeria in the early 1960s. The pattern is called *Olokun* (goddess of the sea).

2 Barbara Brown's carefully calculated placement of line and colour creates the impression of three-dimensional boxes on printed furnishing fabric *Complex*, designed for Heal's, London, around 1967 to 1968.

3 *Brick*, one of Modernist designer Eileen Gray's folding screens (1923), is constructed of black lacquered panels, some with a central square in relief to enhance the surface and soften the geometric severity.

4 This child's dress from 1850s England is trimmed in black velvet in a Greek key design, or 'meander', one of the most basic – and ancient – forms of linear pattern, symbolizing infinity or the eternal flow of things.

5 Nigel Quiney creates an aesthetic statement with his *Cubic* wrapping paper of small geometric shapes, made in London in 1972.

6 In this late 19th-century patchwork quilt, small pieces of fabric in geometric shapes in light, dark and medium tones are sewn together to produce the geometric design known as 'tumbling blocks'.

7 Jacob (Jacques) Dimoldenberg trained in print design in Paris, before moving to Manchester, where he designed fabrics for shirtings, scarves, pyjamas and ties. He created this design for a woven silk tie around 1930.

3

4

5

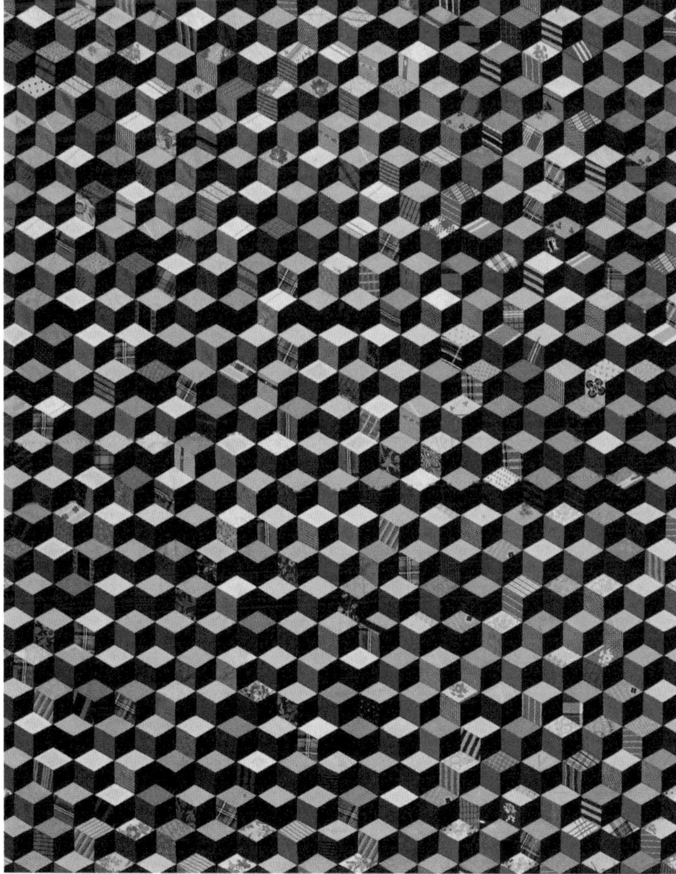

6

7

1

2

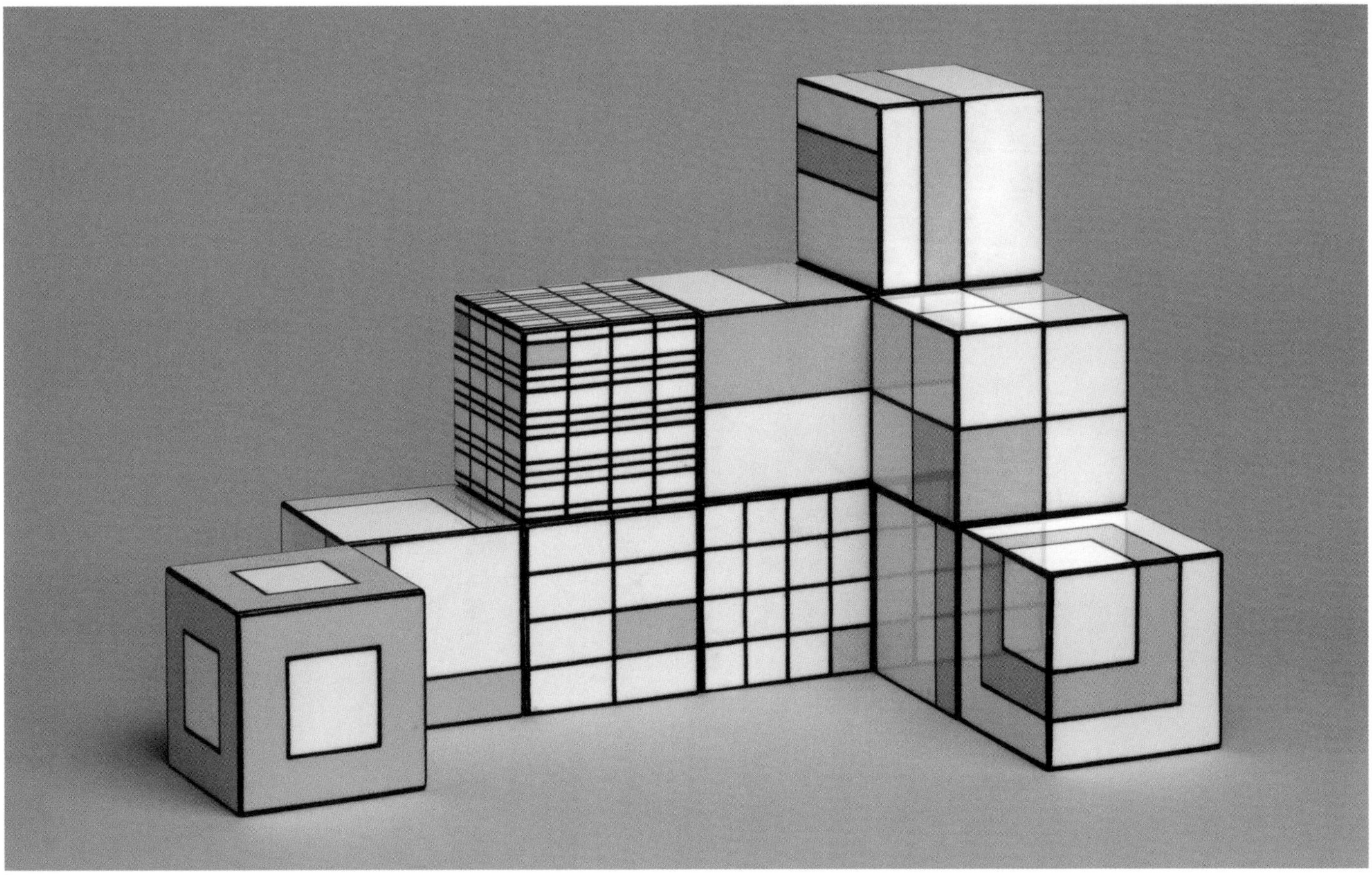

3

1 *Chequers*, a cotton satin furnishing fabric, was designed in 1949 by Terence Conran and displayed at the 1951 Festival of Britain. It was screen printed in Lancashire by David Whitehead.

2 The *Toccata* wallpaper pattern designed by Peter Shuttleworth was produced by Lightbown Aspinall in 1955 for the first range of *Palladio* wallpapers commissioned by Wallpaper Manufacturers, Manchester.

3 Glenys Barton's *Graphic Permutations* was awarded a Diploma of Merit when it was exhibited at the V&A's *International Ceramics* exhibition in 1972. The cubes are slip-cast in bone china with silk-screen decoration.

4 Wendy Ramshaw and David Watkins designed these *Optik Art* earrings, inspired by Dutch artist Piet Mondrian, for a collection of screen-printed Perspex fashion jewellery made in London between 1963–1965.

5 This cotton, designed by J.C. Howarth and jacquard-woven by Turnbull & Stockdale in Lancashire in 1933, gives the illusion of folds through a manipulated matrix of squares.

6 Surprisingly modern in its appearance, this geometric design is included in the 'Mulhouse albums', a collection of 1780s to 1880s textile designs.

7 The optical illusion of *Comet*, a furnishing fabric produced by Morton Sundour in Carlisle between about 1960 and 1970, results from the juxtaposition of concave and convex shapes.

4

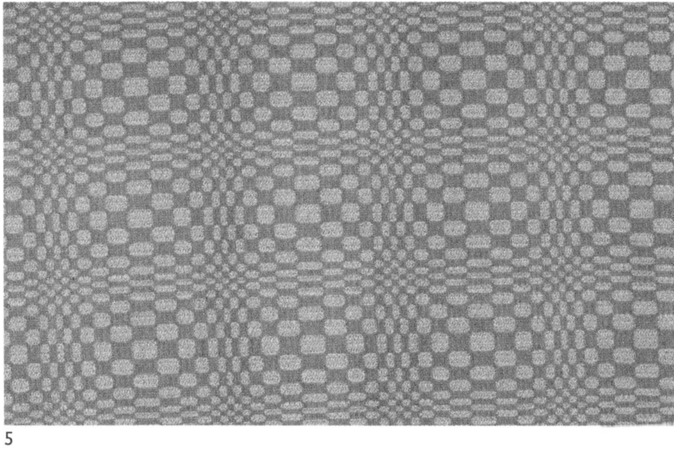
5

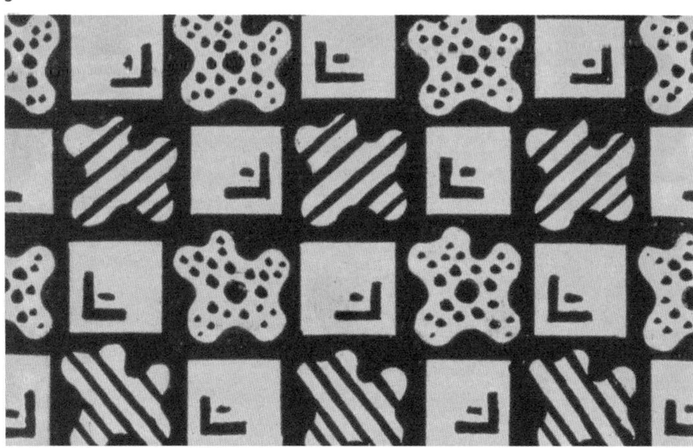
6

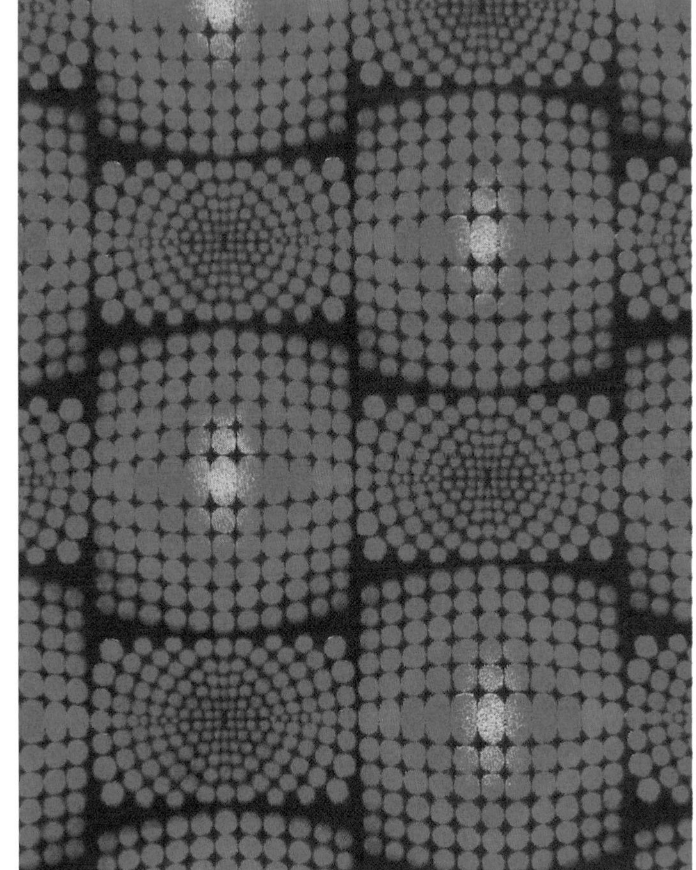
7

1

1 The bold shades and geometric style of Lucienne Day's *Isosceles* design reflected the optimistic mood of post-war Britain when it was produced as a curtain fabric by Heal's in 1955.

2 A simple geometric motif is mixed with a spot of neon to make a fresh design for a tie fabric, by Karin Heath Warming, England, in the 1960s to 1970s.

3 This cigarette case designed by Gérard Sandoz in Paris in 1929 is decorated with a geometric design made of lacquer, a popular medium with artist-jewellers because it did not chip as easily as enamel.

4 Made in 1933 by the Calico Printers' Association, Manchester, the geometric printed cotton design is softened by combining wavy horizontal lines with vertical zig-zags.

5 The textile firm L.F. Foght commissioned some of the best Danish artist-designed textiles. The painter William Scharff designed this screen-printed furnishing fabric *Fyr* (pine tree) in 1956.

6 *Pythagoras*, a furnishing fabric, was designed in 1952 by Swedish architect Sven Markelius, and produced in the 1960s by Nordiska Kompaniet Textilkammare, featuring a maths-inspired print of triangles.

7 *Isotop*, the title of this furnishing fabric of 1955 by Vide Jansson for Eric Ewers, Sweden, alludes to the chemical elements that inspired the Festival Pattern Group at the Festival of Britain.

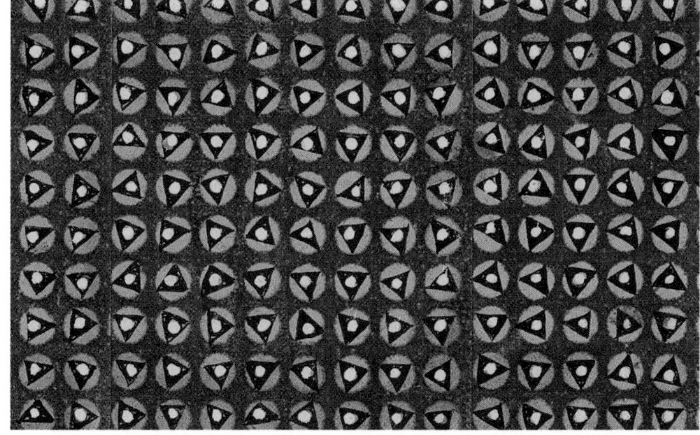

2

3

4

5

6

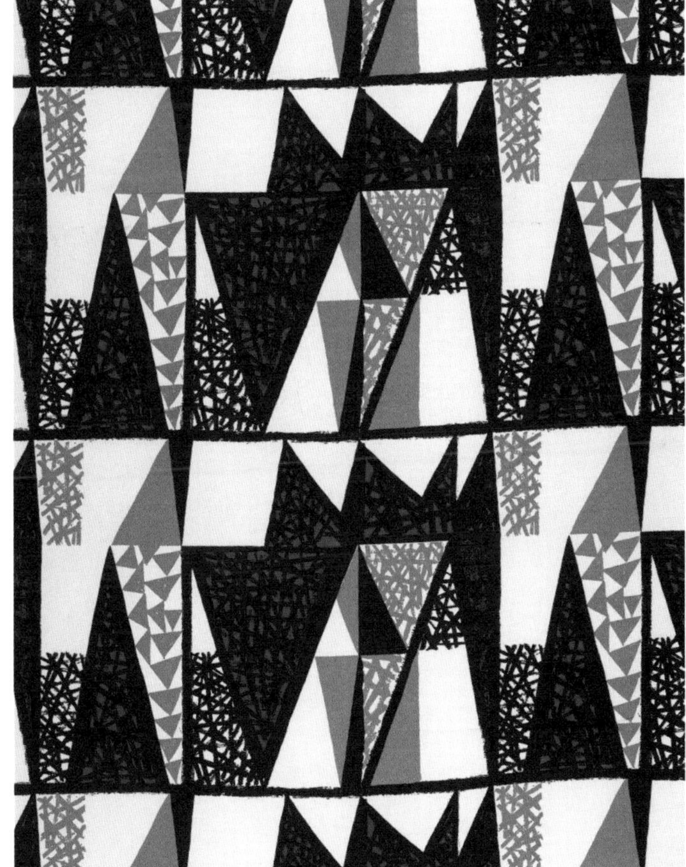
7

1

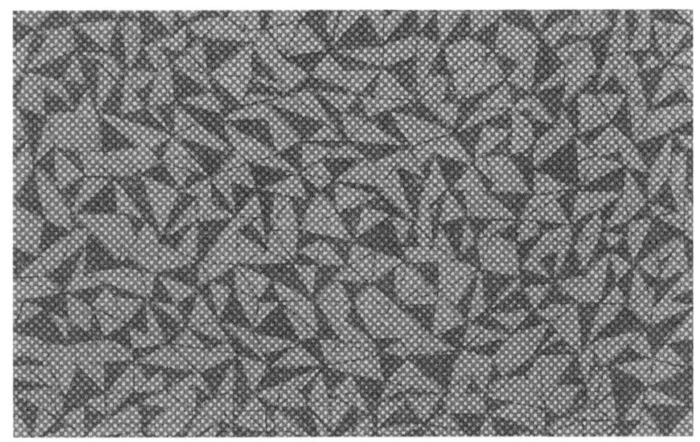

2

3

4

5

6

7

1 Designed by Karin Heath Warming as a tie fabric, this small repeat pattern blurs the line between geometric and maritime signal flag. It was made in England in the 1960s to 1970s.

2 A textile design by Karin Heath Warming combines an all-over graphic design of origami triangles with a Ben Day dot pattern; made in England in the 1960s to 1970s.

3 This detail is from a cotton, resist-dyed, ceremonial skirt cloth (*dodot*), made on the Coromandel Coast of India for the Javanese market in Indonesia.

4 Produced by the Calico Printers' Association, Manchester, in 1929, this warp-printed cotton textile features an Art Deco abstract geometric design.

5 *Roulette* wallpaper of stylized divided pinwheels was designed by artist Deryck Healey for the *Palladio 8* range in 1968 for Sanderson-Rigg, Bridlington, Yorkshire.

6 Decorated with typically Cubist motifs in red and black lacquer and brass, this bangle by Jean Dunand was made in Paris around 1925.

7 This is an early 20th-century fabric from Indonesia, patterned with bands woven with the weft-ikat technique.

8 Sanderson, England, manufactured this roller-printed furnishing cotton in 1928. The alternating dark and bright triangles and small diamonds are typical of 'Jazz Age' patterns.

8

1

2

3

4

1 Art Deco-style *Telemachus* wallpaper was designed by Eddie Squires for the *Palladio 8* series in 1968 for Sanderson-Rigg of Bridlington, Yorkshire.

2 This Korean porcelain flask (1750–1850) has a hexagon pattern above which are bats between bands of scrolls.

3 Featuring a pattern designed to imitate moulded plasterwork, this ceiling paper dating from around 1830 was removed from Clandon Park, Surrey.

4 These hexagonal glazed fritware tiles, decorated in blue on white, were made in Damascus, Syria, in the 14th or 15th century.

5 The *Octavia* screen-printed wallpaper pattern of octagons filled with circles was designed by Inge Cordsen for the *Palladio 8* series in 1968 for Sanderson-Rigg of Yorkshire.

6 This wallpaper pattern designed by Owen Jones interlocks hexagons, rosettes and funky Ys; possibly produced by John Trumble & Co., London, 1850s.

7 With a pattern of linked octagons imitating carving or stucco work, this ceiling paper (*c.*1825–75) is from a house in La Haute Ville, Vaison, France.

8 L. Anton Maix, New York, screen printed Pierre Kleykamp's 1954 design *Infinity* on cotton. Coloured and patterned hexagonal tiles are combined.

9 Small hexagons of brightly coloured woollen cloth make up this detail from a quilt made by Francis Brayley, who served as a private in India, around 1864–77.

5

6

7

8

9

1 Designed by nendo and manufactured in collaboration with Ochiai-Seisakusho, Tokyo, in 2010, the visually arresting yet functional *21400 mm chair* is made from bent and welded powder-coated steel.

2 Designed by Astrid Sampe in 1954, *Windy Way* was screen printed on cotton by Ljungbergs Textiltryck for Nordiska Kompaniet in Sweden. The design is characterized by vertical stripes pierced at intervals with rhythmic diagonals or arrowheads.

3 This printed voile dress fabric with abstract tessellation pattern was manufactured by Tootal Broadhurst Lee, Lancashire, in 1929.

4 Dating from the 1700s, this watercolour rendering for a wallpaper design by Heussner & Co., England, is in the style of a woven textured pattern resembling wicker or rattan.

5 Traditionally made by women throughout the Yoruba region of south-western Nigeria, indigo-dyed cottons (*adire*), like this example (*c*.1964), are decorated using a resist-dyeing technique.

6 This flash of pattern, like an elongated variation on the heraldic ermine design, is from a pattern book used for textiles; from England, designed late 18th to mid-19th century.

7 The silhouette of this Biba dress, made in London in 1973, harks back to the 1930s. The striped black and tan jersey ensemble is cut at alternating angles to enhance the Art Deco illusion.

1

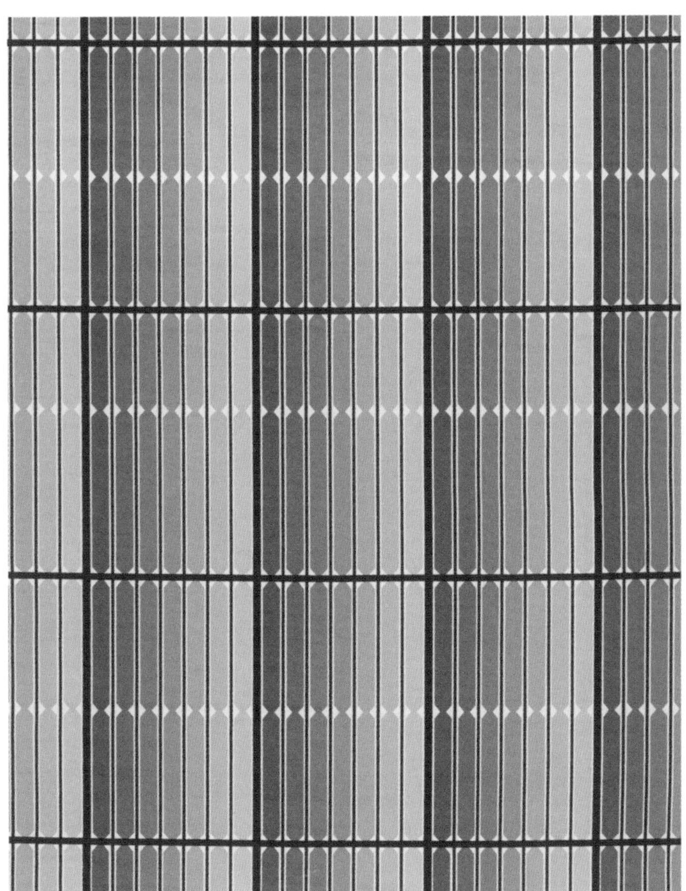

2

3

4

5

6

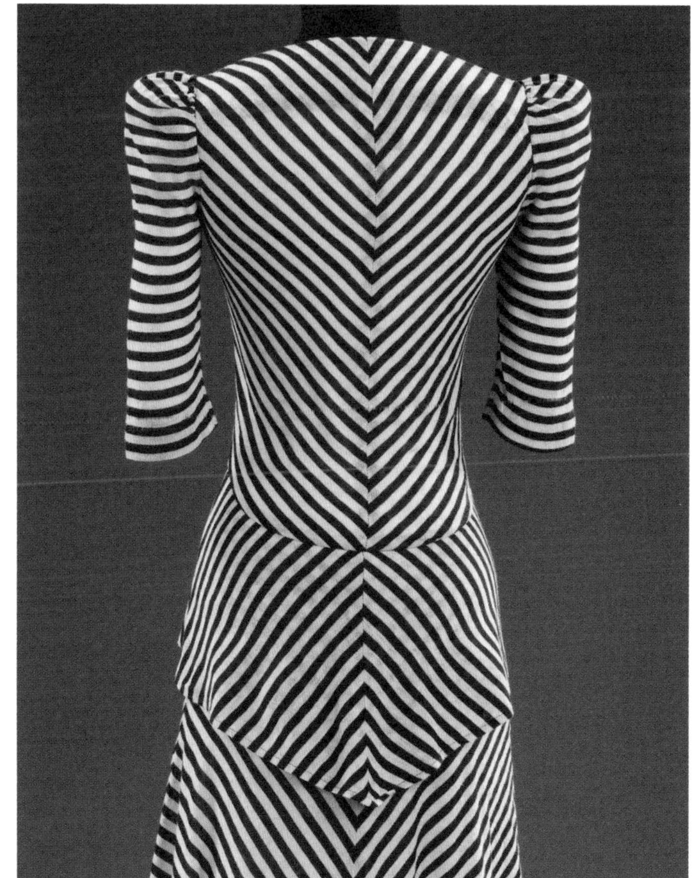
7

1

1 *Galleria*, designed by Barbara Brown and manufactured by Heal's, London, in 1969 for furnishings, features large-scale curves in vibrant colours. It was inspired by the designer's interest in geology.

2 The screen-printed cotton crêpe *Frequency*, designed by Barbara Brown for Heal's in 1969, draws on the movement of the Earth's crust and folds in rock strata.

3 This detail of vibrantly striped mid-20th-century fabric is from the back of a woman's dress from the Afghan-Pakistan border area.

4 Kari Sorteberg, the first permanent designer at Hjula Væveri in Oslo, arranged simple geometric shapes in muted colours in the pattern for this 1956 screen-printed rayon furnishing fabric, one of her many curtain fabrics.

5 René Lalique's Art Deco *Actinia* vase, press-moulded in opalescent glass with blue staining, was made at the Lalique glassworks at Wingen-sur-Moder in Alsace, France, from 1937 to 1947.

6 *Neon* wallpaper designed by Tony Fraser for the *Palladio 9* series in 1971, manufactured by Sanderson, London, was screen printed on vinyl with metallic colours.

7 This wool and cotton jacquard-woven pattern of undulating waves, designed by Élise Djo-Bourgeois, was hand-woven in France for Metz & Co. around 1930. Her designs were popular for modernist interiors.

2

3

4

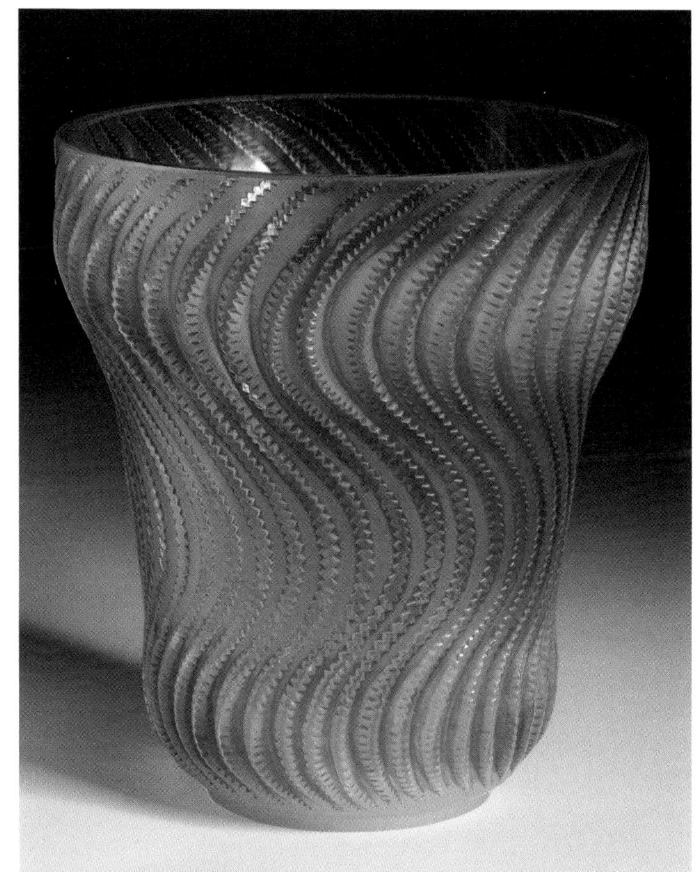
5

6

7

1

2

1 *Ziggurat* wallpaper was designed in 1968 by Margaret Cannon for the *Palladio 8* series, produced by Sanderson-Rigg in Bridlington, Yorkshire.

2 *Mosaic*, a furnishing fabric probably woven in France around 1931, was modern in its use of rayon with cotton and the angular overlapping geometric shapes in its pattern.

3 Designed by Lucienne Day in 1971, *Integration* curtain fabric was screen printed in England for Heal's. Rectangles form the surface pattern, running parallel to the warp and weft, arranged in herringbone fashion.

4 This piece of Rajasthani fabric has been resist dyed to produce a striking zig-zag pattern. It was made in the 19th century.

5 This printed linen, with abstract undulating drapes designed by F. Gregory Brown for William Foxton, London, in 1922, won a gold medal at the 1925 decorative arts exhibition in Paris.

6 Decorated with innumerable small bubbles and geometric shapes cut out on the outer surface, this thick-walled art glass vase by Maurice Marinot was made at the Viard Frères glassworks at Bar-sur-Seine, France, in 1932.

7 English designer Claud Lovat Fraser based this 1920s geometric striped fabric for Willam Foxton on wall paintings discovered on archaeological expeditions to Egypt.

3

4

5

6

7

1

2

3

4

5

6

1 Margaret Cannon designed *Quarto* for a furnishing fabric for the English firm Hull Traders in 1966. The bold geometric design of stylized rosettes is printed on printed cotton sateen.

2 *Broadway East* wallpaper by John Garnett for the *Palladio 9* series, produced by Sanderson-Rigg, Bridlington, is a melting pot of sophisticated Art Deco glamour and style and 1970s disco dancing and hedonism.

3 *Carnival 3* wrapping paper, designed by Nigel Quiney in London in 1967, has a geometric pattern of quatrefoils.

4 Full of colour, this detail is from a child's dress, homemade in Scotland in 1965, with a geometric print evoking the fractured images produced in a kaleidoscope toy.

5 *Sikhara* wallpaper, designed by Peter Jones for the *Palladio 9* series, blends classical Art Deco motifs with sci-fi elements. It was manufactured by Sanderson, London, in 1971.

6 Printed with a kaleidoscopic pattern of stars, circles, squares and diamonds, *Ceramica* wallpaper was designed by Judith Cash for the *Palladio 8* range in 1968 for the Yorkshire-based firm Sanderson-Rigg.

7 Based on copper foil printed circuit boards used in electronics, this screen-printed cotton designed by Eddie Squires for Warner & Sons, England, in 1968, is appropriately entitled *Circuit*.

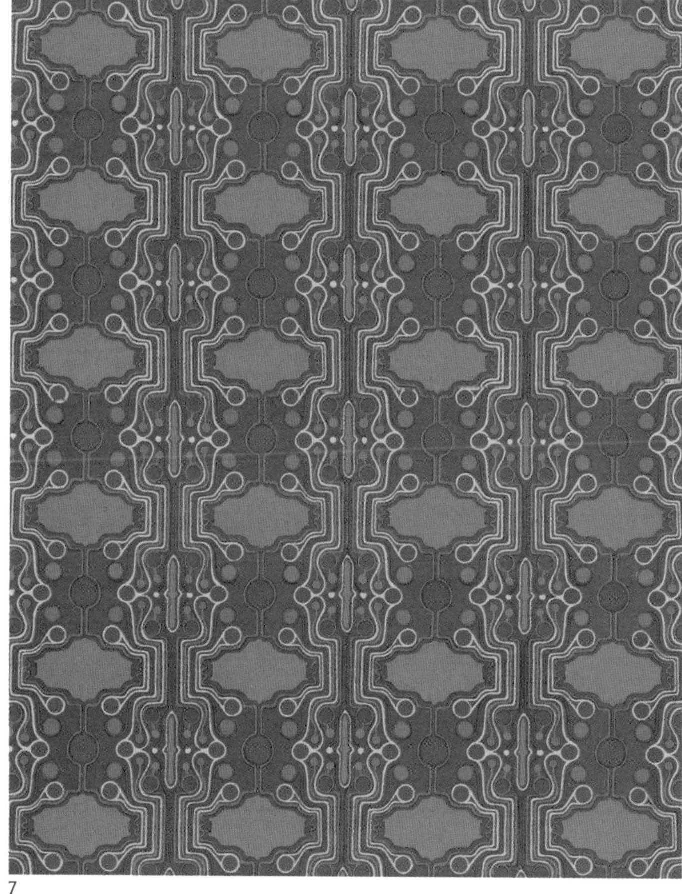

7

1 *Zeppelin* hexagonal wallpaper was designed by Eddie Pond for the *Palladio 9* range produced by Sanderson, London, in 1971.

2 A book illustration by Christopher Dresser shows a snowflake design suitable for a ceiling or dado pattern, from *Studies in Design*, published by Cassell, Peter & Galpin, London, in 1876.

3 Jali screens, such as the one depicted in this drawing from around 1882 taken from a rubbing of a stone decoration in Sikandra, Agra, India, facilitated the circulation of cool air.

4 This portion of a tilework panel, made of yellow sandstone and covered with enamel colours, is from a 14th- or 15th-century tomb in Bukhara in Uzbekistan.

5 Stehli Silks, New York, modernized partly by commissioning contemporary artists. Poster designer Charles Buckles Falls created *Pegs*, which was printed on silk crêpe in 1927.

6 This geometric printed dress fabric was produced by the Calico Printers' Association, Manchester, around 1935.

7 The *Casablanca* sideboard from 1981, designed by Ettore Sottsass for the first collection by Memphis, Milan, combines storage and display and serves as a room divider.

8 Designed by Gay Dulley for Heal's in 1966, this screen-printed furnishing cotton, *Conifer*, features a small-scale pattern of pine cones looking like multicoloured raindrops.

1

2

3

4

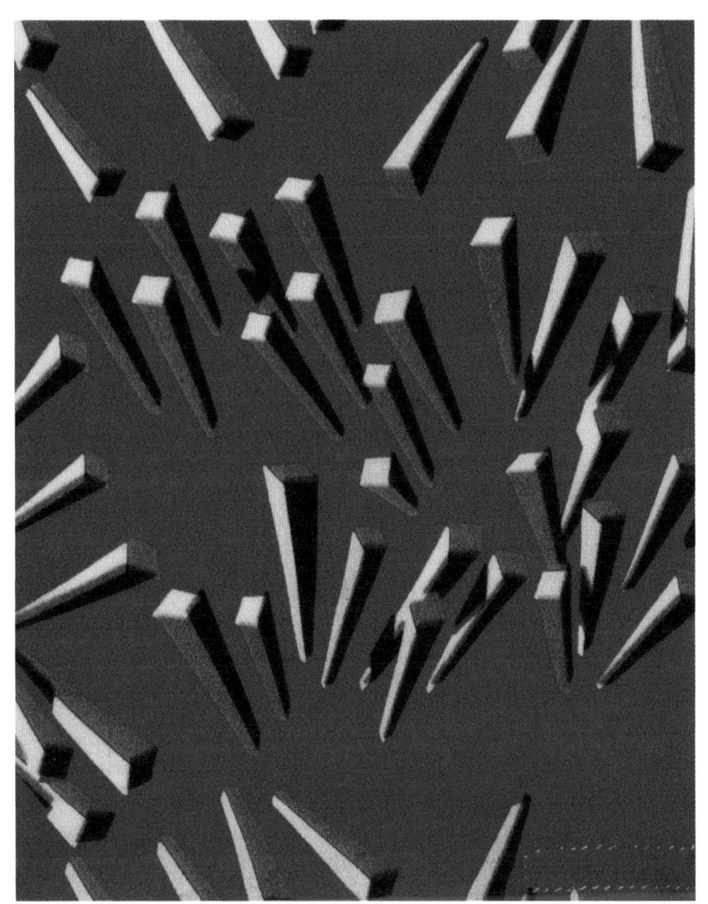
5

6

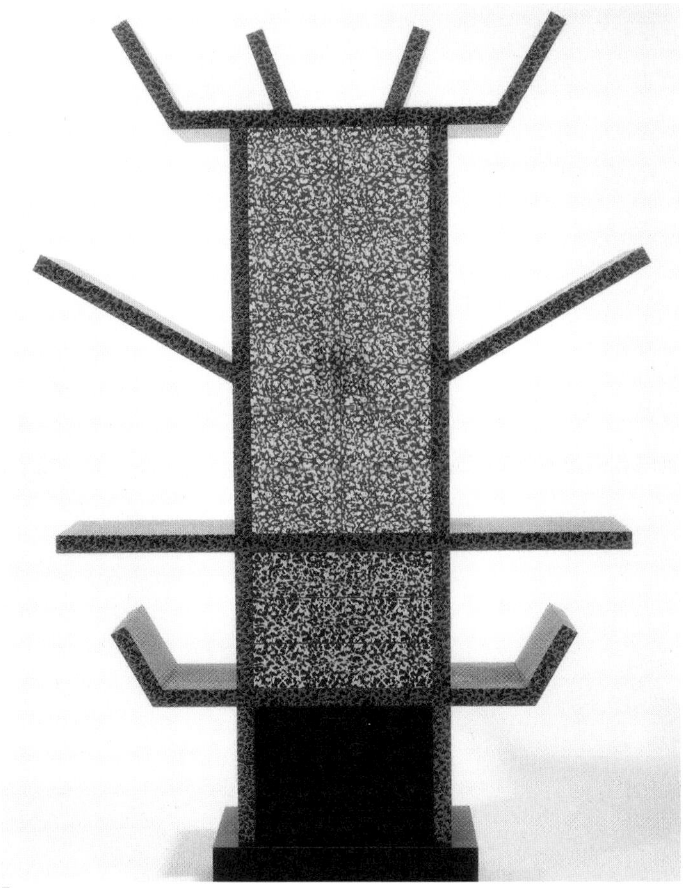
7

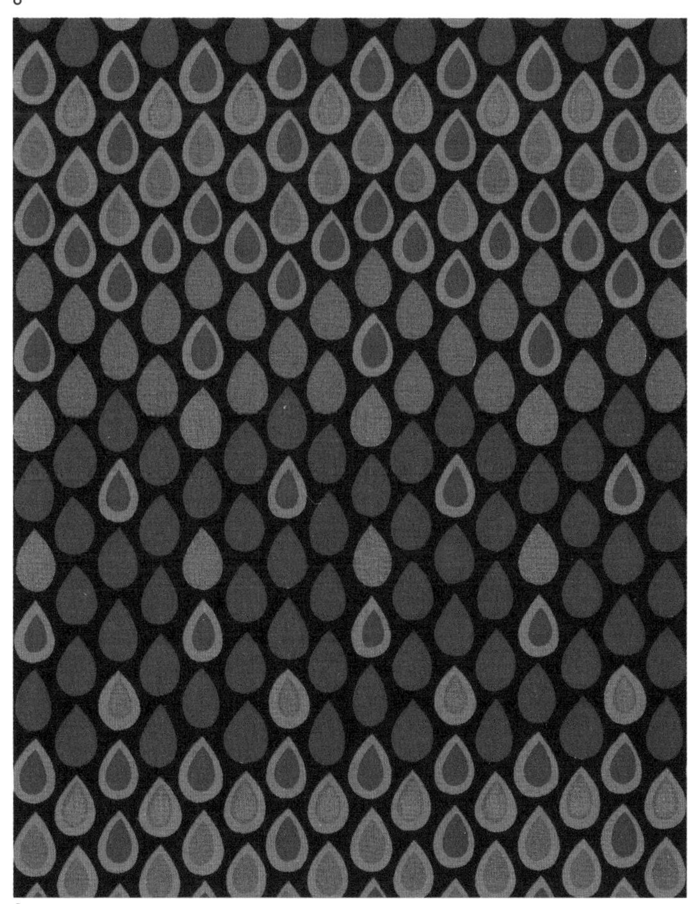
8

1

2

3

4

1 *Tiffany 2* wrapping paper, designed by Nigel Quiney, London, in 1968, expresses the unique artforms found in band posters and album covers of the 1960s.

2 This silk satin tie printed with psychedelic checks in a multitude of colours was made by Frederick Theak, England, around 1970.

3 Created by Mary Yonge in London between the 1960s and 1970s, this design for a printed textile depicts the curves and ripples of an abstract marbled pattern or slice of semi-precious stone.

4 The 1967 'Summer of Love' brought hip new sounds and *Scrolls 3*, a bright psychedelic wrapping paper design with Art Nouveau qualities by Nigel Quiney.

5 Outsize arabesques in vivid colours create the design of this furnishing fabric, *Makula*, by Morton Sundour, Carlisle, from between about 1960 and 1969.

6 *Typhoon 3* wrapping paper, designed in 1969 by Nigel Quiney, contains Art Nouveau-inspired curvilinear shapes to create a psychedelic effect.

7 Nigel Quiney designed *Palisades 2* wrapping paper in London in 1968. Its euphoric whirlpool pattern would have looked right at home at New York's Woodstock festival of 1969.

5

6

7

1

2

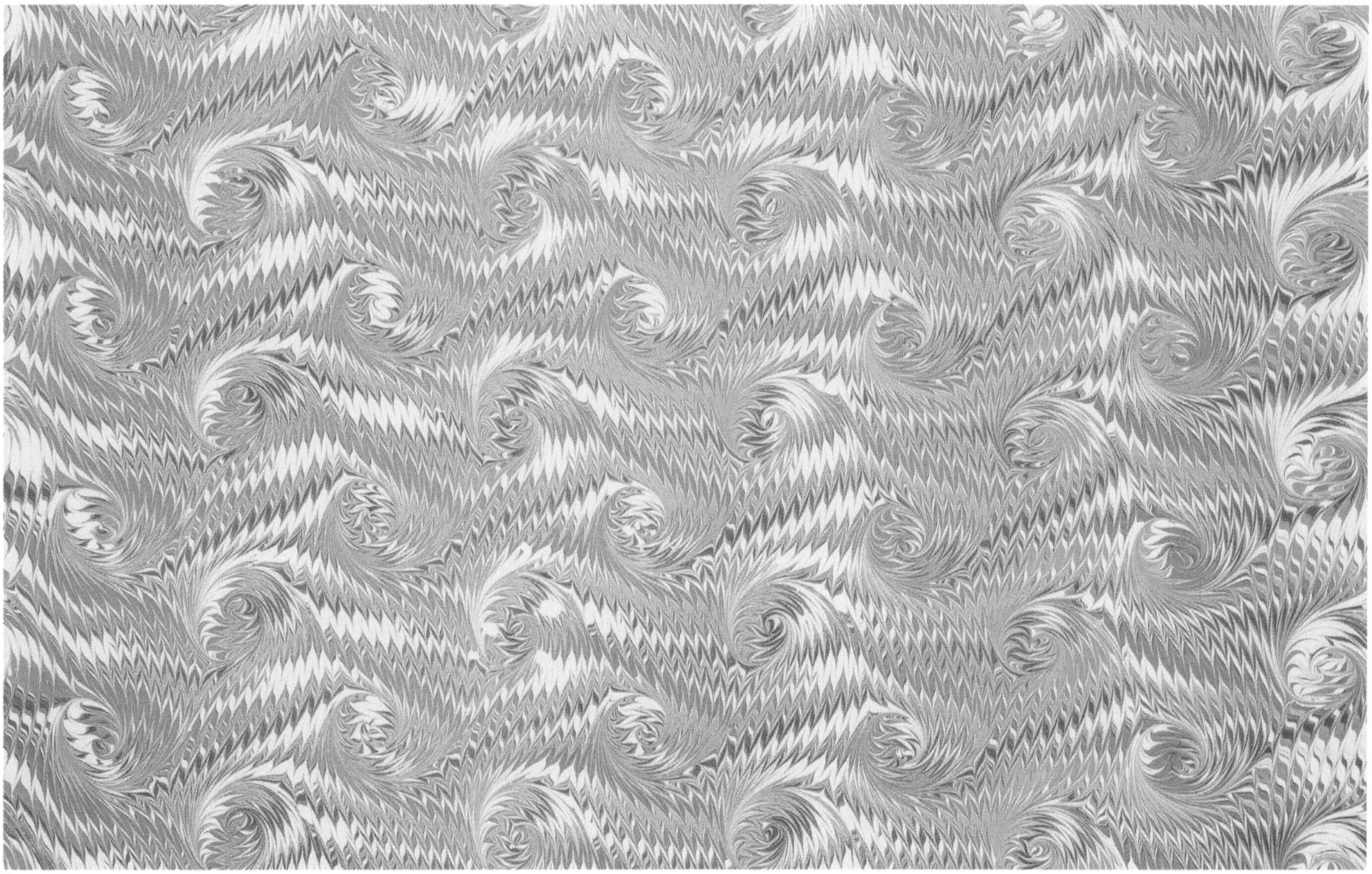

3

1 This decorative drawing is from *Le Castel Béranger*, a folio of lithographs published in Paris by the Librairie Rouam in 1898, by the architect Hector Guimard, one of the most important of French Art Nouveau artists.

2 Each of these hand-blown glass bottles – either rose-water sprinklers or tear catchers – was made in the 19th century, the two blue bottles being Iranian and the centre example being part of Tiffany's *Favrile* glass range made in New York.

3 Douglas Bennett Cockerell of Cockerell & Son, London, produced this marbled paper with a curl pattern for book covers and endpapers in 1938.

4 Dating from around 1860, this is a design for a silk textile in pencil and watercolour with shapes like petals or a cloud formation, by J.D. Cornuaud, France.

5 Intended for book covers and endpapers, this marbled paper with a pebble pattern was produced in the late 19th century by Joseph William Zaehnsdorf's bookbinding firm founded in London in 1842.

6 This marbled paper pattern for book covers and endpapers was produced by Douglas Bennett Cockerell of Cockerell & Son, London, in 1938.

7 The tradition of paper marbling probably began in Turkey or Iran around 1100, and the practice was called *ebru* (clouded paper) in Turkish. This 'shell pattern' marbled paper was produced in England around 1897.

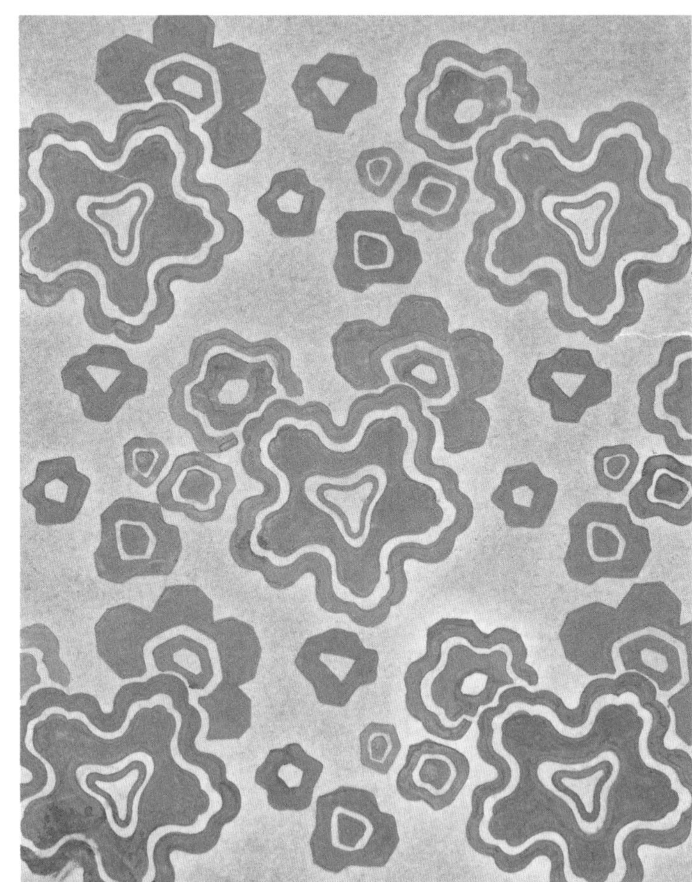
4

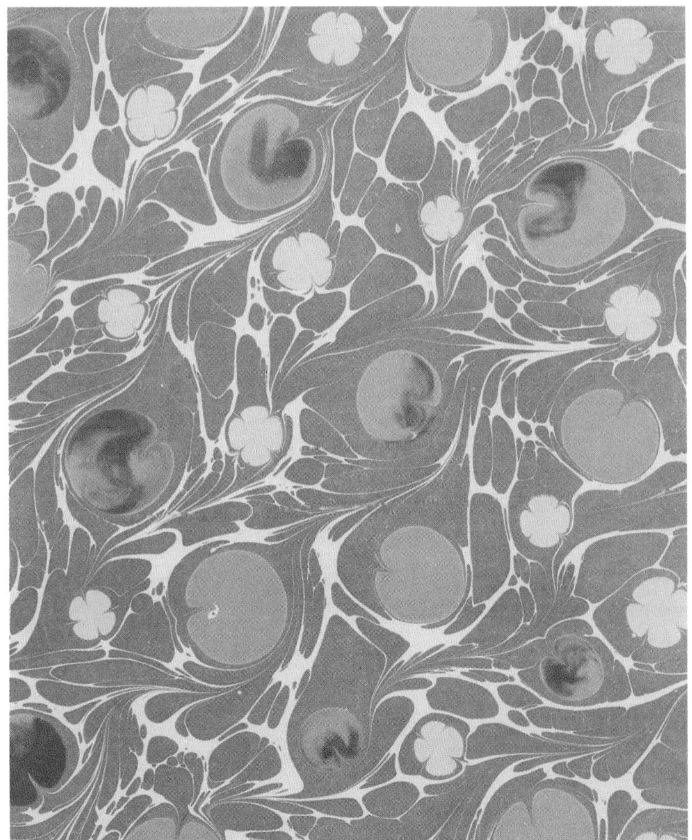
5

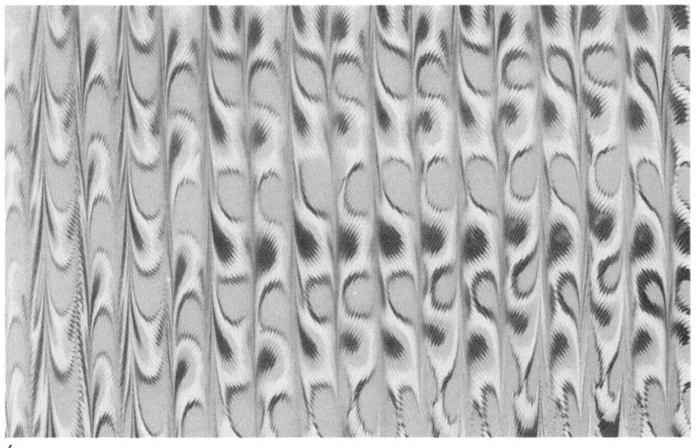
6

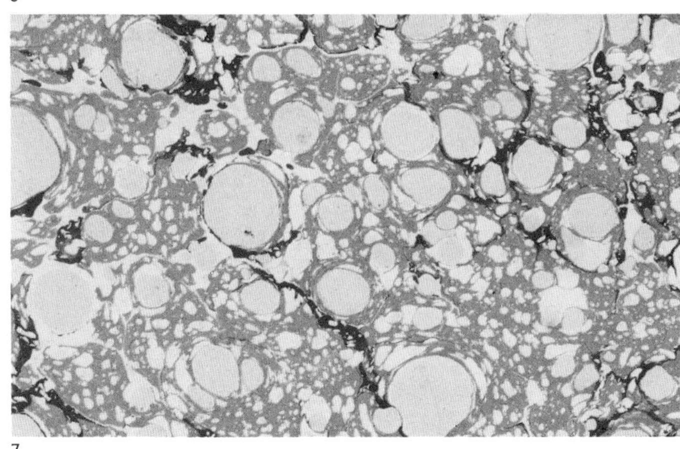
7

1

2

3

1 *Brazil* is a block-printed furnishing fabric designed by Eileen Hunter for Eileen Hunter Fabrics, Surrey, in 1938.

2 Distinguished British bookbinder Douglas Bennett Cockerell was keen to find ways to improve bookbinding materials. In 1928 he approached Morton Sundour to produce a high-quality, water-resistant fabric. This is one of the designs from that collaboration for book cloth.

3 Alexander Morton's son James oversaw collaborations with leading Arts and Crafts designers for Morton Sundour, Carlisle, including the 1928 project with Douglas Cockerell, of which this pattern was a part.

4 Charles Rennie Mackintosh designed this textile for William Foxton, London, in 1928. The abstract design of sprouting bulbs is set in flowing black lines.

5 This design in pen and watercolour by F. Toraud is from a set of early 19th-century designs for Norwich shawls and printed fabrics.

6 Cockerell's 1928 design recalls the decorative old marbled endpapers and book bindings he researched as a master bookbinder, but its simple lines show the fashion for abstract patterns popular with the Art Deco Movement.

7 The furnishing fabric *Pirouette*, made for Morton Sundour in New York before 1960, echoes avant-garde painting of the time.

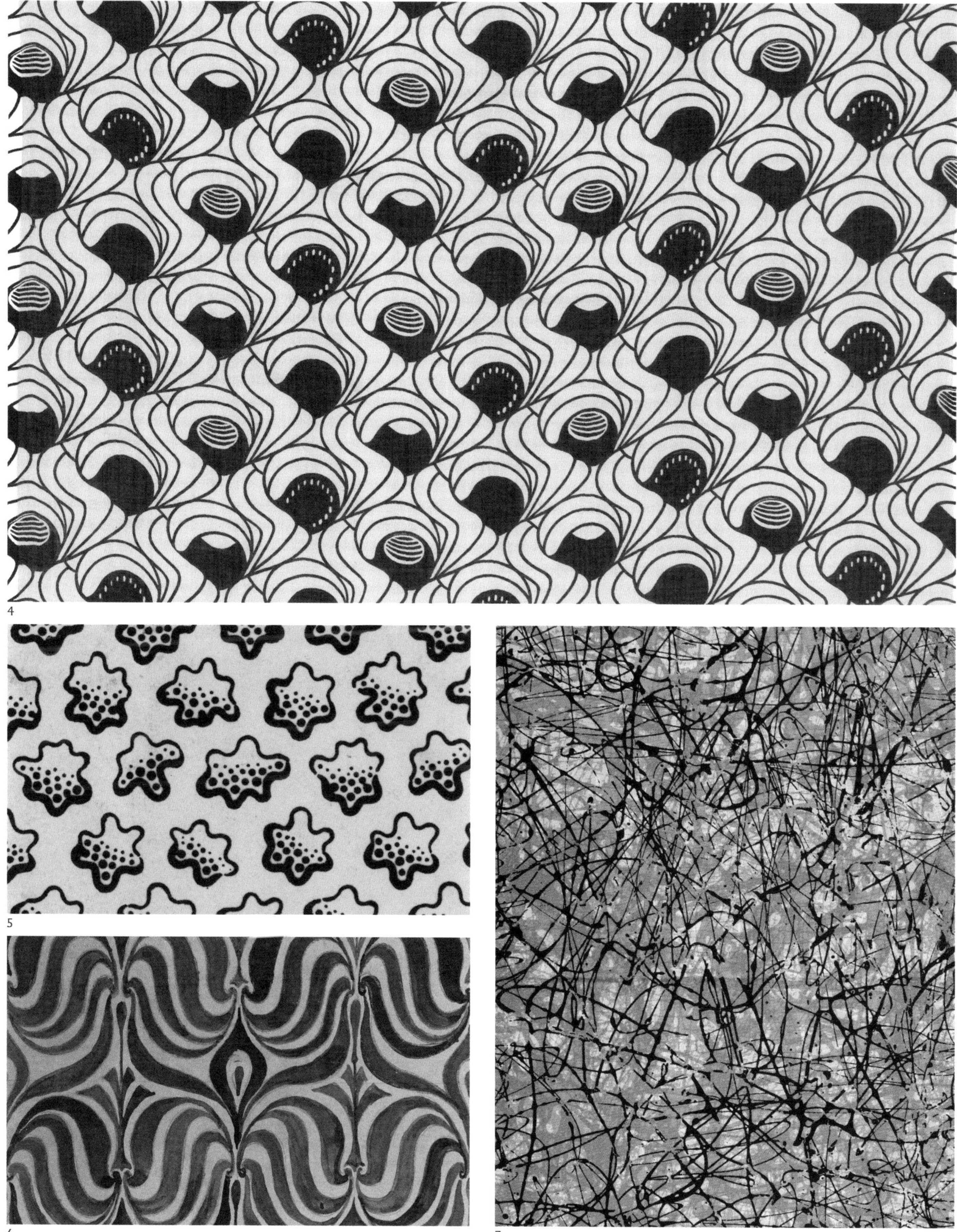

4

5

6

7

# PICTURE CREDITS

More photographs and information about the majority of the objects included in this book can be found by searching the accession numbers listed below on vam.ac.uk/collections.

Cover: E.3685-1915, given by Messrs. Jeffrey & Co.
Frontispiece: T.88-2016, given by Francesca Galloway
7: CIRC.209-1954, given by Heal & Son Ltd, © Robin & Lucienne Day Foundation, courtesy Heal's, London
9: © Timorous Beasties
10: © Timorous Beasties
12: © Timorous Beasties
13: © Timorous Beasties
14: CIRC.175-1954, courtesy of John and Rosemary Pegg
16: 1. CIRC.297-1960, given by Edinburgh Weavers; 2. 29088:96; 3. E.2359-1932, given by Harris & Sons
17: 4. E.3700-1927, bequeathed by J.R. Holliday; 5. M.67-1975, given by Dame Joan Evans; 6. 29088:433; 7. NAL: 38041800072043
18: 1. T.416-1990; 2. T.640-1996, given by Mrs A.C. Rivière; 3. T.72-2004
19: 4. T.218:30-1925; 5. E.2361-1932, given by Harris & Sons; 6. T.38-1919
20: 1. E.313-1974, given by Courtaulds Ltd; 2. CIRC.4-1926; 3. T.137-2004
21: 4. T.219:4-1925; 5. E.2229-1913, given by Sydney Vacher; 6. CIRC.654-1956, given by Miss A. Colby
22: 1. CIRC.307a-1961, © Estate of Graham Sutherland; 2. CIRC.361-1953; 3. T.215-1925
23: 4. T.35-1950, donated by Sir Henry Tate, 4th Baronet
24: 1. CIRC.87-1969, courtesy of Estate of Eero Saarinen; 2. T.183-1957; 3. E.1718-1989, by kind permission of the Estate of Jacob Dimoldenberg
25: 4. E.550-1919, given by Morris and Co.; 5. 121-1899; 6. T.406-1980, given by Manchester Design Registry; 7. CIRC.574-1966, given by the Manchester Design Registry, courtesy of Sanderson Design Group; 8. T.2278-2018, given by Sara Lee Courtaulds
26: 1. T.256-1987, given by Manchester Design Registry; 2. 467&A-1895, bequeathed by Mrs Lyne Stephens; 3. T.110-1953, given by the Kunstgewerbe Museum
27: 4. E.461-1967, given by Miss Mary Peerless; 5. C.720-1935, bequeathed by Herbert Allen; 6. E.467-1967, given by Miss Mary Peerless; 7. E.382-1977, given by Lady Anthea Goodwin and Mr N. Dickin
28: 1. E.641-1974, given by Courtaulds Ltd; 2. T.57-1934; 3. E.1885-1953, given by Morton Sundour Fabrics Ltd
29: 4. CIRC.515-1966, given by the Manchester Design Registry, courtesy of Sanderson Design Group; 5. T.74-1979, given by Manchester Design Registry; 6. C.58-1972; 7. IM.70-1927; 8. T.153-1957
30: 1. E.2326-1932, given by Harris & Sons; 2. E.5164-1919; 3. E.5147-1919; 4. E.68-1961, given by G.P. & J. Baker
31: 5. CIRC.221-1960; 6. E.5165-1919
32: 1. E.2817-1980, given by Shand Kydd Ltd; 2. T.48-1965, given by Madame Elsa Schiaparelli, courtesy of Maison Schiaparelli; 3. T.122-1953
33: 4. T.109-1931, given by the Hon. Marchioness of Bristol; 5. E.2358-1932, given by the Wallpaper Manufacturers Ltd; 6. M.45:1-1980; 7. E.1063-1911
34: 1. CIRC.202A-1949, courtesy of Estate of Enid Marx; 2. T.267-1970, given by Mr Waldo Lanchester; 3. CIRC.5-1959, given by Edinburgh Weavers; 4. T.27J-1952, bequeathed by Lady Cory
35: 5. CIRC.251-1956, given by the Calico Printers' Association; 6. 3289-1901, transferred from the Museum of Practical Geology, Jermyn Street
36: 1. T.131-1976, given by Miss G. Willson; 2. E.1917-1934, given by the Wallpaper Manufacturers Ltd; 3. E.2370-1932, given by Harris & Sons
37: 4. CIRC.652-1962, given by Heal Fabrics Ltd, courtesy Heal's, London
38: 1. T.131:1-2000, gift of the estate of Mr D.A. Butler; 2. IS.64-1978
39: 3. CIRC.42-1954
40: 1. FE.73-2014; 2. 2955-1901; 3. E.3052-1934, given by the artist
41: 4. T.137-1914, given by A.F. Kendrick, Esq.; 5. T.88-1927, given by Mr T.B. Clarke-Thornhill; 6. FE.65-2002
42: 1. IS.142-1950, given by G.P. and J. Baker; 2. T.316-1960, given by Mrs Burton Baldry; 3. E.2852-1913
43: 4. W.43:1-1938, given by Mr A.L.B. Ashton; 5. FE.117-1974, given by Dr Joan Evans
44: 1. 83-1884; 2. 1404-1899; 3. T.517-1996, given by Warner Fabrics
45: 4. T.79-1966; 5. E.802-1915, given by Mr Allan F. Vigers; 6. CIRC.82-1953, given by Mrs Winifred Nicholson; 7. FE.46-2011, given by Edwin Davies
46: 1. T.109-1954, Hart Gift; 2. 1622-1900; 3. E.1856-1934; 4. FE.22-2019, given by Raymond K.P. Ho & Family
47: 5. T.269-1960, given by Mrs Mockett; 6. T.171-1957
48: 1. 4061-1856; 2. T.66-1939, bequeathed by the maker; 3. IS.139-1984, given by Her Majesty Queen Elizabeth II
49: 4. 357-1894; 5. CIRC.97-1937, given by Sidney Mawson; 6. T.52-1953, given by Miss Janet Robertson
50: 1. T.414-1980, given by Manchester Design Registry, © Bianchini-Férier; 2. T.407-1980, given by Manchester Design Registry, © Bianchini-Férier
51: 3. 8342:15, given by Miss Catherine Jones, daughter of the artist; 4. E.607-1919, given by Morris & Co.; 5. 948-1898
52: 1. 1952-1900; 2. CIRC.678-1966, given by Miss Peerless, courtesy of Sanderson Design Group; 3. T.57-1953, given by G.P. and J. Baker Ltd; 4. T.98-1979, given by the Manchester Design Registry, courtesy of Sanderson Design Group
53: 5. E.1419-1979, courtesy of Sanderson Design Group; 6. S.955B-1984; 7. E.2325-1920; 8. E.4043-1915, given by Mr Emslie John Horniman
54: 1. 529-1874; 2. T.141-1919; 3. T.165-1979, given by Miss Mary Peerless
55: 4. E.699-1915, given by Mr Allan F. Vigers; 5. E.1866-1934, given by Wallpaper Manufacturers Ltd; 6. E.1854-1934, given by Wallpaper Manufacturers Ltd; 7. CIRC.232-1958, given by Edinburgh Weavers Ltd; 8. 961-1876
56: 1. M.111-1966; 2. T.67-1973, given by H. W. Garner, Esq.; 3. E.5166-1919; 4. C.100-1967, given by Stuart Durant
57: 5. E.462-1967, given by Miss Mary Peerless;

6. T.29-1965, given from the collection of Mary, Viscountess Harcourt GBE
58: 1. CIRC.401-1930; 2. T.53-1919, given by Morris & Co.; 3. CIRC.416-1966, given by the Manchester Design Registry
59: 4. CIRC.748-1925; 5. E.668-1915, given by Mr Allan F. Vigers; 6. T.426-1990
60: 1. CIRC.317-1960, by kind permission of the Estate of John Drummond; 2. FE.67-2011, given by Edwin Davies; 3. T.11-1933
61: 4. E.475-1919, given by Morris & Co.; 5. T.219:21-1925; 6. CIRC.480-1963; 7. CIRC.105-1966, given by Manchester College of Art and Design
62: 1. CIRC.349-1958, given by Edinburgh Weavers; 2. T.73-1979, given by Manchester Design Registry
63: 3. E.819-1915, given by Mr Allan F. Vigers; 4. C.66-1978, given by D. C. N. Hudson; 5. E.27-1945, given by Mrs Margaret Warner; 6. CIRC.270-1958, given by Turnbull & Stockdale Ltd; 7. T.322-1976, given by Liberty & Co., courtesy Liberty
64: 1. T.192-1997, given by Mr Daniel Manning; 2. E.243-2011, given by Eileen Knowles, © Victoria and Albert Museum, London; 3. T.283-1976, given by Liberty & Co., courtesy Liberty
65: 4. T.161-1957; 5. T.170-1957; 6. T.175-1957; 7. C.234-2018, gift of Ian and Rita Smythe
66: 1. C.65-1978, given by D. C.N. Hudson; 2. CIRC.297-1953, given by Warner and Sons; 3. CIRC.93-1966, given by Manchester College of Art and Design
67: 4. T.10-1990; 5. CIRC.598-1963, given by the Council of Industrial Design, courtesy Heal's, London; 6. CIRC.530-1953, given by Messrs Barnards Ltd; 7. CIRC.246-1951
68: 1. E.70-1961, given by G.P. & J. Baker Ltd; 2. CIRC.247-1966, given by Miss Mary Peerless; 3. 497-1889; 4. T.307:8-1999, given by Heal & Son Ltd, courtesy Heal's, London
69: 5. T.219:22-1925; 6. T.60-2002, given by Gail Caskey Winkler
70: 1. CIRC.2-1976, given by Heal Fabrics Ltd, courtesy Heal's, London; 2. T.174-1957, given by the manufacturer
71: 3. 2560-1901, transferred from the Museum of Practical Geology, Jermyn Street; 4. T.192-1953, given by Mr G. Beale, from the estate of the late Mrs Kate Beale; 5. IS.125-1950, given by G.P. and J. Baker; 6. CIRC.204-1963
72: 1. CIRC.5-1972, given by Heal Fabrics Ltd, courtesy Heal's, London; 2. T.55-1953, given by G.P. and J. Baker Ltd
73: 3. T.223-1948, purchased with Art Fund support; 4. T.275-1983, given by G.P. & J. Baker Ltd; 5. 8342:41, given by Miss Catherine Jones, daughter of the artist; 6. C.1700-1910, Salting Bequest
74: 1. E.68-2018, purchased with the support of the National Heritage Memorial Fund, Art Fund, V&A Members and The Belvedere Trust; 2. E.1412-1979; 3. E.660-1953; 4. E.1069-1977
75: 5. 265-1903; 6. T.178-1967; 7. E.1868-1934, given by the Wallpaper Manufacturers Ltd
76: 1. T.141-1957, given by the manufacturer; 2. FE.56-2017, given by the Central Japan Railway Company
77: 3. FE.18-1997; 4. 274&A-1886; 5. T.312-2002
78: 1. E.3683-1915, given by Messrs Jeffrey & Co.
79: 2. D.1572-1908; 3. D.1575-1908; 4. D.1484-1908
80: 1. E.1424-1979; 2. 1598-1871; 3. T.131-1981, bequeathed by Mrs F.C.C. Treen; 4. E.15-2015, given by James Cohan Gallery, © Trenton Doyle Hancock 2021. Courtesy the artist and James Cohan, New York
81: 5. 2980&A-1901, transferred from the Museum of Practical Geology, Jermyn Street; 6. T.410-1980, given by Manchester Design Registry
82: 1. E.3045-1934, given by the artist; 2. T.11-2002, given by Debra Fram
83: 3. D.1426-1908; 4. T.51-1912; 5. T.104-1987; 6. T.412-1980, given by Manchester Design Registry; 7. T.79-1987
84: 1. T.74-1988, given by Miss D. A. Frearson; 2. D.1457-1908; 3. T.459-2002
85: 4. T.408-1980, given by Manchester Design Registry; 5. CIRC.489-1954; 6. T.1690-2017, given by the Public Record Office
86: 1. E.1403-1979; 2. E.2371-1932, given by Harris & Sons; 3. T.348-1975, given by Mrs G. Sacher
87: 4. T.393-1967
88: 1. E.2230-1913
89: 2. E.1220-2012, given by Eileen Knowles; 3. T.252-1987, given by Manchester Design Registry; 4. 78-1865, bought from the Pourtales Collection; 5. E.5097-1919
90: 1. E.245-2011, given by Eileen Knowles; 2. E.1207-2012, given by Eileen Knowles; 3. Circ.170-1973, courtesy of OK Textiles
91: 4. C.8-1985, given by C.G. Brookes, Esq.; 5. AAD/2009/4, courtesy of Estate of Joyce Badrocke; 6. T.1127-2018, given by Sara Lee Courtaulds
92: 1. M.205-1925, bequeathed by Francis Reubell Bryan; 2. E.2217-1913, given by Sydney Vacher; 3. CIRC.130-1961
93: 4. E.1402-1979; 5. E.3059-1934, courtesy of Estate of Robert Stewart; 6. A.5-1920, given by Lady Cory; 7. E.3059-1934, given by Lindsay Phillip Butterfield; 8. E.3054-1934
94: 1. E.607-1954, given by Mrs G. F. Rawnsley; 2. T.48-1972; 3. T.201-1927, given by Sir Herbert Ingram, Bt, Captain B.S. Ingram MC, and Captain Collingwood Ingram
95: 4. CIRC.659-1956, given by Printex Oy, courtesy Marimekko, design by Maija Isola
96: 1. E.260-1974; 2. C.45-1996, given by Rita Walker; 3. CIRC.468-1966, given by the Manchester Design Registry; 4. CIRC.63-1952, courtesy Liberty
97: 5. E.5139-1919; 6. E.1409-1979; 7. CIRC.377-1970, bequeathed by Mrs G.M. Spear
98: 1. E.392-2019, given by Nigel Quiney; 2. E.387-2019, given by Nigel Quiney; 3. E.496-2019, given by Nigel Quiney; 4. E.493-2019, given by Nigel Quiney
99: 5. T.586-1919, given by Morris & Co.; 6. 414:1228-1885, given by Lady Charlotte Schreiber
100: 1. E.632-1980; 2. CIRC.1-1974, courtesy of John Dove and Molly White; 3. CIRC.172-1973, courtesy of OK Textiles
101: 4. T.259-1926; 5. NAL 95.SS.14-18; 6. C.710-1921, gift of Arthur Myers Smith, Esq., through the National Art Collections Fund; 7. T.88L-1930, given by the Stehli Silks Corporation
102: 1. MISC.4:2-1976; 2. T.396-1988, given by the Descendants of the Storeys of Lancaster
103: 3. CIRC.415-1966, given by the Manchester Design Registry; 4. E.1414-1979; 5. CIRC.72-1953, given by C. Cowles-Voysey, Esq., FRIBA
104: 1. 1216J-1901; 2. 414:1069-1885; 3. CIRC.63-1953
105: 4. CIRC.303-1939, courtesy of The Frank Dobson Estate. www.frankdobsonartist.com; 5. T.99-1959, given by Mrs John C. Taliaferro, Jr; 6. T.5-2003, given from the Everts-Comnene-Logan Collection
106: 1. T.164-1953, given by Morton Sundour Fabrics Ltd; 2. 414:180-1885, given by Lady Charlotte Schreiber
107: 3. E.225-1974, given by Courtaulds Ltd; 4. T.131-1977, given by J.W.F. Morton & Courtaulds Ltd; 5. T.87-1965, given by Mrs P.J. Swann; 6. T.1976-2018, given by Sara Lee Courtaulds
108: 1. T.155-1953, given by Morton Sundour Fabrics Ltd; 2. CIRC.236-1935, © Estate of Duncan Grant. All rights reserved, DACS 2021; 3. E.435-1914, given by M.H. Birge & Sons Co., USA; 4. L.223-1963
109: 5. E.23116-1957, given by Turnbull & Stockdale Ltd; 6. M.134-1951, Cory Bequest; 7. T.181-1962,

given by Miss M.C. Richardson
110: 1. C.346-1921; 2. E.1426-1979; 3. T.208-1953, given by Mrs Gubbins; 4. E.1880-1934, given by the Wallpaper Manufacturers Ltd
111: 5. T.279-1927; 6. E.3710-1927, bequeathed by J.R. Holliday; 7. 964&A-1898
112: 1. T.694-2018, given by Sara Lee Courtaulds; 2. T.223-1981; 3. T.23-1919; 4. CIRC.92-1953, given by Miss Ethel C. Newill
113: 5. 715-1902; 6. 7963(IS)
114: 1. T.40-1919; 2. T.820-1919
115: 3. D.792-1908; 4. 555-1884; 5. T.592-1919
116: 1. E.2226-1913, given by Sydney Vacher; 2. LOAN: GILBERT.345-2008, the Rosalinde and Arthur Gilbert Collection on loan to the Victoria and Albert Museum, London; 3. T.201-2004
117: 4. T.396-1934; 5. T.94-1986; 6. CIRC.100-1960, given by the Henry Francis du Pont Winterthur Museum
118: 1. T.156-2009, given by Sara Lee Courtaulds; 2. E.355-2019, given by Philippe Garner; 3. T.383-2002
119: 4. AAD/2004/9; 5. CIRC.362-1953
120: 1. 919-1873; 2. 3171&A-1853; 3. E.5132-1919; 4. CIRC.118-1957, given by Ramm, Son & Crocker Ltd
121: 5. E.2830-1980, given by Shand Kydd Ltd; 6. CIRC.23&A-1961, given by the maker, © DACS 2021; 7. T.188-1984, given by S. Franses Ltd
122: 1. 29088:151
123: 2. AAD/2004/9; 3. 29088:154; 4. FE.64&A-1984
124: 1. CIRC.24-1961, given by the maker, © DACS 2021; 2. CIRC.482-1956, given by Heal's Wholesale and Export Ltd, © Robin & Lucienne Day Foundation, courtesy Heal's, London; 3. E.892-1979, given by Norma Tapetfabrik, Design: Josef Frank. © Svenskt Tenn, Stockholm, Sweden.
125: 4. CIRC.32-1954; 5. CIRC.135-1950, given by Schiffer Prints, © DACS 2021; 6. T.53-1932
126: 1. T.531:1,2-1996, given by the artist, courtesy Emily Jo Gibbs. Photo: Lol Johnson; 2. 135-1907, given by Mr W.C. Carter; 3. T.631-2018, given by Sara Lee Courtaulds
127: 4. E.1888-1934, given by the Wallpaper Manufacturers Ltd; 5. E.1884-1934, given by the Wallpaper Manufacturers Ltd; 6. C.64:1, 2-2005, given by the American Friends of the V&A Museum through the generosity of Judy Novak; 7. M.333-1983, given by M.J. Franklin; 8. E.1925-1934, given by the Wallpaper Manufacturers Ltd
128: 1. T.88N-1930, given by the Stehli Silks Corporation; 2. A.55-1918, Wheatley Gift; 3. M.204-2007, given by the American Friends of the V&A through the generosity of Patricia V. Goldstein; 4. E.194-1986
129: 5. CIRC.251-1951; 6. CIRC.262-1953, given by Morton Sundour Fabrics Ltd
130: 1. T.308-2002; 2. CIRC.689-1966, given by Morton Sundour Fabrics Ltd; 3. 2135-1899, given by Mr F. Rathbone, Esq.
131: 4. FE.17-1994; 5. T.178-2004; 6. T.184-2004; 7. E.213-1990
132: 1. E.972-1978, given by Dr Emil Rasch, © DACS 2021; 2. T.165-1953, given by Morton Sundour Fabrics Ltd; 3. CIRC.332-1953; 4. T.91-1979, given by the Manchester Design Registry
133: 5. E.1895-1953, given by Morton Sundour Fabrics Ltd; 6. M.32-1939
134: 1. FE.25-2015, purchase funded by Samsung; 2. CIRC.465-1962, given by the Paul Nash Trust
135: 3. T.67-1979, given by Manchester Design Registry; 4. T.266-1968, given by Lady Palairet in memory of Sir Michael Palairet; 5. W.29-2011, purchased by the Outset Design Fund
136: 1. CIRC.86-1960, given by the Henry Francis du Pont Winterthur Museum; 2. T.105-1973, given by the Council of the Salisbury and South Wiltshire Museum; 3. CIRC.670-1966, given by Miss Peerless
137: 4. T.75-1953, given by Mrs Jean Bottard; 5. 246:4/5-1870 and 246:4/6-1870; 6. CIRC.850-1956, given by Edinburgh Weavers Ltd
138: 1. T.26-1966, given by Mr G.F. Wingfield Digby; 2. M.25-1976, bequeathed by Miss J.H.G. Gollan; 3. T.184-1970; 4. E.5102-1919
139: 5. E.477-2019, given by Nigel Quiney; 6. E.259-1974, given by Courtaulds Ltd
140: 1. CIRC.116-1937; 2. T.379-2002; 3. M.20-1976, given by Miss Amy Kotze; 4. CIRC.99-1966, given by Manchester College of Art and Design
141: 5. CIRC.467-1966, given by the Manchester Design Registry
142: 1. E.558-1919, given by Morris & Co.; 2. CIRC.80A-1938, courtesy of Estate of Hans Tidall; 3. T.80-1979, given by the Manchester Design Registry; 4. C.165-1992; 5. T.352-1910
143: 6. CIRC.159-1950; 7. E.312-1984
144: 1. 8387:29; 2. E.23110-1957, given by Turnbull & Stockdale Ltd; 3. 29088:150
145: 4. T.115-1970, given by Miss Catherine Hunt, courtesy Maison Balenciaga; 5. CIRC.285-1938, courtesy of Estate of André Bicât; 6. CIRC.292-1938; 7. CIRC.481-1954, courtesy Liberty
146: 1. C.33-1944, bequeathed by Miss Helena Hill; 2. T.545:3-1999, given by Heal & Son Ltd, courtesy Heal's, London; 3. E.584-1966, given by F. Schumacher & Co., courtesy of VNIP Holdings LLC.; 4. E.445-1988; 5. E.444:3-1988
147: 6. CIRC.822-1967, given by J.W.F. Morton, Esq.; 7. E.444:54-1988
148: 1. CIRC.281-1959, given by Walter Taylor Esq
149: 2. CIRC.175-1954, courtesy of John and Rosemary Pegg; 3. T.280-1927; 4. E.1853-1934, given by the Wallpaper Manufacturers Ltd; 5. E.897-1979, given by Dahls Tapetfabrik, courtesy Thomas Schrader and Hans Schrader
150: 1. T.215-1925; 2. C.375-1914, presented by Lt Col. K. Dingwall, DSO with Art Fund support; 3. E.23180-1957, given by Turnbull & Stockdale Ltd; 4. E.5156-1919
151: 5. E.5108-1919; 6. T.173-2009, given by Sara Lee Courtaulds
152: 1. E.1437-1921; 2. T.11-1935, given by Mrs H.M. Shepherd; 3. E.1604-1921
153: 4. E.1594-1921; 5. E.1938-1921; 6. E.1943-1921; 7. E.1638-1921
154: 1. D.97-1907; 2. D.87-1907; 3. E.194-1986
155: 4. E.1558-1921; 5. D.94-1907
156: 1. E.23125-1957, given by Turnbull & Stockdale Ltd; 2. CIRC.7-1966, given by Oscar Eckhard, Esq.; 3. E.1528-1954, given by Shand Kydd Ltd; 4. M.46, a&b-1914, given by Harvey Hadden
157: 5. 843-1852; 6. T.43-1937, given by Messrs Warners & Sons; 7. T.94A-1930, given by Sir Frank Warner of Warner & Co.
158: 1. E.267-1893; 2. 288-1864; 3. 2716-1856
159: 4. E.1801-1934, given by the Wallpaper Manufacturers Ltd; 5. W.63-1977, purchased by HM Government from the estate of the 6th Earl of Rosebery and allocated to the Victoria and Albert Museum; 6. E.2827-1980, given by Shand Kydd Ltd
160: 1. T.504-1974; 2. W.27:1, 2-1958, bequeathed by Lady Glyn; 3. M.428-1936, gift of the Adelphi Development Company; 4. 28168:5
161: 5. E.1562-1934, given by the Wallpaper Manufacturers Ltd
162: 1. 349-1897; 2. 72370; 3. E.2772-1910
163: 4. 346:1-1896; 5. E.4047-1915, given by Mr Emslie John Horniman
164: 1. E.522-1914; 2. E.195-1937; 3. T.134-1972, given by Warner and Sons
165: 4. 1334-1874, given by Monsieur Paul Balin; 5. NAL pressmark 110.P.37; 6. E.23196-1957, given

by the Hon. Mrs Brian Fairfax-Lucy; 7. E.2778-1910; 8. CIRC.139-1976, given by Heal Fabrics Ltd, courtesy Heal's, London
166: 1. 8336:128, given by Miss Catherine Jones, daughter of the artist; 2. A.576-1910; 3. E.887-1979, given by Cole & Son Wallpapers Ltd; 4. D.721-1908; 5. E.642-1976, given by Cole & Son (Wallpapers) Ltd, courtesy of Cole & Son (Wallpapers) Ltd
167: 6. T.216:31-1925; 7. E.161-1934
168: 1. CIRC.292-1951; 2. 8341:57, given by Miss Catherine Jones, sister of the artist; 3. M.20-1962, given in memory of Mrs C.E. Gladstone, by Lady Alford and Miss Eileen Riddell
169: 4. 7262-1861; 5. 8343:64, given by Miss Catherine Jones, daughter of the artist; 6. E.4033-1915, given by Mr Emslie John Horniman
170: 1. E.4439-1911, presented by George C. Haité, Esq., RBA; 2. E.4423-1911, presented by George C. Haité, Esq., RBA; 3. T.212-1962, given by Mrs I. Gadsby-Toni
171: 4. E.4416-1911, presented by George C. Haité, Esq., RBA
172: 1. E.3399-1908; 2. 1620-1854; 3. E.3495-1908
173: 4. 6908(IS); 5. E.3395-1908; 6. T.206-1920
174: 1. 05648(IS); 2. 0197(IS); 3. 0197(IS); 4. T.215-1925
175: 5. IS.981-1883; 6. E.4424-1911, presented by George C. Haité, Esq., RBA; 7. C.141-1909, given by Sir Charles Marling KCMG, CB
176: 1. A.3-2004, given by the Gilbert Bayes Charitable Trust, by kind permission of the Gilbert Bayes Charitable Trust; 2. T.216:18-1925
177: 3. CIRC.289-1953; 4. E.643-1976, given by Mr Samuel J. Dornsife; 5. E.2957-1918, Richard Phené Spiers Collection of Architectural Drawings; 6. T.9-1915
178: 1. T.91-1999, bequeathed by Clive Scrimshaw; 2. M.188-2007, given by the American Friends of the V&A through the generosity of Patricia V. Goldstein; 3. 8138:2
179: 4. CIRC.465-1966, given by the Manchester Design Registry; 5. E.217-1974, given by Courtaulds Ltd
180: 1. D.770-1908; 2. M.20:1-2017, purchased through the generosity of William & Judith, Douglas and James Bollinger as a gift to the Nation and the Commonwealth; 3. M.10-1962; 4. E.1400-1979; 5. E.165-1934
181: 6. E.163-1934; 7. 1041:2-1869
182: 1. E.166-1934; 2. M.39-1972, formerly in the collection of Charles and Lavinia Handley-Read; 3. E.162-1934
183: 4. W.4 to D-1953, given by Mrs T.H. Minshall
184: T.53-1926
186: 1. IS.100-1955; 2. CIRC.153-1939; 3. CIRC.222 1949, courtesy The House of Scalamandré Archives
187: 4. CIRC.295-1960, given by Edinburgh Weavers, © DACS 2021; 5. CIRC.167-1932, © Raoul Dufy, ADAGP, Paris and DACS 2021; 6. T.260-1987, given by Manchester Design Registry
188: 1. CIRC.4-1940; 2. T.58-1932, given by W. & J. Sloane
189: 3. LOAN: GILBERT.895:1-2008, The Rosalinde and Arthur Gilbert Collection on loan to the Victoria and Albert Museum, London; 4. CIRC.249-1948, by kind permission of the Estate of John Drummond; 5. CIRC.474A-1939, © The Robin and Lucienne Day Foundation, © Robin & Lucienne Day Foundation; 6. A.16-1935, purchased with Art Fund support, the Vallentin Bequest, Sir Percival David and the Universities China Committee
190: 1. E.247-1985, courtesy of Sanderson Design Group; 2. C.453-1940, bequeathed by Miss Amy E. Tomes; 3. CIRC.464-1939, © Angela Verren Taunt. All rights reserved, DACS 2021
191: 4. T.158-2004; 5. T.171-2009, given by Sara Lee Courtaulds; 6. CIRC.73-1938
192: 1. E.42A-1971, given by Mr Roger H.M. Warner; 2. AAD/2009/4, given by Joyce Badrocke, Courtesy of Estate of Joyce Badrocke
193: 4. CIRC.282A-1932, given by the retailers; 5. E.638-1937, given by the artist; 5. T.225-1987, given by Manchester Design Registry; 6. 1811-1869, bequeathed by the Rev. Chauncy Hare Townshend; 7. T.66-1990, given by Miss Olive Budd, courtesy of Estate of Joyce Clissold
194: 1. T.124-1938; 2. T.392-1919; 3. CIRC.118-1915, given by Mr Archibald Anderson
195: 4. T.53-1926; 5. T.648-1919
196: 1. T.459-2018, given by Sara Lee Courtaulds; 2. T.46-1985, given by Mr Nicholas Hill; 3. E.321-1974, given by Courtaulds Ltd
197: 4. W.128-1910, Salting Bequest; 5. E.1766-1914, given by Jeffrey & Co.; 6. CIRC.172-1951
198: 1. CIRC.548-1966, given by the Manchester Design Registry; 2. T.363-1919; 3. 8387:22; 4. 854-1901
199: 5. T.150-1977, given by J W F Morton & Courtaulds Ltd; 6. CIRC.798-1967, given by J.W.F. Morton, Esq.
200: 1. E.205-1974, given by Courtaulds Ltd; 2. CIRC.387-1956, given by the Calico Printers' Association, Manchester; 3. CIRC.74-1950
201: 4. C.426-1934, given by the Secretary of the British Institute of Industrial Art; 5. T.119-2004; 6. W.4-1970; 7. T.53-1926; 8. T.366-1934
202: 1. T.89-1953, given by Miss Elinor M. Pugh; 2. E.1862-1934, given by Wallpaper Manufacturers Ltd; 3. 2390-1901, transferred from the Museum of Practical Geology, Jermyn Street; 4. 38041800167090
203: 5. E.434-1917, given by Mrs William de Morgan; 6. W.4-2005, given by Philip and Elizabeth Hodgson in memory of Kenneth Hodgson; 7. E.329-1974, given by Courtaulds Ltd; 8. E.5311-1958
204: 1. T.36:1-2009, given by Sara Lee Courtaulds; 2. IS.40-1977; 3. 29088:300; 4. T.411-2002
205: 5. T.410-2002; 6. T.128-1937, given by C.F.A. Voysey
206: 1. D.773-1908; 2. T.111-1929; 3. CIRC.495-1954
207: 4. IS.18-1947
208: 1. 691-1872; 2. T.78-2004; 3. T.174B-1931
209: 4. LOAN: GILBERT.1047-2008, The Rosalinde and Arthur Gilbert Collection on loan to the Victoria and Albert Museum, London; 5. T.77-1919, given by Charles T. Garland; 6. 763-1893
210: 1. T.17-1950, given by Mrs R.M. Woods; 2. CIRC.502-1962, given by Mrs R.W. Cave-Orme; 3. T.18-1978, given by the Department of Regional Services; 4. T.384-1972
211: 5. 908 to F-1894 and 894-1897; 6. 1071-1900; 7. E.137-1920; 8. 356-1897
212: 1. T.53-1926; 2. 2815-1901, transferred from the Museum of Practical Geology, Jermyn Street
213: 3. T.256 to B-1967; 4. T.407-2002
214: 1. TN.604-2012; 2. E.690-1993; 3. CIRC.222-1948
215: 4. 29088:539; 5. T.49-1948
216: 1. T.268-1999, given by Heal & Son Ltd, courtesy Heal's, London; 2. IM.258-1920, given by Lady Ratan Tata; 3. 622-1897
217: 4. 8055-1862; 5. 29088:360; 6. CIRC.658-1956, given by Printex Oy, courtesy Marimekko, design by Maija Isola
218: 1. 29088:464; 2. T.86-2004
219: 3. LOAN: GILBERT.35:1 to 13-2008, The Rosalinde and Arthur Gilbert Collection on loan to the Victoria and Albert Museum, London; 4. T.337-1934; 5. T.194-2004
220: 1. CIRC.223-1935, given by Old Bleach Linen Company Limited; 2. CIRC.8-1952; 3. M.1-1918, given by Sir John Ramsden
221: 4. M.59-1996; 5. CIRC.288-1938; 6. T.273-1987, given by Manchester Design Registry; 7. CIRC.333-1953
222: 1. FE.47-2014; 2. T.274-1987, given by Manchester

Design Registry; 3. T.277-1987, given by Manchester Design Registry
223: 4. T.422-1992, © Timorous Beasties
224: 1. T.217-1964; 2. CIRC.214-1960; 3. T.311-2002
225: 4. T.63-1948, given by Brigadier W.T.O. Crewdon CBE, in memory of Mr and Mrs W. Crewdson; 5. IS.2-1967, given by J.B. Fowler
226: 1. T.145-1972, Given by Warner & Sons Ltd; 2. CIRC.112-1939, © Raoul Dufy, ADAGP, Paris and DACS 2021; 3. E.4029-1915, Given by Mr Emslie John Horniman; 4. 2319-1901, transferred from the Museum of Practical Geology, Jermyn Street; 5. CIRC.191-1947
227: 6. 822-1869; 7. T.88-2016, given by Francesca Galloway; 8. CIRC.36-1948
228: 1. E.894:145/1-1978, purchased from the funds of the Capt. H.B. Murray Bequest; 2. T.145:1 to 7-2009, given by Sara Lee Courtaulds; 3. CIRC.249-1939, courtesy Les amis de Paul Mansouroff
229: 4. CIRC.1084-1925; 5. E.245-1974, given by Courtaulds Ltd; 6. C.21&A-1919, given by W.J. de Winton, Esq.; 7. E.894:127/2-1978, purchased from the funds of the Capt. H.B. Murray Bequest
230: 1. 605-1893; 2. 1065:28-1883; 3. E.282-1974, given by Courtaulds Ltd; 4. W.21-1945
231: 5. T.357-2002; 6. 2052-1876; 7. 832-1894
232: 1. E.305-1974, given by Courtaulds Ltd; 2. CIRC.92-1966, given by Manchester College of Art and Design; 3. C.156-1980, given by Mrs R.S. Hughes
233: 4. T.369-1982, given by Misses Audrey and Norah Battye; 5. W.3-2015, purchase funded by Clarissa Ward; 6. T.173-1921; 7. CIRC.466-1953, given by R.N. Christie
234: 1. E.5124-1919; 2. CIRC.336-1948
235: 3. CIRC.313-1953; 4. C.559-1935, bequeathed by Herbert Allen; 5. T.202-1978, given by Mr E.C. Wigan; 6. C.575B&C-1935, bequeathed by Herbert Allen; 7. 622-1897
236: 1. T.18-1963; 2. T.262-1959; 3. FE.113-1997
237: 4. W.34:1, 2-1980; 5. T.20-1923, given by Mrs Watts; 6. CIRC.719-1971, © ADAGP, Paris and DACS, London 2021; 7. CIRC.110-1954
238: 1. E.4037-1915, given by Mr Emslie John Horniman; 2. T.173-1978; 3. M.262-1984; 4. 29088:301
239: 5. CIRC.265-1953, given by Morton Sundour Fabrics Ltd; 6. CIRC.241-1939; 7. E.188-1974
240: 1. CIRC.126-1953, given by Christabel Marillier; 2. M.56-1962, given by Dame Joan Evans; 3. T.247-1987, given by Manchester Design Registry
241: 4. T.341-1934; 5. T.285-2009, given by Sara Lee Courtaulds; 6. E.1886-1934, given by Wallpaper Manufacturers Ltd
242: 1. CIRC.454-1966, given by the Manchester Design Registry; 2. C.73 to C-1972
243: 3. E.4032-1915, given by Mr Emslie John Horniman; 4. 442-1897; 5. ; 5. E.1762-1914, given by Jeffrey & Co.; 6. CIRC.240-1966, given by Miss Mary Peerless
244: 1. E.1841-1934, given by the Wallpaper Manufacturers Ltd; 2. 965-1901; 3. E.1535-1954, given by Shand Kydd Ltd
245: 4. 5466(IS); 5. M.23-1965; 6. E.458:211-1955, given by the Calico Printers' Association Ltd
246: 1. E.404-1917, given by Mrs William de Morgan; 2. CIRC.456-1966, given by the Manchester Design Registry; 3. E.1763-1914, given by Jeffrey & Co.; 4. E.2320-1932, given by Harris & Sons
247: 5. IM.119-1943, given by Col. Wyatt; 6. CIRC.375-1959, given by Messrs Phillips of Hitchin Ltd; 7. T.99-1960
248: 1. T.424-1967; 2. T.269-1966, given by J.W.F. Morton, Esq.
249: 3. T.34-1978, given by Mr F.R. Hutchings, courtesy Natalie Gibson
250: 1. T.79-1927, given by Mr T.B. Clarke-Thornhill; 2. CIRC.452B-1954; 3. T.320-1977
251: 4. 1994-1855; 5. T.76-2004; 6. FE.28-1987
252: 1. CIRC.174-1954, courtesy of John and Rosemary Pegg; 2. T.273-1978, © The Estate of Edward Bawden; 3. CIRC.128-1957, given by Edinburgh Weavers, courtesy Estate of Hans Tisdall
253: 4. T.61-1950; 5. 4860-1858; 6. CIRC.1048-1967, given by Martin Battersby; 7. 1445-1899; 8. IS.11-2004, The Feroza Jamsheed Marker collection of Parsi clothing
254: 1. T.15-1953, given by C. Cowles Voysey, FRIBA; 2. E.1852-1934, given by the Wallpaper Manufacturers Ltd; 3. T.269-1987, given by Manchester Design Registry; 4. E.147-1974
255: 5. E.307-1974, given by Courtaulds Ltd; 6. T.1686-2017, given by the Public Record Office, courtesy of Sanderson Design Group
256: 1. T.443-2018, given by Sara Lee Courtaulds; 2. CIRC.317-1955
257: 3. CIRC.19-1961, given by Miss Bainbridge; 4. CIRC.270B-1951; 5. CIRC.284-1938; 6. IS.1-1965
258: 1. M.820-1926, Lt Col. G. B. Croft-Lyons Bequest; 2. E.509-2019, given by Nigel Quiney; 3. T.361-1970; 4. C.567-1922, given by Stuart G. Davis
259: 5. T.50-1953, given by Rex Silver, Esq. ; 6. T.415-1998, © Crafts Study Centre, University for the Creative Arts, London
260: 1. T.270-1976, given by Liberty & Co., courtesy Liberty.; 2. M.131-1951, Cory bequest; 3. T.188-1922, given by W.L. Collins
261: 4. CIRC.237-1956, given by the Calico Printers Association; 5. CIRC.233-1956, given by the Calico Printers' Association; 6. T.1-1954, given by Mr H. Arnold Ovenden
262: 1. T.264-1974, given by Her Majesty the Queen; 2. 3544-1852; 3. T.171-1992, given by Mr S. Clifford
263: 4. T.772-1972, given by Mrs K. Prater; 5. 63-1852
264: 1. M.62-2003, given by Roger and Geoffrey Munn in memory of their parents; 2. NAL pressmark 49.D.7; 3. T.427-1974, given by Lady Alexandra Trevor-Roper courtesy Maison Schiaparelli; 4. CIRC.377-1948
265: 5. T.35-1946; 6. T.63-1933
266: 1. T.838-2018, given by Sara Lee Courtaulds; 2. W.245:1-1922, Pfungst Gift; 3. T.11-1950
267: 4. M.57-1980; 5. D.598-1887; 6. W.657-1910, Salting Bequest
268: 1. E.484-2019, given by Nigel Quiney
269: 2. E.1876-1934, given by the Wallpaper Manufacturers Ltd; 3. 29088:1; 4. M.16-1978; 5. CIRC.262-1960, given by Miss W.J. Leonard
270: 1. E.1855-1934, given by the Wallpaper Manufacturers Ltd; 2. T.368-1934, given by the British Institute of Industrial Arts; 3. T.3-1960, given by Dr W.A. Kane; 4. 29088:5
271: 5. T.21-1986, given by Miss B. Sander; 6. FE.22-1997; 7. 430580; 8. T.590-2018, given by Sara Lee Courtaulds
272: 1. W.319-1922, Pfungst Gift; 2. T.233-2004; 3. W.24-1972; 4. T.102-1922, given by Alice A. Little
273: 5. M.179:1, 2-1978
274: 1. E.2315-1932, given by Messrs Harris & Sons; 2. M.537-1910, Salting Bequest; 3. 29088:382
275: 4. 29088:359; 5. CIRC.435-1965, bequeathed by Mrs G.Cope; 6. T.53&A-1962, given by The Dowager Lady Swaythling; 7. T.549:3-1999, given by Heal & Son Ltd, courtesy Heal's, London
276: 1. C.478-1914, bequeathed by Myles Burton Kennedy, Esq.; 2. E.302-1974; 3. CIRC.6-1942, bequeathed by Mr Frank Pick; 4. T.238-1960, bequeathed by Frank Ward
277: 5. W.8:1 to 7-2018, given by the American Friends of the V&A through the generosity of Joseph Holtzman; 6. CIRC.37-1940, © The Cedric Morris Foundation / Bridgeman Images
278: 1. FE.33-1983, purchased with the assistance of the

Garner Fund; 2. T.72-1957, Hughes Gift

279: 3. E.9848-1958, given by the Brighton Corporation; 4. T.124-1938; 5. 944-1904; 6. CIRC.1354-1926; 7. 933-1901

280: 1. C.2160-1910, bequeathed by George Salting, Esq.; 2. T.12-1916, given by W.B. Chamberlin through The Art Fund; 3. T.15-1954, given by Messrs Turnbull and Stockdale Ltd; 4. T.64&A-1933

281: 5. 29088:59; 6. T.755-1950, bequeathed by Mr W. Llewellyn Jones

282: 1. 232-1894; 2. 29088:60; 3. 29088:73; 4. T.315-2002

283: 5. T.77:1, 2-2009, purchased with support from a generous individual

284: T.1083-2000, bequeathed by Eddie Squires

286: 1. M.60-1914, given in accordance with the wishes of the late Miss Bernardine Hall; 2. T.79-2001, bequeathed by Eddie Squires

287: 3. C.2-2001, given by Alex Werner; 4. E.2281-1966, given by Mr John B. Fowler; 5. E.2335-1980, given by Shand Kydd Ltd; 6. T.373:1-1999, given by Heal & Son Ltd, courtesy Heal's, London; 7. T.2204-2018, given by Sara Lee Courtaulds

288: 1. 1874T-1899; 2. E.161-1977, given by Arthur Sanderson & Sons Ltd, courtesy of Sanderson Design Group; 3. T.134-1992, given by Margaret Simeon

289: 4. T.26-1980, given by Mr A. Naj-Oleari; 5. T.87E-1930, given by the Stehli Silks Corporation; 6. T.471-1998, courtesy Heal's, London

290: 1. CIRC.39-1969, given by Heal Fabrics Ltd, © Robin & Lucienne Day Foundation, courtesy Heal's, London; 2. C.13-2005, given by Theo Hessing © Theo Hessing; 3. E.525-2019, given by Nigel Quiney, © Nigel Quiney

291: 4. CIRC.2-1962, given by Heal Fabrics Ltd, courtesy Heal's, London; 5. C.52-1969, given by Miss A.L. Reeve; 6. 2216:6; 7. CIRC.486-1954, courtesy of Estate of Robert Stewart, courtesy Liberty.; 8. CIRC.685-1956, given by Edinburgh Weavers Ltd, courtesy of Estate of Olive Sullivan

292: 1. CIRC.45-1970, given by Warner and Sons, © Warner Textile Archive, Braintree District Museum Trust; 2. W.661-2001, given by Adam Carey; 3. CIRC.44-1970, given by Warner and Sons; 4. IS.3:1,2-2015 © Aziz and Suleman Khatri

293: 5. E.952-1978, given by Cole & Son (Wallpapers) Ltd, courtesy of Cole & Son (Wallpapers) Ltd

294: 1. M.4-1969, Pfungst Reavil Bequest; 2. T.11-1954, bequeathed by Mrs Winifred Phillips © Desmond Banks; 3. CIRC.316-1939

295: 4. CIRC.847:1 to 3-1956, given by Mrs Ruth Waterhouse; 5. CIRC.793-1967, given by J.W.F. Morton, Esq.; 6. CIRC.276-1951, courtesy of The Machin Arts Foundation; 7. T.37-2018, purchased with the support of V&A Members

296: 1. W.2-2010, © Victoria and Albert Museum, London; 2. E.885-1978; 3. E.888-1978

297: 4. CIRC.308-1951; 5. FE.48-2014; 6. M.5-2004, © Giovanni Corvaja, courtesy Giovanni Corvaja, Italy; 7. E.886-1978

298: 1. NAL pressmark 49.A.31 2. W.8-1997, courtesy of Tom Dixon; 3. LOAN: MET ANON.5-2007, lent to the Victoria and Albert Museum through the generosity of William and Judith, and Douglas and James Bollinger; 4. NAL pressmark 49.A.31

299: 5. AAD/2002/7/7/17; 6. CIRC.225-1951

300: 1. T.378:3-1999, given by Heal & Son Ltd, courtesy Heal's, London; 2. E.521-2011, given by Julie Verhoeven, courtesy Julie Verhoeven for Galliano Genes. 1991.; 3. CIRC.321-1938, courtesy of the Frank Dobson Estate. www.frankdobsonartist.com; 4. T.539-1999, given by Heal & Son Ltd, © Estate of Paule Vézelay/ Bridgeman Images, courtesy Heal's, London

301: 5. CIRC.133-1961; 6. T.87N-1930, given by the Stehli Silks Corporation; 7. FE.1-2014, given by Isezaki Jun

302: 1. E.2799-1990; 2. T.57-2008, given by Ben Stagg, courtesy www.MarijkeKogerArt.com; 3. T.49-1915, Given by John A. Hay, Esq., in the name of his brother, the late Captain Hay

303: 4. C.1993-1910, Salting Bequest; 5. T.176-2002, courtesy of Sanderson Design Group; 6. FE.14-1987; 7. T.756-1950, bequeathed by W. Llewellyn Jones

304: 1. FE.420:1-1992; 2. T.65-1915, given by Mr T.B. Clarke-Thornhill; 3. E.161-1955

305: 4. T.331-1960; 5. C.123-1986, given by the maker, Form and shape: Grethe Meyer Design / Decoration: *Picnic* design by Ole Kortzau 1982-1983 for Royal Copenhagen; 6. T.1692-2017, given by the Public Record Office; 7. CIRC.372-1975

306: 1. CIRC.109-1957, given by Edinburgh Weavers; 2. CIRC.60B-1953; 3. E.316-2017, given by the artist, © David Faithfull; 4. CIRC.835-1967, given by J.W.F. Morton, Esq., All rights reserved © 2021 Hunter Family Estate

307: 5. E.3010-1930, given by the Arthur Sanderson & Sons' branch of the Wallpaper Manufacturers Ltd; 6. C.256-1986, given by John Clappison and the makers; 7. T.23-1963, bequeathed by Mr J.D. Mayorcas

308: 1. T.63-1979, given by Manchester Design Registry; 2. CIRC.1-1976, given by Heal Fabrics Ltd, courtesy Heal's, London; 3. CIRC.9-1976, courtesy of Estate of Michael Casson; 4. T.76-1990, given by Miss Olive Budd, courtesy of Estate of Joyce Clissold

309: 5. T.166-1970, given by Mr J.B. Fowler; 6. E.960-1978, © The Estate of Edward Bawden; 7. CIRC.322-1959, gift of the Museum of the Fine Arts, Boston, through the wishes of donor Mrs Robert E. Choate

310: 1. T.585-2018; 2. CIRC.75-1957, given by Feinweberei Elsaesser and Co.; 3. CIRC.471-1966, given by the Manchester Design Registry

311: 4. T.414-2002; 5. T.23-1928, given by Mr F. Black; 6. T.263-2018, given by Sara Lee Courtaulds

312: 1. CIRC.482-1954, courtesy Liberty.; 2. IS.31-1970, gift of Mrs Estelle Fuller through The Art Fund; 3. T.422-2002

313: 4. T.170-1988, given by Zika Ascher, © Peter Ascher/Ascher Family Archive

314: 1. 21248; 2. E.315-2017, given by the artist, © David Faithfull

315: 3. T.57-1932, given by W. & J. Sloane; 4. CIRC.150-1954; 5. CIRC.586A-1963, given by Sanderson & Sons Ltd, © The Piper Estate / DACS 2021, courtesy of Sanderson Design Group; 6. C.302-1976, given by Sir Colin and Lady Anderson

316: 1. 245:1-1874; 2. CIRC.201-1957, given by Manifattura JSA; 3. 1600-1899; 4. W.3-1929, given by Mr Marmaduke Langdale Horn

317: 5. T.134-1924; 6. T.421-1934

318: 1. CIRC.639-1956, given by D. Whitehead Ltd, © The Piper Estate / DACS 2021; 2. W.36:1, 2-1981; 3. C.12:1, 2-2001, given by Althea and Imogen Stewart, in memory of their mother, Mrs Emily Margaret Tench Stewart, courtesy Fornasetti – www.fornasetti.com; 4. E.1116-1921, given by Mr Basil Ionides

319: 5. T.157-1958, given by Mrs Jason Westerfield; 6. T.2-1958; 7. E.574-1966, given by the Wallpaper Manufacturers Ltd

320: 1. CIRC.217:1,2-1961, given by Lt Col. P.H.W. Russell; 2. T.308-1966, given by J.W.F. Morton, Esq.; 3. T.5-1933; 4. CIRC.212-1954

321: 5. E.1493-1984, given by Mr John Bonython;

6. C.13-1915, presented by Lt Col. K. Dingwall, DSO, with Art Fund support; 7. T.354-1972, given by Miss J.M. Gibbons and Miss D. Gibbons; 8. E.601-1982, given by Cole & Son Ltd, courtesy of Cole & Son (Wallpapers) Ltd

322: 1. E.2797-1914, given by Mr Henry Butler; 2. T.203-1998, gift of Mrs Ann McColm; 3. FE.27:1 to 25-1981, given by Miss E.P. Cross

323: 4. C.562&A-1920, given by Lieutenant-Colonel Kenneth Dingwall DSO through Art Fund; 5. CIRC.323-1959, given by Calico Printers' Association; 6. W.24:1,2-1917, acquired through the generosity of H.E. Trevor, Esq., with the co-operation of some admirers of David Garrick

324: 1. T.259-1987, given by Manchester Design Registry

325: 2. T.279-1987, given by Manchester Design Registry; 3. T.3259-2018, given by Sara Lee Courtaulds

326: 1. CIRC.221-1951; 2. T.418:1 to 3-1998, given by the designer; 3. CIRC.351-1974

327: 4. C.67-1982, given by Judith Bradfield; 5. CIRC.302-1973, courtesy Lloyd Johnson; 6. T.477:1-1992, given by the manufacturer; 7. E.2354-1980, given by Shand Kydd Ltd; 8. E.444:21-1988

328: 1. T.14-2007, given by Gary Page, courtesy Gerardine and Wayne Hemingway, Hemingway Design, and co-founders Red or Dead; 2. T.394-1974, given by Miss Ruth Ford, courtesy Maison Schiaparelli; 3. 3581-1856

329: 4. E.2409-1980, given by Shand Kydd Ltd; 5. T.557-1994, given by Liberty, courtesy Liberty; 6. T.556-1994, given by Liberty, courtesy Liberty; 7. CIRC.687-1956, given by Edinburgh Weavers Ltd, © The Estate of Keith Vaughan. All rights reserved, DACS 2021

330: 1. T.366-1977; 2. Tile, V&A Refreshment Room; 3. CIRC.154B-1954; 4. T.86-1957, given by Mrs E.A. Hunt of Wrotham, Kent, on behalf of the West Kent Federation of Women's Institute; 5. CIRC.90-1968, given by C.H. Gibbs-Smith

331: 6. T.9-2007, given by Gary Page, courtesy of Gerardine and Wayne Hemingway, Hemingway Design and co-founders Red or Dead; 7. CIRC.324-1938, courtesy of the Frank Dobson Estate. www.frankdobsonartist.com

332: 1. E.596-1996, © Sonia Boyce. All Rights Reserved, DACS 2021; 2. W.51-2005, gift of Bettina and Joe Gleason; 3. CIRC.189-1974; 4. P.56-1977, given in memory of the Hon. Donough O'Brien by his wife the Hon. Rose O'Brien; 5. CIRC.28-1954, By kind permission of the Estate of John Drummond

333: 6. CIRC.266-1974, Design by Dame Zandra Rhodes; 7. W.6-2018, purchased with support from V&A Members, Art Fund and a bequest from Derek Woodman, © Salvador Dali, Fundació Gala-Salvador Dalí, DACS 2021

334: 1. C.318B-1983, courtesy Fornasetti – www.fornasetti.com; 2. E.21-2006, purchased through the Julie and Robert Breckman Print Fund, © Sonia Boyce. All Rights Reserved, DACS 2021; 3. T.2302-2018, given by Sara Lee Courtaulds

335: 4. T.274-1974, given by the designer; 5. T.59-2005, given by the American Friends of the V&A, courtesy Maison Schiaparelli; 6. M.173:1,2-2007, given by the American Friends of the V&A through the generosity of Patricia V. Goldstein

336: 1. E.33B-1971, given by Roger H.M. Warner; 2. S.871-1981, Cyril W. Beaumont Bequest

337: 3. E.1844-1934, given by Wallpaper Manufacturers Ltd; 4. T.219-1992; 5. CIRC.341-1938, courtesy of the Frank Dobson Estate. www.frankdobsonartist.com; 6. CIRC.321-1939; 7. C.2490-1910, bequeathed by George Salting, Esq.

338: 1. T.271-1987, given by Manchester Design Registry; 2. T.395-1974, given by Miss Ruth Ford, courtesy Maison Schiaparelli; 3. CIRC.480-1966, given by the Manchester Design Registry

339: 4. CIRC.474-1966, given by the Manchester Design Registry; 5. T.87O-1930, given by the Stehli Silks Corporation; 6. C.431-1936, Wilfred Buckley Collection; 7. T.87F-1930, given by the Stehli Silks Corporation

340: 1. T.46:1-2017, given by Joanna & Philip Ross in memory of Leah Barnett Ross (nee Lyons); 2. T.87-1930, given by Stehli Silks Corporation; 3. CIRC.360-1964

341: 4. CIRC.489-1974; 5. E.882-1978, given by John Line & Sons Ltd; 6. CIRC.490-1954, courtesy Liberty.; 7. T.231-1987, given by Manchester Design Registry

342: 1. T.402-1999, given by Heal & Son Ltd, courtesy Heal's, London; 2. E.444:45-1988, courtesy of Estate of Roger Nicholson

343: 3. T.350:1-1999, given by Heal & Son Ltd, courtesy Heal's, London; 4. T.2553-2018, given by Sara Lee Courtaulds; 5. CIRC.568-1974 © Estate of Raymond McGrath; 6. T.219-1992; 7. T.392-1934

344: 1. T.276-1987, given by Manchester Design Registry

345: 2. 1198-1888; 3. T.255-2018, given by Sara Lee Courtaulds; 4. 414:192-1885, given by Lady Charlotte Schreiber; 5. T.73-1964, given by Mr Ronald Baker;

346: 1. C.314-1926, bequeathed by Lt Col. G.B. Croft-Lyons FSA; 2. T.60-2010; 3. T.61-1997, given by the designer

347: 4. 86-1899; 5. T.2262-2018, given by Sara Lee Courtaulds; 6. CIRC.1223-1967, given by Terence Conran, Esq., courtesy Natalie Gibson; 7. T.166-1972, given by Warner and Sons

348: 1. T.220-1992; 2 CIRC.795-1968, given by the Council of Industrial Design; 3. E.374:1-1994; 4. T.181-1986, given by Diane Meyersohn, © Meyersohn & Silverstein. All rights reserved, DACS 2021

349: 5. CIRC.465-1948; 6. T.321:2-1999, given by Heal & Son Ltd, © Robin & Lucienne Day Foundation, courtesy Heal's, London; 7. T.97-1927, given by Mr T. B. Clarke-Thornhill; 8. T.271-1983, © Angela Verren Taunt. All rights reserved, DACS 2021

351: CIRC.30-1968, given by Heal & Son Ltd, courtesy Haydon Williams, courtesy Heal's, London

352: 1. E.443-2019, given by Nigel Quiney; 2. 38041800366064; 3. 7964:31

353: 4. T.484-1998; 5. E.1221-2012, given by Eileen Knowles; 6. CIRC.479-1956, given by Heal's Wholesale and Export Ltd; 7. CIRC.267-1967, given by Heal Fabrics Ltd, courtesy Heal's, London; 8. CIRC.56-1972, given by Heal Fabrics Ltd, courtesy Heal's, London

354: 1. T.86-1958; 2. E.1237-2012, given by Eileen Knowles; 3. CIRC.505-1966, given by the Manchester Design Registry, courtesy of Sanderson Design Group; 4. T.412-1934

355: 5. W.19-2010, *Bel Air* designed by Peter Shire in 1982 for Memphis Milano Collection. Courtesy Memphis Srl. www.memphis-milano.com; 6. 29088:86; 7. E.1224-2012, given by Eileen Knowles; 8. E.414:220-1997, given by Mrs Jane Palmer; 9. E.414:180-1997, given by Mrs Jane Palmer

356: 1. CIRC.587-1965; 2. CIRC.31-1968, given by Heal & Son Ltd, courtesy Heal's, London; 3. W.21-1972, given in memory of Charles and Lavinia Handley-Read, by their family

357: 4. T.403-1971; 5. E.463-2019, given by Nigel Quiney; 6. T.427-1980, given by Mr R.W. Hall; 7. E.1695-1989, given by

Maurice Dimoldenberg, son of the designer, by kind permission of the Estate of Jacob Dimoldenberg
358: 1. CIRC.283-1951, Designed by Sir Terence Conran; 2. E.958-1978; 3. CIRC.277 to C-1973, courtesy Glenys Barton, Flowers Gallery, London
359: 4. T.338C&D-1982, given by the designers, courtesy Wendy Ramshaw and David Watkins; 5. CIRC.245-1935, given by Turnbull & Stockdale Ltd; 6. T.159-1988, given by Zika Ascher; 6. E.194-1986; 7. T.2212-2018, given by Sara Lee Courtaulds
360: 1. CIRC.473-1956, given by Heal's Wholesale and Export Ltd, © Robin & Lucienne Day Foundation, courtesy Heal's, London; 2. E.414:160-1997, given by Mrs Jane Palmer; 3. CIRC.329-1972
361: 4. T.474-2002; 5. CIRC.57-1956, given by L.F. Foght, © DACS 2021; 6. T.379-1989, given by Henry Rothschild; 7. CIRC.171-1956, given by Eric Ewers AB
362: 1. E.414:14-1997, given by Mrs Jane Palmer; 2. E.414:168-1997, given by Mrs Jane Palmer; 3. IS.41&A-1988; 4. T.94-1979, given by the Manchester Design Registry; 5. E.5176-1968, given by Wallpaper Manufacturers Ltd, courtesy of Sanderson Design Group
363: 6. M.110-2007, given by the American Friends of the V&A through the generosity of Patricia V. Goldstein; 7. CIRC.332 to C-1963; 8. CIRC.623-1964, given by the London Patent Office
364: 1. E.5127-1968, given by Wallpaper Manufacturers Ltd, courtesy of Sanderson Design Group; 2. C.90-1937; 3. E.32-1971, given by Mr John B. Fowler; 4. 295:1-1900
365: 5. E.5146-1968, given by Wallpaper Manufacturers Ltd, courtesy Inge Cordsen, Livingstone Studio, courtesy of Sanderson Design Group; 6. 8337:174, given by Miss Catherine Jones, daughter of the artist; 7. E.3406-1922, given by Mrs Tremayne; 8. CIRC.565-1954; 9. T.58-2007
366: 1. W.28-2011, purchased by the Outset Design Fund; 2. Circ.587-1954; 3. T.342-1934
367: 4. 7964:3; 5. CIRC.591-1965; 6. 8899A/1145; 7. T.120-2011, given by Barbara Hulanicki, courtesy Barbara Hulanicki Archive
368: 1. CIRC.35-1969, given by Heal Fabrics Ltd, courtesy Heal's, London; 2. CIRC.34-1969, given by Heal Fabrics Ltd, courtesy Heal's, London; 3. IS.140-1965
369: 4. CIRC.128-1956, given by Hjula Veverier AS; 5. CIRC.769-1969; 6. E.231-1977, given by Arthur Sanderson & Sons Ltd, courtesy of Sanderson Design Group; 7. CIRC.46-1936
370: 1. E.5116-1968, given by Wallpaper Manufacturers Ltd, courtesy of Sanderson Design Group; 2. T.220-1931; 3. CIRC.143-1976, given by Heal Fabrics Ltd, © Robin & Lucienne Day Foundation, courtesy Heal's, London
371: 4. 6167(IS); 5. T.325-1934, given by the British Institute of Industrial Arts; 6. C.13-1964, given by Mlle Florence Marinot in memory of Maurice Marinot, all rights reserved – P&V Merat-France; 7. T.440-1934, given by the British Institute of Industrial Arts
372: 1. T.128-1989, given by the makers; 2. E.219-1977, given by Arthur Sanderson & Sons Ltd, courtesy of Sanderson Design Group; 3. E.457-2019, given by Nigel Quiney; 4. B.294-2011, gift of Caroline McIntyre
373: 5. E.230-1977, given by Arthur Sanderson & Sons Ltd, courtesy of Sanderson Design Group; 6. E.5125-1968, given by Wallpaper Manufacturers Ltd, courtesy of Sanderson Design Group; 7. CIRC.802-1968, given by Warner and Sons, © Warner Textile Archive, Braintree District Museum Trust
374: 1. E.243-1977, given by Arthur Sanderson & Sons Ltd, courtesy of Sanderson Design Group; 2. 352-1882; 3. 02195(IS); 3. IS.1052:22-1883; 4. 2054-1899
375: 5. T.87M-1930, given by the Stehli Silks Corporation; 6. CIRC.205-1935, given by Calico Printers' Association; 7. W.14:1 to 6-1990, acquired, in part, with the assistance of Memphis, © ADAGP, Paris and DACS, London 2021; 8. CIRC.247-1967, given by Heal Fabrics Ltd, courtesy Heal's, London
376: 1. E.437-2019, given by Nigel Quiney; 2. T.209-1992, given by Mr A. Yates; 3. E.1217-2012, given by Eileen Knowles; 4. E.405-2019, given by Nigel Quiney
377: 5. T.2272-2018, given by Sara Lee Courtaulds; 6. E.406-2019, given by Nigel Quiney; 7. E.440-2019, given by Nigel Quiney
378: 1. NAL: 19887062; 2. 903-1889, 512-1896, 903-1889; 3. E.3443-1938, given by Mr Douglas Cockerell, MBE, RDI
379: 4. D.4442-1900; 5. E.3855-1932, given by Mr E. Zaehnsdorf; 6. E.3450-1938, given by Mr Douglas Cockerell, MBE, RDI; 7. E.6326:44-1897
380: 1. CIRC.36-1938; 2. E.541B-1971; 3. E.541-1971
381: 4. T.344-1934; 5. E.277-1920; 6. E.541E-1971; 7. T.3255-2018, given by Sara Lee Courtaulds

# INDEX

Page numbers in *italic* refer to illustrations.

# ACKNOWLEDGMENTS

It takes many people to make a publication like this possible, and all are important. First and foremost are the artists and designers – working independently or in studios, workshops and factories – who were responsible for creating the incredible objects included in this book.

I owe a massive thank you both to Marta Di Gioia, Brand Licensing Research Assistant, and to project manager Karen Fick, for their support in bringing this book to life. To Marta for her attention to detail, extraordinary memory, boundless energy and enthusiasm, and for helping me figure out picture layouts. To Karen for her amazing planning abilities that helped me through what could have been an overwhelming process, her understanding of my vision, and her creativity and editing skills.

My gratitude also goes to Peter Dawson at Grade Design for making each page as beautiful as we intended, and special thanks to Hannah Newell, V&A Development Editor, and Julian Honer and Susannah Lawson at Thames & Hudson for their patient commitment to this project. In addition, huge thanks to Kirsty Seymour-Ure for her additional research and copy-editing prowess. For the production of the book, I am extremely grateful to Emma Woodiwiss and Kate Thomas. For their brilliant investigations into the intellectual property rights underlying the objects, I thank Andrew Tullis and Lucy MacMillan.

A heartfelt thanks to the wonderful, helpful and generous V&A curators for their invaluable overview of the text, especially Victoria Bradley, Anna Jackson, Jenny Lister and Lesley Miller. I am also grateful to Alistair McAuley and Paul Simmons of Timorous Beasties for generously allowing us to reproduce their outstanding work and for sharing their design philosophy.

Finally, special appreciation to my friends and family for their encouragement throughout this project and deepest thanks to my parents for taking me to the V&A when I begged them to, aged ten.


# ABOUT THE AUTHOR

Amelia Calver is Licensing Research and Development Manager at the Victoria and Albert Museum, London. Over twenty years of working with international teams of creatives and designers on trend-driven briefs, finding inspiration for a wide range of products, she has cultivated an impressive familiarity with the V&A's extensive collection, particularly of the fabric and wallpaper designs from around the world that have been acquired during the museum's 170-year history.

**Cover**. *Chinese Magpie*, machine-printed wallpaper, designed by William Turner, manufactured by Jeffrey & Co., England, 1915

First published in the United Kingdom in 2021 by
Thames & Hudson Ltd, 181A High Holborn, London WC1V 7QX
in association with the Victoria and Albert Museum, London

First published in the United States of America in 2021 by
Thames & Hudson Inc., 500 Fifth Avenue, New York, New York 10110

Reprinted 2022



Designed by Peter Dawson, www.gradedesign.com



British Library Cataloguing-in-Publication Data
A catalogue record for this book is available from the British Library

Library of Congress Control Number 2021933665

ISBN 978-0-500-48072-4

Printed and bound in China by RR Donnelley